™

References for the Rest of Us!™

Check For DISC
In Back of Book

BESTSELLING BOOK SERIES FROM IDG

Do you find that traditional reference books are overloaded with technical details and advice you'll never use? Do you postpone important life decisions because you just don't want to deal with them? Then our *...For Dummies®* business and general reference book series is for you.

...For Dummies business and general reference books are written for those frustrated and hard-working souls who know they aren't dumb, but find that the myriad of personal and business issues and the accompanying horror stories make them feel helpless. *...For Dummies* books use a lighthearted approach, a down-to-earth style, and even cartoons and humorous icons to diffuse fears and build confidence. Lighthearted but not lightweight, these books are perfect survival guides to solve your everyday personal and business problems.

> *"More than a publishing phenomenon, 'Dummies' is a sign of the times."*
> — The New York Times

> *"...you won't go wrong buying them."*
> — Walter Mossberg, Wall Street Journal, on IDG Books' ...For Dummies books

> *"A world of detailed and authoritative information is packed into them..."*
> — U.S. News and World Report

Already, millions of satisfied readers agree. They have made *...For Dummies* the #1 introductory level computer book series and a best-selling business book series. They have written asking for more. So, if you're looking for the best and easiest way to learn about business and other general reference topics, look to *...For Dummies* to give you a helping hand.

IDG BOOKS WORLDWIDE™

4/98

Praise for *Jazz For Dummies*

"Dirk Sutro, obviously, is madly in love with jazz and its foremost players. It is also more than obvious that he knows what he's talking about."
— "Chubby" Jackson, *jazz bassist*

"When asked, 'What is Jazz?' the great Louis Armstrong replied, 'If you have to ask, you'll never know.' With *Jazz For Dummies,* now you can know one of...America's greatest contributions to world culture."
— Jon Faddis, *jazz trumpeter*

"Dirk Sutro has done an excellent job of conveying to the layman the intricacies and subtle nuances involved in the playing of jazz music. Well done!"
— Charles McPherson, *jazz saxophonist and composer*

"Not only is *Jazz For Dummies* educational, it's fun to read. This book provides an important stepping stone to understanding this complex, profound music. After all, Jazz *is* America's only true art form. It's about time someone did *Jazz For Dummies.* Thanks to Dirk Sutro...it's here!"
— James Moody, *jazz saxophonist*

"*Jazz For Dummies* is a clear, concise, and accurate look at the jazz scene, a major step in demystifying the music and making it more accessible. Long overdue, if you could have just one book about jazz, this should be the one."
— Bobby Matos, *Latin jazz recording artist, percussionist, leader of Bobby Matos & the Afro Cuban Jazz Ensemble*

JAZZ FOR DUMMIES®

by Dirk Sutro

Foreword by Barney Kessel

**IDG
BOOKS**
WORLDWIDE

IDG Books Worldwide, Inc.
An International Data Group Company

Foster City, CA ♦ Chicago, IL ♦ Indianapolis, IN ♦ New York, NY

Jazz For Dummies®

ML
3506
.S94
1998

Published by
IDG Books Worldwide, Inc.
An International Data Group Company
919 E. Hillsdale Blvd.
Suite 400
Foster City, CA 94404
www.idgbooks.com (IDG Books Worldwide Web site)
www.dummies.com (Dummies Press Web site)

Library of Congress Catalog Card No.: 98-86180

ISBN: 0-7645-5081-0

Printed in the United States of America

10 9 8 7 6 5 4 3 2 1

1B/SR/QY/ZY/IN

Distributed in the United States by IDG Books Worldwide, Inc.

Distributed by Macmillan Canada for Canada; by Transworld Publishers Limited in the United Kingdom; by IDG Norge Books for Norway; by IDG Sweden Books for Sweden; by Woodslane Pty. Ltd. for Australia; by Woodslane (NZ) Ltd. for New Zealand; by Addison Wesley Longman Singapore Pte Ltd. for Singapore, Malaysia, Thailand, Indonesia and Korea; by Norma Comunicaciones S.A. for Colombia; by Intersoft for South Africa; by International Thomson Publishing for Germany, Austria and Switzerland; by Toppan Company Ltd. for Japan; by Distribuidora Cuspide for Argentina; by Livraria Cultura for Brazil; by Ediciencia S.A. for Ecuador; by Ediciones ZETA S.C.R. Ltda. for Peru; by WS Computer Publishing Corporation, Inc., for the Philippines; by Unalis Corporation for Taiwan; by Contemporanea de Ediciones for Venezuela; by Computer Book & Magazine Store for Puerto Rico; by Express Computer Distributors for the Caribbean and West Indies. Authorized Sales Agent: Anthony Rudkin Associates for the Middle East and North Africa.

For general information on IDG Books Worldwide's books in the U.S., please call our Consumer Customer Service department at 800-762-2974. For reseller information, including discounts and premium sales, please call our Reseller Customer Service department at 800-434-3422.

For information on where to purchase IDG Books Worldwide's books outside the U.S., please contact our International Sales department at 650-655-3200 or fax 650-655-3297.

For information on foreign language translations, please contact our Foreign & Subsidiary Rights department at 650-655-3021 or fax 650-655-3281.

For sales inquiries and special prices for bulk quantities, please contact our Sales department at 650-655-3200 or write to the address above.

For information on using IDG Books Worldwide's books in the classroom or for ordering examination copies, please contact our Educational Sales department at 800-434-2086 or fax 317-596-5499.

For press review copies, author interviews, or other publicity information, please contact our Public Relations department at 650-655-3000 or fax 650-655-3299.

For authorization to photocopy items for corporate, personal, or educational use, please contact Copyright Clearance Center, 222 Rosewood Drive, Danvers, MA 01923, or fax 978-750-4470.

™ is a trademark under exclusive license to IDG Books Worldwide, Inc., from International Data Group, Inc.

**IDG
BOOKS**
WORLDWIDE

About the Author

Dirk Sutro is a writer and jazz fanatic based in Leucadia, California. He has covered jazz for more than 15 years. He has written and lectured about jazz for the Orange County Performing Arts Center in Southern California. He was the jazz critic for the San Diego edition of the *Los Angeles Times* from 1988 to 1992, and he writes regularly about music for *San Diego Magazine*. Sutro is a regular guest host of *These Days* on KPBS-FM in San Diego, where he frequently interviews musicians. He is a graduate of U.C. Berkeley (BA in English) and San Diego State University (MS in Mass Communications).

Author's Acknowledgments

Endless good vibes to those who have stoked my interest in jazz over the years: Craig Huntington, Jon Hendricks, Todd Barkan and his Keystone Korner, and *San Francisco Chronicle* jazz critic Thomas Albright. Also to those who have encouraged, informed, and inspired me in many ways: My parents Dr. Henry A. and Joann Sutro, Holly Hofmann, Chubby Jackson, Barney and Phyllis Kessel, Bill Wilson, David Littlejohn, James Moody, Charles and Chuckie McPherson, Bob Magnusson, Peter Sprague, Russell Beemer, Tom Judson, and folks at KSDS-FM and KPBS-FM.

Raucous "Bird" solos go out to Mark Butler at IDG Books, who signed me for the project and lent moral support all the way through; project editor (and major music-head) Clark Scheffy, for improving every single page; copy editor Diane Smith; and My Man Berigan, whose critical attentions added countless fine details.

Special thanks to: Cats Meow Records in Oregon; Lou's Records in Leucadia, California, the small store with the big selection; Norman Saks for the inside scoop on Charlie Parker; Stanley and Helen Dance for their legacy of fine writing on jazz; Hannah and Semira, my daughters and lights of my life, and Berta, for her essential role in both of those productions.

ABOUT IDG BOOKS WORLDWIDE

Welcome to the world of IDG Books Worldwide.

IDG Books Worldwide, Inc., is a subsidiary of International Data Group, the world's largest publisher of computer-related information and the leading global provider of information services on information technology. IDG was founded more than 25 years ago and now employs more than 8,500 people worldwide. IDG publishes more than 275 computer publications in over 75 countries (see listing below). More than 90 million people read one or more IDG publications each month.

Launched in 1990, IDG Books Worldwide is today the #1 publisher of best-selling computer books in the United States. We are proud to have received eight awards from the Computer Press Association in recognition of editorial excellence and three from *Computer Currents'* First Annual Readers' Choice Awards. Our best-selling *...For Dummies*® series has more than 50 million copies in print with translations in 38 languages. IDG Books Worldwide, through a joint venture with IDG's Hi-Tech Beijing, became the first U.S. publisher to publish a computer book in the People's Republic of China. In record time, IDG Books Worldwide has become the first choice for millions of readers around the world who want to learn how to better manage their businesses.

Our mission is simple: Every one of our books is designed to bring extra value and skill-building instructions to the reader. Our books are written by experts who understand and care about our readers. The knowledge base of our editorial staff comes from years of experience in publishing, education, and journalism — experience we use to produce books for the '90s. In short, we care about books, so we attract the best people. We devote special attention to details such as audience, interior design, use of icons, and illustrations. And because we use an efficient process of authoring, editing, and desktop publishing our books electronically, we can spend more time ensuring superior content and spend less time on the technicalities of making books.

You can count on our commitment to deliver high-quality books at competitive prices on topics you want to read about. At IDG Books Worldwide, we continue in the IDG tradition of delivering quality for more than 25 years. You'll find no better book on a subject than one from IDG Books Worldwide.

John J. Kilcullen
John Kilcullen
CEO
IDG Books Worldwide, Inc.

Steven Berkowitz
Steven Berkowitz
President and Publisher
IDG Books Worldwide, Inc.

WINNER
*Eighth Annual
Computer Press
Awards ≥ 1992*

WINNER
*Ninth Annual
Computer Press
Awards ≥ 1993*

WINNER
*Tenth Annual
Computer Press
Awards ≥ 1994*

WINNER
*Eleventh Annual
Computer Press
Awards ≥ 1995*

IDG Books Worldwide, Inc., is a subsidiary of International Data Group, the world's largest publisher of computer-related information and the leading global provider of information services on information technology. International Data Group publishes over 275 computer publications in over 75 countries. More than 90 million people read one or more International Data Group publications each month. International Data Group's publications include: **ARGENTINA:** Buyer's Guide, Computerworld Argentina, PC World Argentina; **AUSTRALIA:** Australian Macworld, Australian PC World, Australian Reseller News, Computerworld, IT Casebook, Network World, Publish, Webmaster; **AUSTRIA:** Computerwelt Österreich, Networks Austria, PC Tip Austria; **BANGLADESH:** PC World Bangladesh; **BELARUS:** PC World Belarus; **BELGIUM:** Data News; **BRAZIL:** Annuário de Informática, Computerworld, Connections, Macworld, PC Player, PC World, Publish, Reseller News, Supergamepower; **BULGARIA:** Computerworld Bulgaria, Network World Bulgaria, PC & MacWorld Bulgaria; **CANADA:** CIO Canada, Client/Server World, ComputerWorld Canada, InfoWorld Canada, NetworkWorld Canada, WebWorld; **CHILE:** Computerworld Chile, PC World Chile; **COLOMBIA:** Computerworld Colombia, PC World Colombia; **COSTA RICA:** PC World Centro America; **THE CZECH AND SLOVAK REPUBLICS:** Computerworld Czechoslovakia, Macworld Czech Republic, PC World Czechoslovakia; **DENMARK:** Communications World Danmark, Computerworld Danmark, Macworld Danmark, PC World Danmark, Techworld Denmark; **DOMINICAN REPUBLIC:** PC World Republica Dominicana; **ECUADOR:** PC World Ecuador; **EGYPT:** Computerworld Middle East, PC World Middle East; **EL SALVADOR:** PC World Centro America; **FINLAND:** MikroPC, Tietoverkko, Tietoviikko; **FRANCE:** Distributique, Hebdo, Info PC, Le Monde Informatique, Macworld, Reseaux & Telecoms, WebMaster France; **GERMANY:** Computer Partner, Computerwoche, Computerwoche Extra, Computerwoche FOCUS, Global Online, Macwelt, PC Welt; **GREECE:** Amiga Computing, GamePro Greece, Multimedia World; **GUATEMALA:** PC World Centro America; **HONDURAS:** PC World Centro America; **HONG KONG:** Computerworld Hong Kong, PC World Hong Kong, Publish in Asia; **HUNGARY:** ABCD CD-ROM, Computerworld Szamitastechnika, Internetto online Magazine, PC World Hungary, PC-X Magazin Hungary; **ICELAND:** Tolvuheimur PC World Island; **INDIA:** Information Communications World, Information Systems Computerworld, PC World India, Publish in Asia; **INDONESIA:** InfoKomputer PC World, Komputek Computerworld, Publish in Asia; **IRELAND:** ComputerScope, PC Live!; **ISRAEL:** Macworld Israel, People & Computers/Computerworld; **ITALY:** Computerworld Italia, Macworld Italia, Networking Italia, PC World Italia; **JAPAN:** DTP World, Macworld Japan, Nikkei Personal Computing, OS/2 World Japan, SunWorld Japan, Windows NT World, Windows World Japan; **KENYA:** PC World East African; **KOREA:** Hi-Tech Information, Macworld Korea, PC World Korea; **MACEDONIA:** PC World Macedonia; **MALAYSIA:** Computerworld Malaysia, PC World Malaysia, Publish in Asia; **MALTA:** PC World Malta; **MEXICO:** Computerworld Mexico, PC World Mexico; **MYANMAR:** PC World Myanmar; **NETHERLANDS:** Computer! Totaal, LAN Internetworking Magazine, LAN World Buyers Guide, Macworld Netherlands, Net, WebWereld; **NEW ZEALAND:** Absolute Beginners Guide and Plain & Simple Series, Computer Buyer, Computer Industry Directory, Computerworld New Zealand, MTB, Network World, PC World New Zealand; **NICARAGUA:** PC World Centro America; **NORWAY:** Computerworld Norge, CW Rapport, Datamagasinet, Financial Rapport, Kursguide Norge, Macworld Norge, Multimediaworld Norge, PC World Ekspress Norge, PC World Nettverk, PC World Norge, PC World ProduktGuide Norge; **PAKISTAN:** Computerworld Pakistan; **PANAMA:** PC World Panama; **PEOPLE'S REPUBLIC OF CHINA:** China Computer Users, China Computerworld, China InfoWorld, China Telecom World Weekly, Computer & Communication, Electronic Design China, Electronics Today, Electronics Weekly, Game Software, PC World China, Popular Computer Week, Software Weekly, Software World, Telecom World; **PERU:** Computerworld Peru, PC World Profesional Peru, PC World SoHo Peru; **PHILIPPINES:** Click!, Computerworld Philippines, PC World Philippines, Publish in Asia; **POLAND:** Computerworld Poland, Computerworld Special Report Poland, Cyber, Macworld Poland, Networld Poland, PC World Komputer; **PORTUGAL:** Cerebro/PC World, Computerworld/Correio Informático, Dealer World Portugal, Mac*In/PC*In Portugal, Multimedia World; **PUERTO RICO:** PC World Puerto Rico; **ROMANIA:** Computerworld Romania, PC World Romania, Telecom Romania; **RUSSIA:** Computerworld Russia, Mir PK, Publish, Seti; **SINGAPORE:** Computerworld Singapore, PC World Singapore, Publish in Asia; **SLOVENIA:** Monitor; **SOUTH AFRICA:** Computing SA, Network World SA, Software World SA; **SPAIN:** Communicaciones World España, Computerworld España, Dealer World España, Macworld España, PC World España; **SRI LANKA:** Infolink PC World; **SWEDEN:** CAP&Design, Computer Sweden, Corporate Computing Sweden, Internetworld Sweden, it.branschen, Macworld Sweden, MaxiData Sweden, MikroDatorn, Nätverk & Kommunikation, PC World Sweden, PCaktiv, Windows World Sweden; **SWITZERLAND:** Computerworld Schweiz, Macworld Schweiz, PCtip; **TAIWAN:** Computerworld Taiwan, Macworld Taiwan, NEW ViSiON/Publish, PC World Taiwan, Windows World Taiwan; **THAILAND:** Publish in Asia, Thai Computerworld; **TURKEY:** Computerworld Turkiye, Macworld Turkiye, Network World Turkiye, PC World Turkiye; **UKRAINE:** Computerworld Kiev, Multimedia World Ukraine, PC World Ukraine; **UNITED KINGDOM:** Acorn User UK, Amiga Action UK, Amiga Computing UK, Apple Talk UK, Computing, Macworld, Parents and Computers UK, PC Advisor, PC Home, PSX Pro, The WEB; **UNITED STATES:** Cable in the Classroom, CIO Magazine, Computerworld, DOS World, Federal Computer Week, GamePro Magazine, InfoWorld, I-Way, Macworld, Network World, PC Games, PC World, Publish, Video Event, THE WEB Magazine, and WebMaster; online webzines: JavaWorld, NetscapeWorld, and SunWorld Online; **URUGUAY:** InfoWorld Uruguay; **VENEZUELA:** Computerworld Venezuela, PC World Venezuela; and **VIETNAM:** PC World Vietnam.   5/7/98

Publisher's Acknowledgments

We're proud of this book; please register your comments through our IDG Books Worldwide Online Registration Form located at http://my2cents.dummies.com.

Some of the people who helped bring this book to market include the following:

Acquisitions, Editorial, and Media Development

Project Editor: Clark Scheffy

Acquisitions Editor: Mark Butler

Copy Editor: Diane Smith

Technical Editor: Berlgan Taylor

Editorial Manager: Mary Corder

Editorial Assistant: Donna Love

Editorial Coordinator: Maureen Kelly

Special Help

Constance Carlisle, Suzanne Thomas

Production

Project Coordinators: Valery Bourke, Regina Snyder

Layout and Graphics: Lou Boudreau, Linda M. Boyer, J. Tyler Connor, Angela F. Hunckler, Drew R. Moore, Heather N. Pearson, Anna Rohrer, Brent Savage, Janet Seib, Kate Snell

Photo credits: Everett Collection; Everett/CSU Archives; and Fantasy Inc.; Yamaha Corporation of America, Band and Orchestral Division.

Proofreaders: Christine Berman, Kelli Botta, Rebecca Senninger, Janet M. Withers

Indexer: Steve Rath

General and Administrative

IDG Books Worldwide, Inc.: John Kilcullen, CEO; Steven Berkowitz, President and Publisher

IDG Books Technology Publishing: Brenda McLaughlin, Senior Vice President and Group Publisher

Dummies Technology Press and Dummies Editorial: Diane Graves Steele, Vice President and Associate Publisher; Mary Bednarek, Director of Acquisitions and Product Development; Kristin A. Cocks, Editorial Director

Dummies Trade Press: Kathleen A. Welton, Vice President and Publisher; Kevin Thornton, Acquisitions Manager

IDG Books Production for Dummies Press: Michael R. Britton, Vice President of Production and Creative Services; Beth Jenkins Roberts, Production Director; Cindy L. Phipps, Manager of Project Coordination, Production Proofreading, and Indexing; Kathie S. Schutte, Supervisor of Page Layout; Shelley Lea, Supervisor of Graphics and Design; Debbie J. Gates, Production Systems Specialist; Robert Springer, Supervisor of Proofreading; Debbie Stailey, Special Projects Coordinator; Tony Augsburger, Supervisor of Reprints and Bluelines

Dummies Packaging and Book Design: Robin Seaman, Creative Director; Jocelyn Kelaita, Product Packaging Coordinator; Kavish + Kavish, Cover Design

♦

The publisher would like to give special thanks to Patrick J. McGovern, without whom this book would not have been possible.

♦

Contents at a Glance

Introduction 1

Part I: What Is Jazz? 5

Chapter 1: Listening to Jazz: Altered Ears 7
Chapter 2: Birth of an American Music: Jazz to the 1920s 19
Chapter 3: The Rise of Big Band Swing: The 1930s and Beyond 33
Chapter 4: Bebop to Cool: The 1940s and 1950s 49
Chapter 5: Fractured Forms: The 1960s and 1970s 67
Chapter 6: Latin Jazz: Seven Decades of Spicy Seasonings (1930s to the 1990s) 77
Chapter 7: Jazz Now 89

Part II: Up Front 95

Chapter 8: Saxophonists: Jazz's Main Guard 97
Chapter 9: Trumpeters: Jazz's Bright, Brassy Showstoppers 127
Chapter 10: Vocalists: Swinging without an Axe 147

Part III: Keyboards 167

Chapter 11: Piano and Other Keyboards: Black and White Keys to Jazz 169
Chapter 12: Organists: Cool, Laid-Back Peacekeepers 195

Part IV: Percussion 205

Chapter 13: Drummers: Swingin' through Time 207
Chapter 14: Vibraphonists: Jazz's Musical Rhythm Makers 223

Part V: Strings 235

Chapter 15: The Bassists: Boomers of the Beat 237
Chapter 16: Guitar: Strung Out on Jazz 253

Part VI: More Brass and Reeds 271

Chapter 17: Clarinetists: Leading Licorice Men 273
Chapter 18: Flutists: Mellow Pipers of Jazz 283
Chapter 19: Trombonists: Sliding to the Beat 293

Part VII: The Part of Tens 305

Chapter 20: Ten Trustworthy Jazz Labels 307
Chapter 21: Catching Real Live Jazz 311
Chapter 22: Resources for Further Jazz Enlightenment 323
Appendix A: Starting a Collection 331
Appendix B: What's on the CD? 341

Index 343

Book Registration Information .... Back of Book

Cartoons at a Glance

By Rich Tennant

"The problem with wine tastings is you're not supposed to swallow, and Clifford refuses to spit. Fortunately, he studied trumpet with Dizzy Gillespie."

page 95

page 167

page 5

page 235

page 271

page 205

"Funny—I just assumed it would be Carnegie, too."

page 305

Fax: 978-546-7747 • E-mail: the5wave@tiac.net

Table of Contents

Introduction 1
   Why You Should Read This Book 2
   How to Use This Book 2
   Icons Used in This Book 3
   Bop on, Bold Reader 4

Part I: What Is Jazz? 5

   Chapter 1: Listening to Jazz: Altered Ears 7
      The Origin of the Word *Jazz* 8
         Theories 8
         Controversy 8
      What Is Jazz? 9
         Three key elements 9
         The roots of jazz 11
      What Else Is Jazz? 14
         What is acid, free, *avant garde,* abstract jazz? 14
         What some players say about jazz 15
      Listening to Genuine Jazz 16
         Hearing harmony and melody 16
         Tapping the rhythm section 16
         Picking out the distinctive voices 17

   Chapter 2: Birth of an American Music: Jazz to the 1920s 19
      Basic Ingredients 20
      The First Players 21
         Buddy Bolden (1877-1931) 21
         Other Bolden-era bands 22
      Ragtime 23
         Is ragtime jazz? 24
         Masters of ragtime 24
      First Recording: Original Dixieland Jass Band 25
      Shifting Scene: Chicago in the 1920s 27
         Joe "King" Oliver (1885-1938) 27
         Louis Armstrong (1901-1971) 28
         Jelly Roll Morton (1890-1941) 29
         Bix Beiderbecke (1903-1931) 29
         The Austin High Gang 30
         Members of the Gang 31
         Jimmie Noone and Earl Hines form a band 31
         Other 1920s Chicago sounds 32
         Emergence of swing..32

   Chapter 3: The Rise of Big Band Swing: The 1930s and Beyond 33
      New York: Before the Big Bands 34
      Big Bands Take over Jazz 34
         Fletcher Henderson (1897-1952) 36
         Other big bands from the 1920s 37
         Taking up where Fletcher Henderson left off 38
      Midwest Territory Bands 39
         Bennie Moten (1894-1935) 40
         Other territory bands 40

The Coronation of Duke Ellington (1899-1974) 41
    Royal history: Ellington's early years 41
    The Ellington sound 42
    Ellington's legacy 43
Kings of Swing 43
    Count Basie (1904-1984) sets the swing standard 45
    Benny Goodman (1909-1986) 46
Other Big Bands Come on Strong 47
Keeping the Flame Alive 48

Chapter 4: Bebop to Cool: The 1940s and 1950s 49
Seeds of Change 50
Evolution of the Bebop Sound 51
    Vital music, powerful emotions 51
    Traits of bebop 52
    The bebop scene 52
    Some examples of bebop 54
Bebop and Big Bands 54
    Woody Herman (1913-1987) 55
    Stan Kenton (1911-1979) 55
    Claude Thornhill (1909-1969) 56
Offshoots of Bebop: Cool Jazz and Hard Bop 56
    Los Angeles and West Coast cool 57
        Chet Baker (1929-1988) 58
        Dave Brubeck (born 1920) and Paul Desmond (1924-1977) 58
        Miles Davis (1926-1991) 58
        Gil Evans (1912-1988) 59
        Jimmy Giuffre (born 1921) 59
        Shelly Manne (1920-1984) 59
        Modern Jazz Quartet 59
        Gerry Mulligan (1927-1996) 59
        Shorty Rogers (born 1924) 60
        Howard Rumsey's Lighthouse All-Stars 60
        Lennie Tristano (1919-1978) 60
    New York and hard bop 60
        Gene Ammons (1925-1974) 61
        Art Blakey (1919-1990) 61
        Clifford Brown (1930-1956) and Max Roach (born 1924) 61
        Miles Davis (1926-1991) 62
        Dexter Gordon (1923-1990) 62
        J.J. Johnson (born 1924) 62
        Clifford Jordan (1931-1993) 62
        Jackie McLean (born 1932) 62
        Charles Mingus (1922-1978) 63
        Hank Mobley (1930-1986) 63
        Thelonious Monk (1917-1982) 63
        Lee Morgan (1938-1972) 63
        Sonny Rollins (born 1930) 63
        Horace Silver (born 1928) 64
        Sonny Stitt (1924-1982) 64
        Kai Winding (1922-1983) 64
        Other hard boppers: 65
Rise of the Piano Trio 65
    Red Garland (1921-1977) 66

Ahmad Jamal (born 1930) 66
Bud Powell (1924-1966) 66

Chapter 5: Fractured Forms: The 1960s and 1970s 67
The Early *Avant garde* 67
George Russell (born 1923) and his Lydian Concept 68
Third stream 68
Free jazz versus *avant garde* 68
Two centers for free and *avant garde* jazz 69
The 1960s *Avant garde* 69
Anthony Braxton (born 1945) 70
Eric Dolphy (1928-1964) 70
Archie Shepp (born 1937) 70
Paul Bley (born 1932) 71
World Saxophone Quartet 71
Don Cherry (1936-1995) 71
The Free Jazz Players 71
Beginnings of free jazz 72
Ornette Coleman (born 1930) 72
John Coltrane (1926-1967) 73
Further Free Jazz 74
Electric and Eclectic Fusions 75
Miles Davis (1926-1991) 75
Other fusioneers 75

Chapter 6: Latin Jazz: Seven Decades of Spicy Seasonings (1930s to the 1990s) 77
So, What Is Latin Jazz? 78
Early Latin Influences on Jazz 78
The Cuboppers 79
Machito (1912-1984) and Mario Bauza (1911-1993) 79
Dizzy Gillespie (1917-1993) and Chano Pozo (1915-1948) 80
Chico O'Farrill (born 1921) and his legacy 81
1950s: Latin Jazz Flowering 82
Art Blakey (1919-1990) 82
Woody Herman (1913-1987) 82
Stan Kenton (1911-1979) 82
Perez Prado (1916-1983) 82
Tito Puente (born 1923) 83
George Shearing (born 1919) 83
Cal Tjader (1925-1982) 83
Bossa '60s 84
Gato Barbieri (born 1934) 84
Ray Barretto (born 1929) 84
Willie Bobo (1934-1983) 84
Stan Getz (1927-1991) 85
Astrud (born 1940) and Joao Gilberto (born 1932) 85
Herbie Mann (born 1930) 85
Mongo Santamaria (born 1922) 85
Dave Valentin (born 1954) 86
Spicy, Electric '70s 86
Chick Corea (born 1941) 86
Poncho Sanchez (born 1951) 86
Arturo Sandoval (born 1949) 86
Latin Jazz: The New Generation 87

Jerry Gonzalez (born 1949) 87
Sergio Mendes 87
Danilo Perez (born 1966) 87
Gonzalo Rubalcaba (born 1963) 88
Hilton Ruiz (born 1952) 88
Chucho Valdes (born 1941) 88
A few other Latin flavors worth watching for 88

Chapter 7: Jazz Now **89**
What's the Hap? Diversity 90
What Is Acid Jazz, Man? 90
Neo-Traditionalists 91
Contemporary Jazz 92
Living Jazz Masters 93

Part II: Up Front **95**

Chapter 8: Saxophonists: Jazz's Main Guard **97**
Saxophone Steps Forward 97
The Early Swing Pioneers 99
Sidney Bechet (1897-1959) 99
Benny Carter (born 1907) 100
Coleman "Hawk" Hawkins (1904-1969) 100
Johnny Hodges (1907-1970) 102
Ben Webster (1909-1973) 102
Lester "Prez" Young (1909-1959) 103
Other Swing saxophonists 103
Charlie "Yardbird" Parker (1920-1955) and the Rise of Bebop 106
The making of a legend 106
Bird's recordings 108
Parker's musical legacy 108
Other Bebop Saxophonists 109
Pepper Adams (1930-1986) 109
Earl Bostic (1913-1965) 109
Sonny Criss (1924-1977) 110
Dexter Gordon(1923-1990) 110
Wardell Gray (1921-1955) 111
Johnny Griffin (born 1928) 111
Gigi Gryce (1927-1983) 112
Sonny Rollins (born 1930) 112
Sonny Stitt (1924-1982) 112
Sax in the Fifties: Hard Bop, Cool Jazz 113
Cannonball Adderley (1928-1975) 113
Gene Ammons (1925-1974) 113
Buddy Collette (born 1921) 114
Paul Desmond (1924-1977) 114
Stan Getz (1927-1991) 114
Lee Konitz (born 1927) 115
Harold Land (born 1928) 115
Jackie McLean (born 1932) 115
Hank Mobley (1930-1986) 115
James Moody (born 1925) 116
Gerry Mulligan (1927-1996) 116
Art Pepper (1925-1982) 116
Zoot Sims (1925-1985) 116

Outer Limits: Ornette Coleman (born 1930) 117
Spiritual Search: John Coltrane (1926-1967) 118
On the Cutting Edge 120
    Anthony Braxton (born 1945) 120
    Eric Dolphy (1928-1964) 121
    Julius Hemphill (1940-1995) 121
    Rahsaan Roland Kirk (1936-1977) 121
    Oliver Lake (born 1942) 121
    Roscoe Mitchell (born 1940) 122
    Pharoah Sanders (born 1940) 122
    Archie Shepp (born 1937) 122
    Henry Threadgill (born 1944) 122
Electrifying Saxophones 123
    Eddie Harris (born 1934) 123
    Wayne Shorter (born 1933) 123
    Grover Washington, Jr. (born 1943) 123
The Now Generation 123
    Michael Brecker (born 1949) 124
    James Carter (born 1969) 124
    Kenny Garrett (born 1960) 124
    Joe Henderson (born 1937) 124
    Joe Lovano (born 1952) 125
    Branford Marsalis (born 1960) 125
    Courtney Pine (born 1964) 125
    Phil Woods (born 1931) 125
    A few more 126

Chapter 9: Trumpeters: Jazz's Bright, Brassy Showstoppers **127**
A Trumpet Hails the Birth of Jazz: Buddy Bolden (1877-1931) 127
The Early Innovators 128
    Freddie Keppard (1890-1933) 128
    King Oliver (1885-1938) 129
    Two talented peers: Bix Beiderbecke (1903-1931)and
        Louis Armstrong 130
Father of Modern Jazz Trumpet: Louis Armstrong (1901-1971) 131
    An innovator like no other 131
    Before "Pops" was even knee-high 131
    Louis's first gig 132
    Armstrong breaks out on his own 132
    Armstrong in later years 133
    Armstrong's contemporaries of the '20s and '30s 134
Trumpet Goes Bop 136
    John Birks "Dizzy" Gillespie (1917-1993) 136
    Fats Navarro (1923-1958) and Clifford Brown (1930-1956) 139
    Jazz's Coolest Trumpeter: Miles Davis (1926-1991) 140
The Other Legends 142
    Chet Baker (1929-1988) 142
    Lester Bowie (born 1941) 143
    Tom Harrell (born 1946) 143
    Freddie Hubbard (born 1938) 143
    Lee Morgan (1938-1972) 143
    Woody Shaw (1944-1989) 143
    Clark Terry (born 1920) 144
    Too much talent, too little space 144
Young Brass: A New Generation of Jazz Trumpeters 145

Chapter 10: Vocalists: Swinging without an Axe **147**

Early Vocalists 147
What makes a jazz vocalist? 148
Ida Cox (1896-1967) 149
Alberta Hunter (1895-1984) 149
Ma Rainey (1886-1939) 150
Jimmy Rushing (1903-1972) 150
Bessie Smith (1894-1937) 150
Mamie Smith (1883-1946) 151
Sippie Wallace (1898-1986) 151
Sweet Depression-Era Singers 151
Connie Boswell (1907-1976) 151
Bing Crosby (1904-1977) 152
Annette Hanshaw (1910-1985) 152
Ethel Waters (1896-1977) 152
Golden Years of Swing and Songwriting 153
Billie Holiday (1915-1959) 153
Helen Forrest 154
Other key big band swing singers 154
Singers Go Bebopping 156
Ella Fitzgerald (1917-1996) 157
Eddie Jefferson (1918-1979) 158
King Pleasure (1922-1981) 158
Sarah Vaughan (1924-1990) 159
Eclectic 1950s 160
Jon Hendricks (born 1921) 160
Other jazz singers from the late 1940s and 1950s 161
Frank Sinatra (1915-1998) 163
Brazilian Flavors 163
Into the Modern Era 164
Fringe dwellers and others 164
More in the mainstream 165
Voices for the Future 165

Part III: Keyboards *167*

**Chapter 11: Piano and Other Keyboards: Black and White Keys
to Jazz** **169**

The Rise of Ragtime: "Maple Leaf Rag" And Other Early Jazz Piano 170
Scott Joplin (1868-1917) 170
James P. Johnson (1894-1955) 172
Others from the early ivory front 172
Formative Swing Years 173
Earl "Fatha" Hines (1903-1983) 173
Jelly Roll Morton (1890-1941) 174
Fats Waller (1904-1943) 174
Other pioneers, from ragtime to swing 175
The Boogie Men 176
Flying Next to Bird: The Bebop Pianists 177
Barry Harris (born 1929) 177
Hampton Hawes (1928-1977) 177
John Lewis (born 1920) 178
Thelonious Monk (1917-1982) 178
Bud Powell (1924-1966) 179

Cool, Hard Bop, and Beyond 179
   Dave Brubeck (born 1920) 180
   Kenny Drew (1928-1993) 180
   Bill Evans (1929-1980) 180
   Tommy Flanagan (born 1930) 180
   Ahmad Jamal (born 1930) 181
   Wynton Kelly (1931-1971) 181
   Les McCann (born 1935) 181
   Marian McPartland (born 1920) 181
   Dodo Marmarosa (born 1925) 182
   George Shearing (born 1919) 182
   Horace Silver (born 1928) 182
   Billy Taylor (born 1921) 182
   Bobby Timmons (1935-1974) 183
   Lennie Tristano (1919-1978) 183
   Randy Weston (born 1926) 183
Latin Piano Connections 184
   Eliane Elias (born 1960) 184
   Eddie Palmieri (born 1936) 184
   Hilton Ruiz (born 1952) 185
   Bebo (born 1918) and Chucho Valdes (born 1941) 185
Timeless Classics 185
   Erroll Garner (1921-1977) 185
   Oscar Peterson (born 1925) 186
   Art Tatum (1909-1956) 186
   McCoy Tyner (born 1938) 187
Wide Open Places the Piano's Been 187
   Muhal Richard Abrams (born 1930) 187
   Paul Bley (born 1932) 188
   Marilyn Crispell (born 1947) 188
   Herbie Hancock (born 1940) 188
   Andrew Hill (born 1937) 189
   Abdullah (Dollar Brand) Ibrihim (born 1934) 190
   Keith Jarret (born 1945) 190
   Don Pullen (born 1941) 191
   Horace Tapscott (born 1934) 191
   Cecil Taylor (born 1929) 191
Keys with a Cord 192
Today's Prime Pianists 192

Chapter 12: Organists: Cool, Laid-Back Peacekeepers **195**
Early Jazz Organ 196
   Count Basie (1904-1984) 197
   Fats Waller (1904-1943) 197
   Other early jazz organists 197
The 1960s Groove 198
   Jimmy Smith (born 1925) 199
   Bill Doggett (born 1916) 200
   Johnny "Hammond" Smith (born 1933) 200
   Charles Earland (born 1941) 200
   Richard "Groove" Holmes (1931-1991) 201
   "Brother" Jack McDuff (born 1926) 201
   Jimmy McGriff (born 1936) 202
   Don Patterson (born 1936) 202

Big John Patton (born 1935) 202
Sun Ra (1914-1993) 202
Shirley Scott (born 1934) 202
Lonnie Smith (born 1953) 203
Larry Young (1940-1978) 203
Keepers of the Flame: Jazz Organ Today 203
Joey DeFrancesco (born 1971) 203
Barbara Dennerlein (born 1964) 204
Larry Goldings (born 1968) 204
Greg Hatza 204
John Medeski (born 1965) 204

Part IV: Percussion **205**

Chapter 13: Drummers: Swingin' through Time **207**
Early Jazz Drummers 207
Baby Dodds (1898-1959) 209
Zutty Singleton (1897-1975) 209
Paul Barbarin (1899-1969) 210
Cozy Cole (1906-1981) 210
Dave Tough 210
Modern Colorists 211
Chick Webb (1909-1939) 211
Gene Krupa (1909-1973) 211
Jo Jones (1911-1985) 212
Buddy Rich (1917-1987) 213
Louie Bellson (born 1924) 214
Bop and Post-Bop Drumming 215
Kenny Clarke (1914-1985) 215
Art Blakey (1919-1990) 216
Max Roach (born 1924) 217
Others from '50s and '60s 218
The *Avant garde* 219
Elvin Jones (born 1927) 219
Ronald Shannon Jackson (born 1940) 220
Fusing to Funk and Rock: Tapping New Power 220
Billy Cobham (born 1946) 220
Alphonse Mouzon (born 1948) 221
Tony Williams (1945-1997) 221
Jack DeJohnette (born 1942) 222
Other excellent jazz drummers 222

Chapter 14: Vibraphonists: Jazz's Musical Rhythm Makers **223**
Early Vibraphonists 223
Lionel "Hamp" Hampton (born 1909) 224
Red Norvo (born 1908) 225
Adrian Rollini 227
Vibes in the Modern Era 227
Terry Gibbs (born 1924) 227
Milt "Bags" Jackson (born 1923) 228
Other 1940s/1950s vibes 229
Good Vibes in the '60s 230
Gary Burton (born 1943) 230
Bobby Hutcherson (born 1941) 230

Contemporary Pop/Jazz Vibes 231
    Spyro Gyra and the vibes of Dave Samuels (born 1948) 231
    Steps Ahead and Mike Mainieri (born 1938) 232
From the '50s Forward: Other Happenin' Vibraphonists 232
    Roy Ayers (born 1940) 232
    Eddie Costa (1930-1962) 233
    Victor Feldman (1934-1987) 233
    Jay Hoggard (born 1954) 233
    Gary McFarland (1933-1971) 233
    Buddy Montgomery (born 1930) 234
    Steve Nelson (born 1955) 234
    Cal Tjader (1925-1982) 234
    Also look out for 234

Part V: Strings 235

Chapter 15: The Bassists: Boomers of the Beat 237
New Orleans Jazz's Early Bassists: Playing on the Beat 239
    Wellman Braud (1891-1966) 239
    Pops Foster (1892-1969) 239
    John Kirby (1908-1952) 240
    Walter Page (1900-1957) 240
Jimmy Blanton (1918-1942): First of the Modern Bassists 240
Swing Bassmen 241
    Milt Hinton (born 1910) 241
    Chubby Jackson (born 1918) 242
    Slam Stewart (1914-1987) 242
Building from Blanton: Oscar Pettiford (1922-1960) 242
Big Bad Bassman: Charles Mingus (1922-1979) 243
Mr. Congeniality: Ray Brown (born 1926) 244
Others from the '40s and '50s 245
    Cecil McBee (born 1935) 245
    Red Mitchell (1927-1992) 246
Beyond Bass-ics: The *Avant garde* 246
    Charlie Haden (born 1937) 246
    Niels-Henning Orsted Pedersen (born 1946) 247
    Gary Peacock (born 1935) 247
    Eberhard Weber (born 1940) 248
Connected with Current: Electric Bass 248
    Ron Carter (born 1937) 248
    Stanley Clarke (born 1951) 249
Wild Man on a Mission: Jaco Pastorius 250
Seasoned Stalwarts 250
Back to Bass-ics: Young Cats Worth a Listen 252
    Charles Fambrough (born 1950) 252
    Christian McBride (born 1972) 252

Chapter 16: Guitar: Strung Out on Jazz 253
Early Jazz Guitarists 254
    Lonnie Johnson (1889-1970) 254
    Eddie Lang (1902-1933) 255
    And both together 255
    Other jazz guitarists made contributions during jazz's early years 255

The Parallel Reality of Django Reinhardt (1910-1953) 256
The Rise of Electric Guitar 259
Charlie Christian (1916-1942) Plugs In 259
    Christian's early years 260
    Christian gets his first break 260
    Christian's contemporaries 261
Bebop Guitarists 263
    Kenny Burrell (born 1931) 263
    Bill DeArango 263
    Herb Ellis (born 1921) 263
    Barney Kessel (born 1923) 264
Guitar in the '50s and Forward 265
    Wes Montgomery (1925-1968) 265
    Aaron "T-Bone" Walker 266
    Other cool axmen, '50s forward 266
        Tal Farlow (born 1921) 266
        Grant Green (1931-1979) 266
        Joe Pass (1929-1994) 266
        Gabor Szabo (1936-1982) 267
Heroes of the Electric Guitar 267
    Derek Bailey (born 1932) 267
    Larry Coryell (born 1943) 267
    Al DiMeola (born 1954) 268
    John McLaughlin (born 1942) 268
    Pat Metheny (born 1954) 268
    Lee Ritenour (born 1952) 268
    Terje Rypdal (born 1947) 269
    John Scofield (born 1951) 269
    A few more 269

Part VI: More Brass and Reeds 271

Chapter 17: Clarinetists: Leading Licorice Men 273
Clarinets in New Orleans 274
    Sidney Bechet (1897-1959) 275
Red-Hot Henchmen: Johnny Dodds and Jimmie Noone 276
    Johnny Dodds (1892-1940) 277
    Jimmie Noone (1895-1944) 277
Swinging Licorice: Big Band Clarinet 277
    Benny Goodman (1909-1986) 277
    Artie Shaw (born 1910) 278
    Other important big band clarinetists 278
Bebop: Clarinet Eases from the Spotlight 279
    Joe Marsala (1907-1978) 279
    Jimmy Hamilton (born 1917) 280
Licorice Virtuosity: Buddy DeFranco and Eddie Daniels 280
    Buddy DeFranco (born 1923) 280
    Eddie Daniels (born 1941) 281
Electric and Abstract Licorice 281
    Alvin Batiste (born 1937) 282
    Evan Christopher (born 1970) 282
    Bennie Maupin (born 1940) 282
    Bob Mintzer (born 1953) 282

Chapter 18: Flutists: Mellow Pipers of Jazz **283**
  Early Jazz Flute 284
    Albert Socarras: The first jazz flutist on record 284
    Wayman Carver (1905-1967) 285
  Fifties Flowering: Frank Wess & Co. 285
    Buddy Collette (born 1921) 286
    Herbie Mann (born 1930) 286
    Frank Wess (born 1922) 287
  The '60s and '70s: Jazz Flutists Follow Different Paths 288
    Two Wizards: Rahsaan Roland Kirk (1936-1977) and
      Yusef Lateef (born 1920) 288
  Contemporary Crosswinds 290
    Prince Lasha (born 1929) 290
    Hubert Laws (born 1939) 290
  Flute into the Present 291
    James Newton (born 1953) 291
    Lew Tabackin (born 1940) 291
    Dave Valentin (born 1954) 292
    Other flutists of note 292

Chapter 19: Trombonists: Sliding to the Beat **293**
  Early Trombonists: Beatkeepers and Improvisers 294
    Kid Ory (1886-1973) 295
    Other early titans of trombone 296
  Swingin' Slidemen 296
    Jack Teagarden (1905-1964) 297
    Duke Ellington's heavies 297
    Other kings of swing trombone 298
  Bebop Bosses of the 'Bone 299
    J.J. Johnson (born 1924) 300
    Kai Winding (1922-1983) 302
  Post-Eminent Trombones (After J.J. Johnson) 302
    Ray Anderson (born 1952) 302
    Curtis Fuller (born 1934) 303
    George Lewis (born 1952) 303
    Albert Mangelsdorff (born 1928) 303
    Grachan Moncur III (born 1937) 303
    Roswell Rudd (born 1935) 303
    Steve Turre (born 1948) 304
    A handful of others 304

Part VII: The Part of Tens *305*

Chapter 20: Ten Trustworthy Jazz Labels **307**
  BMG Classics/RCA/Bluebird 307
  Black Saint/Soul Note 307
  EMD/Blue Note Records 308
  Concord Jazz 308
  Fantasy 309
  Uni/GRP/Impulse! 309
  Rhino Records 309
  Sony/Columbia 310
  Ubiquity 310
  PGD/Verve/Polygram 310

Chapter 21: Catching Real Live Jazz **311**
  Making the Most of Your Club Visit 311
  Hittin' the City Scene 312
      Boston 314
      Chicago 315
      Cleveland 316
      Denver 316
      Los Angeles 317
      Montreal 318
      New Orleans 318
      New York City 319
      Oakland (California) 320
      Philadelphia 320
      San Francisco 321
      Toronto 322

Chapter 22: Resources for Further Jazz Enlightenment **323**
  Books 323
  Magazines 325
  Television/Videos 325
  Web Sites 328

Appendix A: Starting a Collection **331**
  One Man's Story 331
  CD, Vinyl, or Cassette? 332
      What about cassettes? 332
      The final question 333
  My Riff on Sound Systems 333
      CD changers and all-in-one systems 333
      Turntables 334
      Other considerations 334
  Starting Your Collection 334
      Avoiding Greatest Hits packages 335
      Deciding which CDs or albums to buy 335
      Expanding your collection 336
  100 Recommended Jazz Titles 336
      Early jazz/New Orleans 337
      Swing/big band 338
      Bebop, hard bop, and related 338
      Singers 339
      Cool/post bop 339
      Abstract/*avant garde* 339
      Electric 340
      Latin 340
      Jazz from the '80s and '90s 340

Appendix B: What's on the CD? **341**

Index *343*

Book Registration Information .... *Back of Book*

Foreword

. . . .

*J*azz has been misunderstood since the beginning. In the early years, jazz's spontaneity and lack of elaborate written music made it seem "less-than" to scholars and classical music fanatics. Big band swing raised questions of black and white at a time when segregation was still very much the norm in America. In its early years, this music wasn't universally accepted: A turning point came when Benny Goodman's Orchestra became the first jazz ensemble to headline at Carnegie Hall in 1938. Next came my generation in the 1940s. I hate labels, because to me, good jazz is good jazz. But when Charlie Parker and Dizzy Gillespie picked up the pace with music the critics called bebop (I was fortunate enough to record with Parker), once again a new form of jazz was misperceived — even by jazz players themselves. Swing band leader Eddie Condon went so far as to call it "slop" in the pages of *Downbeat,* and trumpeter Louis Armstrong said, "First people get curious about it just because it's new, but soon they get tired of it because it's no good." Of course, we know now that Bird and Diz were among jazz's creative giants.

Which brings me to this book. I think the timing is excellent, and the need is great. What passes for "jazz" on the radio is nothing jazz-like to those of us who have spent our lives playing the music. Along with other forms of art and culture, music seems increasingly driven by what appeals to the largest number of people, what sells. Yet people can't appreciate something they don't know. Most people don't know much about jazz. Children don't learn about it in school, they don't play it in school bands because music programs have been cut all over the country, and adults don't hear real jazz on the radio or read much about it in the popular media.

But like I said, jazz has been misunderstood. Most every time I put on some jazz for someone who doesn't know much about it, they are usually impressed. The beat is irresistible. The melodies are beautiful. The harmonies are intricate and intriguing, and the improvisations are phenomenal feats of spontaneous composition.

Jazz For Dummies explains this rich American music in a language everyone can understand. It gives a friendly introduction to some of the most original music in the world. Open it to any page. Read a few paragraphs. Then play something off the CD. If you don't find yourself infatuated enough to wade in deeper . . . well, I guess that you've earned the right to say, as the classic Vernon Duke/Ira Gershwin tune does, "I Can't Get Started."

Barney Kessel
1998

Introduction

This being the modern age and all, analytical thinking is considered a plus. And it can be great, if it cures cancer, prevents polio . . . or shows someone how to have a successful marriage. But in the case of music, too much analysis can scare away people who may actually love the music.

I think jazz has been victimized by too much *heaviosity* (that is, the state of being heavy). Jazz's great players are indeed musical geniuses. Their music is some of the world's greatest music: intellectually, emotionally, and aesthetically. Jazz, though, is a music that most of all, is *felt*. It comes from a musician's heart. Good jazz connects with your heart, or soul, or wherever your feelings live. Improvisation is, for many jazz musicians, the most effective way to communicate — more powerful and more expressive than words.

Jazz is more than 100 years old and has undergone many changes. It has never been music for the masses — not like Madonna or the Beatles. If anything, it has probably become *more* esoteric over time — more complex and less accessible. Jazz is a deep and amazing art form that's still to find a place on a par with some other art forms, such as classical music and 20th century painting. Many people don't listen to jazz simply because they haven't really heard it before, or they don't know a thing about it.

When big band jazz and ballroom swing dancing faded in the year after World War II, the music began to change. A few years later, dozens of intimate jazz clubs died out, too. College jazz programs replaced the clubs as training grounds for jazz, further removing the music from everyday experience. Today, school children seldom hear jazz or learn about it, let alone play it. And radio has all but abandoned the music it popularized during the 1930s and 1940s.

Yet jazz survives among hardcore fans who have the patience to find it in music stores and clubs. And because jazz is deeply emotional music, anyone can connect with it — without knowing everything about it. Trumpeter and bandleader Louis Armstrong can make you laugh, saxophonist Charlie Parker can shoot an electrical jolt up your spine, and vocalist Billie Holiday can make you cry — even if you don't know what key they're playing in, whether or not they are improvising, or even what makes jazz *jazz*.

Why You Should Read This Book

The purpose of this book is to give your brain just enough information so that you can go find jazz you may like, then let it connect with your heart. Yes, jazz can be extremely complicated, sometimes more complicated than classical music — and I do my best to explain the complications and give you insight into jazz's more important concepts. And while volumes have been written analyzing chord combinations, rhythmic changes, scales, solos, and all sorts of musical details, I don't go as deep as your average Ph.D. I do, however, cover just enough history and explanation so that you can get a feel for jazz and begin to appreciate and understand the main varieties.

This book is designed to be detailed enough so that jazz fanatics will find much new and useful information. It is also written so that absolute jazz neophytes can ease into a lifelong love affair with this special American music.

How to Use This Book

There is actually no right or wrong way to use this book. Read it linearly, from front to back, stopping whenever you feel 15 bucks burning a hole in your pocket and you want a tip on a new CD, or spend a little more time and read about a style of jazz or a musician in great depth. Or just browse the Table of Contents and select whatever strikes your fancy — trumpets? drums? bebop? Or just go randomly crazy: Stick your finger in somewhere and see what it finds.

If you are the kind of person who wants to be more methodical, I haven't left you out — I'm thinking of a song written by alto saxophonist Paul Desmond and made famous with the piano stylings of Dave Brubeck — *Take Five:*

- ✔ Part I introduces you to the general history of jazz, and the development and distinguishing sounds of various movements within the overall genre of jazz. It also covers listening to jazz and attempts to define it.

- ✔ Part II introduces you to some of the instruments used to create jazz music, as well as the key players and innovators on these instruments. You're also introduced to great jazz vocalists.

- ✔ Part III fills you in on the keyboards, the players, and their impact on jazz.

- ✔ Part IV tells you about the great drummers and vibraphonists. And you discover how these instruments evolved throughout the history of jazz.

- ✔ Part V covers some history about the bass and guitar. And you're introduced to the great players.

✔ Part VI covers more instruments of jazz: the clarinet, the flute, and the trombone, as well as their artists, past to present.

✔ Part VII is the famous *...For Dummies* Part of Tens. You can find ten great jazz labels, the cities to hear great live jazz, and the valuable resources to expand your mind with even more jazz information.

Each chapter in this book is somewhat self-contained. If you've heard about Charlie Parker and you want to get to him right away, for example, you can go straight to the chapters on bebop and on saxophonists and get a good handle on Charlie Parker's significance, a few recommendations for recordings, as well as a feel for his influence on the jazz world. Or you can begin with chapters on, say, vocalists, drummers, or bassists, and get some general knowledge of key players and give some discs a spin.

If I mention a song, I put it in quotes, for example, "Mary Had a Little Lamb." If I mention a CD title, it's in italics with the label following in parentheses like this: *Mother Goose's Greatest Nursery Hits* (Singing Goose).

This isn't a high school class, and you won't be tested. Don't get hung up trying to remember names, dates, spellings, and flatted fifths. Music is for listening. Jazz is best appreciated by putting on headphones and playing a CD with your eyes closed, or hitting your local club for a taste of the real live item. If there is one piece of advice I can give you, it's this: Get into listening right away.

To put my money where my mouth is, and in case you hardly own any jazz CDs, I've included a starter disc of some great jazz in the back of this book. Sample the music. When you hear something you like, find details in other sections of this book — then head out to your local music store in search of more music in the vein that caught your ear. And if you really want to go wild, take my lists of highly recommended CDs down to your local music store, where you can start a serious jazz collection in an afternoon.

Icons Used in This Book

This book uses a series of icons to point you to specific kinds of useful or interesting information. Here's a list:

This icon highlights a description of the key characteristics of a particular player's sound. Eventually, with some listening and perhaps a little reading, you should be able to identify several players after hearing a few seconds of their music.

This is where I take the liberty of recommending a personal favorite. These recordings may not always be part of every critic's list, but they are the baaaddest (that's a good thing) jazz around, in Yours Truly's opinion.

This icon points out a recording that definitely belongs in your collection — if not now, then at least by Thanksgiving. While author's choices are ones that I'd take to the proverbial Desert Island, Essential music titles are ones that belong in any complete jazz music collection, because they are innovative, rare, or offer important combinations of players.

Not surprisingly, the best people to tell you about jazz are often the players themselves. Here's where you find an anecdote, opinion, or explanation from a current jazz musician.

This icon points out a piece of music that's included on the CD tucked inside the back cover of this book.

This icon points out exactly what you think it does: a tip. In a few places, I offer a bit of advice for collecting, hiring a band, finding a good place to hear live jazz, and so on. This icon points you to these bits of wisdom.

If there's anything anywhere you should remember, I point it out with this icon — in fact, I think I just used it in the previous section.

Bop on, Bold Reader

If jazz is new to you, and you're as impatient as I am, you'll want to hear some great jazz right away. Put the CD in your stereo. Now! Later today, if you're still too pumped to actually do some serious reading, take this book with you to your local music store, grab a handful of CDs, and begin building your collection.

If, however, you're more methodical, like my brother the computer whiz, then by all means start at the front and read cover to cover. You'll get a comprehensive look at the styles and history of jazz — and the players who made it great. And if I've done my job, you'll also get more than facts and a few new words for your vocabulary. I hope you'll also discover many new sources of warm fuzzies — those moments in life when you're listening to a tune and something about it makes the hair stand up on the back of your neck and . . . time seems to stand still.

Part I
What Is Jazz?

The 5th Wave   By Rich Tennant

In this part . . .

You've probably heard of Louis Armstrong or Benny Goodman, but if you want to get into jazz, that's barely scratching the surface. In this section, I give you some important tips for listening to jazz. I also key you in to the music's basic ingredients and some history, from early New Orleans to far-out free jazz cooked up in New York lofts. I take you to the cities where various styles of jazz were born, introduce you to the players who made the music, and offer a few suggestions as to some essential CDs for exploring the history and various movements of jazz.

Chapter 1

Listening to Jazz: Altered Ears

· ·

In This Chapter

▶ How jazz got its name

▶ The three key elements of jazz

▶ What some players say about jazz

▶ Tapping the rhythm section

▶ Listening to genuine jazz

▶ Harmony and melody

▶ Distinctive voices

· ·

*J*azz has a tough time of it in this modern, convenient world. People have grown used to getting everything fast and easy. Restaurants and gourmet food emporia offer speedy take out and drive through — or even delivery. Quickie tune-and-lube shops offer car service with 10-minute fast-or-free guarantees. Vacation photos are back in an hour. And when people get sick, they want the doctor to prescribe rapid relief . . . preferably over the phone.

When it comes to music, many people don't want to work too hard there, either. Most listeners settle for what gets played on the radio. Trouble is, much FM radio music these days is programmed to attract the widest audience possible. Simple melodies and upbeat, brainless lyrics are signs of a potential hit song and bigger advertising dollars for the radio stations.

But there are more satisfying varieties of music. Jazz is one of them. If you are relatively new to it, you may think that jazz sounds complicated, and you may have trouble connecting emotionally. Don't give up. Many current fans felt the same way. I didn't know quite what to make of Miles Davis when I first heard his music — at a time when most of my peers were into Woodstock and acid rock.

The purpose of this chapter is to give you a set of *altered ears*. In this book, I give you just enough information about jazz that you can begin to hear it — and feel it. In Appendix B, you find a detailed guide to songs on the CD that comes with this book. But for the moment, consider jazz in more general terms.

The Origin of the Word Jazz

Jazz. Everyone has some idea of what it sounds like, right? Hip or mellow, hot or cool, Dixieland or *avant garde,* most anyone with a casual interest in music uses the word *jazz*. But just as attempts to clearly define jazz have stirred decades of debate, so the use of the very word *jazz* is a source of controversy.

The word has become a part of American culture. "Jazzy" clothes. Hip clothes. "Jazzy" car. Cool car. Hep cat daddyo. Hip lingo. The Jazz Age. Al Jolson in *The Jazz Singer*. Dixieland jazz, New Orleans jazz, swingin' jazz, live jazz, jive, Benny Goodman, Louis Armstrong, Charlie Parker, Billie Holiday . . . everybody knows jazz, right?

But where did the word come from? Who applied it to music in the first place? Given that it has some tawdry connotations, is jazz a fitting name for this highly dignified American music?

Theories

Origins of the word *jazz* are hazy and theories abound. In its original connotation, "jazz" was "jass." The word came out of bars and bordellos where early jazz was born in places like New Orleans, with its notorious Storyville red light district. Perhaps African Americans coined the term themselves to describe their music during its formative years, when *jazz* was used as a verb. A musician may have said "Jazz it up," when he wanted a band to pick up a song's pace and swing hard. In various literature from the past, the word has been spelled *jasz, jascz, jas, jass, jaz,* and *jazz*.

Or maybe the word, like many others, takes its meaning from its sound, or its sound from its meaning. On that basis, it could mean to hit, or strike, or launch, or some such short, quick stroke or action.

One thing about the word *jazz* is certain. No two people, whether they be writers, historians, musicians, or fans, will agree on exactly what it means, or where it came from.

Controversy

Although jazz is performed by musicians of many colors and melds together elements of many kinds of music, it is essentially African American music. Interwoven with jazz's history is the history of the black experience in America.

Many of the intense feelings surrounding the word *jazz* are valid. Some musicians and writers have objected to the use of the word *jazz,* with its historical context of prejudice and sometimes seamy connotations.

The term *jazz* was initially applied to largely African American music mostly by white writers. And over the years, many white musicians have made more money from the music than its black inventors. Most of jazz's innovators have been African American — Buddy Bolden, Jelly Roll Morton, Louis Armstrong, Lester Young, Coleman Hawkins, Charlie Parker, Dizzy Gillespie, Miles Davis, and Ornette Coleman.

By the mid-'20s, the word *jazz* began to show up in diverse writings about the music and the times. Prior to that, some of the earliest jazz was known as *ragtime,* due its ragged rhythms, as I explain in Chapter 2.

Yet, more than 100 years after the earliest jazz music was made, the word *jazz* is embedded in the national and international consciousness. For simplicity's sake, I assume that most everyone, whether they like it or not, uses the word *jazz* to describe the type of music I cover in this book.

What Is Jazz?

"It Don't Mean a Thing (If It Ain't Got That Swing)." Duke Ellington wrote that song as an homage to jazz. Singer and bandleader Cab Calloway popularized the uptempo tune. And though critics and historians have since expended thousands of words attempting to define jazz, Cab said most of it in 11 words. After all the searching, there are still only a handful of elements musicians and experts commonly accept as defining characteristics of jazz.

Three key elements

Although listeners may not agree on which music and musicians qualify as jazz, at a basic level, you can identify jazz by a few distinguishing traits.

Swing and syncopation

The rhythmic momentum that makes you want to dance or snap your fingers to a good jazz tune is called *swing.* Part of what makes jazz swing is the use of *syncopation.*

When jazz really swings, the beat bombards you, even if the players emphasize the beat by playing right with it some moments, or just before or after it at other times. This technique of placing accents or emphasis in surprising places, is called *syncopation.*

To get a better understanding of what I'm talking about, think of classical music. Classical music is primarily written music — musicians rely on sheet music which shows them phrasing, where the beats fall, and what notes to play. Jazz, on the other hand, is *felt*. Sure, lots of jazz *standards* (songs that are known and played by many musicians) are available as sheet music, but usually only in an outline form showing the basic *changes* (chord structure) of the song and a simple melody. The swing feel and syncopation can't be captured in musical notation, only in live jazz, where players either have the rhythmic stuff, or they don't.

To hear what syncopation sounds like, take a common schoolyard song, for example "Jingle Bells." Sing it the first line the usual way, just like you learned it:

"Jin-gle bells, jin-gle bells, jin-GLE all the way."

The "GLE" on the third "jingle" gets special emphasis (at least that's the way I learned it).

Now sing it a few times and change some accents like this:

"JIN-gle bells, JIN-gle bells, jin-gle...ALL...the way."

Make up your own interpretations. Try it with other songs, say, "Twinkle, Twinkle Little Star," or "Somewhere Over The Rainbow." That's the basic idea behind syncopation. And when you get a few players bouncing these kinds of ideas back and forth, some of them hitting one beat harder, others hitting a different beat harder, you begin to get the magic of great jazz.

Improvisation

Good jazz demands tremendous technical and creative ability because its players invent at least half of the music spontaneously. Famous jazz tunes have familiar melodies set to consistent chord changes, but legendary jazz players from trumpeter Louis Armstrong to saxophonists Lester Young and Charlie Parker made their mark with their phenomenal ability to improvise. The melody and *changes* (the chords) of a jazz tune are just a framework and starting point for exploring the possibilities of a song.

Blues is the most basic structure for improvising in jazz. A basic blues song is made of 12 measures, or *bars*. (Blues that most people can instantly recognize is commonly called *12-bar blues,* each bar, or measure, containing four beats.) Here's a basic blues song, invented on the spot.

Wait . . . before you sing, start tapping your foot slowly and steadily: 1-2-3-4, 1-2-3-4. Each line gets one measure, or group of four beats.

> "Well, I woke up this morning . . .
> took down my Dummies book
> (pause)
> (pause)
> "Well, I woke up this morning,
> took down my Dummies book
> (pause)
> (pause)
> "Put on some Coltrane . . .
> man my soul was shook."
> (pause)
> (pause — and back to the beginning!)

Now, expand the song on your own. Make up a couple more verses and invent your own words, melody, and accents.

Congratulations. You have now completed a basic seminar in improvisation. And while 12-bar blues is just one simple structure used in jazz, you are starting to get a feel for how jazz players invent music within a framework.

Distinctive voices

Additionally, most great modern jazz has another other key feature. Because jazz is so heavily dependent upon improvisation, it is often distinguished by the individual *voices* of its players: their selection of notes, their tone, their rhythmic sense. Miles Davis played trumpet in a muted whisper. Charlie Parker's saxophone had a sharp edge, and he soloed with phenomenal speed and variety. On drums, Jo Jones could invent a symphony of sounds just by using his cymbals.

With a little listening experience, you can easily begin to recognize these distinctive voices of various players. A performer is not only a musician, he is also by definition a composer whose personal style and preferences affect his performance just as much as the structure of the song.

The roots of jazz

Jazz roots run so deep in American culture that further attempts to define the elements of jazz become murky at best. Yet there are a few other facts that need mentioning.

Jazz pulls from the blues

Jazz is partly built on the blues, and some jazz pulls straight from the blues, utilizing the song structures of the traditional blues song structure known as *12-bar blues*. (See the section "Improvisation" a little earlier in this chapter for an example of the 12-bar blues in action.)

In good blues, jazz, and gospel, players listen intently to each other's playing, and have an almost intuitive connection to each other — an uncanny sixth sense felt between musicians. In the gospel church, the preacher sings out a line of sermon, and his congregation tosses it back to him. In blues and jazz, one musician plays or sings something, and another player throws it back in slightly new, altered form, adding a new variation to the theme and exploring a song further. Still another player may take a swing at the musical phrase, even adding a new melodic run. This tradition of call and response, and more simply improvisation, is a big part of jazz.

And by the way, if you're into (or want to get into) the blues, check out *Blues For Dummies,* by Lonnie Brooks and Cub Coda (IDG Books Worldwide, Inc.).

Jazz pulls from European traditions

European musical traditions are also a vital part of jazz. Elements like swing and improvisation found their way into jazz from Africa, but jazz's major instruments, including piano, saxophone (invented in Belgium about 1840 by Adolphe Sax), and assorted horns, came to jazz by way of Europe. Note that if you talk to a *musicologist* — someone who studies origins of music and instruments — you may hear that many European instruments are modified versions of instruments from the Middle East and Africa.

Jazz's basic system of notes is also derived from the European musical tradition. You can think of these notes as all the notes on a piano — together known as the *western chromatic scale.* This is in contrast to many systems of notes from other traditions in Africa and the Middle East which use *quarter tones* — notes that, if they were on a piano, would appear *between* keys — and gaps in scales where western ears would expect to hear a note. Within the western chromatic scale are all the various scales (major, minor, the various modes, and so on) that jazz players use to create melodies and improvise.

But wait, European classical music includes improvisation?

Though jazz is more commonly recognized as music that includes improvisation, what is not widely known among jazz fans is that much European classical music also includes improvisation. Many pieces by Bach, Mozart, and others include a section — called a *cadenza* — where players can invent or embellish melodies within the song's basic structure.

Jazz, however, pulls its use of improvisation from other sources — mostly from various African and folk traditions.

Departures from the Western chromatic scale

Jazz musicians added their own twist to the European scales, or groups of notes. For example, blues is distinguished by *blue notes,* and the sound of these note combinations is popular in jazz as well. To hear what I'm talking about, go to a piano. Find middle C, the note at the center of the keyboard. Now find B-flat, the fifth black note up from C. Play these two at the same time — what you are playing is called a *flat seventh interval.* B-flat is the seventh in relation to C, and adds that blues sound to it. Blue, or *seventh notes,* exist for every note on the piano — not just middle C.

Further departures from the Western chromatic scale (and an arrival at jazz)

Beginning in the 1940s, a lot of jazz musicians began to experiment with more complicated chords and harmonies. Some of these musical combinations aren't found in other forms of music, and they really help give jazz its special sound.

In addition to blue notes, jazz players often use note combinations that can't be produced on a piano. These musicians often bend the note (by bending a string on guitar, or using various techniques on the horns, such as blowing extra hard or using a different valve combination), and slide its pitch higher or lower to make a sound that doesn't exist in the western chromatic scale. These bent notes help give jazz its mystery, tension, and energy.

Another technique is the use of *modes.* Modes are various scales, or series of notes. To hear modes, go to a piano and play the C major scale (all the white notes on a piano starting at middle C and ending on the C one octave higher).

Now, play all the white notes starting on the D above middle C (the white note immediately above middle C) and ending on the D one octave higher. This scale is called the *Dorian mode.* You can hear other modes of the western chromatic scale by starting the same one-octave scale of all white notes on different notes.

However, understanding modal jazz is a bit more complicated because it can apply to entirely new scales that a jazz musician invents for a particular composition. You may hear the term *modal jazz* used to describe a new scale being used in a jazz piece even though the scale doesn't figure neatly into one of the traditional modes of western musical theory. You often hear the term *modal* used to describe jazz that draws from Indian music, which is rooted in scales and modes that help create its centered, meditative sound. In addition, sometimes a group leader may say, "I like these nine notes. Improvise with them any way you want on this tune, but only choose from these nine notes." That's also modal. And guess what? That's okay, and it's part of the invention and innovation that keeps jazz evolving and exciting.

Jazz pulls from African polyrhythms

Polyrhythms are different rhythmic patterns simultaneously played by a jazz band. For instance, a drummer sets up one pattern, a bassist embellishes it, and a third musician adds yet another pattern. Like drumming in many African cultures, jazz gets much of its brilliance from colliding, overlapping, contrasting rhythms. I go into some more detail on the importance of polyrhythms in Chapter 13.

What Else Is Jazz?

Beyond the basic elements I cover in the previous sections, what exactly constitutes jazz varies from one critic, historian, or musicologist to another. Does top-selling saxophonist Kenny G play jazz? Some radio stations say he does, but I don't think so. His music, to me, doesn't swing, and his *voice* (his personal signature sound) on his instrument is bland and undistinguished. A more accurate label for G's music may be *instrumental pop,* and in fact, Kenny G agrees with this opinion in interviews.

What is acid, free, avant garde, abstract jazz?

And what about the new 1990s music known as *acid jazz?* Is it jazz? Not to me. Although some acid jazz is played using traditional instruments, other examples borrow sound electronically from other music, so it tends to have a more layered, electronic sound that's distinct from most of jazz's earthier, spontaneous aura. Acid jazz's rhythms, usually simple and somewhat repetitious, are danceable but don't have the creative power of jazz's polyrhythms. And by the way, acid jazz doesn't sound like anything out of the 1960s, its players don't claim the drug LSD as their source of inspiration, and I give you a bit more detail on the style in Chapter 7.

Does that frantic noise known as *free jazz, abstract jazz,* or *avant garde jazz* really qualify as jazz? By the late 1960s, some musicians attempted to stretch jazz's boundaries by making music with minimal structure and no consistent sense of swing. Ironically, many of these musicians were trained in more traditional forms of jazz, and the music of artists such as Anthony Braxton and the Art Ensemble of Chicago obviously has improvisation, distinctive voices, and polyrhythms in abundance. I think it qualifies as jazz (and I go into a bit more detail on these forms in Chapter 5).

What some players say about jazz

To give some sense of how hard it is to define jazz, I asked several jazz players straight up, "What is jazz?" Here are a few answers:

"Jazz is a music that really allows a person to express his deepest self, his most personal self — Africa being the primary source of jazz. Naturally, improvisation and swing are a part of jazz, improvisation being the key."

> — Harold Land, jazz saxophonist

"I have two definitions: sociological and technical. The sociological definition is, jazz is the music developed primarily by African Americans in the early part of this century in New Orleans, that came from a merging of western musical technique with African sensibilities, and was based on syncopation and improvisation, with rhythm as the primary force. The technical definition is, it's the music that is conceived, performed, and felt simultaneously."

> — Mose Allison, jazz singer and pianist

"That's like asking, 'What is Chinese food?' It's the same thing we eat: green beans, rice, beef. What makes it Chinese is the treatment of the food, the spices, how it is cooked. Loosely, jazz is an interpretation and a treatment of music that employs a great deal of syncopation, a certain bending of notes, a music that is imbued with the blues. You've got heavy emphasis on syncopation, a certain attitude and treatment of notes, tones, and chords, which are not always literally played but implied or bent, and a music that is born and has its origin in blues and gospel, with the emphasis on improvisation — jazz is both written and improvised."

> — Charles McPherson, jazz saxophonist

"I would say that jazz is a musical effort, artistic in nature, which is based on improvisation — which is very unusual in the field of music, where a soloist is capable of taking a standard song with standard chords that have written melodies by the composers, and is able to invent his own melody that would fit perfectly with the original chord changes."

> — Chubby Jackson, jazz bassist

Listening to Genuine Jazz

Now cue up some jazz — a good place to start is the CD that comes with this book. In piano or guitar pieces, listen to the way players use chords to keep the beat. Finally, notice how Louis Armstrong, Lester Young, and other lead instrumentalists wave melodies and solos around the beat.

Hearing harmony and melody

Harmony is the way two or more notes sound together. Obviously, with 88 keys on a piano, the harmonic possibilities are nearly infinite.

Melody is a series of single notes that together make a musical statement. Melody is what most people commonly call the "tune" of a song.

Harmony and melody are vital partners. Within a jazz song, harmony works on several levels. A guitar player or pianist plays chords — combinations of notes. These notes harmonize with each other in various ways. A singer or sax player adds a melody over the chords. So the melody harmonizes with the chords. A bass player adds yet another line of music beneath the chords a primary melody. Yet another layer of harmony.

As you get into jazz by Louis Armstrong, Lester Young, Miles Davis, and other legendary jazz players, listen to each new song a half dozens times in a row . . . or more. First time through, listen with an ear for basic rhythms, chords, and melodies. Then hear how various instrumental parts complement each other. Once you feel comfortable with basic rhythms, chords, and melodies, start paying attention to the ways in which players improvise.

But how can you tell when they are improvising? It's not always easy. Sometimes, even when playing a familiar song, jazz musicians alter the basic melody. Sometimes you'll still recognize it. Other times, familiar songs sound like new songs because of the way jazz musicians reinvent them. In the most common type of jazz song, the band plays the song's signature melody all the way through once before the improvisation begins. Then they usually end the song by playing the melody again.

Tapping the rhythm section

Jazz usually has a juicy beat that you can feel. A basic difference between swing and a stiffer beat stems from the placement of accents. People who are unfamiliar with jazz will often clap on the first and third beat in every group of four. Jazz audiences, by contrast, will usually emphasize two and four, with a looser, swinging feeling that dates back to gospel music in black churches.

Although some jazz has such complex or irregular rhythms that evades the tap of your foot, most jazz has a steady beat, embellished by the drummer and other players. If jazz is tough for you to appreciate, its rhythms offer the easiest point of access.

Listen to Louis Armstrong or some of the other early jazz performers on the CD included with this book. Tap your foot or clap your hands or move your body. Try to feel the music, and listen to the way various instruments carry the rhythms. Although all jazz players tie into the music's rhythms, "rhythm sections" have primary rhythmic responsibility.

To identify the rhythm section, remember that it usually consists of standup bass (or tuba), drums, and sometimes piano or guitar (these versatile instruments can also play harmonies and melodies).

While you tap your foot to the music, concentrate on the drummer. Hear how he fills in assorted rhythms all around the primary beat, usually carried by his right foot as it tromps on a pedal that pounds his bass drum. Listen to the bassist (or, with Armstrong, tuba player), and hear how these bottom-end instruments anchor the rhythms with their steady thumping.

If, once you start tapping your foot, you don't begin to feel the music's power . . . well, go see a music doctor and ask him to prescribe something strong. You need a cure. You are rhythmically challenged!

Picking out the distinctive voices

Jazz's legendary players all have special sounds of their own: Lester Young's smooth, sexy tenor saxophone, Charlie Parker's sharp, speedy alto sax, Miles Davis's muted, whispery trumpet, and Louis Armstrong's spirited cornet and warm, gruff vocals. The joy of getting into jazz comes when you begin to recognize the players' "voices." After only a short while, you'll be able to tell Miles Davis from Dizzy Gillespie, Charlie Parker from Lester Young, Jo Jones from Gene Krupa.

Included on your *Jazz For Dummies* CD are some songs that have been recorded over the years by many great jazz musicians. Among them are "Oleo" and "St. Louis Blues." Eventually, you will be fascinated by comparing various versions of songs — sometimes even several versions by the same musician. You will want to discover, for instance, how Fats Waller's original "Honeysuckle Rose" differs from subsequent interpretations by Oscar Peterson and many other jazz greats. When you begin to feel the rhythms, hear harmonies and melodies, and get an incredible rush from jazz's amazing improvisers . . . then you'll know you are on your way to becoming a bona fide jazz fanatic.

Chapter 2

Birth of an American Music: Jazz to the 1920s

In This Chapter

▶ Basic ingredients blend in New Orleans

▶ Buddy Bolden puts the pieces together

▶ Scott Joplin and his ragtime peers

▶ The Original Dixieland Jass Band makes the first jazz recording

▶ Chicago becomes a center for jazz in the 1920s

▶ Bix Beiderbecke: New horn in town

▶ Jimmie Noone and Earl Hines: Apex Club schooling

▶ Young European Americans listen closely

*W*aves of change swept America between the Civil War and the turn of the century. Agriculture and rural life gave way to industry and urbanization. With the end of the war and slavery, many African Americans moved to American cities.

Life was still relatively simple. Riverboats, steam trains, and gas lamps had not yet been replaced by automobiles, airplanes, and electricity. While some American cities wrestled with a new multicultural identity, New Orleans was more accepting of ethnic diversity due to its roots as a French-ruled city. African Americans, French, Spanish, Europeans, and Native Americans mixed more freely than in most cities, and the atmosphere was conducive to new combinations of culture and fresh forms of expression.

In this cultural gumbo of a city, the earliest jazz was born during the 1880s and 1890s, played primarily by African Americans who brought their blues, spirituals, and worksongs together with European music and instruments (especially brass). Improvisation, the spontaneous invention of rhythms and melodies that is part of authentic African music, was a vital element in jazz from the beginning.

Basic Ingredients

New Orleans, with its rich multicultural history and rainbow population, was the obvious — maybe the only — place for jazz to be born. Consider the ingredients present during the last years of the 19th century:

- ✔ **A mixed population with French, Spanish, African, and West Indian roots — and a cosmopolitan atmosphere.** African music came forcibly to New Orleans via the slave trade, and indirectly via immigrant West Indians who had earlier incorporated African traditions into their culture.

- ✔ **A great concentration of African Americans and other people of color.** In 1880, 55,000 of 210,000 New Orleans residents were non-white. The city was the major population center in the South, and the foremost southern U.S. destination for both imports and exports, boasting of a major transient or "circulating population." This helped to give the city a somewhat more relaxed atmosphere, when it came to race relations, than other U.S. cities.

- ✔ **Brass marching bands, a popular tradition since Louisiana was under French rule.** Before jazz's earliest innovators hit the scene, during the decades after the U.S. Civil War, musicians in marching bands brought brass instruments such as cornets, trumpets, saxophones, and trombones into New Orleans, and into the hands of African American players.

- ✔ **Relaxed attitudes toward people of color.** Despite segregation, people of various races were afforded better-than-average treatment in New Orleans. Elected officials and police officers — more in New Orleans than in other American cities — let the ethnically diverse population mix freely, which meant they also shared musical influences.

People of color in New Orleans who played a lot of the earliest jazz were *creole* (a mix of French and African), *mulatto* (European and African), or sometimes *quadroon* or *octaroon* — a reference to the extent of their African heritage at a time when lighter (that is *less African*) folks received preferential treatment under the law.

- ✔ **A wealth of music including blues, spirituals, marches, popular "Tin Pan Alley" songs from musicals, and opera and classical music heard by Creole jazzmen, often educated in European music.**

- ✔ **African American parade, funeral, and party bands that made music during the late 1800s, using some of the essential elements of jazz: improvisation, swinging multiple rhythms, and ragtime syncopation.**

- ✔ **African American churches throughout the South, where Sunday sermons and gospel singing contained threads of jazz's fabric including call-and-response (back-and-forth interplay between preacher and congregation, or between choir and congregation), improvisation, and swinging rhythms.**

> ✔ **Storyville, the notorious district marked out by local statute for licensed prostitution.** Storyville's night life included dozens of saloons, honky tonks, and houses of pleasure featuring entertainment — including early jazz players.

The First Players

Early jazz was group music featuring collective improvisation. Jazz's first important soloists, such as sax and clarinet man Sidney Bechet, cornetist King Oliver, and trumpeter Louis Armstrong began their careers improvising in these popular bands. Long before the music and its variations moved into the swing era of the late 1920s and 1930s, jazz was primarily the entertainment of the black working class, alongside rags, cakewalks, and other popular music of the day. Early jazz was mostly party music, music made for dancing — as it was for years to come. This music wasn't yet known as *jazz* — the widespread use of that word wouldn't come for several more years, when the Original Dixieland Jass Band made the first jazz recording and lent its name to the genre.

Buddy Bolden (1877-1931)

Cornet player Buddy Bolden cut a colorful figure in New Orleans' African American community. Physically imposing, boisterous, a womanizer, he could play his horn with such power that many claimed it could be heard for miles . . . even across the Mississippi.

In 1895, Bolden put together the first significant jazz band. Bands such as Bolden's were brassy and sassy. Their music was based on the simple, one-two rhythms of marching bands, and many of the players didn't read music. They made loose, frenzied music. Clarinet and cornet players wove improvised melodies in and out of driving, syncopated rhythms laid down by guitar or banjo, bass or tuba, and sometimes drums.

Musical ideas and songs were passed around through casual conversations or jam sessions. Because the music came mostly from feelings and not from the commercial sheet music of the day, it had a free, spontaneous spirit that suited New Orleans and defined jazz. Eventually, during the 1940s and 1950s revival of early jazz, the jazz of New Orleans and 1920s Chicago became known as *Dixieland*. If you've ever heard something called "Dixieland," you have some idea what Bolden's music sounded like.

Though the wax recording cylinder was invented in 1885, the first jazz was not recorded. Instead, the sound of the music survives in stories told by those who were there, and in recordings made years later by musicians who heard or played the earliest jazz.

Beginning in 1906, Bolden's unpredictable, violent antics (such as striking his mother in the head with a porcelain water pitcher) made him a danger to those around him. He moved to a mental hospital where he spent most of the rest of his life. But the basic lineup of early jazz bands such as his — two or three lead horns, plus a three-piece rhythm section — served as the basic small band model for years to come.

Other Bolden-era bands

While Bolden was certainly the local legend, several players were prominent in New Orleans during the late 1800s and early 1900s: John Robicheaux's orchestra, the Onward Brass Band (with cornet/trumpet player King Oliver), the Excelsior band with brothers Lorenzo and Louis Tio, the Original Creole Band (with trumpeter Freddie Keppard), clarinetist George Lewis (who, after the advent of recording, helped re-create early New Orleans sounds on records), trumpeter Bunk Johnson (born in 1889, he was another early New Orleans player who revived early jazz probably similar to Bolden's during the Dixieland craze of the 1940s), pianist Fate Marable (who led bands on Mississippi riverboat cruises beginning in 1907, but who never recorded), and clarinetist George Baquet.

During the teens, many New Orleans players helped jazz evolve from ensemble music dating back to brass marching and funeral bands, to music with collective improvisation and strong solos. Among the best were:

- ✔ **Sidney Bechet.** Jazz's famous clarinetist first recorded with Clarence Williams' big band in 1923, making him the first great jazz soloist on vinyl (he barely beat Louis Armstrong with King Oliver's Creole Jazz Band). Around 1910, when Bechet was only 13, he was already jamming with top bands in New Orleans, and he later became a vital part of the jazz scene in 1920s Chicago. Sample Bechet's music on many CDs, including the excellent *Centenary Celebration-1997: Great Original Performances 1924 To 1943* (Louisiana Red Hot Records).

- ✔ **Baby Dodds.** Born in 1898, Baby Dodds was a drummer *extraordinaire* and brother of clarinetist Johnny Dodds. Baby was never a noted band leader, but he was among the first major drumming men in early bands led by Louis Armstrong and others. Dodds recorded with many of the greats in the 1920s and 1930s and continued playing into the 1950s.

- ✔ **Johnny Dodds.** By some accounts the leading clarinetist in early New Orleans jazz, Dodds was among the first to record his music. A good cross section can be heard on *Johnny Dodds/His Best Recordings/1923–1940* (Best of Jazz).

- ✔ **"Pops" Foster.** Foster's career lasted for more than 60 years. He was never prominent as a leader, but you can find his name and bass-playing on countless albums by other musicians.

✔ **Lil Harden.** Later married to Louis Armstrong, she was an important figure in New Orleans and Chicago jazz of the 1920s. A leading pianist who played with King Oliver and Louis Armstrong, Harden also led bands of her own, and her promotional abilities sped Louis's rise to the top as a band leader and trumpeter.

✔ **Freddie Keppard.** Much of this cornetist's best music went unrecorded, but he was on par with King Oliver in the early days. Keppard became popular in 1920s Chicago, and was also responsible for taking early New Orleans music to the western parts of the United States in later years. Several historical reports state that he turned down the opportunity to record the first jazz record as early as 1915 — apparently, he was afraid his style would be copied.

✔ **Jelly Roll Morton.** Another New Orleans native, Morton, a pianist, was a *Creole,* a Euro-African American, born in 1890. His ancestry can almost be viewed as a model for the roots of jazz itself. Morton was playing clubs by the time he was ten. His style was rooted in ragtime, and he was among jazz's most influential musicians during the teens, 1920s, and 1930s. He was also one of the New Orleans legends who became a part of Chicago's vital scene during the 1920s.

✔ **Albert Nicholas.** Another New Orleans/Chicago original on clarinet, you can hear him on *New Orleans/Chicago Connection* (Delmark) which presents Nicholas playing with great "Dixie-blues" pianist Art Hodes.

✔ **Joe "King" Oliver.** Born in 1885, Oliver was blowing his cornet with New Orleans bands by the early 1900s. He soon led bands of his own, served as mentor to a young Louis Armstrong, and lived another New Orleans-to-Chicago story, as I describe in the section "Shifting Scene: Chicago in the '20s."

✔ **Kid Ory.** A New Orleans original, Ory kept the "tailgate" trombone alive into the 1950s (he was also in 1920s Chicago). For early stuff take a listen to *Kid Ory's Creole Trombone* (ASV/Living Legends). Ory also has some wonderful later recordings, including *Favorites!* (Fantasy).

Ragtime

One argument that persists regarding jazz's early history is whether *ragtime* should be considered jazz. African American culture and the musicians it produced, especially in New Orleans in the 1890s and early 1900s, made little effort to separate ragtime (also called *barrelhouse* or *honky tonk*) from jazz. In fact, they used the word *ragtime* loosely to identify music played by Bolden's band and others.

Is ragtime jazz?

Ragtime, popular during the late 1800s and early 1900s, was named for its ragged rhythms. Like jazz, ragtime counted New Orleans marching band music as one ancestor. Unlike jazz, ragtime contained little improvisation, but it did lend jazz its jaunty, swinging one-two rhythms. And whether ragtime was played by two hands on piano, or by several instruments, the music was rhythmically rich, with syncopated patterns layered over each other, their accents falling in surprising places.

While ragtime shared jazz's loose, syncopated rhythms, it also drew from European traditions. The music was formally composed on paper. It didn't use the simple blues structure common in early jazz, and it had little or no room for improvisation. Depending on the player, ragtime could sound concisely European . . . or it could become a loose, swinging precursor of jazz.

Masters of ragtime

Some of the most popular rags were composed by pianists Scott Joplin ("Maple Leaf Rag"), James Scott ("Hilarity Rag"), and Joseph Lamb ("American Beauty Rag") during the 1890s and early 1900s. Joplin surpassed his peers in later years by penning orchestral works that influenced both jazz and theater music.

By 1910, ragtime was a national phenomenon, and in the quest for popularity, the music became diluted and less challenging. The ragtime era came to a close in 1917 with Joplin's passing, and by the end of World War I, elements of ragtime had merged into more sophisticated varieties of jazz including swing — although you could still hear distinctive rag sounds in the piano playing of Earl Hines, Fats Waller, Count Basie, and others for years to come.

James P. Johnson (1894-1955)

A prolific New York pianist and composer, Johnson was a key player in the cross-pollination between jazz and ragtime.

Johnson's evolution from ragtime to early jazz — in his playing and in his composing — pushed the music in fresh directions. Johnson was the most successful musician to make early player *piano rolls* (those perforated rolls of paper). Heard by countless musicians, his rolls helped spread ragtime and jazz across the country. Johnson's popular compositions "Carolina Shout," "Old Fashioned Love," and the wildly successful "The Charleston" (written for the 1923 Broadway musical *Running Wild*) helped put what little jazz there was in the "Jazz Age" of the early 1920s. Early examples of his playing are available on CD: *Carolina Shout* (Biograph).

Scott Joplin (1868-1917)

Joplin came before the advent of records, so his music, as he played it, survives only on player piano rolls and on CDs of his compositions as played by later pianists. Some of Joplin's original piano rolls have been recorded and released on albums such as *The Entertainer* (Biograph). Of course, the limits of player pianos make these rolls sound stiff and mechanical. If you want more emotional examples of Joplin's music, you can find them on CDs by pianists such as Josh Rifkin's *Best of Joplin's Piano Rags* (Nonesuch) and Dick Hyman (*Joplin's Greatest Hits* RCA). Both of these offer excellent approximations of how Joplin may have sounded in a live setting.

Eubie Blake (1883-1983)

More than any other player, pianist Eubie Blake kept ragtime alive into contemporary times. Born in Baltimore in 1883, he lived for a full century, composing, playing, and recording until late in life. After a long layoff, his 1969 album *The 86 Years of Eubie Blake* (Columbia) found him in fine form.

First Recording: Original Dixieland Jass Band

When jazz musicians finally connected with sound recording studios in a big way during the 1920s, jazz was quickly carried beyond clubs and ballrooms and into America's living rooms. Jazz's most creative players soon relied upon 78 rpm (revolutions per minute) records to document each new development in their style — preserving each new piece of music, making it available to music fans in the United States, and even overseas.

Heavily reliant upon improvisation, jazz could never be effectively captured or passed around via sheet music. But with the advent of records, the new music spread quickly as musicians heard what their peers elsewhere were playing.

So who made the first jazz recording? While African American musicians such as Buddy Bolden, Sidney Bechet, and King Oliver laid the groundwork, the all-white Original Dixieland Jass Band (ODJB), made the first jazz record. The group formed in New Orleans, and after a stint in Chicago, opened at a popular restaurant in New York in 1916. Their performances in New York had an immediate effect on the music scene, so the Victor Talking Machine Company seized on their popularity and recorded the band in early 1917.

The ODJB recording of "Livery Stable Blues," was released and became a hit after two earlier jazzier songs were deemed too "hot" and suggestive. Inspired in New Orleans by King Oliver and other great African American players, the Original Dixieland *Jass* (the original spelling) Band put some solid jazz down for posterity, although it was neither the most powerful early jazz, nor the most proficient.

Led by cornetist Nick LaRocca, who claimed to be jazz's inventor (as did Jelly Roll Morton), this New Orleans band recorded several songs in New York beginning in February of 1917. LaRocca's boasts — and even his choice of the name "Original" for his band — may be offensive to those who know the music's African American heritage. These recordings should nevertheless be a part of your collection. *Original Dixieland Jass Band, Vol. 1* and *Vol. 2* (Jazz Archive) are good starters.

The ODJB, by making the first jazz record, delivered the music to the masses and fueled one of the major events in 20th century American music. But to jazz's African American inventors, the oft-repeated phenomenon of white players capitalizing on black music summed up America's frustrating history of race relations.

Although recordings made by Louis Armstrong and King Oliver in the 1920s are, in my opinion, superior, LaRocca's band turned in some blistering performances. With horns wailing beneath LaRocca's sharp clarinet, and with tubas, percussion, and banjos setting the pace, his band raced through prime vintage jazz.

A bit more on race relations in the early jazz years

It stands to reason that music played by black musicians in New Orleans would not go unnoticed by the general community — especially white musicians. Despite informal occasions where people of all colors mingled, practically all social functions were segregated during the late 1800s. Even Mardi Gras had two Kings — a black "King Zulu" and a white "King Rex."

Yet, by around 1900, most of the established white march-style bands had added more than a little "rag" to their stuff, and the white public began to want more of the music from "downtown" at their dances and parties. By 1910, several white bands played early jazz: among them Tom Brown, Johnny DeDroit, Louisiana Five, and the Brunies Band.

Besides the ODJB, a white group called the New Orleans Rhythm Kings (NORK) made a name for itself, led by clarinetist Leon Rappolo, *tailgate* trombonist George Brunis (see Chapter 19), and cornetist Paul Mares. After their first recordings came out in 1922, they became the most important white band of the time. Their music had a loose, authentic New Orleans feel that set it apart from many rivals.

One essential CD for your collection is *New Orleans Rhythm Kings and Jelly Roll Morton* (Milestone).

Shifting Scene: Chicago in the 1920s

Chicago replaced New Orleans as jazz's happening city during the 1920s. Musicians from New Orleans and elsewhere in the South gravitated toward the rapidly growing Windy City, where bustling clubs and recording studios gave the players a shot at national notoriety.

Recorded at last in Chicago after honing his chops in New Orleans, trumpeter Louis Armstrong became jazz's first famous soloist. Other early New Orleans players who also had essential roles in 1920s Chicago jazz included band leader/pianist Luis Russell, clarinetists Sidney Bechet, Jimmie Noone, Albert Nicholas, Johnny Dodds, drummer Baby Dodds (Johnny's brother), and bassist Pops Foster.

Also in Chicago, a young pianist named Earl "Fatha" Hines brought piano into the age of swing and bebop. Top white Chicago players including cornetist Bix Beiderbecke developed a big following of their own in white venues, and during off hours they traded licks with Armstrong and other African American musicians at late-night jam sessions.

Several elements made Chicago the right place for jazz to make its next major leaps forward. By the 1920s, the music industry was centered in Chicago, with its clubs, live jazz radio broadcasts, and numerous recording studios. Beginning around 1914, leading jazz players gravitated toward Chicago, and the influx was sped by the closure of New Orleans's fabled Storyville district in 1917 at which time many of jazz's innovators headed north in search of work. At the same time, some musicians went west to Los Angeles, east to New York, overseas to perform in London, or toured the South with African American revues.

Joe "King" Oliver (1885-1938)

Joe "King" Oliver earned his coronation. First in New Orleans, then in 1920s Chicago as leader of groups including his Creole Jazz Band, Oliver was a powerhouse cornet player who conquered his leading competitors — Manuel Perez and Freddie Keppard — in a *cutting contest,* outduelling both men in an improvising jam session.

Trumpeters of the 1920s used plungers or mutes over the bells of the horns to achieve a wailing "wah-wah-wah" sound reminiscent of the sound of voices rising and falling during a gospel church service. Oliver was renowned for the mutes, cups, and glasses he used to get his signature sound.

King Oliver and Louis Armstrong smoke on the *1923 Louis Armstrong/King Oliver* (Milestone), and Oliver's Creole Jazz Band is red hot on the *Okeh Sessions* (EMI) album. The way energy zings back and forth between players, and the presence of key players such as brothers Johnny Dodds (clarinet) and Baby Dodds (drums), who would later record with Armstrong, makes Oliver's early recordings doubly important.

King Oliver/The Quintessence (Fremeaux & Associates) is a fine collection of music made by Oliver between 1923 and 1928. This two-CD set revisits the loose, sweaty feel of Storyville on a hot, humid summer night, with currents of people spilling in and out of clubs, music echoing through the streets, and sweet magnolia in the air.

Time and again on *Quintessence,* you hear early jazz's essential elements: syncopation (placement of accents at surprising points around the primary one-two beat); collective improvisation, with horn players inventing interwoven strands of melody; rhythmic tension created between rhythm section instruments such as piano, banjo, and drums, and between the rhythm section and other instruments; and bent, sliding notes that hit tones between the standard 12 tones on a piano. Slide trombones, cornets, and clarinets, especially, slide often from one note to another several steps away.

Louis Armstrong (1901-1971)

In Chicago, Louis Armstrong became a star by blowing sharp solos on trumpet and cornet. While his mentor, King Oliver, played a powerful midrange, bluesy cornet, and legendary cornetist Freddie Keppard was penetrating and nimble, Armstrong combined elements from both with a special something of his own. Armstrong was the top trumpeter of his time and set the standard for the new generation of trumpeters in the next decade.

Yet Armstrong was much more than a virtuoso instrumentalist. He was a charming band leader loved by fans of all colors — and he was the first important jazz vocalist. Listening to Armstrong's vocal and instrumental improvisations, you can hear jazz's connections to blues and gospel. When Armstrong solos, you can also hear how his instrumental phrasings grow from the way he sings, in the same way that later solos by Lester Young, Coleman Hawkins, and Miles Davis had warm, human overtones.

Essential early Armstrong includes anything he did with his Hot Five and Hot Seven groups, including the CDs *Hot Fives* and *Hot Sevens Vols. 1, 2,* and *3* (all on Columbia). Mostly made in Chicago between 1925 and 1928, these recordings capture jazz's emerging giant soloist.

Jelly Roll Morton (1890-1941)

Yet another New Orleans legend who made his fame in Chicago, Morton recorded what I consider to be his era's hottest jazz, with his Red Hot Peppers in 1926 and 1927. What strikes me about the Peppers (including Kid Ory on trombone, Omer Simeon on clarinet, and Johnny St. Cyr on banjo) is their tremendous dynamic range, their use of loud/soft and fast/slow contrasts, their sense of swing, and the wild imaginations of the soloists. In particular, Morton is a major talent and innovator as a songwriter — not surprising given that his formative years included broad exposure to European music as well as early New Orleans jazz.

The *Birth of the Hot* (RCA/Bluebird) CD starts with Morton's frenzied "Black Bottom Stomp" but downshifts for "Smoke House Blues," a slow, sexy tune that has horns wrapping sensuous melodies around each other. "The Chant" is taken at breakneck tempo, as Oliver and his hornmen invent sharp melodic lines above Simeon's wailing clarinet.

Included on the *Jazz For Dummies* CD is a cut from Morton that captures him on the cusp between his early New Orleans sound and the swing era soon to come.

Bix Beiderbecke (1903-1931)

Maturing musically around the same time as African American jazz legends like Armstrong and clarinetist Sidney Bechet, Bix Beiderbecke was Armstrong's white alter ego. Like Armstrong, Beiderbecke was a trumpeter and cornetist, and he was the first famous white jazz soloist and band leader. Inspired by Armstrong and other innovators, but also by classical composers including Claude Debussy, Beiderbecke had a distinctive sound — delicate and lyrical.

Born in Davenport, Iowa, Beiderbecke was a teenage pianist who taught himself cornet by listening to the Original Dixieland Jass Band's Nick LaRocca and other leading players. But he soon left LaRocca behind to find an elegant, mature style of his own. After moving to Chicago in 1921, Beiderbecke was smitten with the torrid jazz scene. He was in awe of fellow cornetists King Oliver and Louis Armstrong, but he didn't copy them. In 1923, Beiderbecke formed a band called The Wolverines, and later in St. Louis, Missouri, launched another band with leading St. Louis saxman Frankie Trumbauer. By 1925, Beiderbecke was making magical records of his own, but he spent a significant part of his meteoric career in commercial *"sweet"* dance bands or concert bands that afforded him little space for his *hot* jazz solos.

Beiderbecke had a major impact on jazz. He helped create and popularize Chicago-style jazz. His imaginative use of the cornet's middle range (as opposed to gruff lows and squealing highs emphasized by others) inspired Red Nichols, Bunny Berigan, and many other cornetists and trumpeters. His innovative ensemble arrangements pointed the way toward more intricate group arrangements by Fletcher Henderson and other big band leaders during the late 1920s and early 1930s. And his dreamy, melodic compositions for piano were forerunners of impressionistic jazz made by Bill Evans, Miles Davis, and other 1950s *cool jazz* players (see Chapter 4).

Beiderbecke died from pneumonia in 1931 after years of chronic alcoholism and poor health — during an eight-year career, he made music that helped shape jazz for years to come, music that still sounds vital today. After his passing, Beiderbecke became a legend of mythic proportions as Beiderbecke bands and fans sprung up across the nation, paying tribute to his life and music. In 1938, novelist Dorothy Baker's *Young Man with a Horn* was loosely inspired by Beiderbecke, and helped make him one of the most romantic figures of the Roaring Twenties.

Give Beiderbecke a listen on *Bix Beiderbecke—1924–1930* (Best of Jazz), as well as *Bix Beiderbecke, Vol. 1: Singin' the Blues* (Sony).

The Austin High Gang

Following the lead of legends such as Bix Beiderbecke, King Oliver, Earl Hines, and Jimmie Noone, Chicago's Austin High Gang (so named because some of them attended the same high school) of young white players made jazz in the spirit of their idols. Members of the high school clan included drummers Gene Krupa and Dave Tough, clarinetist/violinist Frankie Teschemacher, cornetist Jimmy McPartland — and a young clarinetist named Benny Goodman whose fame would surpass them all.

Dedicated and enthusiastic, the Austin High Gang checked out their African American counterparts in clubs and late-night jams, looking up to them as mentors. Some of these white jazzmen also looked up to the white New Orleans Rhythms Kings — who had in turn been inspired by King Oliver and his bands.

Eventually, the Gang split over philosophy: Should the music be made by small groups in basic 1-2-1-2 rhythms, or larger ensembles that could explore more complex rhythms and arrangements? Some small bands stayed with the simple rhythms of early New Orleans, while early big bands moved toward rhythmic variety, complex chord changes, and intricate arrangements.

Austin High Gang figures such as Tough, Krupa, and Goodman were among those who opted for the new swing style pioneered by African American musicians including Noone, Hines, arranger/saxophonist Don Redman, and drummer/band leader Ben Pollock.

Members of the Gang

The list of guys who were a part of the Austin High Gang:

- **Benny Goodman.** Like riverboat pianists Jess Stacy and Joe Sullivan, Goodman was a young jazz player with extensive musical training. He studied classical clarinet as a boy, and listened to leading New Orleans clarinetists as he developed a jazz style of his own. Goodman played in Ben Pollock's band in Chicago, and later led legendary big bands of his own (see Chapters 3 and 17 for more on Goodman and big bands).

- **Pee Wee Russell.** A fresh voice on clarinet, and a veteran of early Southwestern jazz bands, Russell was a prime Chicago-style jazz player, but he also fit in effectively with younger bebop and *avant garde* jazz players such as bassist Charlie Haden and pianist Steve Kuhn during the 1960s. Catch him on the CD *Clarinet Strut* (Drive Archive).

- **Jack Teagarden.** On his horn and as a singer, Teagarden was a swing-era master with roots in blues. He led a big band during the early 1940s, but his larger legacy is as a durable swing trombonist in bands including Louis Armstrong's all-star ensembles of the 1950s. Hear him on *Jack Teagarden 1928–1943* (Best of Jazz).

- **Drummers Dave Tough and Gene Krupa, saxophonist Bud Freeman, and guitarist/session organizer Eddie Condon.** This group of guys all took to jazz first as teenage fans, and then as musicians. Krupa brought drums into the spotlight as a star of Benny Goodman's 1930s band, and later bands of his own. Tough was a less-famous but well-respected swing drummer in the big bands of Tommy Dorsey and Benny Goodman, and adapted to bebop with Woody Herman in the 1940s.

Jimmie Noone and Earl Hines form a band

Jimmie Noone is one of the most important clarinetists of the 1920s. A key player in New Orleans during jazz's formative years, he was a vital link between the older New Orleans style and emerging swing.

Noone led the house band at Chicago's Apex Club, which set a new standard for the post-New Orleans ensemble. In that band, pianist Earl "Fatha" Hines experimented with *trumpet-style* voicings on piano — playing spare, melodic lines like a trumpeter. Noone's group also featured the unusual *front-line* (as opposed to the background rhythm section of drums and bass) of alto sax, clarinet, and piano. Through his influence on clarinetists Buster Bailey and the young Benny Goodman, Noone also changed the approach to the clarinet, helping the instrument move into the swing movement of the next decade. Introduce yourself to Noone on *Apex Blues* (Decca).

Hines cared little for ragtime and wasn't steeped in blues, as were other early jazz players. He thought of the piano as more of a "little orchestra." He later became an important Chicago player and leader of some of swing's hottest big bands. His orchestra of the late 1930s became a healthy incubator for the fledgling bebop revolution of the early 1940s.

Hines's recordings in the 1920s with Louis Armstrong are some of jazz's unquestioned classics. Among them, *Louis Armstrong and Earl Hines* (Sony) is a winner.

Other 1920s Chicago sounds

Collecting jazz is an almost infinite proposition, but several other jazz recordings from the 1920s capture great music, excellent musicianship, and the transformed spirit of New Orleans. I recommend these artists:

- **Barney Bigard.** He took clarinet lessons from Lorenzo Tio, one of Buddy Bolden's peers, in New Orleans during the teens. In Chicago, he had a big impact on swing clarinetists of the 1930s. *Clarinet Lament* (Topaz) presents a solid cross section of his best work.

- **Luis Russell.** An early New Orleans pianist/arranger, Russell moved to Chicago in the 1920s and eventually led one of the hottest early big bands. He was a greatly overlooked innovator of his time. A good start is *Luis Russell 1926–1934* (Storyville).

- **Clarence Williams.** This pianist/singer was one of the major band leaders in New Orleans before moving to Chicago during the 1910s. His music is covered on several CDs. His bands include many important soloists, such as Albert Socarras, who improvised one of the earliest jazz flute solos on a 1929 recording with Williams.

Emergence of swing

In Chicago by 1923, the records of King Oliver, New Orleans Dixieland Jass Band, Jelly Roll Morton, Kid Ory, Clarence Williams (with Sidney Bechet) and Doc Cook (with Freddie Keppard and Jimmie Noone) and the New Orleans Rhythm Kings helped spread the New Orleans approach across the nation. It seemed that Louisiana musicians had a special feeling for the blues, and the hippest jazz musicians attempted to capture the feel of the New Orleans/Chicago pioneers.

By the late 1920s and early 1930s, early jazz made by giants like Morton, Bechet, Oliver, Armstrong, and Beiderbecke evolved into big band swing. And while many of the better players continued an almost subterranean small band presence, stemming from countless jam sessions in the smaller clubs and in the homes of jazzophiles around the country, swing arrived with a big band bang.

Chapter 3

The Rise of Big Band Swing: The 1930s and Beyond

In This Chapter

▶ Expanded lineups: Big bands dominate the jazz scene

▶ Fletcher Henderson swings New York

▶ Midwest *territory bands:* Jazz spreads to the heartland

▶ Duke Ellington ascends to the throne

▶ Kings of swing enjoy mainstream success

▶ Keeping the flame alive

*N*ew Orleans was a never-ending Mardi Gras of primal jazz through the teens, until the city shut down the Storyville red-light district. Jazz players then headed north to Chicago in search of work and wider exposure through records and radio. Chicago swung through the 1920s. Hot New Orleans jazzmen like trumpeter Louis Armstrong, cornetist Joe "King" Oliver, and pianist Jelly Roll Morton rolled into Chi-town and turned up the juice, while homegrown jazz giants like Benny Goodman came of age musically.

Spread by records and radio, jazz was a part of popular music by the 1930s. Larger jazz ensembles added new dimensions to the music. In the Southwest and in New York City, big bands replaced smaller New Orleans groups. Expanded ensembles fronted by drummer Ben Pollack, pianists Fletcher Henderson, Benny Moten, and Duke Ellington, and bassist Walter Page took to stages and radio airwaves with at least a dozen players seated in sections: brass (trumpets, trombones); woodwinds (clarinet, saxophones); rhythm (drums, bass, piano, and guitar); and, often a singer. It was the beginning of an era of music that remains the favorite of many jazz fanatics today.

New York: Before the Big Bands

The Big Apple became jazz's capital during the late 1920s and early 1930s, but it had been a vital jazz city since the turn of the century. Several artists sealed New York's place in early jazz history:

- **James P. Johnson (1894–1955).** Blending the primal power of blues with the more elaborate song structures of ragtime and classical music, Johnson was an innovative pianist and founding father of ragtime — as well as one of jazz's first great composers. Born in New Brunswick, New Jersey, he was writing sophisticated original music and playing it in New York by the teens (see Chapter 2). Whereas New Orleans jazz was loose and largely spontaneous, the music that Johnson played in New York City's upscale nightclubs was meticulously composed.

- **James Reese Europe (1881–1919).** Europe laid the groundwork for the greatest big bands of the 1930s with music he made in 1913 and 1914. Europe composed pieces for ensembles as large as his 50-piece Hell Fighters Band, yet he infused the music with ragtime's rhythmic momentum. His bands also served as a training ground for early jazz musicians. Europe proved that tightly composed music played by a big band could swing even harder than ragtime's careful compositions.

- **Will Marion Cook (1869–1944).** Yet another major mentor to young musicians (including clarinet/saxophone player Sidney Bechet and pianist/bandleader Duke Ellington), Cook was a classical violinist who led the 50-piece New York Syncopated Orchestra. Cook was African American, and he wanted his orchestra to capture some of the raw power of authentic African music. He believed that James Europe had watered down African American music for the sake of commercial success. Cook also helped open Broadway productions to black players.

Born in the plantation South, the best New Orleans jazz was played by African Americans. New York City jazz was made from a slightly different recipe. Big bands in New York City didn't really swing until the Original Dixieland Jazz Band (see Chapter 2) came up from New Orleans in 1916. New York players began to transform the feel of their music by heating it up with New Orleans and Chicago flavors and rhythms.

Big Bands Take over Jazz

Thanks to Chicago's radio and recording outlets, jazz was a part of America's national culture by the end of the 1920s. Heading into the Great Depression years of the early 1930s, jazz's new popularity and expanded big band lineups meant more work for jazz players. But the fledgling recording business that had given jazz a big boost in the 1920s came tumbling down with the stock market crash of 1929. By 1931, RCA was the only company making many jazz records — it also had the foresight to venture into commercial radio with NBC.

As recording dropped off, jazz reached the masses over the airwaves. In 1933 the Casa Loma Orchestra, an outgrowth of Detroit's Jean Goldkette band, made the first appearance on radio by a swing band. As live jazz broadcasts became more common in the 1930s, more bands gained exposure. And as the recording industry bounded back, big band swing rose to new heights of popularity. Bands and recording companies now had multiple access to listeners: records for home playback, a rejuvenated jukebox industry, live remote radio broadcasts, and big band concert tours (by train and bus) through all parts of the country on an ever-improving road system.

Initially, two types of big bands were prominent:

- **Rougher blues-oriented bands from the Midwest and Southwest, featuring riffing horn sections and boisterous sax solos.**

- **Smoother bands whose pedigree was split between commercial pop and swinging dance music featuring hot soloists in the tradition of early jazz.** These bands were prevalent in big cities such as New York and Chicago. They featured intricate written arrangements and musicians who could read complex big band "charts," or sheet music.

The larger ensembles had broad repertoires that included popular songs from Broadway musicals, many of which eventually became "standards" in the jazz musician's repertoire. Big band arrangers such as Don Redman (with Fletcher Henderson) and Duke Ellington carefully crafted the music to make dramatic use of expanded lineups. The advent of big bands achieved two results that seem at odds:

- **More complex and evocative arrangements used instrument groupings to maximum effect.** Brass sections rubbed against reeds, harmonies, and rhythms bounced back and forth between horn sections, and tighter rhythm sections of piano, drums, bass, and rhythm guitar swung like crazy. The CD *Legendary Sidemen* (Topaz) captures the synergy between sensitive arrangers and gifted soloists.

- **While big band charts were tighter and more complex, the bands also became showcases for star soloists.** Earlier New Orleans bands like ones led by Louis Armstrong and King Oliver used little in the way of written arrangements, thereby allowing various players to improvise simultaneously, with only short breaks for solos. The new big bands had tight, written arrangements that left specific spaces for soloists to stretch out.

Although many American cities had growing jazz scenes, and Chicago was still strong, New York was the heart of the music industry by the late 1920s, and it was in New York that some of the finest big bands flourished.

Fletcher Henderson (1897-1952)

Listening to Henderson's big band, you can hear jazz evolving from early New Orleans style to sophisticated swing. Georgia-born Henderson grew up listening to the blues of Bessie Smith and Ma Rainey, and the big bands he led in New York beginning in 1923 swung with a rootsy, bluesy feel — a feel absent from tighter ragtime and dance bands.

Yet Henderson's ensembles were also far more polished than the so-called Midwest *territory bands* (see the section "Midwest Territory Bands" later in this chapter) of his day. They always played in tune and many of the musicians read music — essential, because the ensemble relied upon tight arrangements by Don Redman and others. But despite its musical literacy, the band lent its own interpretation to songs, stamping them as their own with improvised solos by star players.

Henderson's orchestra pointed the way toward famous big bands of the 1930s — which played tight compositions containing wide open spaces for extended solos. Don Redman — a saxophonist, clarinetist, and sensitive arranger — was a key to Henderson's success.

Henderson had a gift for spotting talent: In 1924, he recruited Armstrong from New Orleans, and the combination of Redman's charts and Satchmo's virtuosity gave the music a hot, new sound. On songs such as "Copenhagen," Redman's arrangements pit trombone and trumpets against sax and clarinets in an energetic push-pull. Songs were tightly scripted to spotlight soloists such as Armstrong and saxman Coleman Hawkins.

Initially, Henderson's band was much stiffer than its New Orleans counterparts such as Jelly Roll Morton's Red Hot Peppers, but the arrival of Louis Armstrong loosened things up. Redman, as well as Henderson, sax/trumpet player Benny Carter, and arranger Bill Challis came up with consistently solid arrangements in subsequent years. The band showcased a steady stream of great soloists: trumpeters Joe Smith, Rex Stewart, and Tommy Ladnier; trombonists Benny Morton, Charlie Green, Jimmy Harrison, and J.C. Higginbotham; saxophonist Chu Berry; and clarinetist Buster Bailey.

Henderson's peak period is captured on *The Fletcher Henderson Story/A Study In Frustration* (Columbia/Legacy), a four-CD set.

Comparing Henderson's music with jazz recorded by Jelly Roll Morton's Red Hot Peppers during the same period can give you a tangible idea of the difference between classic New Orleans-style jazz (Morton) and New York big band swing (Henderson). Morton brought opera and classical influences into his music, but his arrangements, while tight, were never as intricate or inventive as Redman's arrangements for Henderson.

On the other hand, Morton's band *swung harder.* He employed all seven Peppers to maximum effect, making great use of contrast, harmony, rhythmic tension, and multiple interwoven melodies (known as *polyphony*).

While Henderson's band was key to the transition from New Orleans jazz as exemplified by Morton and others, and vintage big band swing played by Duke Ellington and Count Basie's bands, Henderson never quite put it all together. Even when Armstrong takes the lead, Henderson's band sounds stiff and methodical on its tight arrangements, never attaining the heat of Morton's Peppers.

The next wave of big bands, during the early 1930s, successfully combined two essential qualities of jazz: the relentless swing of New Orleans jazz, and Redman-inspired arrangements that orchestrated all instruments for maximum effect — but also gave star soloists a special role.

Other big bands from the 1920s

Henderson's was not the only big band trying on new styles, he just had the best "tailor" of the time in Don Redman. Other bands also squeezed a new sound from the uptight "sweet" dance band formula. In Chicago, drummer/band leader Ben Pollack hired some of the brightest lights (clarinetist Benny Goodman, trumpeter Jimmy McPartland) from the white Chicago Jazz scene. Working from Detroit, the Jean Goldkette Orchestra toured constantly. Stealing the spotlight from everyone was the media-hyped "King of Jazz" himself, Paul Whiteman — regarded by many jazz players as a pop icon more than a serious jazzman. A few details:

- **Jean Goldkette (1899–1962).** Goldkette was a French-born booking agent who fronted a popular dance orchestra that played a few early swing tunes featuring hot solos — especially in its road shows. None of the recordings really capture what the band could do on stage. Goldkette's orchestra employed many outstanding jazz musicians including cornetist Bix Beiderbecke, violinist Joe Venuti, trombonist Tommy Dorsey, and saxman/clarinetist Jimmy Dorsey. Members of Goldkette's later group, the Orange Blossoms, formed the core of saxophonist Glen Gray's Casa Loma Orchestra.

- **Ben Pollack (1903–1971).** Pollack was the original drummer with the New Orleans Rhythm Kings, which collaborated with New Orleans legend Jelly Roll Morton. Pollack's bands were early ventures into swing that included future stars such as clarinetist and bandleader Benny Goodman, trumpeter Harry James, saxman Bud Freeman, and trombonist/arranger Glenn Miller. In 1934, members of Pollack's band joined singer Bob Crosby's (Bing's brother) popular swing ensemble.

- **Paul Whiteman (1890–1967).** Whiteman was undoubtedly the best-known orchestra leader of the 1920s. Playing music midway between ragtime and the height of swing, Whiteman's dance band was one of the most popular — and most emulated — bands of the 1930s. Among Whiteman's star soloists were Bix Beiderbecke, trombonist Jack Teagarden, trumpeter Bunny Berigan, and guitarist Eddie Lang.

- **The Casa Loma Orchestra (formed 1927).** Led by saxophonist/clarinetist Glen Gray, the orchestra was a cooperative effort formed in 1927 by musicians from Jean Goldkette's orchestra. Under Gray's guidance, and with the arrangements of guitarist Gene Gifford, the Casa Loma Orchestra became one of the first popular white swing bands. And swing they did! Give a listen to *Maniac's Ball* (Hep).

Taking up where Fletcher Henderson left off

Chick Webb, Jimmie Lunceford, Cab Calloway, and Andy Kirk were among bandleaders who snatched Henderson's swing baton and carried it confidently into the 1930s.

- **Cab Calloway (1907–1994).** The "Hi-De-Ho" man mesmerized audiences with his wild jazz, flip-flopping hair, big smile, warm vocals, and excellent big bands he fronted beginning at Harlem's Cotton Club in the 1930s. *Are You Hep To The Jive?* (Columbia) is classic, also go for *Jumpin' Jive* (Jazz Archives).

- **Benny Carter (born 1907).** Saxophonist, trumpeter, composer, arranger, Carter has played a part in nearly every phase of jazz's development. During the early 1930s, he played and arranged for Fletcher Henderson and McKinney's Cotton Pickers. He flew off to London during the mid-1930s to become a staff songsmith and arranger for the BBC dance orchestra, eventually having a tremendous influence on the jazz of Western Europe. Upon his return to the United States, Carter led a popular big band in New York City — and his career continues in the 1990s. Early essentials from the Carter catalog include *Benny Carter 1929–1940* (Best of Jazz) and *Advanced Swing* (Drive Archives).

- **Lionel Hampton (born 1909).** A jazz institution as both a musician and bandleader — the most famous of all jazz vibraphonists, whose bands have consistently been wild, swinging, and unpredictable. From the early years, look for the albums *Slide, Hamp Slide* (Drive Archives) and *Lionel Hampton 1939–40* (Classic Jazz).

- **Earl Hines (1903–1983).** Hines led one of the Midwest's most popular 1930s big bands, home-based at Chicago's Grand Terrace hotel. His music was more influential in some ways than Ellington's from the same period. NBC radio's Blue Line carried the Hines band to points west and south of Chicago. *Earl Hines 1934–1937* (Classic Jazz) is a winner, and if the 1930s RCA stuff is ever reissued, grab it.

✔ **Andy Kirk (1898–1992).** Kirk's Clouds of Joy group featured the arrangements and piano of Mary Lou Willams. Unlike its Kansas City peers, the band relied less on collective riffing and more on Williams's imagination. Although some of the band's stuff was so-so, when they swung — behind such soloists as saxman Don Byas, trumpeter Howard McGhee, and especially the wonderful inventions of Williams — they really swung. Sample some of the band's most buoyant moments on *12 Clouds of Joy* (ASV/Living Legends).

✔ **Jimmie Lunceford (1902–1947).** Flashy showmanship and tight, swinging musicianship were the trademarks of Lunceford's band, one of the hottest of its era beginning with a 1934 stint at New York's fabled Cotton Club. Short on great soloists but long on stage presence, the band put down some of the era's best music when it played trumpeter/vocalist Sy Oliver's lyrical arrangements — Oliver was lured away to Tommy Dorsey's band in the early 1940s. Check out the Lunceford unit's peak Oliver years on *Rhythm Is Our Business* (ASV/Living Legends).

✔ **McKinney's Cotton Pickers (formed 1923).** After the band plucked ace arranger Don Redman from Fletcher Henderson in 1927, the Pickers stepped up the pace. By the time they recorded the following year, they were swinging hard and tight to Redman's charts, hard enough to be ranked with the more famous Ellington and Basie bands. Get hold of *The Cotton Pickers* (Jazz Archives).

✔ **Chick Webb (1909–1939).** Powered by the diminutive Webb's dynamic personality and drumming, his orchestra was best known for songs featuring a young singer named Ella Fitzgerald. But Webb's band was one of the most amazing all-around swing machines, dominating "battle of the bands" competitions. In one notorious encounter, Webb and his crew blew away the rival Benny Goodman big band (with Gene Krupa on drums). Give *Spinnin' the Webb* (Decca) a good spin.

Midwest Territory Bands

While New York big band jazz was heating up, big bands of a different stripe shredded their way through the Midwest. After Storyville shut down in New Orleans in the teens, musicians migrated north — to Chicago, but also to several towns strung along the Mighty Mississippi river, a central artery through big band territory. Even in the teens, New Orleans jazz had drifted upriver to northern cities, carried by riverboat bands and 78 rpm records.

During the mid-'20s, while Fletcher Henderson's orchestra was on the rise in New York, dozens of famous and not-so-famous big bands tore up stages in San Antonio, Dallas, Oklahoma City, Tulsa, Memphis, St. Louis, and Omaha. These competitive, regional bands were known as *territory bands,* and their members were loyal, sticking together so they could make it to the next town and earn a few dollars.

Bennie Moten (1894-1935)

Moten was a ragtime pianist who formed a band in Kansas City and first recorded in 1923 with a six-piece New Orleans-style lineup. By 1924, he was back in a studio, this time in Camden, New Jersey, with an expanded 10-piece ensemble — only two pieces shy of Fletcher Henderson's big band across the Hudson River in New York City.

Moten's music grew out of early jazz and blues, with impromptu *head arrangements* (short melodic themes) that led into extended improvisational jams. Moten's band had a buoyant rhythm section that served as a model for great big band rhythm sections over the next two decades.

The early Moten band is well represented on *Bennie Moten: 1923–1932* (Best of Jazz). After 1929 Moten served mostly as leader, turning piano duties over to Bill "Count" Basie, an eventual legend who modeled his own 1935 band after Moten's. Setting a new high standard for big band jazz, Moten's ensemble made its last and best recordings in New Jersey in 1932. Arrangements by saxophonist Eddie Barefield and guitarist Eddie Durham alternated welling ensemble passages with sizzling solos by trumpeter Oran "Hot Lips" Page, saxophonist Ben Webster, and others.

Other territory bands

Other territory bands swung hard with that loose, wide-open blues feel. Recording was not common in the Midwest, so much of this music (with the exception of Moten's on RCA) is not well documented. Even though their recorded legacies were small, their reputations still loom large even today.

- **Troy Floyd.** Troy Floyd's nine-piece San Antonio ensemble had tight arrangements and a smooth, less bluesy feel than its peers, as captured on recordings from 1928 and 1929.

- **Walter Page's Blue Devils.** Hailing from Kansas City, the Blue Devils featured top players including trombonist/arranger Eddie Durham, trumpeter Oran "Hot Lips" Page, and singer Jimmy Rushing. Though the band only recorded once, it gave Moten's band some hot competition on stages in Missouri, Kansas, and Nebraska — that is, before Moten stole many of Page's musicians.

✔ **Jesse Stone's Blues Serenaders.** This group recorded four bluesy tunes in 1927 that cooked like crazy, with horns playing simultaneous lines of melody over loose, relaxed rhythms.

✔ **Alphonse Trent.** Alphonse Trent's all-black band broke color barriers with a longstanding gig at the all-white Adolphus Hotel in Dallas during the 1920s, and reached a radio audience with live shows on a Dallas station. The eight tunes recorded by the 12-piece band are tough to find.

Dozens of other territory bands covered America's heartland with early big band jazz during the mid-'20s, but most were never recorded. To hear some of the more obscure big band jazz from the period, pick up one of these compilations: *Real Kansas City of the '20s, '30s, & '40s* (Columbia), *Kansas City Legends* (Jazz Archives), and *Kansas City Style* (Topaz).

The Coronation of Duke Ellington (1899-1974)

Jazz's heroes ascended to mythic heights mostly on the basis of prodigious soloing abilities. And for overall impact on 20th-century jazz, Edward Kennedy "Duke" Ellington is easily worthy of his title.

Royal history: Ellington's early years

Born in 1899, Ellington initially wanted to be a painter, which may help explain the colorful sweep of his music. He entered jazz as a ragtime pianist, and his long career covered the peak period of New Orleans jazz; the late-1920s prime of Midwest territory bands; New York's prime big band period of the 1930s and early 1940s; the mid-'40s advent of bebop; 1950s cool jazz; and 1960s free jazz.

Like some other New York musicians of the big band era, Ellington had strict, formal music training. Growing up in Washington, D.C., he heard and played in polite "sweet" dance bands at elite capitol social functions.

Ellington moved to New York in 1922 and two years later took over Elmer Snowden's band, a six-piece unit typical of the time. Inspired by James P. Johnson's classically-influenced ragtime compositions, Ellington began to write for his band.

By 1926, Ellington's group had grown to 12 pieces, but the music was stiff, like a pale version of King Oliver or Jelly Roll Morton's New Orleans-style recordings from the same period. Early Ellington compositions leave room for soloists such as trumpeter Bubber Miley, but they sound young compared to his later creations. Miley's gruff trumpet pushed Ellington toward a rougher, more spontaneous ensemble music in the spirit of the New Orleans style. By the late 1920s, Ellington's subtle orchestrations of horn sections began to swell under solos by Miley, alto saxman Johnny Hodges, clarinetist Barney Bigard, trombonist Tricky Sam Nanton, and others.

Some of Ellington's best early music is on the two-CD *Okeh Ellington* (Columbia), including the cuts "Black and Tan Fantasy," "Mood Indigo," and "East St. Louis Toodle-Oo," with horns wailing beneath Miley's solo.

During the 1920s in live performances at Harlem's Cotton, Club Miley and Nanton blew loose, sweat-soaked solos that enhanced the group's "Jungle Band" reputation — for the music it played behind elaborate dance performances.

The Ellington sound

Ellington's songs can be tough to follow from sheet music, but even a small amount of listening should start your lifetime love affair. The more you listen, the more you appreciate how delicate melodic themes (*motifs* or *motives*) are stated, modified, and restated again in new forms. Ellington was a master at using his sections (trumpets, trombones, saxes and woodwinds, rhythm section) to weave thick, rich tapestries of sound. Always, his music moves with a loose, steady swing.

Ellington creates waves of tension by pitting sections against each other, then making them "play nice" together. Blaring trumpets cut across silky smooth saxes, melodies are batted back and forth, tempos change for dramatic emphasis, and the music swings with syncopated rhythms (rhythms that don't fall on the beat, but nonetheless emphasize it) — all classic characteristics of jazz.

Ellington made his musicians partners in the creative process, and his music gained power from their input. Ellington often composed at a piano with the band around him, playing snatches of a song, asking bandmembers to improvise their parts. Ellington would then write down the solos, and they often stuck: For example, saxman Johnny Hodges would rarely change his successful solos, unless and until he had a better idea. Satisfied creatively, and generously compensated, many of them remained in Ellington's orchestra for years.

Ellington was among the first big band leader to use a singer's voice as an instrument on a par with all the others, when Adelaide Hall sang wordless melodies on "Creole Love Call." Ellington also used the standup bass in bold new ways. Phenomenal bassists such as Jimmy Blanton and Oscar Pettiford were virtuosos on a par with saxophonists and trumpeters, and Ellington put them to work as full musical partners, not just keepers of the beat.

As Ellington's composing matured, his songs became masterful ensemble pieces for a dozen or more distinctive voices, as well as showcases for star soloists. While Fletcher Henderson, Chick Webb, Jimmy Lunceford, and other big band leaders of the 1920s advanced the music beyond the rougher New Orleans and Midwest/Territory sounds, Ellington elevated the art of big band music to new heights of sophistication. His music wasn't just entertainment: He often composed with a message in mind, and many of his compositions were meditations on his experiences as an African American.

Ellington's legacy

In the 1920s, Ellington's band began a five-decade reign as king of the big bands. Ellington wrote dozens of songs around the orchestra's consistently stellar soloists, and he and his longtime writing partner Billy Strayhorn did all the arranging. Although big bands faded from popularity following World War II, Ellington wrote and recorded great jazz through two more decades. Such was his creativity that over the course of his career, he effectively collaborated with artists in most of jazz's major styles.

More than any other jazz player, Ellington (shown in Figure 3-1), through his orchestras and his compositions, helped elevate jazz to the status of American classical music. His music is respected internationally on a level with great classical composers.

If you can find it, one of the best of the Ellington ensemble's best recordings is *Live at Fargo, 1940* (Jazz Classics), recorded on a chilly winter night in North Dakota. It captures the raw heat of a dance hall setting, with Ben Webster's saxophone sounding especially good. Made on a portable machine, this album nonetheless has good sound quality. Blanton's bass booms through. Rex Stewart's muted trumpet wails. Barney Bigard's clarinet snakes in and out of the music, Sonny Greer's drums pound out primal rhythms, and Ellington's sensuous horn and woodwind arrangements can be heard in all of their stunning glory.

Other great Ellington: *Beyond Category: the Musical Genius of Duke Ellington* (RCA), *Far East Suite* (RCA), and *Hot Summer Dance* (Columbia).

Kings of Swing

Recording industry pressure divided big band music somewhat along color lines. Black bands were encouraged to play *hot* and *loose*, white bands to play *light* and *sweet*.

Figure 3-1:
Duke
Ellington
(photo:
Everett
Collection).

But the music of trombonist Jack Teagarden, clarinetist Pee Wee Russell, guitarist Eddie Lang, and white bands like the New Orleans Rhythm Kings, the Casa Loma Orchestra, and Chicago's so-called "Austin High Gang" (drummer Gene Krupa, clarinetist Benny Goodman, and others) proved that loose, hot swing could be played by both black and white bands. On the other side of the racial line, sales of *hot* big band swing by African American bands to fans both white and black proved that recording companies were wrong in trying to market blues and jazz strictly as "race music" for black listeners.

Yet, even with the revival of smaller, independent jazz recording labels in the mid-'30s, the music was still divided along racial lines — in the same way that the South was still segregated. Packaging and marketing helped white bands gain wide popularity with white audiences. But as they succeeded commercially, they never forgot where the music came from. They openly acknowledged the African American roots of the music.

Of course, serious fans and players of all ethnic backgrounds could hear the real truth: After all, great music is great music.

Count Basie (1904-1984) sets the swing standard

Perhaps the greatest of the great swing bands was Count Basie's. From the start, Basie, shown in Figure 3-2, was bound for big band greatness. He came up through Walter Page's Blue Devils and Bennie Moten's band, both among the hottest of the larger ensembles of the late-'20s and early-'30s. Basie left Moten's band in 1935, just before Moten's death, and just when big band swing was about to hit the big time nationally.

Figure 3-2:
Count Basie
(photo:
Everett
Collection).

By 1936, Basie was leading his own smaller band in Kansas City, Missouri, which included drummer Jo Jones, saxophonist Lester Young, and blues singer Jimmy Rushing. Live radio broadcasts of the band caught the attention of agents and Decca Records. On the verge of commercial success, in 1937 Basie expanded his group to a full-size swing band. In the Kansas City tradition, everything was arranged around a smooth-but-swinging rhythm section (piano, bass, drums, and rhythm guitar) and arrangements that left plenty of room for stellar soloists like Young.

Basie's arrangements were still in the loose Midwest style, with "heads" or signature melodies serving as the basis for collective and individual improvisation. But the sections worked tightly together, giving the effect of easygoing precision. Even today, the Basie band's tight, trademark sound is still respected and emulated by newer big bands.

Introduce yourself to the Count on *Basie: Golden Years — Volumes 1–3* (Jazz Archives). Or go all out with the *Complete Count Basie Decca Recordings 1937–1944* (Decca) and the *Essential Count Basie Volumes 1–3* (Columbia). And for an example of how inventive and resilient Basie and his bands were over the years — even after the Big Band era tailed off in the 1950s and 1960s — pick up the *Complete Atomic Basie* (Roulette/Capitol) from the early 1960s or *Farmer's Market Barbecue* (Original Jazz Classics) from the 1970s.

Benny Goodman (1909-1986)

Benny Goodman may have not have led the most innovative of the big bands, but he took big band swing to new heights of popularity and led the way in showcasing star soloists. Goodman openly expressed his admiration for early African American swing bands, such as Fletcher Henderson's — Goodman even hired Henderson and his arranger Edgar Sampson.

Goodman's music was more precise and less spontaneous than some of the better black bands, but he had an ear for gifted players, the music swung hard, and Goodman played a fine clarinet.

The apex of Goodman's big band career came between 1936 and 1939, when his band included trumpeters Harry James, Bunny Berigan, and Ziggy Elman, pianists Jess Stacy and Teddy Wilson, drummers Davey Tough and Gene Krupa, and vibraphonist Lionel Hampton. Goodman's popularity and commercial success gave him the leverage to field one of the first high-profile integrated orchestras. You can hear some of Goodman's African American guest stars on *Clarinet a la King, Volume 2* (Columbia), *On the Air/ 1937–38* (Columbia), and *Sing, Sing, Sing* (RCA).

You can also hear the triumphant peak of Goodman's career and collaboration with black players on *Live at Carnegie Hall 1938* (Sony). Drummer Gene Krupa swings the band hard, and guests from the Basie and Ellington bands help power the music to new heights. This was also the first time a jazz orchestra played the prestigious, conservative concert hall. It marked the arrival of jazz as a respected music everywhere in society.

Other Big Bands Come on Strong

While Basie and Goodman were the powerhouses of big band swing, several other great bands kept the beat going.

- ✔ **Charlie Barnet (1913–1991).** A sax man with a love of Ellington's sound, Barnet had several hits. He was an outspoken champion of integration, and he led what was probably the first white big band to play the Apollo Theatre in Harlem. Check out *Swell & Super* (Drive Archive), *Wings Over Manhattan* (Vintage), and *Charlie Barnet 1935–1944* (Best of Jazz).

- ✔ **Bob Crosby (born 1913).** A bandleader and vocalist (brother of Bing Crosby), he helped Chicago-style jazz evolve into sophisticated big band swing. He also lead a New Orleans-style small group called the Bobcats. Get hold of *Bob Crosby Orchestra & the Bobcats* (ASV/Living Legends).

- ✔ **Jimmy Dorsey (1904–1957).** This Dorsey brother was a solid Chicago-style jazz clarinetist. He was also a good saxophonist, and one of the first to use the alto sax in jazz. Dorsey's most successful big bands featured singers, starting with Bob Eberly and Helen O'Connell. *Contrasts* (Decca) catches his band at its 1930s peak.

- ✔ **Tommy Dorsey (1905–1956).** Known for his warm tone on trombone, Dorsey was also instrumental (like his brother) in early Chicago jazz and its transition to 1930s big band swing. His orchestra was one of the smoothest and most popular, and its stars included trumpeter Bunny Berigan, saxman Bud Freeman, and a teen singer named Frank Sinatra. Find a copy of *17 Number Ones* (RCA).

- ✔ **Harry James (1916–1983).** James was a top big band trumpeter, although not on a par with Buck Clayton, the star trumpeter in Basie's band. James led a modern swing band in the 1950s featuring saxophonist Willie "The Lion" Smith. Get *Harry James 1937–1939* (Classic Jazz) or, from the 1950s, *Harry James: Silver Collection* (Verve).

- ✔ **Gene Krupa (1909–1973).** A central figure in Chicago's "Austin High Gang," Krupa was the first famous jazz drummer — with Goodman's band, and later fronting a big band of his own. He employed innovative trumpeter Roy Eldridge (who also sang with the band), as well as Anita O'Day, an innovative swing singer. Check out *Drum Boogie* (Columbia), or, from the late '50s, *Drummer Man* (Verve), with Eldridge and O'Day.

✔ **Artie Shaw (1910).** Like Benny Goodman, Artie Shaw was a gifted clarinetist, and his big band was among the best in the late 1930s, although it never achieved the wide popularity of Goodman's. Shaw was a visionary risk-taker. He experimented with strings, hired rising players such as drummer Buddy Rich, pianist Johnny Guarneri, trumpeters Oran "Hot Lips" Page and Roy Eldridge, and in the 1940s, was among the few bandleaders to take a legitimate crack at playing bebop (see Chapter 4) with a big band. Start with *Indispensable Artie Shaw* (RCA) and *Irresistible Swing* (Drive Archives).

Keeping the Flame Alive

During World War II, popular music began to change, and big band swing's popularity began to wane. Many musicians were drafted into the military, taken from their music (although some played in military jazz ensembles). Lengthy strikes by the musicians' union put a halt to recording during the war. In some cities, a special tax was imposed on dance halls.

And in Harlem, frenetic new jazz that would be known as bebop was being invented during the mid-'40s by Dizzy Gillespie, Charlie Parker, Thelonious Monk, and others at Minton's Playhouse and Monroe's Uptown House.

The music of Ellington and Goodman's bands was so strong, the bands and the music endured for several more years. Meanwhile, band leaders like Woody Herman, Stan Kenton, and Claude Thornhill heeded the call of bebop. They began to take big band music in exciting new directions.

Chapter 4

Bebop to Cool: The 1940s and 1950s

• •

In This Chapter

▶ Bebop: Jazz takes a new direction

▶ Big bands take some boppish cues

▶ Off-shoots of bebop: *Cool jazz* and *hard bop*

▶ Piano trios produce peak creativity

• •

*J*azz, like any art form, runs in cycles. Innovative art is rarely born in a vacuum, and the birth of bebop combined artistic forces with social and historical events. As World War II wound down in the mid-'40s, the country was in a state of flux, and the jazz scene was in disarray. During the war, fans and musicians alike had been drafted away from the music. The recording ban enforced by the musicians' union in a battle over royalties put a halt to recording from 1942 to 1944. New taxes on cabarets and dance halls forced many venues to cut back on costs — which often meant hiring smaller bands.

In New York City clubs, backrooms and apartments, where young jazz musicians began experimenting with new ideas during the mid-'40s, the influences were diverse. Some young boppers appreciated the swing of bands led by drummer Chick Webb or pianist Count Basie, but preferred the more innovative music of Duke Ellington and Artie Shaw's orchestras. Young boppers also studied the music of pianist Art Tatum and saxophonist Coleman Hawkins, who had already explored advanced harmonies, altered chords, and chord substitution — all hallmarks of bebop. Swing saxophonist Lester Young had already shown that jazz could be played with many subtle variations. Drummer Jo Jones, the catalyst in Count Basie's big band, had revolutionized the rhythm section's role with complex new rhythmic combinations. Guitarist Charlie Christian and bassist Jimmy Blanton also came up through swing and had a significant impact on bebop with their revolutionary soloing techniques.

Ban on recording

The recording bans were instituted by the American Federation of Musicians in a dispute over artists' royalties. The AFM demanded that recording companies pay royalties to musicians not only for the sale of records to the public, but for records played by profitable radio stations. The ban applied only to instrumental music, so singers (who were not union members) continued to make records and gain popularity.

A second ban, in 1948, was not quite as effective as the first one, but it pretty much put an end to swing bands that had survived. By this time, independent labels were about to boom, and the major recording companies had plenty of material stockpiled for release during the one-year ban.

While bebop was truly a revolution in jazz, it *seemed* even more revolutionary than previous movements for several reasons:

- As the war ended and musicians and fans returned from years of military duty, the whole country looked different to a lot of people.

- With the recording ban from 1942 to 1944 (in a dispute over artists' royalties), bebop had already evolved for a couple years before it was recorded. As a result, when the music finally made it to vinyl, it was more mature than most new styles, and it sounded radically different.

- African American musicians were well aware of the rise of popular white jazz musicians and integrated bands. Some of the black players wanted to return to their roots, to play music that might be a more pure reflection of their culture.

Seeds of Change

Kansas City and the Midwest territory bands (see Chapter 3) produced many of the swing era's top soloists: saxmen Coleman Hawkins, Lester Young, Herschel Evans, and Ben Webster. Most of the graduates of the territory bands moved on to Chicago or New York, and to prominent parts in big bands led by Duke Ellington, Fletcher Henderson, Count Basie, and others.

Now, the Midwest dispatched a fresh creative force to New York: a saxophonist by the name of Charlie Parker. A natural-born musical genius, even Parker went through a cataclysmic period of adjustment when he hit New York. At bebop jam sessions, players deconstructed standard tunes and rebuilt them with new chords and revised melodies. They put completely new songs to chords from old standards, or played familiar jazz tunes in unfamiliar keys. They intentionally put strangers through complex music played at breakneck speed. Parker's grasp of music theory was basic compared with his new peers, but true to his nickname ("Bird"), he soared above them all.

Evolution of the Bebop Sound

In 1945, after months of experimental jam sessions, Parker and trumpeter Dizzy Gillespie recorded some of their most famous and influential tunes. "Shaw 'Nuff," "Salt Peanuts," "Hot House," and other cuts heralded the new, daredevil form of jazz that became known as *bebop*.

Parker and Gillespie made a perfect pair. Parker was the pure creative genius who could play most anything he heard, even if he couldn't read music or explain theories behind complex chords and melodies. Gillespie was more cerebral, methodically considering how to re-invent jazz, then implementing his ideas in his compositions, arrangements, and playing. Where Parker was brooding, moody, and unreliable, Gillespie had a bright, sunny disposition that helped bebop catch the attention of the media and of jazz fans.

Initially, bebop's wild, free departure from the restrictions of big band swing met with much criticism. The sound seemed noisy and disorienting to some fans and critics. But as bebop spread, critics, audiences, and veteran players began to view the music's complexity and occasional dissonance as challenging and progressive rather than vulgar. Not only was the music revolutionary, but the smaller format of its bands marked a significant shift, and by the late 1940s, big bands were waning.

Vital music, powerful emotions

Bebop conveys a multitude of emotions — there is sadness, but also joy, and a fair amount of humor. New York City, including Harlem, was a dense, noisy, urban place, with people packed together, car horns honking, skyscrapers under construction, subway cars running underground, and street vendors hawking their wares. Bebop sounds like the life pulse of this teeming American metropolis where cultures collided in frightening and beautiful ways.

Many songs from the height of the bebop era have strange names, such as "Klacktovedsedsteen" and "Ornithology." Savvy listeners can detect snatches of melody from other songs, even children's songs, inserted into solos. Artists created complete new songs by substituting new chords and melodies over the basic structures of popular songs of the time such as "I Got Rhythm" and "How High The Moon."

Wherefrom "bebop"?

The word bebop probably came from the "be-boppity-boppity-boo" sound of the melodies and rhythms played by Charlie Parker and Dizzy Gillespie. Like other labels such as *jazz* and *swing, bebop* is difficult to define.

Also like other labels, *bebop* was not coined by musicians, but by writers. Throughout the history of jazz, a tension has existed between the African Americans who make most of the creative breakthroughs and white scholars who analyze and categorize the art. Ultimately, jazz does not fit neatly into categories, and labels for styles within the music are attempts to describe complex musical sounds that really must be heard to be felt and understood.

Traits of bebop

Bebop has longer, more complicated stretches of melody and improvisation than earlier forms of jazz. It is staccato music — it uses strings of short, choppy eighth and sixteenth notes. Each line of a solo by Charlie Parker or Dizzy Gillespie may start somewhere surprising and wind up in an even more unexpected place.

Bebop's sound was radical, but the bebop group was in many ways a streamlined version of a classic swing-era big band. In big bands, sections played melodic themes in unison or tossed them back and forth, and small-group teammates such as Parker and Gillespie did the same thing.

One main difference between bebop and swing is in the rhythm section: bass, drums, piano, and sometimes guitar. Bop drummers like Kenny Clarke shifted primary timekeeping duties from bass drum to cymbals and snare. Shimmering cymbal sounds lend the music a lighter, effervescent aura. By keeping time on their cymbals, drummers could change gears quickly as a song took surprising twists and turns. Freed from primary timekeeping duties, drummers put together several layers of rhythm, and they worked more closely with soloists, supporting and challenging them.

The bebop scene

A whole crew of gifted jazz players came out of bebop's formative years in New York City. In addition to Charlie Parker and Dizzy Gillespie, jam sessions in basements, backrooms, and tiny apartments, and later in New York clubs such as the Downbeat and Spotlite, included these players among others:

- **Tadd Dameron (1917–1965).** A pianist and composer, Dameron wrote several famous bebop tunes including "Hot House," and he played fine, fleet bebop on several albums from the 1950s and early 1960s. Two of them were for Riverside, available as *Fats Navarro and the Tadd Dameron Orchestra* (Milestone).

- **Barney Kessel (born 1923).** A leading cool, swing, and bebop guitar man, Kessel recorded (and jammed after-hours) with Parker in Los Angeles in 1947. He also played alongside Parker at producer Norman Granz's legendary Jazz at the Philharmonic concerts. Catch Kessel on *Complete Charlie Parker on Dial* (Jazz Classics).

  Kessel went on to make eclectic music of his own, often with bop leanings. Some of Kessel's best music as a leader is on *To Swing Or Not To Swing* (Original Jazz Classics).

- **Howard McGhee (1918–1987).** For hot all-star bop, you can't beat *Maggie: The Savoy Sessions* (Savoy). By 1960, McGhee could still deliver the goods, as you can hear on the 1960 *Maggie's Back in Town* (Original Jazz Classic).

- **Fats Navarro (1923–1950).** A young bop trumpeter inspired by both Parker and Gillespie, Navarro died at 34 , but he had already recorded more than 150 songs, many with groups other than his own. Among his personal bests are *Nostalgia* (Savoy) and the two-CD *Complete Blue Note and Capitol Recordings of Fats Navarro and Tadd Dameron* (Blue Note).

- **Oscar Pettiford (1922–1960).** Pettiford ranks among the top three innovators on bass, coaxing an array of sounds from his instrument with both *pizzicato* (plucked) and *arco* (bowed) techniques. Good examples of his gift are on *Oscar Pettiford Sextet* (Discovery).

- **Bud Powell (1924–1966).** Among modern pianists, Powell comes closest to Parker's improvised melodies. A true giant whose creativity was cut short by personal problems, Powell still made some of bebop's most innovative recordings. Get *The Amazing Bud Powell Vols. 1 & 2* (Blue Note) and *Bud Plays Bird* (Roost).

- **Sonny Stitt (1924–1982).** In the shadow of Bird, Stitt is my favorite underappreciated bebop saxophonist. His improvisations sparkle with freshness and energy, and his technique is flawless. You've got to hear *Kaleidoscope* (Original Jazz Classics).

Other players who participated in the bebop scene, but whose roles are often overlooked, include saxophonist Coleman Hawkins, trumpeters Harry "Sweets" Edison, Cootie Williams and Al Killian, and drummers Shelly Manne and Buddy Rich. Pianist Thelonious Monk and drummer Kenny Clarke often formed the nimble nucleus of early bop jam sessions — which were held in spite of musicians' union rules about when and where a union member could play.

Some examples of bebop

Charlie "Yardbird" Parker and Dizzy Gillespie made dozens of recordings. Here are some essential examples of their music, and some other vital bebop titles:

- ✔ *The Complete Dial Sessions* (Jazz Classics) is one of my favorite Parker collections. Four CDs catch Parker in a Los Angeles studio in 1946 and 1947, just before personal troubles landed him in Camarillo State Hospital. During the sessions, he was emotionally distraught, but he played brilliantly despite the pain that comes through the music (for example, he misses his cue to play the melody for "Lover Man").

- ✔ *Dizzy Gillespie 1945–1946* (Classics 935) is another excellent example of bebop in its prime. Gillespie tears through signature tunes such as "Salt Peanuts," "Shaw 'Nuff," and "Night in Tunisia." and the cast also includes Charlie Parker, Lucky Thompson, Milt Jackson, Al Haig, Don Byas, Sid Catlett, Charles Mingus, and Ray Brown.

- ✔ *The Bebop Era* (Columbia), with Cootie Williams, Dizzy Gillespie, Woody Herman, Claude Thornhill, Charlie Parker, and the Metronome All Stars.

- ✔ *Bop Begins* (Topaz) with Dizzy Gillespie, Don Byas, Dexter Gordon, Oscar Pettiford, Charlie Parker, and Coleman Hawkins.

- ✔ *Masters of Jazz Vol.2: BeBop's Greatest Hits* (Rhino) with Dizzy Gillespie, Charlie Parker, Kenny Clarke, Bud Powell, and Thelonius Monk.

- ✔ *Complete Dial Masters: Modern Jazz Trumpets* (Jazz Classics) Diz, Fats Navarro, Sonny Berman, Serge Chaloff, Lucky Thompson, and Milt Jackson.

- ✔ *The Bebop Boys: Navarro/Stitt/Powell* (Indigo).

Bebop and Big Bands

World War II's end and the advent of bebop brought major changes to the sound of big bands. Between the draft, which took musicians and fans away from the music, the recording ban, which kept new jazz away from the public, and a cabaret tax that forced some clubs to close, the national jazz scene was ready for revival.

Big bands led by Duke Ellington and Benny Goodman remained popular among fans of swing, but three other big band leaders took a different tack.

Woody Herman (1913-1987)

Clarinetist/saxophonist Herman led one of the most popular swing bands of the early 1940s, but by 1946 he had put together the first bop-oriented big band, called the Herd. Herman's Herd played the occasional swing tune, but originality became its hallmark. Longer songs like "Summer Sequence" and "Lady McGowan's Dream" by arranger Ralph Burns were showpieces, and the band was especially strong in the sax section. Stan Getz was featured on "Lemon Drop," and Al Cohn, Zoot Sims, and Serge Chaloff were among the Herd's other sensational saxophonists. Herman was one of the few leaders who kept a series of strong big bands going through the 1950s and 1960s.

Graduates of Herman's various Herds constitute a veritable Who's Who of swing, bop, and cool jazz: bassist Chubby Jackson; arrangers Neal Hefti and Ralph Burns, saxophonist Gerry Mulligan (also a prolific arranger), saxophonists Al Cohn, Stan Getz, Serge Chaloff, Zoot Sims, and Flip Phillips; trumpeter brothers Conte and Pete Candoli and Shorty Rogers; trombonist Bill Harris and vibraphonists Red Norvo, Terry Gibbs, and Marjorie Hyams.

Essential Herd CDs include: *Blues on Parade* (Decca), the bebopping *Thundering Herds 1946–1947* (Columbia) and *Wildroot Broadcasts of 1945* (Artistry). And, from the 1950s, *The Herd Rides Again . . . In Stereo* (Evidence). Also pick up the 1960s-era *Verve Masters, Vol. 54* (Verve), and the 1970s *Woody and Friends* (Concord) with several guest artists.

Stan Kenton (1911-1979)

Stan Kenton was one of jazz's most popular and controversial figures of the 1940s, 1950s, and 1960s. Scorned by some swing and bop purists, Kenton augmented his big band with extra brass, violins, or percussion, and he built a reputation for offbeat compositions, provocative arrangements, and fantastic soloists.

At various times, Kenton's band including saxophonists Lee Konitz, Art Pepper, Zoot Sims, and Pepper Adams, trumpeters Chico Alvarez and Maynard Ferguson, guitarist Laurindo Almeida, drummer Shelly Manne, trombonist Kai Winding, singers Anita O'Day and June Christy, and arrangers Pete Rugolo, Shorty Rogers, Neal Hefti, and Johnny Richards. Kenton also gave something back to the jazz community, participating in several university-level music education programs.

Three great Kenton albums to start with are *Cuban Fire* (Capitol), *Kenton in HiFi* (Capitol), and *Adventures in Time* (Capitol).

Claude Thornhill (1909-1969)

Emerging as a leader during the late swing era of the 1940s, Thornhill was a pianist and arranger who created a fresh big band sound featuring striking arrangements by Bill Borden and Gil Evans. With gifted players like saxmen Lee Konitz and Gerry Mulligan, the band borrowed from bebop and from classical music. Thornhill's use of french horn, bass clarinet, and tuba during the 1940s inspired Miles Davis's 1949 *Birth of the Cool* (Capitol). You'll want a copy of *Claude Thornhill and his Orchestra* (Jazz Hour).

Offshoots of Bebop: Cool Jazz and Hard Bop

Bebop offered sharp contrast to earlier swing, but it also borrowed from previous periods of jazz. During the 1950s, new strains of jazz developed that both borrowed from bop and veered away from it.

In California, a gentler, sweeter sort of jazz called *cool jazz* emerged, played primarily by white musicians. Cool jazz borrowed bright melodies and swinging rhythms from the earlier swing era, but it also utilized some of bop's harmonic and rhythmic subtleties. And in New York City, *hard bop,* a bluesy, driving, stripped-down variant of bebop, became the predominant jazz style, played predominantly by black artists.

Music critics love to give labels to movements, implying that each is discrete and self-contained. In truth, boundaries are fuzzy, and players from both coasts respected and played with each other and swapped ideas.

New York pianist Lennie Tristano played with beboppers including Dizzy Gillespie and Charlie Parker, yet during the 1950s his music took on a cooler aura that was more common to California. Trumpeter Miles Davis recorded *Birth of the Cool* (Capitol), which lent its name and laid-back vibe to the new California jazz. But during the 1950s, Davis himself stayed in New York and played dark, brooding hard bop.

African American players including bassist Red Callendar, drummer Chico Hamilton, pianist Hampton Hawes, and saxophonist/clarinetist Buddy Collette have been affiliated with both hard bop and cool. White jazz musicians like saxophonists Pepper Adams, Frank Strozier, and Phil Woods moved easily between swing, cool, and hard bop elements, and often played with black hard boppers.

While there was cross-pollination, each movement had a distinctive feel. Cool jazz was more concise and carefully choreographed. Hard bop relied more upon spontaneous improvisation around looser arrangements. It's the difference between Art Blakey's Jazz Messengers (hard bop) and Howard Rumsey's Lighthouse All-Stars (lighter cool jazz).

Los Angeles and West Coast cool

Jazz recording and publishing have been based mostly in New York City (and to a lesser extent Chicago) since the 1930s and 1940s, leaving the West Coast as a smaller satellite scene. But in 1947, Charlie Parker recorded his famous Dial sessions in Los Angeles, and by the 1950s, the West Coast had a hip jazz scene in L.A. and San Francisco.

As Los Angeles matured and became a center for movies, culture, and the arts, many major recording companies opened offices there. During the late 1940s and 1950s, the city became a hub for jazz musicians seeking club dates, studio work including movie soundtracks, and recording contracts.

While many of the musicians who came to Southern California were veterans of swing or bebop, in this new setting they developed a mellow and melodic style during the 1950s that became known as *cool*. California cool jazz drew not only from swing and bebop, but also from the intricate harmonies and melodies of 20th century classical composers including Maurice Ravel and Claude Debussy. Arrangers such as Ralph Burns, Gil Evans, and Gerry Mulligan composed epic classically inspired pieces that were never intended for dance halls. Famous as bop's co-creator, Dizzy Gillespie paid close attention to California, and even wrote arrangements for Boyd Raeburn's late '40s California big band.

California cool jazz included trumpeters Chet Baker and Shorty Rogers, drummer Shelly Manne (his Los Angeles night club, Shelly's Manne-Hole, was a hot spot for California jazz), and saxophonist Jimmy Giuffre. Gerry Mulligan (baritone sax), Lee Konitz (alto saxophone), and Kai Winding (trombone) were also among players who shaped a mellower West Coast sound during the 1950s in small groups that left lots of space in the music.

West Coast jazz tends to be romantic and reminiscent of California coastal sunsets. It doesn't seem that far-fetched to imagine that the mellow, sunny atmosphere had some influence on jazz that was parallel to the influence one imagines busy, noisy, dirty New York City had on its hometown players (see "New York and hard bop" later in this chapter).

Chet Baker (1929-1988)

Baker was a leading creative force in California cool jazz. He was known for a whispery, Miles Davis-like tone. Over the course of his career, he played with Charlie Parker, as well as with several major cool schoolers including saxophonists Gerry Mulligan, Jimmy Giuffre, Bud Shank, and Stan Getz, pianists Bill Evans and Russ Freeman, and drummer Shelly Manne. Baker's extensive catalog of great music includes *The Pacific Jazz Years* (EMD/Blue Note), *Young Chet* (EMD/Blue Note), *The Art of the Ballad* (Prestige), and *Chet Baker in Paris, Vol. 2* (PGD/Verve). For some West Coast-style bebop, listen to Baker in a group with alto saxman Art Pepper on *The Route* (Pacific Jazz), and to hear what it sounds like when left and right coasts collide, get *Chet Baker in New York* (Original Jazz Classics).

Dave Brubeck (born 1920) and Paul Desmond (1924-1977)

This piano/sax pair wowed both hipsters and college kids during the 1950s and 1960s. Brubeck, who studied with composer Darius Milhaud, brings eclectic classical influences to his compositions, and Desmond's light, airy tone was perfect for the melodic music they made together. Get *Time Out* (Sony), which contains some of their experiments with odd time signatures. Also find *Jazz at Oberlin* (Original Jazz Classics), *Jazz Impressions of Eurasia* (Sony), and, for proof that Brubeck is still a vital creative force in the 1990s, *Young Lions, Old Tigers* (Telarc).

Miles Davis (1926-1991)

Trumpeter Miles Davis is a key connection between the 1940s and 1950s in jazz. Davis played and recorded with Charlie Parker, Dizzy Gillespie, and other beboppers, but always had a cooler, laid-back sound. In 1949, his cool style found full expression on his *Birth of the Cool* (Capitol) album, with intricate arrangements for a nonet by Gil Evans and others.

The lineup included baritone saxophonist Gerry Mulligan, alto saxman Lee Konitz, and trombonists J.J. Johnson and Kai Winding. Against a new, nearly symphonic backdrop arranged by Evans, Davis painted spare, minimalist lines of improvised melody. He knew that *space* (absence of playing) is as important as sound, that each carefully selected note would have all the more impact if he left room for it to resonate.

Through the 1950s, Miles Davis refined his whispery, muted sound and his mid-range open sound in small groups with one of the great quintets in jazz history featuring John Coltrane on tenor sax, pianist Red Garland, bassist Paul Chambers, and drummer Philly Joe Jones. Their classic series, really more in the vein of hard bop, was originally released on Prestige Records and includes *Cookin'*, *Workin'*, *Steamin'*, and *Relaxin'* (all are now available on CD on the Original Jazz Classics label).

Gil Evans (1912-1988)

The most famous arranger of cool jazz, Evans helped artists scale new heights of creativity. For trumpeter Miles Davis, Evans crafted a series of lyrical settings on *Miles Ahead* (Sony), *Porgy and Bess* (Sony), and the landmark *Sketches of Spain* (Sony). Also check out Evans's own *Out of the Cool* (GRP/Impulse!) and *Individualism of Gil Evans* (Verve). Later in his career, Evans also experimented by blending electronic effects with the music of a large jazz ensemble, as on *Priestess* (Verve), featuring saxophonist Billy Harper.

Jimmy Giuffre (born 1921)

Equally adept on clarinet and saxophonists, Giuffre was one of the most innovative West Coast jazzmen. After stints in several 1940s big bands, Giuffre recorded some fine music in experimental trios and quartets, making unusual use of reeds, bass, guitar, and piano. Good early Giuffre can be heard on *The Jimmy Giuffre 3* (Atlantic), and his later prime is captured on *Conversations with a Goose* (Soul Note). Also look for *Gerry Mulligan in Paris Vols. 1 and 2* (BMG/Disques Vogues).

Shelly Manne (1920-1984)

The best of the California cool drummers during the 1950s and 1960s, Manne was also an influential bandleader and owner of the famous Shelly's Manne-Hole jazz club. Hear him with pianist Andre Previn on *My Fair Lady* (Original Jazz Classics), with guitarist Barney Kessel on *Poll Winners: Straight Ahead* (Original Jazz Classics), and with a crew of classic California cool players on *West Coast Sound Vol. 1* (Original Jazz Classics). Manne also played fiery hard bop, as on *Shelly Manne and his Men at the Blackhawk,* a five-CD series (Original Jazz Classics).

Modern Jazz Quartet

While not based on the West Coast, the "MJQ" was the epitome of cool jazz. Pianist John Lewis and vibraphonist Milt Jackson had experience playing 1940s bebop, but, with Lewis's classically-inspired compositions, the MJQ became something of a traveling chamber group. Their music was wildly creative, and the group also achieved wide acclaim. Their playing was so tight that it sounded telepathic, yet they could also wring maximum emotion from a ballad. Listen to *Pyramid* (Atlantic), *Lonely Woman* (Atlantic), and *Topsy: This One's for Basie* (Pablo).

Gerry Mulligan (1927-1996)

A key player on California's cool scene, Mulligan was a talented pianist, composer, and arranger best known for his big smooth sound on baritone sax. He made some of his best music with trumpeter Chet Baker and valve trombonist Bob Brookmeyer. Look for *The Best of Gerry Mulligan with Chet Baker* (Pacific Jazz), *Gerry Mulligan Quartet at Storyville* (Pacific Jazz),

California Concerts #1 and *#2* (Pacific Jazz). Mulligan also made several good albums teamed with other solid sax players. For a sampling, find *Gerry Mulligan Meets the Saxophonists* (PGD/Verve).

Shorty Rogers (born 1924)

Shorty came up through big bands led by Woody Herman and Stan Kenton and became a top trumpet/fluegelhorn player and bandleader in 1950s West Coast cool jazz. Get Shorty on *Portrait of Shorty* (BMG/RCA), as well as on *Shorty Rogers Quintet* (VSOP), and on Shelly Manne's *The Three and "The Two"* (Original Jazz Classics).

Howard Rumsey's Lighthouse All-Stars

Drummer Howard Rumsey (born 1917) launched his career during the 1940s with Stan Kenton's orchestra. After bouncing through various bands, he landed as leader of the house band at the Lighthouse Cafe in Hermosa Beach in Southern California. Over the years, Rumsey's Lighthouse All-Stars served as a vital training ground for a crew of important California cool players. Lighthouse All-Stars included trombonist Frank Rosolino, trumpeter Conte Candoli, Stu Williamson, and Shorty Rogers, multi-reedmen Bob Cooper, Bud Shank, Jimmy Giuffre, and Buddy Collette, pianists Claude Williamson, Sonny Clark, and Hampton Hawes, and drummers Shelly Manne and Stan Levy. Several CDs chronicle the music: *In the Solo Spotlight* (Original Jazz Classics), *Sunday Jazz a la Lighthouse* (Original Jazz Classic), and *Lighthouse All-Stars: Oboe/Flute* (Original Jazz Classics) are all good.

Lennie Tristano (1919-1978)

Tristano's experiments during the late '40s and early '50s with dense harmonies, exotic melodies, and freeform improvisation were the forerunner of 1960s free jazz. Saxophonists Lee Konitz and Warne Marsh helped make Tristano's music sound ethereal. The pianist's sliding, shifting rhythms give the music an elusive quality reminiscent of pianists such as Bill Evans and Keith Jarrett who came later. Check out *Intuition* (Capitol) with Warne Marsh, and, for early experiments in overdubbing multiple piano parts, get *The New Tristano* (Rhino).

New York and hard bop

Some of the hard boppers were graduates of 1940s bebop, including drummers Max Roach and Art Blakey and tenor saxophonists Sonny Rollins and Dexter Gordon. Others were relative newcomers searching for new sounds. The new generation included several players from outside New York City and especially from Detroit and Philadelphia. The Motor City produced bassist Paul Chambers, drummers Louis Hayes, and Elvin Jones, trumpeters Thad Jones and Donald Byrd, pianists Barry Harris and Tommy Flanagan, guitarist Kenny Burrell, baritone saxman Pepper Adams. Philadelphians included, trumpeters Clifford Brown and Lee Morgan, pianists McCoy Tyner and Bobby Timmons, saxmen John Coltrane, Benny Golson and Jimmy Heath, and drummer Philly Joe Jones.

Think of hard bop as a cooler bebop . . . or hotter cool jazz. It doesn't have bebop's frantic, restless feel, but it's not as mellow as cool jazz either. Hard bop has a sense of urgency and passion, a deep, brooding aura that seems to indicate that these predominantly African American players living in New York City had quite different experiences from their predominantly white cool jazz counterparts in California.

Gene Ammons (1925-1974)

The sax-playing son of boogie woogie piano legend Albert Ammons, Gene Ammons broke into jazz playing bebop with Billy Eckstine's 1940s big band and became one of jazz's great balladeers. His big, warm tenor sax did wonderful things with romantic standards. But hear for yourself on *The Happy Blues* (Original Jazz Classics), *Gene Ammons Story: Organ Combos* (Prestige), and with Dexter Gordon on *The Chase!* (Prestige).

Art Blakey (1919-1990)

Drummer/band leader Art Blakey was the granddaddy of hard bop. With pianist Horace Silver, he founded the Jazz Messengers in 1953, and after Silver left the following year, Blakey took over and led the band through four decades of innovative jazz.

Blakey and the Messengers defined hard bop, and, with his unerring eye for raw talent, Blakey helped launch the careers of countless players who came through his band. Over the years, the Messengers included saxophonists Jackie McLean, Bobby Watson, Johnny Griffin, Billy Harper, trumpeters Kenny Dorham, Terence Blanchard, and Bill Hardman, and pianists Cedar Walton, Bobby Timmons, and Joanne Brackeen. Trumpeter Wynton Marsalis and his saxophone-toting brother Branford are two other famous Blakey alums.

Start with *A Night at Birdland Vols. 1 and 2* (EMD/Blue Note) featuring Clifford Brown on trumpet, Lou Donaldson on alto sax, and Silver on piano. Also get *The Jazz Messengers at the Jazz Corner of the World* (EMD/Blue Note), featuring trumpeter Lee Morgan and tenor saxophonist Hank Mobley.

Clifford Brown (1930-1956) and Max Roach (born 1924)

Trumpeter Clifford Brown and drummer Max Roach had one of jazz's most prolific partnerships during the 1950s, prior to Brown's premature passing in an auto accident.

Brown's career began after he toured Europe with vibraphonist Lionel Hampton's band. An example of this early Brown is *Jazz Immortal* (Pacific Jazz) with saxophonist Zoot Sims. But Brown hit his creative peak when he teamed up with the more seasoned Roach beginning in 1954. Brown combined Dizzy Gillespie's verve and range with Fats Navarro's sense of melody and burnished tone. Roach was one of bop's most original drummers, and the most complete, with solid technique and an intuitive sense of timekeeping. His playing propelled saxophonists Charlie Parker and Sonny Rollins through some of their best music.

Together, Brown and Roach made a perfect pair, and in just over two years, they produced several fabulous albums. Go get *Roach & Brown in Concert* (GNP), *Brown/Roach, Inc.* (EmArcy), and *Study in Brown* (EmArcy).

Miles Davis (1926-1991)

Okay, so I already listed Davis in the cool jazz section, but you have to know this: Davis's mid-'50s quintet made a string of albums with one-word titles like *Cookin', Workin', Steamin',* and *Relaxin'* (all available on Original Jazz Classics) that epitomized brooding hard bop. Just one more example of how these labels that get assigned to jazz movements are ultimately inadequate to define the many individual contributions the artists make.

Dexter Gordon (1923-1990)

Breaking into jazz as a New York City bebopper in the mid-'40s, Gordon was an ace alto saxman for 30 years, mixing Charlie Parker's speed and inventiveness with Lester Young's laid-back, sleepy sound. *The Chase!* (Stash) catches Gordon running down late '40s bebop. His Blue Note albums from the 1960s, including *Doin' Alright, Dexter Calling,* and *Go!* are some of the finest examples of gritty hard bop.

J.J. Johnson (born 1924)

A driving force in 1940s bebop, Johnson was one of the few trombonists who could keep up with Dizzy Gillespie and Charlie Parker. Johnson was jazz's most talented trombonist during the 1950s, composing, arranging, and playing music with a bluesy, hard bop feel, utilizing unconventional instrumentations and harmonies. Get *Mad Bebop* (Savoy), *Early Bones* (Prestige), and *The Eminent Jay Jay Johnson, Vols. 1 and 2* (EMD/Blue Note).

Clifford Jordan (1931-1993)

Smooth and full-bodied, Jordan's sound on tenor saxophone is distinctive. During the 1950s, he collaborated with original beboppers such as Charles Mingus and Max Roach and made several excellent albums of his own. *Blowing in from Chicago* (EMD/Blue Note) is his auspicious debut, and *Spellbound* (Original Jazz Classics) is more vintage mid-'50s Jordan.

Jackie McLean (born 1932)

One of the grittiest alto saxophonists in 1950s hard bop, McLean was one of Art Blakey's Jazz Messengers from 1956 to 1958. On his own, he made excellent albums including *Swing, Swang, Swingin', Tippin' the Scales,* and *Bluesnik* (all on EMD/Blue Note).

Charles Mingus (1922-1978)

Jazz's unconventional genius of standup bass and a masterful composer with ambitious ideas, Mingus played 1940s bebop with raw power and went on to explore a vast array of formats. He was one of the first jazz musicians to start his own recording label (with Max Roach), and one of the first to utilize studio overdubbing to add extra instrumental tracks.

Jazzical Moods (Original Jazz Classics) gives you Mingus's take on cool jazz, with saxophonist John LaPorta. *Charles Mingus Quintet plus Max Roach* (Original Jazz Classics) finds him brooding over some bluesy hard bop. *Blues and Roots* (Atlantic) is hard-driving soulful jazz with a gospel spirit. *Mingus Dynasty* (Columbia) catches the monster bassman in 1960, on the cusp of a new decade of breakthroughs.

Hank Mobley (1930-1986)

With roots in rhythm and blues, Mobley became one of the hippest tenor saxophonists playing 1950s hard bop. Mobley played with greats including drummers Art Blakey and Max Roach and pianist Horace Silver. The best of his 1950s output includes *No Room for Squares* (EMD/Blue Note) and *Workout* (Blue Note).

Thelonious Monk (1917-1982)

Commonly associated with 1940s bebop, Monk was one of the few pianists with an instantly recognizable style. Like Charlie Parker, Monk threw away all rules when he invented his loose, loping style. His *Genius of Modern Music Vols. 1 & 2* (EMD/Blue Note) is essential 1940s music, and you should also treat yourself to *The Complete Blue Note Sessions* (EMD/Blue Note), a phenomenal four-CD set.

Other essential albums by Monk are *Brilliant Corners* (Original Jazz Classics), with trumpeter Clark Terry, saxophonists Ernie Henry and Sonny Rollins, bassist Oscar Pettiford, and drummer Max Roach — the title track is incredible! *Monk with Trane* (Original Jazz Classics) is one of the great all-time jazz albums. *Misterioso* (Original Jazz Classics) is his first recording with his own quartet, and *Blues Five Spot* (Milestone) catches Monk during a live club date.

Lee Morgan (1938-1972)

Following the premature passings of Clifford Brown in 1956 and Fats Navarro in 1958, Morgan became one of hard bop's leading trumpeters. *Candy* (EMD/Blue Note), *Cornbread* (EMD/Blue Note), and *The Sidewinder* (EMD/Blue) are essential Morgan CDs.

Sonny Rollins (born 1930)

On tenor saxophone, Rollins played some of the most vital hard bop of the 1950s and 1960s. He had genuine bebop experience, playing with trumpeter Fats Navarro and pianist Bud Powell in 1949. Rollins came into his own during the 1950s with a series of powerhouse recordings, and he kept the momentum going into the 1960s (after a break from 1959 to 1961). You need copies of *Work Time* (Original Jazz Classics), *Sonny Rollins Plus 4* (Original Jazz Classics), with Max Roach and Clifford Brown, and *Saxophone Colossus and More* (Original Jazz Classics).

Horace Silver (born 1928)

Pianist/composer Silver was on the leading edge of hard bop, and has matured into patriarch status as evidenced by the title of his album *Hardbop Grandpop* (GRP/Impulse!). Drawing from the bebop of pianist Bud Powell before him, Silver plays in a bluesier style emphasized by rhythmic left-hand chord patterns. Silver also gets credit for co-founding the Jazz Messengers with drummer Art Blakey — the definitive hard bop band.

Start your Silver wares with *Song for my Father* (EMD/Blue Note), with trumpeter Carmell Jones and saxophonist Joe Henderson, and *Tokyo Blues* (EMD/Blue Note), with saxophonist Junior Cook and trumpeter Blue Mitchell. Also get *Further Explorations* (EMD/Blue Note).

Sonny Stitt (1924-1982)

Sonny launched his career on alto sax, borrowing heavily from Charlie Parker, but soon developed a voice of his own on both alto and tenor. Stitt's output during the 1950s and 1960s ranges from bebop to bluesy hard bop to early soul jazz. You'll want copies of *Sonny Stitt at the Hi-Hat* (Roost) and *Boss Tenors* (Verve), as well as *Sonny Stitt and the Top Brass* (Atlantic) which catches him in a rare nonet format held together by great arrangements.

Kai Winding (1922-1983)

Kai Winding is perhaps best known as J.J. Johnson's cool jazz counterpart on their shared recording dates. Captivated by bebop, Winding had a major impact on Stan Kenton's orchestra with his unusual vibrato. Winding played on trumpeter Miles Davis's landmark *Birth of the Cool* (Capitol), and he frequently collaborated with J.J. Johnson during the mid-'50s. *Kai Winding Solo* (Verve) catches the trombonist in his prime.

Circuit riders: A vehicle for soloists

Beginning with 1940s bebop, jazz has been dominated by small, nimble groups that leave lots of room for soloists. Think of it as the *circuit rider* approach: A band plays a *head arrangement,* in which a melodic theme is stated at the start, or *head,* of a tune. Then the soloists take turns "riding" the circuit, with the rhythm section providing transportation in the form of steady chords and rhythms. Saxophonists most often front these small, facile jazz units. Prime examples from the hard bop era are Dexter Gordon, Gene Ammons, Lee Morgan, Hank Mobley, and Sonny Stitt.

Other hard boppers:

Other hard boppers worth your eventual attention include:

- ✔ **Curtis Fuller (born 1934).** A soulful, bluesy trombonist, Fuller is among the handful of trombonists who have made fine albums as leaders. Hear Fuller on *Curtis Fuller with Red Garland* (Original Jazz Classics), and especially on *Blues-Ette* (Savoy) and *Blues-Ette, Part 2* (Savoy).

- ✔ **Joe Henderson (born 1937).** Playing in a style that encompasses the history of jazz saxophone, from swing to bebop and hard bop, Henderson recorded his first album as a leader during the early 1960s and has since made consistently solid music. Essential Henderson includes *Page One* (EMD/Blue Note), *Inner Urge* (EMD/Blue Note), and *The Kicker* (Original Jazz Classics).

- ✔ **Yusef Lateef (born 1920).** One of jazz's most versatile musicians, Lateef plays saxes, flute, and oboe, and draws from a variety of jazz influences, as well as directly from African music. Lateef's launched his career during the 1950s and 1960s with hard bop albums including *Morning* (Savoy), *Cry!/Tender* (Original Jazz Classics), and *The Three Faces of Yusef Lateef* (Original Jazz Classics).

- ✔ **Wayne Shorter (born 1933).** Also somewhat in the shadow of more famous players, Shorter has had a major impact on several phases of jazz beginning with 1950s hard bop and its 1960s successors. A member of Art Blakey's Jazz Messengers during the early 1960s, Shorter also made several good albums of his own, including *Blues a la Carte* (Vee Jay), *Juju* (EMD/Blue Note), *Speak No Evil* (EMD/Blue Note), and *Adam's Apple* (EMD/Blue Note).

- ✔ **Mal Waldron (born 1926).** Another underappreciated jazzman, Waldron played some of the most interesting hard bop piano during the late '50s and early '60s. Waldron collaborated with bassist Charles Mingus and accompanied singers Billie Holiday and Abbey Lincoln. Among his own best recordings are *One and Two* (Prestige), *Mal 2* (Original Jazz Classics), and *Black Glory* (Enja).

Rise of the Piano Trio

Piano is one of jazz's original instruments, but in the realm of improvisation, it has been played most inventively in small-group formats — especially trios — that leave maximum latitude for the pianist's creations. The trio tradition began with Art Tatum in 1940, after Earl Hines had elevated the piano to lead roles during the 1920s. With the advent of extended improvisations in bebop, hard bop, and cool jazz — and the long-playing record format to capture them — the leading pianists of the 1950s took the jazz pianist's art to new heights. Trios were the predominant vehicle.

Red Garland (1921-1977)

A bebop pianist who backed Charlie Parker and others giants during the 1940s, Garland matured into one of hard bop best pianists during the 1950s and early 1960s. Hear him on *Garland of Red* (Original jazz Classics) and *Red Garland at the Prelude, Vol. 1* (Prestige), as well as on trumpeter Miles Davis's mid-'50s albums on Prestige including *Cookin'*, *Workin'*, and *Steamin'*. You can also catch Garland playing with the great saxophonist John Coltrane on the *Jazz For Dummies* CD.

Ahmad Jamal (born 1930)

Using a spare, melodic approach on piano parallel to what Miles Davis was doing on trumpet, Jamal developed an understated approach that pulls maximum emotion from a minimal number of notes. For a taste of Jamal's long, lyrical improvisations, get *Ahmad's Blues* (GRP) and *Ahmad Jamal Trio* (Epic).

Bud Powell (1924-1966)

Inspired by saxophonist Charlie Parker and trumpeter Dizzy Gillespie, as well as bop pianist Thelonious Monk's new harmonies, Powell was the quintessential bebop pianist. He played beautiful rapid-fire melodies and improvisations with his right hand, while his left pumped out provocative chord changes. Catch Powell with trios on *Inner Fire* (Elektra), *Jazz at Massey Hall, Vol. 2* (Original Jazz Classics), and *The Amazing Bud Powell, Vol. 3* (EMD/Blue Note).

Chapter 5

Fractured Forms: The 1960s and 1970s

. . . .

In This Chapter

▶ Early rebellions

▶ The jazz revolution

▶ Ornette Coleman and the birth of *free jazz*

▶ John Coltrane's meditations

▶ Free jazz focal points: Chicago and New York

▶ Electric, eclectic fusions

. . . .

*W*hen the black-and-white 1950s faded into the Technicolor 1960s, jazz already came in many flavors. Hard bop players from the 1950s, such as drummer Art Blakey and his Jazz Messengers, were still going strong. Trumpeter Miles Davis played brooding hard bop into the 1960s, but he soon plugged into electric rock and funk and sparked a fusion revolution. And Duke Ellington, Benny Carter, Coleman Hawkins, Count Basie — giants from jazz's Golden Age of the 1930s — were still making vital music.

The Early Avant garde

As early as 1949, though, some jazz players began to experiment with looser, freer forms that left more latitude for improvisation. Pianist Lennie Tristano's 1949 recordings of the songs "Intuition" and "Digression" on *Crosscurrents* (Capitol) marked one of the earliest adventures into free jazz. In a sextet alongside saxophonists Lee Konitz and Warne Marsh, Tristano stepped outside jazz's familiar boundaries for some extended improvisations that hailed a new freedom.

In the realm of big bands, Stan Kenton's 1940s and 1950s ensembles played long, complex pieces inspired by 20th Century classical music, on albums such as *City of Glass* (Capitol) and *Innovations Orchestra* (Capitol).

Through the 1950s, cool jazz and driving hard bop dominated, but a few players following Tristano explored freer forms. Saxophonist Jimmy Giuffre's 1955 *Tangents in Jazz* (Capitol), 1961 *Thesis* (Verve) and 1963 *Free Forms* (Columbia); pianist Cecil Taylor's 1956 *Jazz Advance* (Blue Note) and 1959 *Looking Ahead* (Original Jazz Classics); and bassist Charles Mingus's 1956 *Jazz Composer's Workshop with Teo Macero* (Savoy) were among the recordings that set the stage for 1960s free jazz.

George Russell (born 1923) and his Lydian Concept

Farther on the fringe, pianist/composer George Russell began developing his "Lydian Chromatic Concept of Tonal Organization" during the 1940s, composing pieces that often used Afro-Cuban elements for Dizzy Gillespie, Charlie Ventura, Artie Shaw, Claude Thornhill, and other band leaders.

Russell's theories translated into complex, unconventional compositions. His music made innovative use of the big band format and pointed the way toward 1960s *avant garde* and free jazz, and the notion of orchestrating jazz with the same subtleties as classical music. Sample Russell's music on the *Jazz Workshop* (Bluebird), *Stratusphunk* (Original Jazz Classics), *The Outer View* (Original Jazz Classics), and *Electronic Sonata for Souls Loved by Nature* (Soul Note).

Third stream

Experiments in combining jazz with classical music are known as *Third stream,* and the movement was spearheaded during the 1950s and 1960s by Modern Jazz Quartet leader John Lewis as well as composer Gunther Schuller. One excellent example of this genre is the CD *The Birth of the Third Stream* (Sony), including music by Lewis, trombonist J.J. Johnson, composer George Russell, saxophonist Jimmy Giuffre, and bassist Charles Mingus. One of Lewis's most successful efforts is *Jazz Abstractions* (Atlantic), with saxophonists Eric Dolphy and Ornette Coleman helping bring the music to life.

Free jazz versus avant garde

Lennie Tristano, George Russell, Cecil Taylor, John Lewis and others had opened jazz up to all sorts of new ideas. Building on their groundwork, new music soared with the spirit of the 1960s as young players explored fresh ways to express their innermost feelings in music. The decade was one of introspection in America; fittingly, the new *avant garde* and free jazz tended to be moody and contemplative.

Although the terms *free jazz* and *avant garde* are often used interchangeably, they refer to two types of music that can sound very different. *Avant garde* jazz is experimental, but it also usually has structure. It may sometimes sound chaotic, but it is often elaborately composed in advance. Free jazz, by contrast, is exactly that — free, with no (or few) rules. Free jazz can sound like anarchy, because that's what it is: the most direct expression of feelings in music.

Two centers for free and avant garde jazz

Chicago and New York became the centers for free jazz beginning in the 1960s and 1970s. In Chicago, a group of African American jazz players led by pianist Muhal Richard Abrams founded the Association for the Advancement of Creative Musicians (AACM) in 1965. The AACM is a collective nonprofit support group for players of various types of experimental black music, including jazz. Its membership includes: the Art Ensemble of Chicago, Anthony Braxton, Chico Freeman, Henry Threadgill, and numerous other free and *avant garde* jazz innovators. AACM presents concerts, takes jazz into city schools, and maintains its own music school.

The Knitting Factory is New York City's newer answer to the AACM. Opened as a club in 1987 by Michael Dorf, it has since grown into a recording label and professional association for experimental musicians. Players recorded by the Knitting Factory Works label include: Rashied Ali (onetime Coltrane drummer), Anthony Braxton (also an AACM member), Don Byron, Anthony Coleman, Mark Dresser, the Jazz Passengers, Junk Genius (a San Francisco band), Roscoe Mitchell, and Roy Nathanson.

Both of these groups have Internet sites that give lots of information on their programs and biographies on many of the participating musicians.

- Knitting Factory Web site: www.knittingfactory.com.
- AACM Web site: www.centerstage.net/chicago/music/whoswho/ aacm.html.

The 1960s Avant garde

Giants of the 1960s *avant garde* include Anthony Braxton, Eric Dolphy, Albert Ayler, Archie Shepp, Paul Bley, Julius Hemphill, and Don Cherry. Some of them also played all-out free jazz, but here are some details on their more structured tendencies:

Anthony Braxton (born 1945)

With his cardigan sweaters and wire-rimmed specs, Braxton looks like a college math professor, and his music is as perplexing as advanced calculus. Sometimes playing unaccompanied, other times composing epic works that are symphonic in their precision and complexity, Braxton, who plays alto sax and other wind instruments as well as piano, has made some of jazz's most unconventional music since the mid-'60s. An early member of the AACM (Association for the Advancement of Creative Musicians), he played with many of the *avant garde*'s leaders: saxophonist Joseph Jarman, pianist Muhal Richard Abrams, pianist Marilyn Crispell, drummer Gerry Hemingway. Hear *For Alto Saxophone* (Delmark), *Dortmund/Quartet 1976* (Hat Art), and *Six Monk's Compositions/1987* (Black Saint).

Eric Dolphy (1928-1964)

An associate of fellow saxophonists Ornette Coleman and John Coltrane, Dolphy was also on the leading edge of the late '50s and early '60s *avant garde*. Together in Coltrane's group, Dolphy and Coltrane were among the earliest saxophonists to solo until they felt they were finished — which may be 10 minutes or an hour or longer. Through his association with composer Gunther Schuller, Dolphy also had a hand, or horn, in early '60s experiments at combining jazz with elements of classical music. Alto was his main instrument, but he also played bass clarinet and flute. Hear Dolphy's wild leaps of imagination on *Here and There* (Original Jazz Classics), *Out There* (Original Jazz Classics), and *Far Cry* (Original Jazz Classics), and on several Coltrane albums including *Impressions* (GRP/Impulse!).

Dolphy also made numerous free jazz albums (see "The Free Jazz players" later in this chapter) as a leader beginning in 1960. *Out To Lunch* (Blue Note), recorded months before his death in 1964, features some of his wild, free blowing, with its dark, haunting undertones.

Archie Shepp (born 1937)

On tenor and soprano saxes, Shepp has been part of jazz's *avant garde* since the start. He played with Cecil Taylor and Don Cherry during the early 1960s, and led bands of his own that included trombonists Roswell Rudd and Grachan Moncur and vibraphonist Bobby Hutcherson. Check out *Archie Shepp in Europe* (Delmark), *Four for Trane* (GRP/Impulse!), *On This Night* (GRP), and *Magic of Ju-Ju* (GRP/Impulse!).

Paul Bley (born 1932)

On piano, Bley plays a lighter, dreamier style of *avant garde* jazz than peers such as fellow pianist Cecil Taylor and saxophonists John Coltrane and Ornette Coleman. Early on, he played with 1950s cool and hard bop musicians such as trumpeter Chet Baker and saxophonist Jackie McLean, but by the 1960s, Bley veered toward jazz fringes. Look for *Improvisations: Introducing Paul Bley* (Original Jazz Classics), *Paul Bley with Gary Peacock* (ECM), and *Copenhagen and Harlem* (Arista).

World Saxophone Quartet

For longevity and innovation in *avant garde* jazz, it's tough to top this group. Since the 1970s, the group, including alto saxophonists Oliver Lake and Julius Hemphill, tenor saxophonist David Murray, and baritone saxophonist Hamiett Bluiett, has produced a string of provocative albums of original music and re-vamped classic jazz. Their music combines jazz, blues, and gospel with authentic African rhythms and instruments. Good starters include *Steppin' With* (Black Saint), *W.S.Q.* (Black Saint), and *Plays Duke Ellington* (Elektra).

Don Cherry (1936-1995)

Jazz's leading trumpeter in the late '50s and early '60s *avant garde,* Cherry composed and played music that drew from both international and classical sources. He has also inspired many musicians who came through his bands. Pluck Cherry's *Symphony for Improvisers* (EMD/Blue Note) and *Art Deco* (A&M).

The Free Jazz Players

Free jazz is called "free" because it liberates players from traditional structures, such as melodic themes, patterns of chords, and restrictions on the duration or format of improvisations. Many free jazz pieces begin with a musical theme, then, as in other forms of jazz, the players take turns soloing. But a song's structure can be loose or virtually non-existent. Bandmates may improvise collectively, or one at a time. Shifts in the music may occur spontaneously, instead of from a leader's cue or sheet music. Free jazz players may also use their instruments in unconventional ways to produce unusual sounds — such as when a horn player intentionally *overblows* to produce moans, shrieks, and cries.

Beginnings of free jazz

In 1959, saxophonist Ornette Coleman broadsided jazz listeners with music that marked the arrival of free jazz, on his album *Shape of Jazz to Come* (Atlantic). That same year, another saxophonist named John Coltrane pushed the limits of hard bop in the direction of free jazz on his album *Giant Steps* (Atlantic). By the sixties, these two had become leading figures of *avant garde* and free jazz.

Free jazz brought even greater freedom of form, as well as fresh combinations of instruments. One of Ornette Coleman's groups included two electric guitarists, previously unheard of in jazz. Henry Threadgill's Very Very Circus has employed unconventional lineups such as two tubas, two electric guitars, a french horn, and drums behind the leader's saxophone — listen to his *Spirit of Nuff Nuff* (Black Saint)

Ornette Coleman (born 1930)

Think of Coleman's music as parallel to abstract painting, art with no tangible "subject." Instead, feelings, impressions, and emotions are the subjects. Coleman's music has only the loosest structure, sometimes as scant as a simple strand of melody, or repeated funky rhythms. Players improvise practically all the music.

Harmolodics, as Coleman calls his musical system, lets musicians respond to their intuitions and to each other as they invent new harmonies and melodies on the spot. Like many jazz fans, I find Coleman's music difficult to appreciate. It requires open ears and an open mind, but the emotional and intellectual rewards are great.

Ornette Coleman's music can be jarring, but it has traits in common with other jazz:

- ✔ **Improvisation.** To the max!
- ✔ **Distinctive voices.** Coleman's sound on alto saxophone is revolutionary in its sharp tone and soaring improvised melodies.
- ✔ **Swing.** Coleman may fly away from any sort of structure, but Charlie Haden on bass and Billy Higgins on drums swing hard through several sections on *The Shape of Jazz to Come* (Atlantic), laying down a loose, grooving foundation for Coleman's liberal creations.

Coleman's *The Shape of Jazz to Come* (Atlantic), from 1959, strikes some of the first notes of the new forms of jazz that would follow during the next decade. Coleman's bandmates — drummer Billy Higgins, cornetist Don Cherry, and bassist Charlie Haden — also became important purveyors of the new, free jazz.

Compared with some of the frantic free jazz that followed, Coleman's *Shape* album has an austere, mythic beauty. In his quest for fresh jazz, which continues today, Ornette Coleman may be responsible for some odd and annoying music, but he is never boring. Other recommended experiments by Coleman are his albums *Free Jazz* (Rhino/Atlantic) and 1990s *Tone Dialing* (Harmolodic/Verve).

John Coltrane (1926-1967)

In the 1960s, like major innovators such as Charlie Parker, Dizzy Gillespie, Duke Ellington, and Louis Armstrong before him, saxophonist John Coltrane turned jazz on its ear. Unlike Ornette Coleman, who played loose, free jazz almost from the start, Coltrane had his roots firmly in jazz tradition. Following early experiences with Dizzy Gillespie, Thelonious Monk, and Miles Davis, 'Trane took off in a different direction that led to music as free, in its own way, as Coleman's.

Coltrane's music was progressive, but it was also deeply spiritual. Increasingly during his prime years in the early 1960s (he died in 1967), Coltrane conceived music as a spiritual offering. In fact, the spiritual power of his music is so great that in San Francisco, the Church of John Coltrane uses it as a basis for its services.

At first, tenor saxophone was Coltrane's main instrument, but he eventually made some of his best music using the higher-pitched, mysterious-sounding soprano sax — an instrument that hadn't been used much in jazz since Sidney Bechet in the 1920s and 1930s. As Coltrane's music climbed into higher octaves, it scaled new heights of spiritual passion.

You'll want to tap Coltrane's 1950s music eventually, but in my opinion, his best and freest jazz was produced during the 1960s. As his creativity soared, Coltrane surrounded himself with players who were on his wavelength, especially explosive drummer Elvin Jones and bassist Jimmy Garrison.

Key elements of Coltrane's music:

- ✔ **Free, soaring solos.** He works familiar melodies, as on "Greensleeves," into his solos, but he also goes far outside a song's written chords. His solos were longer than almost any that came before him.

- ✔ **Odd sounds.** Squeals, squawks, and other sounds that others might consider "noise" are artfully integrated into his solos, extending their emotional range and intensity.

✔ **A meditative approach called *modal*.** Coltrane met Indian sitar player Ravi Shankar during the 1960s, and the deep, meditative aura of Coltrane's modal works is parallel to the Indian classical form known as *raga*. Influenced in part by this meeting, Coltrane wrote songs centered on single scales, or modes, instead of complex chord changes. Improvisers were freer to play straight from their feelings because they didn't need to follow predetermined chord changes.

John Coltrane's 1960s prime lasted for seven years and produced dozens and dozens of recordings. Any of this music is worth owning eventually, but *A John Coltrane Retrospective* (Impulse!), a three-CD set, is an excellent place to begin. It includes landmark Coltrane songs such as "Naima," "Spiritual," "I Want To Talk About You," and "A Love Supreme."

Further Free Jazz

For additional details on specific players, check the chapters on individual instruments. But here are some basics on a few others whose music was vital to free jazz during 1960s and 1970s:

✔ **Art Ensemble of Chicago.** A product of the AACM (Association for the Advancement of Creative Musicians), the Ensemble, like the World Saxophone Quartet, plays jazz seasoned with other musical spices (especially African), and adds a variety of unusual instruments. *Tutankhamun* (Black Lion) is a good example of their early (circa-1969) music.

✔ **Andrew Hill (born 1937).** Pianist extraordinaire whose music marks the murky line between latter-day bebop and free jazz, Hill is a talented composer who plays spectacular spontaneous improvisations. Hear him on *Point of Departure* (Blue Note).

✔ **Pharoah Sanders (born 1940).** He's among leading post-Coltrane/ Dolphy players of free jazz. His deep, dark legacy includes the 1969 album *Karma* (Impulse!).

✔ **Sun Ra (1914–1993).** He claimed he was from another galaxy, and his jazz was otherworldly. Live performances with his Arkestra were a spectacle of costumes, movement, and sound; the music is equally stunning — try any of his 1960s recordings on the Evidence label.

✔ **Cecil Taylor (born 1929).** Taylor's wild attacks on the ivories make for some raw, emotional piano music on albums including *Unit Structures* (Blue Note).

✔ **A few others.** Peruse your local music store for CDs by these other free players: reedmen Arthur Blythe, Henry Threadgill, David Murray, and John Zorn, trumpeter Lester Bowie, pianists Don Pullen and Marilyn Crispell, violinist Leroy Jenkins, trombonist George Lewis, drummer Sunny Murray, and guitarists Sonny Sharrock and James "Blood" Ulmer.

Electric and Eclectic Fusions

Avant garde and free jazz constituted one jazz tributary that flowed during the 1960s. Another stream blended jazz with rock, funk, and other styles and became known as *fusion* or *electric jazz*.

Although some fans and critics dismiss fusion for not being genuine jazz, it has all the hallmarks. Musically, there's no question it is jazz: it swings, includes extensive improvisation, and features soloists with distinctive voices. In fact, many of the first musicians to play fusion had played more traditional acoustic jazz before they went electric.

Miles Davis (1926-1991)

Trumpeter Miles Davis's 1960s albums *In a Silent Way* (Sony) and *Bitches Brew* (Sony) started a revolution. Davis, who had played unplugged bebop and cool jazz during the 1940s and 1950s, teamed his trumpet with electric instruments and utilized elements from funk and rock. His bandmates included electric guitarists such as John McLaughlin, and jazz pianists like Herbie Hancock and Chick Corea — only with Miles, they played *electric* piano.

Playing his trumpet through electronic effects, Davis got a haunting, echoey sound, and he sprayed delicate lines of improvised melody against the canvas of throbbing, pulsing sounds provided by his bands.

Throughout his career, Davis had a knack for discovering raw talent. Countless musicians who participated in Davis' early electric sessions went on to play essential parts during the next phase of jazz fusion. Among them were keyboard players Chick Corea, Herbie Hancock, and Joe Zawinul, saxophonist Wayne Shorter, guitarist John McLaughlin, and drummers Tony Williams and Lenny White.

Other fusioneers

In addition to Davis's key recordings, here are some other players to hunt down at your local music store:

- ✔ **Chick Corea (born 1941).** Corea played with Miles Davis and went on to fusions of his own, leading the group Return to Forever. *Light As A Feather* (Polygram) blends Corea's electric piano with Brazilian rhythms and Flora Purim's light, airy vocals. *Hymn of the Seventh Galaxy* (Polygram) takes fusion in a more electrifying rock direction.

- ✔ **The Crusaders.** During the 1970s, parties were just as likely to pop with the Crusaders as with hard rock. *Scratch* (MCA) is an all-time electric jazz-funk party classic.

- ✔ **Herbie Hancock (born 1940).** *Headhunters* (Columbia) is one of Hancock's all-time top electric jazz/funk recordings, but I'm also partial to his 1974 *Thrust* (Priority), which includes the beautiful song "Butterfly."

- ✔ **Freddie Hubbard (born 1938).** This talented trumpeter made one of my all-time favorite electric jazz albums. *Red Clay* (available as an import on KUDU) came out in 1970 and captured my emotions in a major way.

- ✔ **John McLaughlin (born 1942).** Mahavishnu Orchestra was guitarist McLaughlin's electrifying jazz/rock fusion band, and its albums *Inner Mounting Flame* (Columbia) and *Birds of Fire* (Columbia) are electric jazz classics.

- ✔ **Grover Washington, Jr. (born 1943).** On my friend Brad Shuster's mega-watt system, saxman Washington's 1975 *Mister Magic* (Motown) split our eardrums. It is one of the most important albums to merge jazz with funk and soul — great solos, rock-solid rhythms.

- ✔ **Weather Report.** Led by keyboardist Joe Zawinul and saxman Wayne Shorter, this electric jazz group really soared after bassist Jaco Pastorius came aboard. *Black Market* (Columbia) makes my all-time A-list of electric jazz and has been a vital part of my collection since its 1976 release.

- ✔ **Other neon names from 1960s and 1970s jazz fusion include:** Donald Byrd (trumpet), Stanley Clarke (bass), Billy Cobham (drums), Larry Coryell (guitar), Al DiMeola (guitar), Eddie Henderson (trumpet), Allan Holdsworth (guitar), Alphonso Johnson (bass), Alphonse Mouzon (drums), Johnny Hammond Smith (organ, synthesizer), Tower of Power, and anything on the CTI label, which defined its own smooth soul/jazz sound during the 1970s.

Chapter 6

Latin Jazz: Seven Decades of Spicy Seasonings (1930s to the 1990s)

● ●

In This Chapter

▶ Just what is Latin jazz?

▶ Early "Latin" influences on jazz

▶ The Cuboppers: Machito and Chano Pozo

▶ Latin and jazz embrace in the 1950s

▶ Simmering in the bossa sixties

▶ Looking at the present — Latin jazz's latest generation

● ●

*B*ossa nova, Cubop, calypso, mambo, salsa, cha-cha-cha. Almost since the
beginning of jazz, Latin rhythms have spiced up the music. Of course,
jazz's basic rhythmic roots are African, but the music has a tradition of
rhythmic variety dating back to New Orleans, where the cultural mix included African, French, Hispanic, and assorted tropical flavors.

Beginning in the 1930s, Latin rhythms and melodies worked their way into
jazz on a regular basic. Afro-Cuban players came to New York and inspired
jazz musicians like Dizzy Gillespie and Charlie Parker. In turn, American big
band leaders including Cab Calloway, Chick Webb, and Duke Ellington
influenced some sizzling arrangements by Machito, Mario Bauza, and other
giants of Latin music. American jazz players seasoned their rhythmic mix by
adding in unusual Latin rhythmic patterns, and Latin players found themselves experimenting with traditional 1-2-3-4 swing jazz rhythms and getting
a sense of jazz's earthy roots in blues.

So, What Is Latin Jazz?

Latin can be a misleading word. Latin jazz is a catchall phrase that refers to mergers of American jazz with musical elements from Cuba, Puerto Rico, the Caribbean, and various South American cultures. Of course, some forms of Latin music have more specific origins. *Salsa* refers to Mexican hot sauce and also to spicy Afro-Cuban dance music. *Bossa nova* and *samba* are Brazilian, and *mambo* is Cuban. So Latin jazz incorporates a variety of elements — mostly rhythmic — from several locales outside the United States and mostly in the southern hemisphere. Afro-Cuban and South American influences account for the vast majority of rhythms and other musical elements that constitute Latin jazz. (Icelandic and Alaskan music hasn't impacted jazz, as best I can tell.)

"Machito and Mario Bauza really created Afro-Cuban jazz, and they called it Afro-Cuban. Bauza was very upset when people called it 'Latin jazz'," says Bobby Matos, who leads a contemporary Afro-Cuban ensemble. "Latin really means Brazilian, Colombian, South American — but most people mean Afro-Cuban when they say it. Paquito D'Rivera is one 'Latin' player who actually uses stuff from Venezuela and Brazil."

Latin jazz encompasses Machito's big band music from the 1940s and 1950s, as well as Cal Tjader, Airto Moreira, Tito Puente, Tito Rodriguez, Charlie and Eddie Palmieri, Mongo Santamaria, Hilton Ruiz, Carlos "Patato" Valdes, Paquito D'Rivera, David Sanchez, and hot young bands with weird names like Bongo Logic.

Latin jazz also includes Dizzy Gillespie, Illinois Jacquet, George Shearing, Duke Ellington, Horace Silver, Gil Evans and Miles Davis.

Early Latin Influences on Jazz

Jelly Roll Morton, the pianist and band leader who helped create New Orleans jazz, utilized Caribbean rhythms. In his music from the '20s, you sometimes hear his left hand play a Latin pattern known as a *habanera*. Blues was a source of inspiration for early jazz musicians, and blues composer W.C. Handy used Latin rhythms in his famous "St. Louis Blues," a standard jazz tune since he published it in 1914. And Scott Joplin, the ragtime pianist and composer, used a tango-like pattern in his composition "Heliotrope Bouquet."

In the 1930s, bandleaders Don Azpiazu and Xavier Cugat helped popularize Cuban dance music called *rhumba*. Cugat had a hit hit in 1935 with Cole Porter's "Begin the Beguine," and continued to play light, commercial Latin jazz into the 1950s. His music wasn't really jazz, but Cugat helped introduce America to Latin rhythms, setting the stage for Latin jazz musicians such as percussionist/bandleader Tito Puente and pianist Perez Prado.

Among Latin musicians who had an impact on early jazz was Alberto (or Albert) Socarras (also one of the first jazz flutists), who led Latin jazz bands during the 1930s and hired jazz musicians like singer Cab Calloway and Cuban percussionist/composer Mongo Santamaria.

Some swing bands used Latin flavors occasionally during the 1930s. Duke Ellington played songs written by his Puerto Rican trombonist Juan Tizol, including the famous Ellington anthem "Caravan." But it wasn't until the 1940s in New York that Latin elements began turning up in jazz in a significant way.

The Cuboppers

New York in the 1940s had almost as eclectic a culture as New Orleans in the 1920s. It was an obvious birthplace for new forms of jazz. Saxophonist Charlie Parker and trumpeter Dizzy Gillespie, the inventors of bebop, were the first famous jazz players to make major use of Latin flavors. In turn, Cuban immigrants in New York merged bebop into their music, and the cultural exchange between American jazz players and recent immigrants created something called *Cubop* — blazing bebop played over Afro-Cuban rhythms.

Cubop doesn't follow rigid rules. The music may move to Latin rhythms, then switch to the 1-2-3-4 of big band swing. But Gillespie, in particular, had a close relationship with Latin music and musicians. Cuban band leader Mario Bauza played with Cab Calloway's band (which for some time included Gillespie), and Bauza later hooked Gillespie up with Cuban percussionist Chano Pozo. Pozo played with Gillespie, and Gillespie and Parker both played and recorded with Latin band leader Machito. Some of the most intriguing jazz happens when popular songs by composers like Irving Berlin, Harold Arlen, and George and Ira Gershwin get reworked in a Latin groove.

Machito (1912-1984) and Mario Bauza (1911-1993)

Bauza was key player in the early '40s fusion of jazz with Latin influences. Bauza had played trumpet in swing bands led by Don Redman and Cab Calloway, and he acted as musical director in drummer Chick Webb's band. Bauza and his brother-in-law Machito (given name: Frank Grillo) were both Cubans who came to the United States. Three years after Machito arrived in the United States in 1937, he started his own band called The Afro-Cubans. The next year, 1941, Bauza joined The Afro-Cubans as writer, arranger, and trumpeter.

Collaborating with American jazzmen like Gillespie and Parker, Machito and Bauza helped create Cubop — the merger of Afro-Cuban music and American bebop jazz. I think Cubop encompasses some of the most amazing and under-appreciated jazz.

The Original Mambo Kings (Verve) album featuring Machito's ensemble is one of the hottest big band jazz recordings. Machito and his orchestra stir up a storm behind sax players Flip Phillips and Charlie Parker, and trumpeters Mario Bauza and Dizzy Gillespie. And Gillespie also plays some mean Latin jazz with his own ensemble (a stellar crew that includes trombonist J.J. Johnson, saxophonists Hank Mobley and Lucky Thompson, plus the congas — Latin hand drums — of Mongo Santamaria).

Infectious rhythms on this recording keep the music grooving and fuel some of Phillips and Parker's finest improvisations. It's fresh 1940s Cubop, a new blend never heard before. Songs on this CD include Bauza's composition "Tanga," the first Afro-Cuban jazz composition, according to Afro-Cuban bandleader Bobby Matos.

The *Original Mambo Kings* was recorded during the late 1940s and early 1950s, and you can hear how much the music is inspired by American big band jazz. Horn sections stir up a storm of contrasts and harmonies, and tight arrangements support great soloists. Overall, the sound is reminiscent of ensemble work in bands led by Count Basie, Duke Ellington, and Benny Goodman.

The team of Machito and Bauza endured for decades, ending in 1976 because of a disagreement. Excellent later examples of the band's percolating dance music can be heard on *Machito Plays Mambos and Cha-Chas* (Palladium), while Cubop's jazzier side is evident on *Machito Live at the North Sea Jazz Festival* (Top Ten Hits). Also check out Machito's *Kenya* (Palladium Latin Jazz) and Bauza's *The Tanga Suite* (Messidor).

Dizzy Gillespie (1917-1993) and Chano Pozo (1915-1948)

Obviously it takes two to tango, or in this case, Cubop. Gillespie was a leading force from the jazz side of the music. Much of the credit for bringing Afro-Cuban influences to jazz goes to Chano Pozo, a Cuban percussionist who came to New York City in 1947.

Gillespie was into Afro-Cuban rhythms years before bebop. In 1939, he and Bauza played together in band leader Cab Calloway's trumpet section, and Gillespie also played a brief stint in flutist Alberto Socarras's somewhat commercial Afro-Cuban big band. Gillespie carried the Afro-Cuban connection into bebop and Cubop. After he and saxophonist Charlie Parker had made many recordings and performed numerous times together, Gillespie struck out on his own.

As leader of a bebop big band, he continued to utilize Latin rhythms. Modeled on Billy Eckstine's big band, which brought together many key players during the early days of bebop, Gillespie's first band splintered apart in 1945. But he soon assembled another band, with a key difference — a new emphasis on Cuban rhythms.

Gillespie then hired Pozo, whose percussion and vocal style could be traced through Cuba and back to West African voodoo cults that arrived in Cuba with the slave trade during the 18th and 19th centuries. Pozo had ancient roots, but he also loved playing the new kind of jazz. His 15-month collaboration with Gillespie during the late-1940s produced the definitive examples of Cubop.

Machito had proven that Afro-Cuban bands (and their fans) took quite naturally to jazz influences. Now Gillespie and his band carried Cubop to a broader American jazz audience. The best examples of Gillespie and Pozo's association are *Dizzy Gillespie and His Big Band In Concert* (GNP) and *Diz 'n' Bird at Carnegie Hall* (Roost/Blue Note).

Besides being essential examples of Afro-Cuban-flavored jazz, these performances are important for the ways in which arranger/composers John Lewis, Tadd Dameron, and George Russell adapted bebop's harmonies, rhythms, and speedy tempos to the big band format. On the GNP disc, dating from 1948, "Emanon" is a good example of how jazz drummers collaborate with Cuban percussionists — it was a natural merger that became common in years to come. Drummer Joe Harris plays standard jazz rhythms and Pozo embellishes them, then they switch roles, lending the music a loose, loping feelng. Meanwhile, Charlie Parker also maintained his Latin love affair. Much of his Cubop is included on *South of the Border* (Verve), a compilation of music including his collaborations with Machito's orchestra.

Chico O'Farrill (born 1921) and his legacy

Like Bauza and Pozo, composer, arranger, and trumpeter Chico O'Farrill was born in Cuba and came to the United States at the height of Gillespie's fascination with Cubop. O'Farrill arrived well-versed in both Afro-Cuban rhythms and American big band jazz, and as a result, he soon had plenty of work. Benny Goodman, Machito, Dizzy Gillespie, and Stan Kenton were among bandleaders who used O'Farrill's compositions.

In early 1950s New York, O'Farrill soon earned the respect of musicians, and had a significant impact on jazz through the decade. Since then, he has gone through several more productive phases that produced great Latin jazz and compositions. O'Farrill has a hand in *The Original Mambo Kings* (Verve) as arranger, composer, and conductor. His own recordings from the late 1940s and early 1950s — summarized on the CD *Cuban Blues* (Verve) — are also essential. Musicians on this CD are an eclectic blend: African-Americans such as trumpeter Roy Eldridge, saxophonist Flip Phillips, bassist Ray Brown, drummer Jo Jones, plus Mario Bauza and a host of Latin percussionists.

Recording quality on both *The Original Mambo Kings* and *Cuban Blues* is excellent, especially considering the technology of those times. Don't deny yourself. Get a hold of these CDs and turn your friends on to some hip music they probably haven't heard.

1950s: Latin Jazz Flowering

Machito, Dizzy Gillespie, and Chano Pozo set a torrid Afro-Cuban pace, and momentum carried into the 1950s, and many bandleaders followed the lead of these earlier guys and kept the spices flowing. During the 1950s, Latin elements also turned up in the driving, bluesy jazz called *hard bop,* and in mellower California *cool jazz* as the mambo beat became popular.

Art Blakey (1919-1990)

Given that the Latin influence is largely a rhythmic one, it makes sense that a leading drummer like Art Blakey would be fascinated by it. Blakey, longtime leader of the Jazz Messengers, experimented with all sorts of rhythms beginning in the 1950s. *Orgy in Rhythm, Vols. 1 & 2* (EMD/Blue Note) is powerful, percussive music incorporating Latin and Afro-Cuban rhythms. Blakey also plays a prominent part on pianist Horace Silver's recording, *Horace Silver Trio, Vol. 1: Spotlight on Drums* (EMD/Blue Note), along with Latin percussionist Sabu Martinez.

Woody Herman (1913-1987)

Bandleader Woody Herman and his Herd recorded songwriter Ralph Burns's Latin-flavored "Bijou" during the 1940s. During the 1950s, Herman teamed with Latin percussionist Tito Puente on *Herman's Heat and Puente's Beat* (Evidence).

Stan Kenton (1911-1979)

Pianist/arranger/bandleader Stan Kenton experimented with Latin rhythms — get hold of *The Innovations Orchestra* (EMD/Blue Note), with Kenton's 37-piece ensemble including Brazilian guitarist Laurindo Almeida, conga player Carlos Vidal, and trumpeter Chico Alvarez. Also check out *Cuban Fire* (EMD/Blue Note), another hot Kenton big band session.

Perez Prado (1916-1983)

Also check out Latin pianist Perez Prado on *Havana 3 a.m.* (BMG) and *Mondo Mambo* (Rhino). Prado and Machito team up with vocalist Beny More on *The Most from Beny More* (BMG/RCA), and there's some fine Cuban big band music from the 1950s on *Tumbao Cubano: Cuban Big Band Sound* (Palladium). Also look for Cuban guitarist Arsenio Rodriguez' *Leyendas* (Sony), as well as Puerto Rican vocalist Tito Rodriguez' *Live at Birdland* (Palladium).

Tito Puente (born 1923)

A category unto himself, Puente has been the single most prolific player of Latin jazz since the 1950s. As a percussionist (primarily timbales, but also vibes, congas, bongos, and other tools), Puente has worked with countless leading players including percussionists Machito, Mongo Santamaria, Willie Bobo, and Carlos "Patato" Valdez. As a leader, Puente's own albums have featured talents as diverse as saxophonist Mario Rivera, flutist Dave Valentin, and rising young pianist Hilton Ruiz.

Always keeping the "Latin" before the "jazz," Puente has made an amazing string of recordings that feature a mix of original Latin jazz tunes and re-worked jazz standards, always with hot, driving rhythms. Add some essential zing to your collection with *Dance Mania* (BMG), *El Rey* (Concord Picante), *Salsa Meets Jazz* (Concord Picante), and *Royal T* (Concord Picante).

George Shearing (born 1919)

In a small-group setting, pianist George Shearing also went Latin with great results during the 1950s, collaborating with Cuban percussionists Armando Peraza and Willie Bobo. Shearing was already popular, so his Afro-Cuban music reached a wide audience. Some of his best Latin jazz is on *The Best of George Shearing* (EMD/Blue Note).

Cal Tjader (1925-1982)

Tjader's contributions to Latin jazz were twofold: He played melodic vibes that blended seamlessly with Latin rhythms; and, as a leader, he selected great combinations of players and Latin-flavored material. Check out his 1954 *Tjader Plays Mambo* (Original Jazz Classics), and subsequent albums including *Black Orchid* (Fantasy), *Latin Concert* (Original Jazz Classics), *Latino* (Fantasy), *El Sonid Nuevo* (Verve), and *Primo* (Original Jazz Classics).

And later, more than any American jazzman of the 1960s and 1970s, Tjader was a vital creator of fresh Latin jazz. He played with great Latin percussionists like Willie Bobo and Mongo Santamaria, and kept his Latin fascination going strong over the course of several albums. His later work includes *Primo* (Original Jazz Classics), *Descarga* (Original Jazz Classics), *La Onda Va Bien* (Concord Picante), and *A Fuego Vivo* (Concord Picante).

Bossa '60s

The reedy sound of saxophones and flutes fits naturally with Latin rhythms, especially those from Brazil and other parts of South America. So it's not surprising that saxophonists including Stan Getz and Gato Barbieri and flutists like Herbie Mann, and, more recently, Dave Valentin, have been among the most adept at blending Latin elements into their jazz. However, one of the first people to make a case for bossa in the United States was Astrud Gilberto with her recording of "Girl from Ipanema."

Gato Barbieri (born 1934)

Born in Argentina, Barbieri has blended eclectic international sounds and rhythms into his jazz since the late 1960s. *El Pampero* (BMG/RCA) is excellent early Barbieri, while more recent gems include *The Third World Revisited* (Bluebird), *Chapter 3: Viva Emiliano Zapata* (GRP/Impulse!), with arrangements by Chico O'Farrill, and *Para Los Amigos* (A&M).

Ray Barretto (born 1929)

Like Cuban percussionist Chano Pozo before him, Barretto broke into jazz jamming with New York City's top players. He played in Tito Peunte's band, but he also played with jazzmen including pianist Red Garland, saxophonists Lou Donaldson and Gene Ammons, and guitarist Kenny Burrell — as well as Cal Tjader.

Barretto directed the Latin jazz of the Fania All Stars during the 1960s, and has made a string of fine Latin jazz albums into the 1990s. His music is distinguished by a lighter, gentler feel than 1950s Cubop or early '60s bossa nova. Check out Barretto on *Carnaval* (Fantasy), *Handprints* (Concord Picante), *Taboo* (Concord Picante), as well as on Ammons' *Boss Tenor* (Original Jazz Classics) and Donaldson's *Blues Walk* (EMD/Blue Note).

Willie Bobo (1934-1983)

Schooled as Machito's go-for and later as a member of bands fronted by Tito Puente and Cal Tjader, Bobo has added Latin percussion to a wide array of jazz. A two-CD re-issue of Bobo's *Unos, Dos, Tres* and *Spanish Grease* (PGD/Verve) albums is a 1960s classic. Also look for *Talkin' Verve* (PGD/Verve) and *Latino!* (Fantasy) with vibist Cal Tjader and percussionist Mongo Santamaria.

Stan Getz (1927-1991)

Getz connected with Latin-loving vibraphonist Cal Tjader on *Stan Getz with Cal Tjader* (Original Jazz Classics). After his seminal early 1960s sessions with Joao Gilberto, Getz maintained passionate about Latin rhythms, as you can hear on *The Best of Two Worlds* (Sony) — a reunion with Gilberto — as well as *Apasionado* (A&M).

Astrud (born 1940) and Joao Gilberto (born 1932)

Astrud's 1963 collaboration with husband Joao Gilberto, Brazilian composer Antonio Carlos Jobim, and American saxophonist Stan Getz produced warm, breezy Latin jazz of lasting quality. Get *The Astrud Gilberto Album* (PGD/Verve) as well as her *Look at the Rainbow* (PGD/Verve). Also find *The Legendary Joao Gilberto* (World Pacific), as well as *Getz and Gilberto* (Mobile Fidelity), essential albums of early '60s bossa jazz.

Herbie Mann (born 1930)

Mann, a flutist, was one of the most inventive at merging jazz and Latin music in the '60s. Earlier, he had led the Afro-Jazz Sextet and visited Brazil and Africa, and by the time of his 1960 *Flute, Brass, Vibes and Percussion* (Verve), his music utilized an eclectic array of Latin elements — particularly Brazilian and Afro-Cuban. *Brazil Blues* (United Artists) is another Mann collection of exotic sounds (including xylophone-like marimba). *Do the Bossa Nova* (Atlantic) helped hail the start of the national bossa craze, and Mann later diversified his cultural base even farther on the '70s albums *Reggae* (Atlantic) and *Brazil: Once Again* (Atlantic).

Mongo Santamaria (born 1922)

For his prolific output as a leader of his own bands and with countless other musicians, Santamaria, a percussionist and composer, deserves to be ranked among jazz's top players. His compositional hits include "Afro Blue" and "Parati," both Latin jazz standards. Born in Havana, Cuba, Santamaria came to New York City in 1950 and made a mark recording Afro-Cuban jazz and playing with pianist George Shearing. He later worked with Latin jazz leader/vibraphonist Cal Tjader as well as with Dizzy Gillespie, Chick Corea, Hubert Laws, even harmonica monster Toots Thielemans. Heat up to Santamaria's rhythms on *Afro-Roots* (Prestige), *At the Black Hawk* (Fantasy), *Skins* (Milestone), *Soy Yo* (Concord), and on Tito Puente's *Top Percussion* (BMG).

Dave Valentin (born 1954)

Valentin melded Latin elements with jazz beginning in the 1970s. In fact, he got his start during his teens playing Latin clubs in New York City and has delivered a steady stream of solid Latin-flavored jazz ever since. Catch him on *Kalahari* (GRP) and *Tropic Heat* (GRP), as well as with fellow flutist Herbie Mann on *Two Amigos* (GRP). Valentin's *Red Sun* (GRP) is an intriguing amalgam of Latin, jazz, and funky grooves.

Spicy, Electric '70s

While many top creators of 1960s Latin jazz kept going strong into the 1970s and 1980s, younger players came along with new hybrids. Latin rhythms, especially the mambo, lent a strong influence to funk and soul jazz sounds of the early 1970s.

Chick Corea (born 1941)

Electric instruments used by jazzmen such as pianist Chick Corea added new twists to Latin jazz. Corea's *Light as a Feather* (Polydor) is a seamless merger of electric jazz with the Brazilian rhythms of percussionist Airto Moreira and wild exotic vocals of Flora Purim. Corea's later album *My Spanish Heart* (Polydor) has a mellower, more romantic Latin vibe.

Poncho Sanchez (born 1951)

Sanchez learned about Latin jazz under a master: He was a member of Cal Tjader's band for several years beginning in 1975, spicing up albums such as *La Onda Va Bien* (Concord Picante) and *Gozame! Pero Ya* (Concord Picante). Sanchez began leading his own bands during the early 1980s, producing some of the decade's hottest Latin jazz. *Papa Gato* (Concord Picante), *Fuerte!* (Concord Picante), *Chile Con Soul* (Concord Picante), *Para Todos* (Concord Picante), and *Soul Sauce: Memories of Cal Tjader* (Concord Picante) are among more recent winners by Sanchez.

Arturo Sandoval (born 1949)

A protégé of Dizzy Gillespie, Cuban-born trumpeter Sandoval began making hot Latin jazz in Cuba in the 1970s — first as a member of the Orquesta Cubana de Musica Moderna (also including saxophonist/clarinetist Paquito D'Rivera), then as part of Irakere, a leading Cuban jazz ensemble. Sandoval toured with Gillespie's band during the early 1980s and made his solo recording debut in 1982. Sandoval plays Gillespie-like bebop over scintillating Latin rhythms, and he's also made some straight-ahead jazz albums). Check out *Danzon* (UNI/GRP), *Arturo Sandoval & the Latin Train* (UNI/GRP), *No Problem* (Jazz House), and *Hot House* (N2K), as well as dueling with his mentor Dizzy on Gillespie's *To a Finland Station* (Original Jazz Classics).

Latin Jazz: The New Generation

Maybe it's the Internet, maybe it's CNN and MTV, but culture is becoming more global and less regional. Just as people living in remote parts of the world know about designer clothing and Hollywood movies, different types of music from various parts of the world can spread quickly. Latin jazz from the 1980s and 1990s covers a tremendous range of influences. Some players uphold the tradition of Cubop or bossa nova or other styles from past decades, but there are also new combinations of Latin rhythms, jazz, and other influences. Here are a few of the most interesting purveyors of Latin jazz from the most recent two decades.

Jerry Gonzalez (born 1949)

A top latter-day bebop trumpeter, also an excellent percussionist, Gonzalez founded the Fort Apache Band, an innovative Latin jazz ensemble that does tangy things to famous jazz tunes by players such as pianist Thelonious Monk, saxophonist Wayne Shorter, trumpeter Miles Davis, and other legendary figures. Get *The River Is Deep* (Enja), *Rhumba Para Monk* (Sunnyside), *Obatala* (Enja), and *Pensativo* (Milestone).

Sergio Mendes

Beginning with *Brasil '66,* this Brazilian bandleader has had streaks of commercial success in the United States, but his big bands have also made some red hot music, combining excellent arrangements with solid musicianship and a variety of Brazilian-flavored vocals. Get *Sergio Mendes and Brasil '66* (A&M) and the newer *Brasilerio* (Elektra).

Danilo Perez (born 1966)

Perez, a pianist, was fortunate enough to play with trumpeter Dizzy Gillespie during the late 1980s, and has made several good recordings of his own including *Danilo Perez* (Novus) and *The Journey* (Novus).

Gonzalo Rubalcaba (born 1963)

A young, promising pianist born in Havana, Cuba in 1963, Rubalcaba has already caused quite a stir. But hear for yourself on *Live in Havana* (Messidor), *Mi Gran Pasion* (Messidor), *The Blessing* (EMD/Blue Note), and *Rapsodia* (EMD/Blue Note).

Hilton Ruiz (born 1952)

Yet another promising young jazz pianist, Ruiz (a protégé of pianist Mary Lou Williams) has already made an impressive string of Afro-Cuban–jazz albums. Check out *El Camino* (Novus), *A Moment's Notice* (Novus), and *Manhattan Mambo* (Telarc).

Chucho Valdes (born 1941)

Born in Cuba, this bandleader/pianist founded the Cuban jazz ensemble Irakere in the 1970s, and he also plays wonderful Afro-Cuban–flavored jazz piano. Get your hands on Valdes's *Lucumbi: Piano Solo* (Messidor) and *Solo Piano* (EMD/Blue Note).

A few other Latin flavors worth watching for

The number of excellent Latin players is too large to go into depth on every one, so here's a list of a few more worth your time:

- Afro-Cuban All-Stars, *A Toto Cuba Le Gusta* (Nonesuch)
- Azymuth, *Crazy Rhythm* (Milestone)
- Bongo Logic, *Tipiqueros* (RykoLatino)
- Conrad Herwig, *The Latin Side of John Coltrane* (Astor Place)
- Bobby Matos, *Footprints* (Ubiquity), also featuring Jerry Gonzalez
- Manny Oquendo and Libre, any of their albums are worth your time
- Mario Rivera, *El Commandante/The Meringue Jazz* (RTE)
- John Santos and the Machete Ensemble (including their album *Machete* on Xenophile)
- Charlie Sepulveda, *The New Arrival* (Groovin' High)
- Carlos "Patato" Valdes, *Ritmo Y Candela II: African Crossroads* (Round World Music), a 1998 Grammy nominee

Chapter 7

Jazz Now

. . . .

In This Chapter

▶ Jazz is still a vibrant and diverse sound

▶ Acid jazz

▶ Neo-traditionalists

▶ "Contemporary" or "lite" jazz

▶ Living masters

. . . .

So you find yourself trying to make it as musician in the 1990s. Maybe even a jazz musician. What a daunting task! Think of the legacy you have to live up to: Louis Armstrong, Lester Young, Duke Ellington, Charlie Parker, Miles Davis, John Coltrane . . . the list of players whose music has stood the test of time is already long.

Does that mean there's no more creative room left? No — just different modes of creativity to explore. Classical music fans continue to love Bach, Mozart, and Beethoven — centuries after they penned their most famous pieces. Opera buffs are still crazy about Puccini, Verdi, and Rossini.

Working within the framework of phenomenal works of genius, contemporary composers, musicians, and great opera singers give each performance fresh life by channeling the music through their own emotional and interpretive filters. Jazz's legends may have set some great precedents, but there is much room left for creativity and new sounds . . . especially given that jazz, unlike classical music, is substantially based on improvisation.

Jazz is now more than 100 years old if you take Buddy Bolden's circa-1895 New Orleans band as the starting point. Because of its longevity, jazz has matured from new, raw music into a classical style in its own right.

What's the Hap? Diversity . . .

America, jazz's birthplace, is more complex and culturally diverse today than ever. Jazz is growing in many fresh directions. Some young players make music within the boundaries of basic jazz styles such as early New Orleans, swing, bebop, cool . . . and not-so-basic *avant garde* and *free* jazz. Others move fluidly between styles. And still other young talents combine jazz with other musical influences, or use jazz as a jumping off point for ventures into some of the latest electronic sounds.

From my point of view amidst the scene, there doesn't appear to be a focus — no single, new, creative direction, as existed with bebop or cool jazz. Perhaps today's world is *too* diverse — too unified by the Internet and television — for a lone revolutionary style of jazz to emerge. But more than ever, jazz celebrates diversity in a diverse world.

Jazz traditions are still handed down the old-fashioned way. Although big bands, the original "colleges" for young jazz players, have been replaced by collegiate jazz degree programs, young players continue to get the real education for their craft by performing and recording with seasoned mentors. Saxophonists Benny Carter and Sonny Rollins, bassist Milt Hinton, drummers Max Roach and Elvin Jones, and pianist Oscar Peterson began their careers decades ago and are still going strong in the 1990s, often teaming with younger musicians to make vital music.

And jazz, like fashion, goes through cycles. In the same way that sixties fashions made a comeback in the 1990s (anyone see the movie *Austin Powers*?), budding players have latched onto earlier forms of jazz as a basis for fresh new music. Perhaps the most prominent of these is the style known as Acid Jazz.

What Is Acid Jazz, Man?

Acid jazz combines sounds from jazz, soul, funk, and even contemporary hip-hop. It was born in London dance clubs, and it is music meant for moving and grooving. DJs often spin acid jazz records at *raves* — the all-night 1990s version of the 1960s "happening."

Some acid jazz utilizes digital equipment to *sample* earlier sounds for use in new music — a sample is a swatch of existing music that is digitally incorporated or transformed into new music. An acid jazz producer like the popular Greyboy may take an electric bass part from a 1970s piece, tweak it electronically so you probably don't even recognize it, then build a new song by adding several layers of instrumentation with the sample as the foundation.

Much acid jazz, contrary to its mysterious and spacey name, is actually earthy music that hits you at a gut level. One name for some Acid Jazz is *groove,* due do its digable, danceable beat.

And although it wasn't called "acid" when it was recorded during the 1970s, some good, funky jazz from that decade, especially the early half, has been the major inspiration for acid jazz. As a result, much of it is being re-issued on CD. Trumpeters Donald Byrd and Miles Davis, guitarist Grant Green, vibraphonist Roy Ayers, organist Charles Earland, and saxmen Houston Person and Lou Donaldson are among earlier jazz heavies cited as inspirations by the new acid jazzers.

If you don't know a thing about acid jazz, the best way to get into it is to buy one of several compilation CDs. From labels like Ubiquity, Instinct, BGP, PGD/Hollywood, and Irma come some great introductory CDs — collections of 15 or more songs by a variety of artists.

Among acid jazz artists to look for: Greyboy, Gang Starr and Tribe, Jamiroquai, Incognito, Snowboy, Galliano, the James Taylor Quartet (no, not *that* James Taylor), Brand New Heavies, Medeski, Martin and Wood, A Tribe Called Quest, Digable Planets, Count Basic, Night Trains, Mother Earth, Chris Bowden, EM&I, Money Mark, Slide Five, Soul Bossa Trio, Spiritual Vibes.

Neo-Traditionalists

While some players push for new combinations of jazz-rooted sound, others continue in the tradition of classic unplugged jazz.

Trumpeter Wynton Marsalis led a wave of young jazz traditionalists that became known as the *Young Lions* during the 1980s. Others in this crowd were pianists Marcus Roberts and Kenny Kirkland, Wynton's saxophonist brother Branford, guitarists Mark Whitfield and Kevin Eubanks, trombonist Robin Eubanks (Kevin's brother), bassists Robert Hurst III and Reginald Veal, drummers Jeff "Tain" Watts and Herlin Riley, trumpeters Wallace Roney, Ryan Kisor, James Zollar, Roy Hargrove, Terence Blanchard (like Wynton, a former member of Art Blakey's Jazz Messengers), organist Joey DeFrancesco, and saxophonists Jesse Davis, Javon Jackson, Scott Hamilton (who often records with his older mentors), Joshua Redman (son of tenor saxman Dewey Redman), and Coltrane-inspired Courtney Pine.

Wynton Marsalis's efforts are especially noteworthy. As head of jazz programs at New York's Lincoln Center, Marsalis has staged numerous fine jazz concerts — showcasing fresh new music, as well as revamped early jazz like the kind heard on his *The Fire of the Fundamentals* CD (Columbia).

Some of the Lincoln Center music and/or musicians (including an orchestra conducted by Marsalis) have also gone on the road, bringing first-rate jazz to several American cities. Meanwhile, Marsalis continues his own career as one of jazz's most provocative artists. His intricate three-CD suite, *Blood in the Fields* (Sony), expresses many moods and moments from the African-American experience. He is also a fine classical player, and continues to perform and record with his own small groups. Marsalis has also written books and hosted a television show about music for kids on PBS. With all of his projects, Marsalis is modeling how jazz musicians can take their art to new listeners, including the next generation of young players.

Marsalis and his peers make solid jazz and put across a dignified image — always meticulously dressed and well-rehearsed. Most of them are still going strong as they move into mid-career. Now a new generation is coming up. Many are progeny of legendary jazz players. Drummer T.S. Monk is the son of famous bebop pianist Thelonious Monk. Saxophonist Ravi Coltrane is John Coltrane's son; singer Miki Coltrane is his daughter.

Other promising young jazz musicians who've already made a mark include bassists Christian McBride, Anthony Cox, and Avishai Cohen; guitarists Charlie Hunter and Fareed Haque; singers Kevin Mahogany, Kurt Elling, and Claire Martin; saxophonists Ivo Perelman, James Carter, Peter Apfelbaum, Kenny Garrett, Mark Turner, David Sanchez, Dave Ellis, Mark Shim, Antonio Hart, Greg Tardy, and Chris Potter; trumpeters Nicholas Payton (check out his album with New Orleans veteran Doc Cheatham, on Verve), Tim Hagans, Peck Almond, and Marcus Printup; and pianists Danilo Perez, Cyrus Chestnut, and Brad Mehldau; cornetist Robert Mazurek and drummers Kenny Washington and Kenny Wollenson.

Contemporary Jazz

The name is misleading — much "contemporary jazz" really isn't jazz in the truest sense. Players in this category, such as Kenny G, have struck gold, but their music is more appropriately described as "gentle instrumental." It doesn't swing like genuine jazz, and while it includes improvisation, the spontaneous inventions of "contemporary jazz" players are mild compared with the creations of more pure jazz players.

While I disagree with the use of the word *jazz* to describe some of this music, a few legitimate jazz players have opted to play this more popular, radio-friendly variety of music. And given that there is a blurring of boundaries between what many critics would call *genuine* jazz and *contemporary* jazz, it is possible that music fans who first gravitate to contemporary jazz will eventually wind up working their way back through jazz's history into more ambitious, and in my opinion, rewarding music.

Contemporary jazz's roots are in the various varieties of fusion jazz — so-named for the combination of jazz and rock influences — that evolved during the 1970s. Seasoned jazz musicians such as Miles Davis, Herbie Hancock, and Wayne Shorter plugged in and began playing electric music that melded jazz with rock, funk, and soul (see Chapter 5).

A few players who moved away from acoustic jazz and into lighter, funkier jazz during that decade — such as Grover Washington, Jr., and Chick Corea — are still making good music.

Meanwhile, the 1980s brought a whole new realm of players who only played light, "contemporary jazz," but who had no experience playing genuine jazz. As part of their revamped marketing campaigns, FM radio stations have a new name for contemporary jazz: *smooth jazz*. I've also heard the terms *lite jazz,* and even *the quiet storm.*

Among today's smooth jazz stars are saxophonists Boney James, Richard Elliott, Candy Dulfer, and Dave Koz; guitarists Mark Antoine, Chuck Loeb, Peter White, and Ottmar Liebert; trumpeters Rick Braun and Chris Botti; singers Marilyn Scott and Bobby Caldwell; keyboard players Keiko Matsui, Bobby Lyle, and Bob James; pianists David Benoit and Sergio Salvatore; Latin-based players the Gypsy Kings, Juan Carlos Quintero, and Roberto Perera, and banjo man Bela Fleck.

While some of these players are a little *too* smooth for my taste, some other artists in the contemporary category make more challenging music. Among my favorites: the Yellowjackets, Spyro Gyra, Fourplay, the Rippingtons, keyboard player Joe Sample, drummer Dave Weckl, guitarist Denny Jiosa, saxophonists George Howard, Kim Waters, and Grover Washington, Jr.

Living Jazz Masters

While young upstarts offer hope for the future of jazz, I think the best jazz today comes from living legends and seasoned pros. These are players ranging in age from their 40s to their 80s who have survived jazz's brutal coming of age and are currently in their prime. Here are a few personal favorites and a suggested release by each of them:

- Howard Alden/Jimmy Bruno, *Full Circle* (Concord)
- Michael Brecker, *Two Blocks from the Edge* (Impulse!)
- Randy Brecker, *Into the Sun* (Concord)
- Dee Dee Bridgewater, *Dear Ella* (Verve)
- Gary Burton, *Astor Piazzolla Reunion* (Concord)

- Ron Carter, *The Bass and I* (Blue Note)
- Mino Cinelu, Kevin Eubanks, and Dave Holland, *World Trio* (Intuition)
- Olu Dara, *In The World: From Natchez to New York* (Atlantic)
- Jack DeJohnette, *Oneness* (ECM)
- Eliane Elias, *The Three Americas* (Blue Note)
- Charlie Haden and Hank Jones, *Steal Away* (Verve)
- Charlie Haden and Pat Metheny, *Beyond the Missouri Sky* (Verve)
- Herbie Hancock and Wayne Shorter, *1+1* (Verve)
- Joe Henderson, *Big Band* (Verve)
- Bill Holman Big Band, *Brilliant Corners: The Music of Thelonious Monk* (WEA).
- Jazz Messengers, *The Legacy of Art Blakey* (Telarc)
- Peter Leitch, *Up Front* (Reservoir)
- Mingus Big Band, *Que viva Mingus* (Dreyfus)
- John Scofield, *A Go Go* (Verve)

Part II
Up Front

"The problem with wine tastings is you're not supposed to swallow, and Clifford refuses to spit. Fortunately, he studied trumpet with Dizzy Gillespie."

In this part . . .

Unlike classical music or opera, which are pre-planned, with parts written for the players, jazz is largely improvisational music. Musicians may play your favorite popular song, but they'll take it apart and put it back together in fresh ways. Or they'll play something completely wild, the likes of which you never imagined. Given that jazz is so spontaneous, its talented players and vocalists are as important as the composers and back leaders behind the music. Legendary players such as Louis Armstrong, Charlie Parker, and John Coltrane and vocalists like Ma Rainey, Billy Holiday, and Ella Fizgerald "compose" much of what they play and sing on the spot, in their improvised solos and intuitive interpretations of melodies.

The important players and vocalists from each stylistic period are covered in this part, including some history of the saxaphone and trumpet and how these instruments made it into the music.

Chapter 8
Saxophonists: Jazz's Main Guard

. . . .

In This Chapter

▶ Sax meets jazz in the 1920s big bands

▶ Early saxmen offer a sweet introduction to jazz

▶ Charlie "Yardbird" Parker is the heavyweight champ

▶ John Coltrane takes a spiritual journey

▶ The *avant garde* expresses emotion with sound

▶ The 1990s offer retro forms plus fresh ideas

▶ Living legends still make great music

. . . .

"**S**axophone is one of the important instruments in jazz, because it emulates the human voice quite well," says saxophonist Charles McPherson, a disciple of the late, great jazz saxman Charlie Parker. "I'm sure this is why it was such an attractive instrument to musicians at the very inception of the music."

In the hands of Charlie Parker or John Coltrane, a saxophone expressed the full range of human emotions, with whispers, shrieks, shouts, squeals, and even giddy laughter. Parker's 1946 rendition of "Lover Man," recorded as he bottomed out on heroin, is a gut-wrenching cry from the soul. John Coltrane's "Meditation" ponders a Higher Power. Abstract pieces by Anthony Braxton, Oliver Lake, and Arthur Blythe evoke raw feelings, colors, and imagery.

Saxophone Steps Forward

Today, if you give most anyone three seconds to name a jazz instrument, most would name the saxophone. Yet early jazz bands and their precursors, the parade and funeral bands of the deep South, did not utilize saxophone. Instead, the clarinet (as played by Sidney Bechet, who incidentally also played sax, Benny Goodman, Artie Shaw, and Jimmie Noone) — was the original reed instrument in jazz.

Essential facts about the sax

Adolphe Sax patented his design for the horn in Belgium in 1846, an attempt to improve on the sound of the clarinet. Initially, it was used in symphonic and chamber music. Some African music, one of jazz's ancestors, employed various horns, but nothing like a saxophone.

A soprano sax is straight and resembles a clarinet; alto and tenor saxes are the ones that look like, well . . . saxes. They have the classic curved shape and upturned, flared bell most people visualize when they think "saxophone."

Alto is the smaller horn with the higher pitch and sharper sound. Tenor is the larger, mellower-sounding sax. You can recognize it by the extra hump in the neck, near the mouthpiece.

Most saxophone mouthpieces are made of hard rubber (a few players prefer metal ones), and are similar to a clarinet's mouthpiece. There's a small clamp for attaching a reed, which vibrates when the player blows across it.

Early *C-melody* saxophones, favored by players such as Jack Pettis and Frankie Trumbauer, had a range between alto and tenor. No one uses them today (a possible opportunity for a young player to create a "new" sound).

Of the seven major types of saxophone, alto and tenor are most prominent in jazz. They all look different (see the figure in this sidebar), but they all have six keys and use similar fingerings. A master of one variety of saxophone can play the others.

soprano

alto

(Illustration courtesy of Yamaha Corp. of America, Band and Orch. Div.)

tenor

baritone

(Illustration courtesy of Yamaha Corp. of America, Band and Orch. Div.)

Saxophone began to sneak into jazz during the late 1920s. Perhaps because of the human qualities of its tone and expressive range, the instrument soon became the darling of jazz, the star of jam session battles that lasted for hours. Soaring above piano, bass, and drums, saxophonists played a lead role in small groups, many of which spun off from big bands during the late 1930s.

The Early Swing Pioneers

Early saxophone solos by musicians such as Sidney Bechet (who is also known for his clarinet prowess), Johnny Hodges, Jimmy Dorsey, Don Redman, Harry Carney, Barney Bigard, Ben Webster, and Coleman Hawkins are good places for an introduction to jazz saxophone. Some players, including Bechet, played and improvised in an early New Orleans style, although saxophones didn't really become widely used in jazz until the 1920s. Other players, such as Hodges, Hawkins, and Webster, went further — they became some of the first soloists featured in big bands and small groups.

Sidney Bechet (1897-1959)

Bechet was born in New Orleans and was already a top jazz player in his teens. Like some other early jazz horn specialists, he had a light, fleet sound distinguished by a wavering vibrato. He played with cornetist Louis Armstrong, pianist Clarence Williams, and saxman Johnny Hodges, but Bechet was a strong soloist who stood out in most any setting. With the revival of traditional jazz during the 1940s, Bechet enjoyed a career revival that lasted through the 1950s and produced several solid recordings although seldom equaling his earlier jazz for pure energy and spirited improvisation.

Although cornet/trumpet player Louis Armstrong is commonly credited as jazz's first great soloist, Bechet was a significant early improviser in his own right. On soprano sax or clarinet, Bechet blew up a storm of twisting, turning improvised lines that intertwined around lines invented by such frequent bandmates as pianists Jelly Roll Morton and Clarence Williams, guitarist Teddy Bunn, trumpeter Tommy Ladnier, clarinet/saxman Mezz Mezzrow and, of course, the great Louis Armstrong himself.

Bechet's improvisational gift is an example of his genius for jazz. Another is his rhythmic gift, his uncanny sense of swing as evidenced in his sensitive use of syncopation — the way accents in his solos frequently fall just before or after the beat, while still helping to move the music relentlessly ahead.

At least 30 CDs of Bechet's music are available, including *The Chronological Sidney Bechet/1923–1936* (Classics), *An Introduction to Sidney Bechet/His Best Recordings 1923–41* (Best of Jazz), *The Best of Sidney Bechet* (EMD/Blue Note), *Great Original Performances 1924–1943* (Louisiana Red Hot Records), as well as an extensive multi-volume series on the Masters of Jazz label.

Benny Carter (born 1907)

Carter was one of the first great alto saxophonists (along with Johnny Hodges), but also a well-respected trumpet player and one of jazz's best arrangers and composers over his long and ongoing career. As a multi-instrumentalist he was invaluable to the bands of the 1920s and early 1930s. As an arranger, Carter was one of the most important in building the big bands of the swing period.

Carter's saxophone style took a different course than that of Hodges. Both men are pure originals, with Carter's playing and tone a little more tart compared to Hodges's cream. Carter solos in long lines and sneaks up on the tune.

Still performing and recording, Carter sounds and swings great. A tour of some of his later work can be quite a trip. Start with *3, 4, 5: The Small Group Sessions* (Verve), a 1950s Carter anthology, with some Verve all stars. *Jazz Giant* (Original Jazz Classics) with tenorman Ben Webster and trombonist Frank Rosolino has solid performances all around. One of Carter's all-time top dates co-stars Dizzy Gillespie: *Carter/Gillespie, Inc.* (Original Jazz Classics). Another is *Further Definitions* (GRP/Impulse) featuring saxophonists Phil Woods, Charlie Rouse, and Coleman Hawkins playing Carter's arrangements. Carter's latest CDs are also excellent — try *New York Nights* (Music Masters).

Coleman "Hawk" Hawkins (1904-1969)

Taking apart the structure and melody of the song "Body and Soul," re-assembling it in a smooth but complex solo, Coleman Hawkins pointed the way toward modern sax improvisation — the year was 1939. Five years later, trumpeter Dizzy Gillespie, saxophonist Charlie Parker, and a few others began creating the challenging new bebop style (see Chapter 4). Hawkins, a tenor saxophonist generally associated more with 1930s and 1940s swing than 1940s bebop was so advanced that he had no troubl playing with these new revolutionaries.

Whereas Lester Young's saxophone solos came out in phrases of unpredictable length, Hawkins usually belted his out in uniform bunches of notes. Both players had strong roots in blues, as evidenced by Young's soulful feel, and Hawkins' recordings with blues singers Ma Rainey and Bessie Smith. But Hawkins was more of a traditionalist, his style rooted in the steadily swinging rhythms of 1920s big bands such as Fletcher Henderson's, where Hawkins first hit the big time as a soloist when he joined in 1924.

Musically, Hawkins was the most advanced among the top saxophonists of the 1930s. He helped elevate his instrument from a vaudeville novelty outshone by the trumpet, to a key instrument for improvisation in both small and large bands. After Hawkins' arrival, the saxophone replaced the trumpet as jazz's leading instrument.

"Hawk was the first modern jazz saxophonist," says Jessie Davis, a rising young saxophonist who has closely examined the music of the great jazz saxophone players. "What made him unique first and foremost was his sound: big, airy, also sweet, mellow, pretty. He was a rhythmic player. He played in the style they call swing. Prez [Lester Young] is definitely a melodic player."

Charlie Parker was bebop's hottest saxophonist and is generally regarded as bop's founding father, but Hawkins also gets credit, by many accounts, for leading the first bebop recording session in February of 1944. Trumpeter Dizzy Gillespie, drummer Max Roach, and bassist Oscar Pettiford were among the bebop pioneers joining Hawkins on the CD *Rainbow Mist* (Delmark).

During a career that stretched from the mid-'20s to the mid-'60s, Hawkins recorded with most of jazz's leading lights: saxophonists Lester Young, Ben Webster, Benny Carter, Chu Berry, Don Byas, Johnny Hodges, Sonny Rollins, and even the *avant garde* John Coltrane; as well as pianists Bud Powell, Oscar Peterson, Thelonious Monk, Billy Taylor, Red Garland, Tommy Flanagan, and Duke Ellington; guitarists Kenny Burrell, Django Reinhardt, and Herb Ellis; trumpeter Roy Eldrige, bassist Oscar Pettiford, and vibraphonist Lionel Hampton.

Hawkins's 1948 recording of "Picasso," included on *Verve Jazzmasters 34/ Coleman Hawkins* (PGD/Verve), is an unusually spare, spacious tribute to the great cubist painter. Hawkins, in a radical departure from his norm, plays unaccompanied. Hawkins's big tenor sound on this CD hints at the subsequent sound of saxophonist John Coltrane.

Other great recordings featuring Hawkins include: *Retrospective* (RCA/ Bluebird) an excellent cross section of the great man's career, featuring big band and combo work of the 1940s to the 1960s; *Bean and the Boys* (Prestige) another excellent compilation featuring bop selections and modern swing of the 1950s; *Duke Ellington Meets Coleman Hawkins* (GRP/Impulse!); *Coleman Hawkins Encounters Ben Webster* (Verve); and *Blues Wail: Coleman Hawkins Plays the Blues* (Prestige) a set of excellent all-star dates.

Johnny Hodges (1907-1970)

Although other accomplished saxophone players predated Hodges, his efforts on alto saxophone (particularly in Duke Ellington's band, where he spent most of his career, beginning in 1928) made him among the very first to utilize the saxophone as a lead instrument in jazz.

For your first experience of Hodges, try his 1928 recording, with Ellington's band, of "The Mooche," included on *Okeh Ellington* (Sony). Hear how Hodges elevates sax to a more prominent role and how he improvises around the song's signature melody and chords. Also notice how he interacts with the other players: rhythmically (with bass, drums, and piano) and melodically (trading riffs with the other horns).

You can also catch Hodges on *Duke Ellington 1928–1929* (Classics), on the three-CD *Early Ellington/1926–1931* (Decca), and on *Johnny Hodges 1928–41* (Best of Jazz). For an introduction to early Hodges in a small group, try *Hodge Podge* (Legacy/Epic), where he plays both soprano and alto saxes. *Passion Flower* (Bluebird) is great '40s Hodges, *Used to Be Duke* (Verve) finds him going strong in the 1950s, and *Triple Play* (Bluebird) shows he still had good stuff during the late 1960s, a few years before he died.

You can hear Hodges's budding warm, whispery tone, and dreamy, sexy playing on slower songs. Listen to how he takes a tune's signature melody and gives it a fresh spin with each new round of soloing. Smooth slides through a series of notes — known as *glissandos* — are another Hodges hallmark that became common in the playing of later saxophonists.

Ben Webster (1909-1973)

Next to Coleman Hawkins and Lester Young (both products of 1920s Midwestern "territory" bands), Ben Webster was the most influential tenor man of his era and kept making good music almost until his death in 1973. Webster's raw, tough tone was a powerful tool that he applied equally well to both ballads and rowdier tunes. If not a tremendous risk-taker, Webster was one of the most sensitive, evocative of all saxophonists.

Of his many recordings, essentials include *Best of Ben Webster 1931–44* (ASV/Living Legend), an excellent summation of early work, *Music with Feeling* (PGD/Verve), a fine example of Young's hoarse tenor with a string orchestra, *Soulville* (PGD/Verve), an excellent outing with pianist Oscar Peterson's trio, *King of the Tenors* (PGD/Verve), also with Peterson, as well as trumpeter Harry Edison and alto saxman Benny Carter, and *Plays Duke Ellington* (Storyville).

One of my favorite Webster cuts is his version of Billy Strayhorn's "Chelsea Bridge," from *Soul of Ben Webster* (PGD/Verve), recorded in 1958. Pure emotion oozes from his horn. Each wavering note fades into whispers of breath, almost as if Webster is speaking through his horn.

Lester "Prez" Young (1909-1959)

Young's sound is as smooth and sweet as maple syrup. Each note melts into the next, and each phrase, or group of notes, ends with a slow, sensuous *vibrato* — a wavering sound. One of his most important breakthroughs was varying the length of his phrases, whereas his peers on tenor, such as Ben Webster and Coleman Hawkins, conformed their solos more to consistent-length groups of notes. Countless players since have counted Young as a primary influence. The budding Charlie Parker learned Young's solos note-for-note.

Quirky, shy, easily hurt, Young was criticized early in his career for having a thin, ethereal tone, at a time when Coleman Hawkins' big, bold sound was in fashion. Young often outshone his peers in the legendary *cutting contests* of the day. One famous contest included Young, Evans, Ben Webster, and Hawkins, who was in town with Fletcher Henderson's band. By all accounts, the session lasted all night, with each man taking solos again and again. By morning, only Young was still standing, blowing steady streams of fresh improvisations.

Young's sweet sound is preserved on dozens of recordings. Of these, the best to start with are the ones he made with Count Basie's band beginning in 1937. Must-have recordings of Young include Count Basie's *Original American Decca Recordings* (Decca), which also includes saxophonists Herschel Evans and Chu Berry. Young also did great work with Billie Holiday, beginning with *The Quintessential Billie Holiday, Volumes 3* and *4, 1936–1937* (Sony). Also check out several albums documenting Young as a leader, including *The Lester Young Story* (Jazz Archives), *Lester Young and Charlie Christian* (Jazz Archives), with the legendary guitarist, and *The Jazz Giants '56* (PGD/Verve). Other great Prez includes *Master Takes* (Savoy), *Complete Aladdin Sessions* (EMD/Blue Note), and *Lester Young & the Piano Giants* (PGD/Verve).

Other Swing saxophonists

Other fine saxophonists of the swing persuasion abound. Here are a few of them:

Chu Berry (1910-1941)

A 1930s peer of Ben Webster, Lester Young, and Coleman Hawkins, Berry was a premiere soloist in big bands led by Benny Carter, Teddy Hill, Fletcher Henderson, and Cab Calloway. Check out Chu on *Berry Story* (Jazz Archives) and *Blowing Up A Breeze* (Topaz), as well as *Cab Calloway/1938–1939* (Classics) and Cab *Calloway/1939–1940* (Classics).

Don Byas (1912-1972)

Some fans don't know his music well, but among players, his name comes up constantly. An Oklahoma-born tenor saxman seasoned in 1930s big bands led by Andy Kirk, Lucky Millinder, Lionel Hampton, and others, Byas made some sensational music as a leader, walking a tightrope between smooth, luscious swing and speedy, complex bebop. Check out *Introduction to Don Byas/1938–46* (Best of Jazz), *A Night in Tunisia* (Black Lion), *Autumn Leaves* (Jazz House), *Don Byas, Vol. 2/1945* (Classics).

Arnett Cobb (1918-1989)

Yet another soulful Texas tenorman, Cobb did his journeyman jazz with Texas big bands and vibraphonist Lionel Hampton's band during the 1940s. Later, he made several fine albums of his own, including *Blows for 1300* (Delmark), *Blow, Arnett, Blow* (Original Jazz Classics), *Smooth Sailing* (Original Jazz Classics), and, with pianist Red Garland, *Blue And Sentimental* (Prestige).

Eddie "Lockjaw" Davis (1922-1986)

Swinging, soulful, bopping tenor man who hit his stride during the 1950s, Davis is an under-appreciated musician's favorite who has played with jazz legends ranging from Louis Armstrong to Count Basie. Check out *The Eddie Lockjaw Davis Cookbook Vols. 1–3* (Original Jazz Classics), *Smokin'* (Original Jazz Classics), *Trane Whistle* (Original Jazz Classics), and *All of Me* (SteepleChase), *Heavy Hitter* (32Jazz). Also catch him going horn-to-horn with fellow tenorman Johnny Griffin on *Tenor Scene* (Original Jazz Classics).

Illinois Jacquet (born 1922)

He's from Louisiana, not Illinois, but Jacquet is one of the great Charlie Parker-derived bop/swing tenor and alto saxophones. He was vibraphonist Lionel Hampton's counterpart on the Hampton signature song "Flying Home," and he also played in Count Basie's and Cab Calloway's bands. Try *The Blues: That's Me!* (Original Jazz Classics), *Illinois Jacquet* (Sony), *Flying Home: The Best of the Verve Years* (Verve), as well as Hampton's *Lionel Hampton 1942–1944* (Classics) and, from producer Norman Granz's live Jazz at the Philharmonic concert series, *The First Concert* (Verve).

Budd Johnson (1910-1984)

Another saxman whose career covered 1930s/1940s swing and 1950s-forward bop, Johnson was a Texas tenor/soprano who played with many of the greats, ranging from Louis Armstrong to Dizzy Gillespie. Check out *Let's Swing* (Original Jazz Classics).

Flip Phillips (born 1915)

Speedy as the beboppers when he wanted to be, tenor saxophonist Phillips was more into his consistently sweet tone than his swiftness. Phillips came into jazz just before bebop began in the mid-'40s and played in bands led by clarinetist Benny Goodman, vibraphonist Red Norvo, and best of all Woody

Herman, whose bands showcased a string of great soloists. *Flip Wails: The Best of the Verve Years* (PGD/Verve) gives a good overview. His recent CD with young saxman Scott Hamilton *Sound Investment* (Concord Jazz) and the 1986 *The Claw: Live at the Floating Jazz Festival* (Chiaroscuro) prove that Phillips still had good stuff in the fifth decade of his career.

Russell Procope (1908-1981)

His name seems to be everywhere in histories of jazz's early decades: Procope played with giants ranging from pianist Jelly Roll Morton to band leaders Chick Webb, Fletcher Henderson, and more. Procope also did some superb alto sax work in bassist John Kirby's late '30s/early '40s sextet. Check out *The Persuasive Sax of Russell Procope* (Dot), as well as several CDs worth of music with the John Kirby's swing combo on *John Kirby 1939–1940* (Classics).

Ike Quebec (1918-1963)

Longtime swing tenor-man who broke in with drummer Kenny Clarke, saxman Benny Carter, bandleader Cab Calloway, and others during the late '40s and early '50s, Quebec has fared well over the long haul. With the 1990s advent of acid jazz, has enjoyed a revival of the soulful, bluesy 1960s recordings he made with folks like saxman Stanley Turrentine, guitarist Grant Green, and organist Jimmy Smith. Get your hands on *Heavy Soul* (EMD/Blue Note), *Blue and Sentimental* (EMD/Blue Note), *Ike Quebec/1944–46* (Classics), and *Ballads* (EMD/Blue Note).

Paul Quinichette (1916-1983)

Known for his swinging smooth-as-syrup Lester Young-like sound, tenor saxophonist Quinichette came up during the 1940s and early 1950s with pianist Jay McShann, bluesman Johnny Otis, and Count Basie's big band. Among his own recordings, *On the Sunny Side* (Original Jazz Classics) is a good one to start with, while *Cattin' with Coltrane & Quinichette* (Original Jazz Classics) offers a great contrast in tenor styles.

Willie Smith (1910-1967)

Not to be confused with Willie "The Lion" Smith (who plays piano), this Smith plays alto in the 1930s swing style. He was a star of Jimmy Lunceford's big band from the late '20s to early '40s, and in Harry James's orchestra for several years during the 1940s, 1950s, and 1960s. He didn't leave a legacy as a leader, but some his best saxophone can be found on *Willie Smith/1925–1937* (Classics) and *Willie Smith/1938–40* (Classics).

Buddy Tate (born 1913)

Another in a long line of Texas tenors, Tate developed his sound during the late '30s and early '40s in big bands led by Count Basie, Andy Kirk, and others, and went on to lead several groups of his own. Check out *Buddy Tate and his Buddies* (Chiaroscuro), *Texas Twister* (New World), and *Swinging Scorpio* (Black Lion).

Bob Wilber (born 1928)

A traditional jazz revivalist, saxophonist/clarinetist Wilber has helped spread the early jazz gospel of clarinet giant Sidney Bechet (his mentor). During the 1950s and 1960s, he played early New Orleans jazz and swing with Eddie Condon and Bobby Hackett, and as co-founder of the World's Greatest Jazz Band. Try *Duet* (Progressive) with pianist Dick Wellstood, *Bob Wilber & Bechet Legacy* (Challenge), and *Soprano Summit Live at the Concord* (Concord).

Charlie "Yardbird" Parker (1920-1955) and the Rise of Bebop

And then there was Bird. Most jazz fans and critics, if asked to name the single most important jazz musician of the 20th century, would choose Charlie Parker (see Figure 8-1).

Parker got his nickname while on a road trip with Jay McShann's band, according to the famous bandleader. When the car Parker was riding in ran over a mangy chicken (a "yardbird," as he called it), Parker insisted they pick it up. He had it cooked for dinner that night, and from then on friends called him "Yardbird," or just "Bird."

A troubled genius who never made peace with personal demons, Parker nonetheless played brilliantly throughout his career; great musical moments accompanied even his most difficult, depressing times.

Born in Kansas City in 1920, Parker died in 1955, his early demise a result of lifelong substance abuse. "Bird Lives" read the graffiti that appeared in the weeks following his death, which ended his 10-year prime as modern jazz's major force. His short career makes his major contributions seem even more impressive. Influenced by Lester Young in Kansas City (the young Parker learned many of Prez's solos note-for-note), Parker went to New York City with Jay McShann's band in 1941, joined pianist Earl Hines's band, and met Dizzy Gillespie, who was to become his partner in the invention of a cerebral new form of jazz labeled *bebop*.

The making of a legend

Charlie Parker's earliest recordings were blues-rooted sessions with fellow K.C.-man Jay McShann's band. Even then, he began to depart from conventional ways of playing in his search for fresh combinations of notes and chords, combining complex melodies and improvisations with lightning speed.

Figure 8-1:
Charlie
Parker
(photo:
Everett
Collection).

As a budding young player, Parker paid his dues. Prompted by a poor showing at a jam session featuring prominent players at Kansas City's Reno Club (legend has it that Parker was forced from the stage by a cymbal flung at him in disgust by drummer Jo Jones), he practiced incessantly. His endless practice sessions included learning to play blues in every key — not just the three or four common jazz keys.

Ready to bite the Big Apple, Parker moved from Missouri to New York City in 1939. Lacking a union membership card, he went to work washing dishes at Jimmy's Chicken Shack, where jazz pianist Art Tatum was the featured entertainment.

Parker joined pianist Earl Hines's orchestra in 1942 where trumpeter Dizzy Gillespie was already playing. Parker and Gillespie soon left Hines's ensemble, but they teamed again briefly in 1944 in pianist and singer Billy Eckstine's big band. Between 1944 and 1947, Eckstine's band, with various lineups, was the simmering test tube for radical new jazz experiments. Besides Charlie Parker and trumpeter Dizzy Gillespie, the group's giants included, at various times, trumpeters Fats Navarro, Miles Davis, and Kenny Dorham; saxmen Gene Ammons and Dexter Gordon; drummer Art Blakey; and singer Sarah Vaughan.

Bird's recordings

Although Parker and Gillespie recorded together with various bands both large and small during the mid-'40s, they hit their prime as bebop collaborators in 1944 and 1945. Playing together in such clubs as the Three Deuces, the Hi-de-Ho Club, and the Savoy Ballroom, the pair seasoned their new bebop sound, sweating through nightly sets and after-hours jams. Gillespie and Parker made many records together in 1944 and 1945. These early "sides," as collectors call 78 rpm records, received a lukewarm reception from critics. To some jazz writers, Parker and Gillespie's music sounded, at first, like chaotic nonsense — it was too fast and complex for many listeners to comprehend.

The Complete Dial Sessions (Jazz Classics), a four-CD set, offers an emotionally charged introduction to prime Parker. This set includes three takes of Gillespie's "A Night In Tunisia," two of George Gershwin's "Embraceable You," two of Parker's "Ornithology," three of his "Moose the Mooche," and four of "Relaxin' at Camarillo," Parker's tribute to his stint in a mental hospital. All of these are stunning in their variety and originality.

Sweet Love, Bitter is a forgotten jazz movie that should be acquired by all Parker fans. Dick Gregory stars as a saxophone genius named Eagle, modeled on Bird.

Parker's musical legacy

Parker may have been quirky and deeply troubled, but his music was marked by innovation on several levels.

Parker's marvelous sound on alto is not subtle or soft, like many of the great tenors of his era. Hard-edged, his tone cuts through thickets of other instruments. You can make a more intimate connection by paying attention to every detail: breath rushing over reeds, phrases ending in gently wavering vibrato. Even his fastest, densest solos have logic and structure. Listen carefully and you can hear each musical phrase tell a complete "story," with a beginning, middle, and end. His influences were not only his predecessors in jazz, but also some of the great classical composers. Parker was fascinated with the music of composers Bela Bartok, Igor Stravinsky, Arnold Schoenberg, Paul Hindemith, and Edgard Varese.

Parker's improvisations, although initially limited by the three-minute length of the 78 rpm format, offer endless variety. He took famous songs and re-invented their signature melodies in fresh but familiar ways. He used the chords from popular songs such as "What Price Love?" and "How High The Moon" and composed new melodies of his own over the chords. On "Home

Cookin','" he combined sections from George and Ira Gershwin's "'S Wonderful" and pianist Fats Waller and Andy Razaf's "Honeysuckle Rose" to render yet another original Parker.

Essential Parker recordings to add to your collection include *Bird's Best Bop on Verve* (PGD/Verve), *Bird Plays the Blues* (PGD/Verve), *Rockland Palace* (Jazz Classics), and *Bird at the Hi-Hat* (Cema/Capitol), a fantastic, fairly well recorded live date that captures the essence of a typical club gig. *Charlie Parker with Strings: The Master Takes* (PGD/Verve) records Parker cushioned by symphonic sound. *Bird and Diz* (PGD/Verve) has Parker with pianist Thelonious Monk and drummer Buddy Rich. *Jazz at Massey Hall* (Original Jazz Classics) captures one of the great bebop concerts, with bassist Charles Mingus, pianist Bud Powell, and drummer Max Roach. *Yardbird Suite: The Ultimate C. Parker* (Rhino) captures some of the best of the best, from studio recordings and live broadcasts — this is a must have.

Other Bebop Saxophonists

Charlie "Yardbird" Parker was clearly the ringleader among bebop saxophonists — and among jazz musicians in general. Yet he didn't invent bebop in a vacuum. He drew from many players who came before him, and he inspired — and was inspired by — several saxophonists who were his peers. Here are several who were actually on hand during bebop's mid-'40s invention in the clubs of New York City — or who advanced the bop style during the 1940s and early 1950s.

Pepper Adams (1930-1986)

Adams was a unique hard bop innovator, and one of the few baritone sax players to negotiate hard bop's combination of drive and precision. He coled a hard bop combo with trumpeter Donald Byrd on *10 to 5 at the 5-Spot* (Original Jazz Classics) and had an *Encounter with Zoot Sims* (Original Jazz Classics). He performed into the 1980s with *Conjuration/Fat Tuesday's Sessions* (Reservoir).

Earl Bostic (1913-1965)

Blending bebop and swing with soulful rhythm and blues, Bostic was revered by fellow saxmen for his knowledge of horns and mouthpieces and how to get an amazing range of tones from a sax. *The Best of Earl Bostic* (King/Deluxe) gives you a slice of this alto saxmaster's 1950s prime.

MUSICIANS SPEAK

Bird lives

Parker's playing was the ultimate merger of emotion, technique, and genius. Here's why some prominent jazz saxophone players are still in awe of his music.

"I was about 14 or 15 when I first heard him at a dance in Detroit. He was my hero even at that age. He would be pretty much like Bach is to classical music; he's that important. Listeners should buy anything by Charlie Parker. Every record he ever made is worthwhile."

— *Charles McPherson,* who overdubbed Parker-like sax parts for the movie *Bird*

"I first heard him in the '40s. I don't remember the tune, but I do remember that when I came out of the Air Force, I joined Dizzy Gillespie's big band, we were on the road for a while, and we wound up in Chicago doing a one-nighter. Charlie Parker was a guest artist, and it was outasight."

— *James Moody,* saxophonist

"Once I heard him, I automatically knew that there was something special about his playing, but I didn't really know how to identify it. 'Bird With Strings' was the first recording I had. That should be your first Charlie Parker album. There's an interplay between him and the ensemble. He was masterful at utilizing the language of the saxophone. It's almost like he's talking to you. He'd start a phrase, and he'd always end it."

— *Jesse Davis,* saxophonist

"Bird was from another planet. The times he grew up in, the inspiration of the great musicians around him, such as Coleman Hawkins, Lester Young, Ben Webster, Johnny Hodges, inspired him. Charlie Parker was a spontaneous improviser. You didn't know what he would play next. He developed his technique to the virtuosic point to execute anything he could hear. That's the essence of jazz."

— *Joe Lovano,* saxophonist

Sonny Criss (1924-1977)

A first generation Parker devotee, Criss developed a softer, breathier style of his own on alto sax. Listen to *Intermission Riff* (Original Jazz Classics), *Saturday Morning* (Xanadu), and *Portrait of Sonny* (Original Jazz Classics).

Dexter Gordon (1923-1990)

While Bird was bopping in New York, Gordon was among Los Angeles saxophonists exploring the new, complex, speedy idiom. He was probably the first tenor saxophonist who could sustain the pace of Parker's alto.

Known as "Long Tall Dex," Gordon stood 6-foot 5-inches and blew a mean tenor inspired by alto saxophonist Parker's speed and musical genius, and by tenor saxman Lester Young's sleepy, fluid improvisations and emotional ways with a melody.

Gordon was in Louis Armstrong's band during the early 1940s, but felt his true calling when he joined singer/pianist Billy Eckstine's band in 1944 and began blowing early bop with bandmates Parker and trumpeter Dizzy Gillespie. He spent the years between 1962 and 1976 in Europe, where jazz players were revered. Unlike peers who flamed out prematurely, Gordon was a powerful player until a few years before his death in 1990 — leaving a vast catalog of fine CDs featuring his slurry, whispery tone.

Essential Gordon includes: *Dexter Rides Again* (Savoy), with several of bebop's best 1940s players; *One Flight Up* (EMD/Blue Note), including then-young trumpeter Donald Byrd and a teenage Nils-Henning Orsted Pedersen on bass; *Bouncin' with Dex* (SteepleChase); and *Homecoming: Live at the Village Vanguard* (Sony) also featuring trumpeter Woody Shaw. For Gordon in a mellower mood, get *Ballads* (EMD/Blue Note), *Dexter Gordon, Vol. 2/1944–46* (Masters of Jazz), *Live at Carnegie Hall/Complete* (Sony), and *Go!* (EMD/Blue Note).

Wardell Gray (1921-1955)

Born in Oklahoma City, a graduate of bands led by pianist Earl Hines, saxman Benny Carter, singer/pianist Billy Eckstine, and Count Basie, Gray was a bebopping tenor sax peer of Dexter Gordon and Teddy Edwards under the influence of alto saxman Charlie Parker. He also played with trumpeter Tadd Dameron, as well as Swing King Benny Goodman, before he died at the age of 34 in 1955. Gray also wrote the tune "Twisted," popularized by singers including Joni Mitchell and Annie Ross.

Some of Gray's best recordings were made with Gordon during the late 1940s. Good Gray CDs for your collection include: *Wardell Gray Memorial, Vols. 1* and *2* (Original Jazz Classics), as well as *Bebop Masters* (Indigo), with bop pianist Dodo Marmarosa and bassist Red Callender.

Johnny Griffin (born 1928)

A speedy Chicago-born bebop tenor man, Griffin initially bopped behind vibraphonist Lionel Hampton and with pianists Thelonious Monk and Bud Powell, Jazz Messengers' leader Art Blakey, drummer Jo Jones, and fellow tenorman Arnett Cobb. From 1960 to 1962, Griffin also co-led a quintet with fellow saxman Eddie "Lockjaw" Davis. Wielding his Parker-influenced chops, Griffin goes horn-to-horn-to-horn with saxophonists John Coltrane and Hank Mobley on *A Blowing Session* (EMD/Blue Note), bops on his own on *The Congregation* (EMD/Blue Note), and improvises like crazy on his 1990s *Cat* (PGD/Verve).

Others to get your hands on include *Do Nothing 'Til You . . .* (Original Jazz Classics), *Chicago/New York/Paris* (PGD/Verve) with rising young talents bassist Christian McBride and trumpeter Roy Hargrove, as well as Art Blakey and the Jazz Messengers' *1957 Edition featuring Johnny Griffin* (BMG/RCA).

Gigi Gryce (1927-1983)

Warming his chops in New York City alongside drummer Max Roach, pianist Tadd Dameron, and trumpeter Clifford Brown, Gryce, an alto saxophonist, became a leading proponent of bluesy 1950s hard bop. He recorded with pianist Thelonious Monk and bassist Oscar Pettiford, and recorded a handful of solid albums as a leader during the 1950s. *Gigi Gryce & The Jazz Lab Quintet* (Original Jazz Classics) and *Rat Race Blues* (Original Jazz Classics) are essential listening, and you'll also find Gryce on *The Clifford Brown Sextet in Paris* (Original Jazz Classics), and on *Thelonious with John Coltrane* (Original Jazz Classics).

Sonny Rollins (born 1930)

Still in his teens during bebop's formative 1940s years, Rollins grew into his own sound over several decades and dozens of fine tenor sax albums. Among saxophonists with roots in bebop, Rollins, who also names saxophonist Coleman Hawkins as a major inspiration, has been one of the most enduring and prolific, giving an idea what may have been possible for saxman Charlie Parker, or trumpeters Clifford Brown and Fats Navarro, had they survived through a normal lifespan — Rollins even made a brief 1960s foray into free jazz.

The Rollins section of your collection can grow for years, but here's where to start: *Work Time* (Original Jazz Classics); *Tenor Madness* (Original Jazz Classics), with John Coltrane; *Way out West* (Original Jazz Classics — the title track is included on the *Jazz For Dummies* CD); *A Night at the Village Vanguard, Vols. 1 and 2* (EMD/Blue Note); *The Bridge* (Bluebird), including guitarist Jim Hall; *East Broadway Run Down* (GRP/Impulse!) — and that's barely up through the mid-1960s! From more recent years, check out *Silver City* (Milestone) and *+3* (Milestone), a set of all-new music released in 1996 and also featuring young pianist Stephen Scott, veteran pianist Tommy Flanagan, and drummer Jack DeJohnette.

Sonny Stitt (1924-1982)

Man, this alto saxophonist could blow. *Kaleidoscope* (Original Jazz Classics), recorded during the early '50s, is one of my all-time favorite albums. Stitt was a Parker-influenced player who played with singer/pianist Billy Eckstine's band during bop's mid-'40s formative years. Also check out *Sonny*

Stitt with Bud Powell and J.J. Johnson (Original Jazz Classics); *Prestige First Sessions, Vol. 2* (Prestige); *Stitt Plays Bird* (Atlantic); with trumpeter Dizzy Gillespie and Rollins on *Sonny Side Up* (PGD/Verve); *Endgame: Constellation* (32Jazz); and *In Case You Forgot How Bad He Was* (32Jazz), a last blast of awesome alto and tenor recorded only weeks before he died in 1982.

Sax in the Fifties: Hard Bop, Cool Jazz

Some seasoned players who had been on hand for bop's invention in the 1940s took the music into new areas during the 1950s. Under the influence of blues and soulful rhythm and blues, these 1950s players took off from Charlie Parker and played a slightly laid-back bop known now as *hard bop*. Meanwhile, Davis's *Birth of the Cool* album inspired several musicians to play a more melodic, mellow form of jazz that became known as *cool*. See Chapter 4 for more on these movements, and read on for some details on the players.

Cannonball Adderley (1928-1975)

A physical and creative giant of blues-like bop alto saxophone, Adderley produced a long line of consistently solid recordings during the 1950s and '60s. *Presenting Cannonball* (Savoy) was his first and indicated what greatness was yet to come.

A milestone in Adderley's career came when he joined the Miles Davis All Star Sextet in the late 1950s. He turned out some of the best of his own albums using Davis's personnel: the beautiful *Portrait of Cannonball* (Original Jazz Classics) with pianist Bill Evans and drummer Philly Joe Jones, *Somethin' Else* (Blue Note) with Miles Davis himself, and *Cannonball in Chicago with John Coltrane* (EmArcy) is a legendary tete-a-tete between two sultans of sax, also featuring the Davis rhythm section.

Nancy Wilson/Cannonball Adderley (Capitol) finds him spelling the fine vocalist. Adderley also contributed to the *soul jazz* craze with the *Cannonball Adderley Quintet in San Franscico* (Original Jazz Classics), featuring the hit "Dis Here", and *Mercy, Mercy, Mercy* (Capitol), including the hit-song title track.

Gene Ammons (1925-1974)

Chicago-born Ammons brings the Windy City's bluesy vibe to bop, as well as slower, soul-jazz — which means he's popular again with young 1990s acid jazz fans. On hand for bop's 1940s formative years when he blew his tenor sax with singer/pianist Billy Eckstine's band, Ammons blossomed during the 1950s.

Give a listen to *Greatest Hits/The '50s* (Original Jazz Classics); *The Happy Blues* (Original Jazz Classics), *Boss Tenor* (Original Jazz Classics), *Late Hour Special* (Original Jazz Classics), *Gene Ammons/Legends of Acid Jazz* (Prestige), and *Soul Summit* (Prestige) recorded with organist Brother Jack McDuff and saxophonist Sonny Stitt.

Buddy Collette (born 1921)

Equally adept on tenor sax, clarinet, and flute, Collette has been a vital part of the Los Angeles jazz scene since the 1950s when he was a close friend and mentor to bassist Charles Mingus. Earning early kudos in bands fronted by Louis Jordan, Benny Carter, Chico Hamilton, and others, Collette's put some great music to tape. Try *Man of Many Parts* (Original Jazz Classics) with guitarist Barney Kessel and bassist Red Callender, and *Nice Day* (Original Jazz Classics) with pianist Don Friedman and drummer Shelly Manne.

Paul Desmond (1924-1977)

Pianist Dave Brubeck gets most of the credit, but alto saxman Desmond actually wrote the cool 1950s anthem "Take Five," popularized by Brubeck's group which included Desmond. Born in New York City, Desmond's best playing had much of the lighter, gentler feel more commonly associated with California. Sample some of Brubeck and Desmond's early quartet music on *Brubeck and Desmond in Concert* (Fantasy) as well as *Jazz Goes to College* (Sony) and *Time Out* (Sony), which includes the famous "Take Five." After he left Brubeck, Desmond led his own excellent sessions, including *Pure Desmond* (Sony), *Take Ten* (Bluebird), and *Two of a Mind* (Bluebird) with baritone saxman Gerry Mulligan.

Stan Getz (1927-1991)

A sensitive tenor man with a soft, lush sound, Getz was a key player in the early 1960s merger of jazz with Latin rhythms — especially bossa nova (see Chapter 6). He recorded dozens of albums, and many of them are excellent. *Roost Quartets* (Roulette) is early 1950s Getz. *Hamp and Getz* (Verve) teams him with the great vibraphonist, Lionel Hampton. Also try *Stan Getz and J.J. Johnson at the Opera House* (Verve), *Getz and Gilberto* (Mobile Fidelity), *Live at Montmartre* (SteepleChase), and *People Time* (Verve). Also check out "Prezervation" from the album of the same name (Original Jazz Classics) on the *Jazz For Dummies* CD.

Lee Konitz (born 1927)

Another member of trumpeter Miles Davis's *Birth of the Cool* (Capitol) crew, alto/soprano saxophonist Konitz collaborated with other cool colleagues during the 1950s including fellow saxmen Warne Marsh, Gerry Mulligan, and Jimmy Giuffre, as well as free-jazz pioneer and pianist Lennie Tristano. Among Konitz' coolest stuff is *Subconscious-Lee* (Original Jazz Classics), *Konitz Meets Mulligan* (Pacific Jazz), *Live at the Half Note* (Verve), *The Lee Konitz Duets* (Original Jazz Classics), and *The Lee Konitz Nonet* (Roulette).

Harold Land (born 1928)

Another in a long line of Texas tenors, Land became known during the 1950s and '60s as a vital member of the Los Angeles jazz scene. He launched his career playing bluesy hard bop with a band led by trumpeter Clifford Brown and drummer Max Roach, and later worked with bassist Curtis Counce, vibraphonist Bobby Hutcherson, and trumpeter Blue Mitchell. Landmark Land albums are: *Harold in the Land of Jazz* (Original Jazz Classics), *Mapenzi* (Concord), as well as the Hutcherson's 1970 *San Francisco* (Blue Note).

Jackie McLean (born 1932)

Earning early stripes with trumpeter Miles Davis, bassist Charles Mingus, and drummer Art Blakey's Jazz Messengers, McLean was among the few 1950s alto saxophonists to develop a distinctive (although Charlie Parker-inspired) sound in the aftermath of bebop's mid-'40s invention.

You can hear his biting, probing alto on dozens of recordings he made as a leader beginning in the mid-'50s. McLean also went through a free-jazz phase during the 1960s. *Jackie's Bag* (Blue Note), *Let Freedom Ring* (Blue Note), *One Step Beyond* (Blue Note), *Jacknife* (Blue Note) and *Demon's Dance* (Blue Note) are among many McLean classics. Some of his newest albums are also worth checking out, such as *Hat Trick* (EMD/Blue Note) and *Dynasty* (Triloka).

Hank Mobley (1930-1986)

A sleeper of a saxman, Mobley is not that well known considering his lengthy record of collaborations with top players and consistently high quality of his own recordings. A bluesy tenor saxman who worked with trumpeter Dizzy Gillespie, drummer Max Roach, and drummer Art Blakey and pianist Horace Silver's original Jazz Messengers, Mobley puts down solid solos on *Soul Station* (Blue Note), *Workout* (Blue Note), *A Slice of the Top* (Blue Note), *Best of Hank Mobley* (Blue Note), *Jazz Message of Hank Mobley, Vol. 1* (Savoy), and *Reach Out!* (Capitol).

James Moody (born 1925)

Moody has become a spiritual man whose music has sounded steadily happier since the late 1940s. "Moody's Mood for Love" is a warbling staple of his live shows, but he wields mean saxes (tenor, alto, soprano) and flute. Some of his early bop solos can be heard on the 1948 *Dizzy Gillespie and His Big Band* (GNP). Among Moody's own albums, look for *Hi-Fi Party* (Original Jazz Classics), *Last Train from Overbrook* (Argo), *Never Again* (Muse), *Young at Heart* (WEA/Warner), and *Moody Plays Mancini* (WEA/Warner).

Gerry Mulligan (1927-1996)

Probably nobody has done more for (or with) the baritone sax. Born in New York, Mulligan became a vital founding father of the cool jazz sound, playing on trumpeter Miles Davis's *Birth of the Cool* (Capitol), and also contributing key arrangements, eventually recording with, and/or arranging for, a long list of heavies including trumpeter Chet Baker, band leader Stan Kenton, pianist Thelonious Monk, saxophonists Paul Desmond, Ben Webster, Stan Getz, and Johnny Hodges, pianist Dave Brubeck — even Duke Ellington's orchestra. *The Arranger* (Columbia) catches Mulligan's arranging genius. Also worth checking out is *What Is There to Say* (Columbia), *Gerry Mulligan Meets Ben Webster* (Verve), and *Soft Lights and Sweet Music* (Concord).

Art Pepper (1925-1982)

Dark currents in Pepper's cool, sometimes fragmented bop mirrored the ups and downs of a tough life. A California native, he was a part of L.A.'s vital 1940s/1950s scene, and he played in orchestras led by Benny Carter and Stan Kenton. Best bets include *Discoveries* (Savoy), *The Artistry of Pepper* (Pacific Jazz), *Art Pepper + Eleven: Modern Jazz Classics* (Original Jazz Classics), *The Trip* (Original Jazz Classics), and *Straight Life* (Original Jazz Classics).

Zoot Sims (1925-1985)

A cool/bop chameleon, Sims had a prolific career that spanned five decades beginning in the 1940s. Clarinetist Benny Goodman, saxophonists Jimmy Giuffre, Stan Getz, John Coltrane, and Sonny Rollins, and many other top players were among his cohorts. *Morning Fun* (Black Lion), *Zoot Sims and the Gershwin Brothers* (Original Jazz Classics), *Zoot Plays Soprano* (Pablo), *Blues for Two* (Original Jazz Classics), and *On the Korner* (Pablo) offer a good overview. Also hear Sims with Woody Herman's late'40s Herd on *Keeper of the Flame: Complete Capitol Recordings* (Capitol).

Outer Limits: Ornette Coleman (born 1930)

When Ornette Coleman burst on the jazz scene playing his strange brand of jazz during the late '50s, many fans and musicians were baffled — or outraged. Here was music that sometimes sounded like outright chaos. Eventually, Coleman called his concept *harmolodics,* but his explanations of his freeform style could be even more elusive than the music itself. Although younger than saxophonist John Coltrane, Coleman gets some credit for inspiring Coltrane to play some spirited free jazz of his own during the 1960s. (See Figure 8-2.)

Since his earliest recordings, Coleman (who also pulls out a trumpet or violin on occasion) has assumed the position of forefather of free jazz — highly regarded by some fans and critics, still disdained by others. His music, with its sudden shifts in direction, shrieking, wailing horns, and improvisations that can go on forever without reaching a tangible destination, is an acquired taste. But even beginning jazz fans may find that an occasional helping of Coleman can open their minds and ears to new ways of thinking about, and listening to, jazz. Through the 1990s, Coleman is still a force — recording and playing occasional live dates with primal power.

Figure 8-2:
Ornette
Coleman
(photo:
Everett
Collection).

The Shape of Jazz to Come (Atlantic), released in 1959, lives up to its futuristic title, and is really the place to start with Coleman. *Free Jazz* (Rhino) has a herd of top jazz players going wild together. *At the Golden Circle in Stockholm, Vol. 1* (Blue Note) is a searing 1965 live performance, *Opening the Caravan of Dreams* (Caravan of Dreams) is spunky mid-'80s Coleman, and *Tone Dialing* (Harmolodic/Verve) and *Sound Museum* (PGD/Verve) prove he still had hot stuff in 1995. *The Best of Ornette Coleman* (Blue Note) offers a concise intro to his music.

Spiritual Search: John Coltrane (1926-1967)

Of the post-Parker generation of saxophonists, John Coltrane, who played tenor and soprano, stands bell and mouthpiece above his modern peers. Coltrane played in groups with Miles Davis and Dizzy Gillespie, as well as quirky pianist Thelonious Monk. Coltrane had a two-year stint with trumpeter Dizzy Gillespie's big band, but unlike some earlier saxophonists, he came of age musically mostly in small groups, not big bands — a growing trend in jazz during the late '40s and '50s. (See Figure 8-3.)

Coltrane's quest on saxophone was as much spiritual as technical. After he quit using drugs in the 1950s, his music and composing took on increasingly spiritual aspects, as evidenced in song titles such as "Out of This World," "Amen," "Offering," and "A Love Supreme." Because his music was as much about feeling as technique, he expanded the sound of the saxophone to find expression for his innermost impressions of life.

Coltrane's inventions on saxophone were numerous:

- **New sounds.** He ventured into abstract territory, mixing honks, squeals, bleats, and the sound of his breath rushing through the horn, together with odd musical fragments.

- **Small groups.** The elbow room afforded by small, varied, creative partnerings of musicians freed Coltrane to pursue his loftiest musical ambitions.

- **Modal compositions.** He pioneered, along with trumpeter Miles Davis, a meditative musical approach called *modal* inspired in part by Indian music (see Chapter 1). The idea was to explore all possibilities for playing scales in a single key, instead of changing keys mid-song.

- **Diverse influences.** His use of African rhythms and musical ideas was his tribute to jazz's roots. At a time — the 1960s — when diverse cultural groups were claiming equality as Americans, some of Coltrane's music gave a moving, emotional account of the hardships felt by African-Americans living in 20th-century America.

✔ **Used soprano sax.** Coltrane revived soprano saxophone, with its high reedy sound, as an important jazz instrument. Like earlier soprano saxophonists, Coltrane closely studied the soprano sax music of Sidney Bechet, before branching in his own directions. He paved the way for subsequent soprano sax players, including Wayne Shorter.

✔ **Rhythmically, he invented new combinations.** Paired with powerful drummers such as Elvin Jones, Coltrane let his timing collide with the timing of his bandmates to create powerful tension.

✔ **Heavy improvisation.** Coltrane also freed jazz from traditional structure, so that some songs were entirely improvised.

By the time John Coltrane died in 1967 — during the rise of various parallel revolutions in the arts, culture, literature, and politics — he had already left a substantial body of recorded music.

"My Favorite Things" (on the Atlantic album by the same name) is one of my all-time favorite Coltrane tunes, and a far cry from Julie Andrews in *The Sound of Music*. First comes the recognizable melody, as revised by Coltrane. Then he's off into round after round of a solo inspired by the song, but far beyond it in complexity and creativity.

Figure 8-3: John Coltrane (photo: Everett Collection).

Other essential Coltrane CDs range from radio broadcasts with Gillespie in 1951, to sessions with Miles Davis including the famous *Kind of Blue* (Columbia) album, to several recordings as a leader of his own groups, culminating with *Expression* (Impulse!), *Stellar Regions* (Impulse!), and *Interstellar Space* (GRP), made the year of his death, and featuring some of his wildest explorations.

Among the many Coltrane recordings you should consider for your collection are *Standard Coltrane* (Original Jazz Classics), *Afro Blue Impressions* (Pablo), *Blue Train* (Blue Note), *Soultrane* (Original Jazz Classics — be sure to take a listen to "Theme for Ernie" from this album, included in the *Jazz For Dummies* CD), *Giant Steps* (WEA/Atlantic), *My Favorite Things* (WEA/ Atlantic/Rhino), *Complete Africa/Brass Sessions* (Uni/Impulse!), *A Love Supreme* (Uni/Impulse!), *Meditations* (Uni/Impulse!), *Live at the Village Vanguard Again* (Uni/Impulse!).

On the Cutting Edge

By the late '60s and early '70s, *avant garde*/free jazz was in full swing (see Chapter 5). Taking cues from John Coltrane, Ornette Coleman, and others, saxophonists opened up a new abstract side of jazz based on sound, feeling, texture, more than on melodies or traditional chord changes. Their music is challenging, but also rewarding. It requires some dedicated listening and an open mind. But if you can get past your ingrained expectations of what music should be, you can have some amazing alternative listening experiences.

Anthony Braxton (born 1945)

Looking like a professor with his wire-rim glasses and cardigan sweaters, Braxton approaches free jazz with a mathematician's fascination for complex forms and structures. Many of his albums, in fact, include diagrams of the musical structures he devised for the pieces.

Affiliated with Chicago's AACM (Association for the Advancement of Creative Musicians), Braxton has been a central figure in the creation of some far-out jazz — as a leader and with leading players including keyboardist Chick Corea, saxophonist Julius Hemphill, bassists Dave Holland and Nils-Henning Orsted Pedersen, and violinist Leroy Jenkins. Take a chance on *New York/Fall 1974* (Arista), *Dortmund/Quartet 1976* (Hat Art), *Six Monk's Compositions/1987* (Black Saint), *and Charlie Parker Project 1993* (Hat Art).

Eric Dolphy (1928-1964)

Soulmate of saxophonists John Coltrane and Ornette Coleman, Dolphy was a powerhouse on alto sax and bass clarinet — and a pioneer at playing *avant garde* jazz on flute. Dolphy apprenticed in bands led by bassist Charles Mingus and drummer Chico Hamilton, recorded with Coleman, and was part of Coltrane's early '60s group. Start with *Outward Bound* (Original Jazz Classics), *Out There* (Original Jazz Classics), *The Great Concert of Eric Dolphy* (Prestige), *Jitterbug Waltz* (Casablanca), *Vintage Dolphy* (GM Recordings), and *Late Date* (Verve). Live Trane (BYG) catches Coltrane and Dolphy in fine form in 1965.

Julius Hemphill (1940-1995)

A vital force in New York loft jazz during the 1970s, alto/soprano saxophonist Hemphill has composed and played some wildly inventive jazz, both on his own and as a member of the World Saxophone Quartet. *Dogon A.D.* (Freedom) is prime early Hemphill with saxophonist David Sanborn on hand too — before he opted for a commercial/pop approach. *Fat Man and the Hard Blues* (Black Saint) is another eclectic Hemphill project — a *tour de force* all-saxes effort. *At Dr. King's Table* (New World Records) is Hemphill, circa 1997. Also sample the World Saxophone Quartet's *Revue* (Black Saint) and *Plays Duke Ellington* (Elektra).

Rahsaan Roland Kirk (1936-1977)

Not exclusively *avant garde,* Kirk is situated here because his music was eclectic. Whether playing saxes, flute, clarinet, manzello, nose flute — or two or three instruments at once — his music was a sophisticated blend of ancient African folk music, American pop, blues, early New Orleans jazz, and several more recent jazz idioms. Hear him on *Kirk's Work* (Original Jazz Classics), *Bright Moments* (Rhino), and numerous other recordings, mostly from the 1960s and 1970s. Also be sure to read more on Kirk in Chapter 18.

Oliver Lake (born 1942)

On various saxes and flute, Lake is a deep well of endlessly inventive improvisations. One-fourth of the original World Saxophone Quartet, he has been a leading free jazz player, as well as experimented with synthesizers and more structured forms of jazz. *Heavy Spirits* (Freedom), *Expendable Language* (Black Saint), and *Again and Again* (Gramavision) give a good intro to Lake's music. Also hear the World Saxophone Quartet's *Revue* (Black Saint), *Plays Duke Ellington* (Elektra), *Breath of Life* (WEA/Atlantic), *Takin' It 2 the Next Level* (Justin Time), and *Four Now* (Justin' Time).

Roscoe Mitchell (born 1940)

Member of the barrier-breaking Art Ensemble of Chicago, multi-saxophonist Mitchell is one of the most consistently imaginative free-jazz players. Mitchell and the Art Ensemble's music moves easily between authentic African rhythms and sounds, early jazz and blues, bebop, and free abstract music where emotions and tonal colors take precedent over structure and formal melody. Try Mitchell's *Nonaah* (Nessa) and *The Flow of Things* (Black Saint), as well as the Art Ensemble's *Fanfare for the Warriors* (Atlantic) and *Spiritual* (Black Lion).

Pharoah Sanders (born 1940)

A sometime collaborator with saxophonist John Coltrane during the 1960s, Sanders subsequently explored a variety of jazz forms with mixed results. *Karma* (Impulse!) is a freeform effort from 1969 that also features vocalist Leon Thomas. *Jewels of Thought* (MCA/Impulse!), *Thembi* (MCA/Impulse!), *Message from Home* (Verve), *Welcome to Love* (Alfa/Evidence), *Crescent With Love* (Evidence), are vital works by Sanders, while *Rejoice* (Evidence) explores African pop rhythms and melodies including light, effervescent juju music. Alice Coltrane's *Journey in Satchidananda* (Impulse!) also showcases Pharoah's stellar playing alongside Coltrane's harp.

Archie Shepp (born 1937)

Blending bluesy 1950s hard bop and farther out free jazz, Shepp is one of jazz's most durable and prolific saxophonists, doubling on tenor and soprano. On the 1963 *The New York Contemporary Five* (Storyville), he's off to a strong start. Shepp keeps the flame lit through *On This Night* (GRP), *Trouble in Mind* (SteepleChase), *Looking at Bird* (SteepleChase), and the 1991 *Swing Low* (Plainisphare).

Henry Threadgill (born 1944)

Not only is Threadgill a great saxophonist whose style ranges freely from swing and bop to abstract jazz, but he has assembled some of the most unusual jazz groups. One of these groups featured Threadgill with drums, two tubas, french horn, and a pair of wailing guitars — check it out on *Spirit of Nuff . . . Nuff* (Black Saint). Best of all, he has a sense of humor that comes across in his music — a quality lacking in some all-too-serious *avant garde* jazz. *When Was That?* (About Time) and *Carry The Day* (Sony) capture earlier Threadgill. More recent Threadgill worth hearing is *Where's Your Cup* (Sony).

Electrifying Saxophones

Keeping pace with peers such as trumpeter Miles Davis and pianists Herbie Hancock, Chick Corea, and Joe Zawinul, saxophonists began playing electric jazz/rock and jazz/funk during the 1960s. Davis's bands alone included a string of talented saxophonists between the late '60s and late '80s who experimented with electric and synthesized sounds.

Eddie Harris (born 1934)

Among saxophonists trained in serious jazz who eventually plugged in, Eddie Harris was a pioneer. His 1967 album *The Electrifying Eddie Harris* (Atlantic) is hailed by some as the first electric sax album. Harris was also hot on *Swiss Movement* (Atlantic), a popular 1969 collaboration with keyboard player Les McCann that produced the hit "Compared to What?"

Wayne Shorter (born 1933)

A serious jazz man dating back to his stint in Art Blakey's Jazz Messengers, Shorter was also one of the most successful at combining jazz with rock and funk influences in electric settings — first with Miles Davis on albums including *Bitches Brew* (Columbia), and later with Weather Report, which still stands as one of the great all-time electric jazz bands. Get hold of Shorter's *Speak No Evil* (Blue Note), *Adam's Apple* (Blue Note), and *Native Dancer* (Columbia), *Wayne Shorter/This Is Jazz #19* (Sony), as well as Weather Report's *Mysterious Traveler* (Columbia) and *Black Market* (Columbia), and pianist Herbie Hancock's *VSOP Quintet* (Columbia). Also catch Shorter with Davis during the 1960s on *Miles Smiles* (Sony).

Grover Washington, Jr. (born 1943)

Tops among mid-'70s funk-jazz saxophonists, he's a solid jazz player, where going electric or straight-ahead acoustic. *Mister Magic* (Motown) is his 1970s classic, *Winelight* (Elektra) is another finger-popping collection, and *Then and Now* (Columbia) proves he can play pure, unplugged jazz too.

The Now Generation

The 1990s generation of saxophonists has extended the 1980s revival of unplugged jazz as played during the 1930s and 1940s, including early swing music, Parker's and Gillespie's revolutionary bebop, and the West Coast

Cool jazz from the 1950s. The present generation of saxophonists is almost completely devoted to making jazz the old fashioned way: without electric instruments. These are some of the best of the current crop — some of them are relatively newcomers, others have been around awhile and are at the peak of their powers.

Michael Brecker (born 1949)

Best known for fiery electric pop/jazz, tenor saxophonist Brecker is also a solid player in straight-ahead acoustic bop settings. On saxes and EWI (electronic wind instrument), he supplied wailing sax in The Brecker Brothers (with his trumpet-playing brother Randy), and in the electric jazz band Steps Ahead. Get *Michael Brecker* (MCA/Impulse!), *Two Blocks from the Edge* (Uni/Impulse!), and *Tales from the Hudson* (Uni/Impulse!), as well as on *The Brecker Brothers Collection, Vols. 1* and *2* (RCA).

James Carter (born 1969)

A young, talented tenor saxophonist, Carter captures the history of jazz in his playing. Probably the most promising among the new generation of saxophonists, Carter was born in Detroit and made his big-time debut (while still in his teens) in 1986 with Wynton Marsalis. Well versed in traditional styles, Carter has also played with leading *avant garde*/free jazz figures such as trumpeter Lester Bowie and saxophonist Julius Hemphill. Watch for even greater things from him in the future.

But for now, hear Carter on *JC on the Set* (DIW/Columbia), *The Real Quietstorm* (WEA/Atlantic), and *Conversin' with the Elders* (WEA/Atlantic).

Kenny Garrett (born 1960)

Another Young Lion whose career took off in the '80s, Garrett (a Miles Davis "find") has been prolific. *Triology* (Warner Brothers) is good stuff, *Songbook* (WEA/Warner Brothers) catches a maturing player circa '97, and you should also give a listen to a younger Garrett on trumpeter Davis's electrifying late-'80s *Amandla* (Warner Brothers) album.

Joe Henderson (born 1937)

A gold medalist when it comes to longevity and quality, Henderson has maintained a consistently high standard through four decades as a smooth, soulful latter-day bebopper. A graduate of bands led by pianists Horace Silver and Herbie Hancock, Henderson has a warm, deeply emotional way with a tenor saxophone, yet he's not afraid of occasional forays into freeform jazz. Hear him on *Page One* (Blue Note), *In 'N Out* (Blue Note), *The Kicker* (Original Jazz Classics), *The State of the Tenor* (Blue Note), and *Joe Henderson Big Band* (PGD/Verve), a solid 1996 effort, at a time when first-rate big bands are far between. Also try *Ballads & Blues* (EMD/Blue Note) and *Porgy & Bess* (PGD/Verve).

Joe Lovano (born 1952)

Lovano launched his career during the 1970s playing soul jazz, and was also a member of big bands led by Woody Herman and Mel Lewis. He also has a spacey side nurtured by time spent with bassist Charlie Haden and others. Lovano has hit an impressive peak in the 1990s, turning out a steady stream of great albums as a leader, collaborating with all sorts of other top players, writing a bunch of fine original music. *Landmarks* (Blue Note), *Tenor Legacy* (Blue Note), and *Rush Hour* (Blue Note) are solid bets. Also get *Celebrating Sinatra* (EMD/Blue Note), a 1997 tribute album made especially poignant by the great singer's passing in 1998.

Branford Marsalis (born 1960)

Chided by older brother Wynton for touring with rock star Sting and taking the job as first director of comedian Jay Leno's *Tonight Show* band, Marsalis is nevertheless among the best of his generation on tenor and soprano saxophones — a bluesy, soulful player whose music packs more emotional wallop than Wynton's. *Scenes in the City* (Columbia), *Trio Jeepy* (Columbia), and *The Beautyful Ones Are Not Yet Born* (Columbia) are all good.

Courtney Pine (born 1964)

A Brit with a bent toward earlier sax giant John Coltrane, tenor/soprano saxophonist Pine has made solid recordings in the 1980s and 1990s. *Journey to the Urge Within* (Antilles) is a good place to start, and on the more recent *Modern Day Jazz Stories* (PGD/Verve), Pine mixes serious new jazz with electronic samples of earlier jazz and other music to create a hip-hop/techno/jazz hybrid.

Phil Woods (born 1931)

Woods is a mid-career master with a lengthy list of great recordings. Schooled in bands led by trumpeter Dizzy Gillespie and drummer Buddy Rich, Woods is a fleet alto specialist in a contemporary Charlie Parker mode. *Pairing Off* (Original Jazz Classics) is prime 1950s Woods, *Phil Woods/Lew*

Tabackin (Omnisound) is a 1980 collaboration with the under-appreciated flutist/saxophonist, *Bop Stew* (Concord) tosses Woods together with phenomenal trumpeter Tom Harrell, and *My Man Benny, My Man Phil* (Musicmasters) is one of my all-time favorite saxophone albums, teaming Woods with legend saxman/bandleader Benny Carter.

A few more

Here are a few others who will no doubt continue to bring new sounds to the scene:

- ✔ **Joshua Redman (born 1969).** Son of tenor saxman Dewey Redman, Joshua Redman — also a tenor saxophonist — has plenty of potential; he's still looking for a voice. *Wish* (Warner Brothers) offers testimony to his talent.

- ✔ **Javon Jackson (born 1965).** Another alum from Art Blakey's Jazz Messengers, tenor saxophonist Jackson is a latter-day 1950s hard bopper. *Me and Mr. Jones* (Criss Cross) is solid earlier Jackson, while his 1997 *Good People* (Blue Note) showcases a more mature player in a broader context.

- ✔ **Bobby Watson (born 1953).** A seasoned graduate of Art Blakey's Jazz Messengers, Watson keeps the drummer's driving, soulful spirit alive in his own music. *Post-Motown Bop* (Blue Note) is a prime example of alto saxophonist Watson's Post-1950s bop.

- ✔ **Chris Potter (born 1971).** Among the youngest of the current sax set, Potter has already chalked up impressive performances — on his own, and with drummer Paul Motian, pianist Marian McPartland, and other seasoned players. *Concentric Circles* (Concord) is one of the alto saxman's best recordings as a leader.

- ✔ **Craig Handy (born 1963).** An up-and-coming tenor saxophonist who has played with pianist Herbie Hancock and Art Blakey's Jazz Messengers, Handy has also made good music as a leader, such as *Introducing Three For All & One* (Arabesque).

- ✔ **Richie Cole (born 1948).** A spunky alto saxophonist who combines technical finesse with an upbeat spirit, Cole has made several albums of unadulterated jazz since the late 1970s. Try *Kush: The Music of Dizzy Gillespie* (Heads Up).

- ✔ **Jesse Davis (born 1965).** A young alto saxophonist who apprenticed in bands led by masters (Chico Hamilton, Illinois Jacquet), Davis is coming into his own. *As We Speak* (Concord), *High Standards* (Concord), and the 1998 *First Insight* (Concord) are best bets.

Chapter 9

Trumpeters: Jazz's Bright, Brassy Showstoppers

* *

In This Chapter

▶ Early jazz trumpeters

▶ The father of jazz trumpet: Louis Armstrong

▶ Bebop trumpeters

▶ Young brass: a new generation of jazz trumpeters

* *

More than any other jazz instrument, the trumpet played a vital role as jazz made rapid technical and creative advances beginning in the 1920s (see Chapters 1 and 2). In the hands of leading men named Bix and Louis, the trumpet (and its cousin, the cornet) became jazz's leading voice and transformed it with brassy improvisations.

A Trumpet Hails the Birth of Jazz: Buddy Bolden (1877-1931)

Beginning in the 1890s, New Orleans cornet player Buddy Bolden led what some experts say was the first genuine jazz band. Raised amid that great jazz city's rich multi-cultural gumbo, including African American celebrations with music and dancing in Congo Square, Bolden orchestrated some of the earliest inklings of what people now refer to as *jazz*.

Born in 1868, Buddy Bolden grew up singing in church and playing cornet. In 1895, Bolden organized a band, and his bold playing earned him the title "The King." In *cutting contests* where players pitted their improvisational skills against each other, Bolden consistently outdid everyone, and his band reigned supreme in New Orleans until 1907. His career ended tragically when Bolden — a dedicated drinker and womanizer — snapped. He behaved erratically, talking nonsense, even hurled a water pitcher at his mother's head. He spent most of his remaining years in a mental hospital.

Bolden's band served up several flavors of music, drawing from the cultural diversity of New Orleans — polkas, ragtime (including pianist and composer Scott Joplin's famous "Maple Leaf Rag"), and some blues — at bars, dance halls, fairs, and outdoor parties. Like many early jazzmen, Bolden couldn't read music, and feeling was far more important than technique. Though reading music would later be vital to jazz's development, Bolden's spirit and spontaneity are important characteristics of all great jazz. Bolden's trumpet sound was even bolder than that of the young Louis Armstrong, according to some who heard both men blow during the first two decades of a new century.

Sadly, Bolden apparently made no recordings, although aficionados still fantasize about finding a long-lost Edison cylinder in an attic somewhere. (Edison cylinders were made of wax, with a stylus that moved through grooves as the cylinders spun — a precursor to vinyl records and record players.) In any case, descriptions of Bolden's music are based on hearsay, and on the playing of musicians from Bolden's time who recorded during the 1920s. While experts disagree as to the sophistication of his technique, no one questions the *power* of his music, or the fact that he was on to something fresh and exciting — a new sound with African rhythms and roots that compelled folks to pile on to the dance floor.

As young trumpeters, Louis Armstrong and King Oliver both heard Bolden. And while they may have initially been bowled over by his big sound, they soon took what he did to the next level.

The Early Innovators

In the earliest jazz bands, cornet (and, in the 1920s, trumpet) was the logical lead instrument. It had the loudest, sharpest sound, cutting through the cacophony of brass-and-drum funeral, marching, and party bands.

Freddie Keppard (1890-1933)

Band leader and cornetist Freddie Keppard was second only to Buddy Bolden among jazz's earliest innovators in New Orleans. He followed Bolden, but came before Joe "King" Oliver. Bolden, Keppard, and King Oliver are among early New Orleans cornetists whose inventions later inspired the great Louis Armstrong as he re-invented cornet as a modern star soloist. While there are no known recordings of Bolden, Oliver and Keppard made numerous recordings. You can find Freddie Keppard on *Legend* (Topaz).

Brassy cousins

Technically, the difference between a cornet and a trumpet is the interior shape of the twisted brass tubing: In a cornet, it widens continually from the mouthpiece to the bell; in a trumpet, the tubing stays the same size from mouthpiece to bell. The cornet fits in well with early New Orleans bands, where it was one among several instruments in a musical democracy.

The cornet fell out of favor for many years, and in the past few decades has been used primarily by various Dixieland re-creation bands. However, a few modern players have picked it up, among them Nat Adderley and Warren Vache.

The trumpet's sound is brighter and more commanding that that of the cornet — useful qualities for Armstrong, a pioneer soloist. More recently, the flugelhorn (shown in top figure) — another member of the trumpet family — has been utilized by trumpeters such as Freddie Hubbard, Chet Baker, Clark Terry, and especially Art Farmer. The flugelhorn is slightly larger, and its sound is fuller, warmer, and mellower than trumpet (shown in bottom figure) — particularly effective for ballads. Hubbard's big, sweet sound on flugelhorn became a centerpiece of mellow 1970s soul-jazz, and top players including Tom Harrell still use the instrument on a variety of tunes ranging from slow and soft to uptempo bebop.

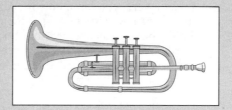

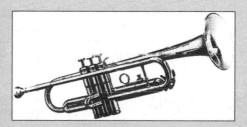

King Oliver (1885-1938)

A native of New Orleans, Oliver began performing in 1905. In the early 1920s, as the jazz scene shifted from New Orleans to Chicago (see Chapter 3), Oliver went with it and made some of his best recordings in the Windy City. His group included trumpeter Louis Armstrong, clarinetist Johnny Dodds, and pianist Lil Harden.

Oliver wasn't a pioneering soloist on the order of Beiderbecke or Armstrong. His contribution was more as mentor to Armstrong and as a leader of bands whose members, at times, included several legendary players: clarinetists Sidney Bechet and Barney Bigard, and future members of Armstrong's Hot Five band, including Johnny Dodds (clarinet) and Baby Dodds (drums). As for Oliver, he never hitched a ride to popularity aboard radio and records. Late in life, he earned his living as a janitor.

Start with Oliver's *Great Original Performances/1923–1930* (Louisiana Red Hot Records), a collection remixed with newer technology that brings out subtle nuances in the music. Also check out *King Oliver and his Orchestra/ 1929–1930* (BMG/RCA) and *King Oliver/1930–1931* (Classics).

Two talented peers: Bix Beiderbecke (1903-1931)and Louis Armstrong

Beiderbecke was an early master of the cornet, and one of the first white jazz players who jammed with African Americans, who accepted him as a solid jazzman with an original voice. During the prime of his short life, Beiderbecke was a white counterpart to Louis Armstrong. Handsome and hard-partying, Beiderbecke served years later as a romantic posterboy for the so-called "jazz age," though he never came close to Armstrong's artistry, fame, or overall lasting impact on the music.

Beiderbecke and Armstrong became friends as teenagers. They even jammed together, and they remained friends until Beiderbecke's death. Beiderbecke took the cornet to new places. His bright tone and lyrical improvisations stood out in any musical setting, and his feel for the music — his sense of swing and spontaneity — was as important as his sound.

"Louis was a soloist par excellence. Bix had a different approach," says Randy Sandke, a trumpeter and jazz historian who has studied, played, and recorded the music of both men. "Louis was really into standing in front of his big band and doing his show. Bix was a more lyrical player. Louis was a dramatist, Bix was a poet."

"There are times with both Louis and Bix when they're the only ones swing-ing," Sandke says, describing the loose but steady forward momentum of good jazz. "Their rhythmic sense is so strong, they carry the rest of the band. This trait is sometimes taken for granted today, but it was originally found in only a few individuals, Louis Armstrong probably being the most important."

Beiderbecke can be heard on *Bix Lives* (RCA) and on two different collec-tions on Columbia: *Bix Beiderbecke, Vol. 1: Singin' the Blues,* and *At the Jazz Band Ball, Vol. 2.* These recordings give the best introduction to his sound and include some recordings he made behind bandleaders Paul Whiteman and Jean Goldkette.

Father of Modern Jazz Trumpet: Louis Armstrong (1901-1971)

"Pops" was Louis Armstrong's nickname, and he was unquestionably the father of modern jazz trumpet. Armstrong, more than any other jazz musician, was a rare combination of instrumental, comedic, compositional, and vocal ability. He also delivered a healthy dose of charisma and charm that helped him put his act across to all audiences — white and black, young and old.

An innovator like no other

Armstrong was the first genuine jazz legend. He was the first modern jazz soloist, playing a lead role, taking more and longer solos than supporting bandmates. Early bands, including King Oliver's, were more of a collective effort. Armstrong utilized a small group format such as his Hot Five, and used his ensembles as showcases for a star soloist (in this case, himself). Armstrong's concept of organizing a band and the music around solos has become one of the key characteristics of modern jazz.

Armstrong vastly extended the trumpet's useful range. He could play high notes that none of his peers could touch — and that few players of today can reach.

"His sense of rhythm was his main contribution," says current jazz trumpeter Jon Faddis. "His sense of rhythm was unparalleled, because it had that natural beat to it that made you want to get up and dance."

"Louis Armstrong is the one musician who taught the world how to *swing,* and by that I mean most of the music going on in the 1920s had more of a steady two-beat feel. Louis taught musicians, on songs such as 'Struttin' With Some Barbecue,' and on his solos, to extend the melodic line and create a solo. Before that, no one played extended improvisations."

Armstrong also made the trumpet, not the cornet, the leading brass instrument. As a boy, Armstrong started on cornet, but after he switched to trumpet for good around 1927, cornet all but disappeared from jazz.

Before "Pops" was even knee-high

Armstrong was raised in a poor section of New Orleans — for his first five years by his grandmother Josephine, then by his mother, Mary Ann, or "Mayann" as she was often called. She was deeply religious, and she took young Louis to church where gospel music was a main feature of the services.

His first instrument was a tin horn that he used to gain attention while driving a coal delivery wagon. He got so good he could blow a tune without the mouthpiece, and he soon graduated to a cornet he bought for five dollars in a pawnshop. By age 12, when Armstrong fired a pistol into the air on New Year's Day and was reprimanded to the Colored Waif's Home for Boys, he had already developed a strong admiration for King Oliver. More minor crimes kept Armstrong in and out of the reform school, which had at least one big plus: a school band within which young Louis could develop his talent.

Louis's first gig

Armstrong was working with professional musicians by the time he was in his teens, and he joined pianist Fate Marable's band, performing aboard a riverboat on the Mississippi. By his early twenties, it was commonly known in New Orleans jazz circles that Armstrong could *cut* any trumpeter — outplay them at the legendary *cutting contests,* where soloists improvised head to head until one took a clear advantage.

In 1918, Armstrong replaced his early idol King Oliver in Kid Ory's band, and in 1922, in an unusual move, Oliver summoned Armstrong to Chicago to join the Creole Jazz Band as his sidekick cornetist. Armstrong recorded 41 cuts with the band in 1923, but he soon outstripped Oliver's abilities on cornet.

At the urging of his second wife, Lil Hardin, a pianist and member of Oliver's band, Armstrong joined Fletcher Henderson's big band as featured soloist in New York in 1924. Armstrong's impact was immediate — the band began to swing like never before.

A Study In Frustration: The Fletcher Henderson Story (Columbia) is a three-CD collection that includes important Armstrong performances from 1924. When Armstrong solos on the songs "Everybody Loves My Baby" and "Sugarfoot Stomp," momentum picks up noticeably. Although the big band includes three trumpeters, Armstrong is clearly the star and he takes all the key solos. You can also hear the band's and Armstrong's evolution on these CDs. From November 1924, when Armstrong recorded "Everybody Loves My Baby" with the band, to May 1925, when several more songs featuring Armstrong were recorded, the orchestra and Armstrong both improved remarkably. Driven by Armstrong's swinging solos and his lead-role carrying melodies, the group, over a period of six months, began playing with new confidence, and Armstrong's solos grew bolder and more complex.

Armstrong breaks out on his own

In 1925, Armstrong returned to Chicago, where he formed his own group (the Hot Five, and later Hot Seven) and began recording as a leader.

Comparing Armstrong's 1923 recordings with Oliver's group to the recordings Armstrong made with his Hot Five in 1925, you can hear the transition from old-style ensemble playing, to a new, more modern jazz centered on the soloist — and he was still only 24 years old. Limited to three minutes per song by the 78 rpm record format, Armstrong couldn't stretch out like later trumpeters, but he still took the art of the solo to new highs.

On *The Hot Fives* (Columbia), Armstrong's first recordings as a leader, his hip solo kicks off "Cornet Chop Suey," an original Armstrong composition. Bold and bright, his horn rallies the troops, and once they fall in behind him, Armstrong carries the melody and takes a second catchy solo. "You're Next," another Armstrong original, showcases his trumpet on a dark, funereal dirge that gradually takes on a happier tone as Armstrong solos and the other players elegantly embroider his inventions.

By the end of the 1920s, with his Hot Five and Hot Seven, Armstrong had completed what most experts believe to be his most important recordings.

Armstrong in later years

After the 1920s, Armstrong became more of an entertainer and less of a jazz innovator. He sang frequently, popularizing the jazzy style of improvising known as *scat*. When he scats, you can hear parallels with his trumpet solos: his sense of swing, the longer melodic lines he improvised, and even specific patterns of notes.

Armstrong's later sessions captured a mature, concise trumpeter, able to get his message across with far fewer notes. Among his finest later recordings are his sessions on the Decca label during the 1940s; several RCA sessions during the 1930s and 1940s, compiled on *The Complete RCA Victor Recordings; The Louis Armstrong Collection, Vol. 4: Louis Armstrong and Earl Hines,* (Columbia), a synergistic pairing of "Pops" with the great pianist; *Armstrong/ Ellington: Together For The First Time* (Mobile Fidelity); and of course *Hello Dolly,* (Kapp) his charming take on the Broadway musical.

Armstrong (see Figure 9-1) opened up jazz for improvisers, and helped spread this largely African American music to wide audiences. As an all-around entertainer and jazz innovator, he was one of the century's two or three most important artists. Take a listen to Armstrong's "Riff Blues" on the *Jazz For Dummies* CD right now to whet your appetite for the great player's sound.

Figure 9-1:
Louis
Armstrong
(photo:
Everett
Collection).

Armstrong's contemporaries of the '20s and '30s

Chicago, with its vibrant recording and radio scene, made big band swing a national phenomenon during the late 1920s and early 1930s. While Armstrong was undoubtedly the most influential trumpeter of his time, others played important parts in the evolution of the instrument and jazz in general:

✔ **Henry "Red" Allen (1908–1967).** Armstrong's peer in New Orleans, Allen was one of jazz's most innovative early soloists. He played in bands led by cornetist King Oliver, pianist Luis Russell, and pianist Clarence Williams, and made several recordings. Check out *Henry "Red" Allen/1929-1933* (Classics) and *Henry "Red" Allen/1937–1941* (Classics).

✔ **Bunny Berigan (1908–1942).** A top trumpeter during 1930s big band swing, Berigan was a part of Benny Goodman's hot mid-'30s ensemble. He also worked for trombonist Tommy Dorsey, and later led a band of his own. Give a listen to *The Pied Piper* (Bluebird).

MUSICIANS SPEAK

Louis Armstrong: Musical genius and role model

"His innovative work took place in the late 1920s, and it opened up jazz for all other musicians," says trumpeter Jon Faddis, who, as a boy during the early 1960s, chose trumpet as his instrument after seeing Armstrong on *The Ed Sullivan Show.* "When he was laying down his stuff with the Hot Five, nothing like that had ever been heard before, and he influenced all the other instruments, not just trumpet: saxophone, clarinet, trombone, piano, bass, drums.

"At that time, it was very rare to see black artists treated with any respect on television," Faddis says. "Nat King Cole had a TV show, but you mostly had *Amos and Andy,* and various 'step-and-fetchit' characters in film.

"My parents had asked me, if I could play an instrument, which one would it be? My sister played piano, so it couldn't be that. My friend down the street played trombone and sax, so it couldn't be that. Another friend played drums, so it couldn't be that.

"Then I remembered Louis on *Ed Sullivan,* and how everyone admired the way he played and sang, so I said, 'trumpet.' Next thing I knew, my parents had bought me a trumpet and were making me take trumpet lessons."

Now a top trumpeter in his own right, Faddis says Armstrong's vintage solos still amaze him.

"I ask students to play some Louis, and they can't do it. The things he was doing are still very difficult to re-create. Could I play the high notes he could play? Yes . . . in my own way."

✔ **Buck Clayton (1911–1991).** First with Basie, later on his own, Clayton was one of jazz's most prolific swing-style trumpeters, with a career that lasted from the 1930s through the 1980s. An elegant, melodic player, Clayton was an imaginative arranger and soloist, as you can hear on *The Classic Swing of Buck Clayton* (Original Jazz Classics) and *Buck Clayton in Paris* (Vogue).

✔ **Harry "Sweets" Edison (born 1915).** A soulful, bluesy player, Edison was a member of Count Basie's big band from 1938 to 1950, and made consistently solid recordings through several more decades. *Jawbreakers* (Original Jazz Classics) is hot early 1960s stuff, while *Edison's Lights* (Original Jazz Classics), shows he was just as electrifying during the late 1970s.

✔ **Roy Eldridge (1911–1989).** Eldridge made a name for himself in 1930s New York City, playing with banjo/guitar player Elmer Snowden, McKinney's Cotton Pickers, Teddy Hill, and Fletcher Henderson. He was in drummer Gene Krupa's hard-swinging early 1940s big band, and added excellent solos to numerous albums over five decades. Eldridge's fleet, musically advanced solos, with their startling, powerful bursts, pointed the early way toward bebop. During the advent of bebop, Eldridge continued to swing, and he played beautiful, melodic solos at a time when Dizzy Gillespie and others were experimenting with the frenetic new forms. Try *Little Jazz* (Sony) and *Roy Eldridge in Paris* (Vogue).

✔ **Tommy Ladnier (1900–1939).** One of the best of the New Orleans trumpeters, Ladnier worked for Fate Marable, King Oliver, and other top bandleaders before becoming a top soloist in Fletcher Henderson's late 1920s big band.

✔ **Red Nichols (1905–1965).** In 1920s New York, Nichols played with reedman Jimmy Dorsey, trombonist Miff Mole, and other notables, and he eventually led a band that at various times included many major jazz musicians such as clarinetists Benny Goodman and Pee Wee Russell, trombonist Jack Teagarden, and drummer Gene Krupa. Pick up *Red Nichols, Vol. 1* (Classic Jazz), as well as several other volumes on the Classic Jazz label.

✔ **Hot Lips Page (1908–1954).** A star soloist in Midwest "territory" bands led by Walter Page and Bennie Moten during the late '20s and early '30s, Page also played briefly with Count Basie and was in Artie Shaw's early '40s big band. *The Chronological Hot Lips Page/1938-1940* (Classics) is a good place to start with this top early trumpeter.

✔ **Cootie Williams (1910–1985).** Over the years, Duke Ellington's big bands had several hot trumpeters, and Williams was among the best in the 1930s. Other top Ellingtonian trumpeters include Bubber Miley, Rex Stewart (who actually played cornet), Ray Nance, Shorty Baker, Cat Anderson, Al Killian, and Clark Terry, who had one of the longest, most versatile careers of any of them.

Trumpet Goes Bop

Jazz entered a new phase during the 1930s as big band swing became widely popular and soloists became the stars of the leading big bands. But while bands led by Duke Ellington, Count Basie, Benny Goodman, and others kept playing swing into the 1940s, a new sound was on the rise in New York clubs such Minton's Playhouse and Monroe's Uptown. In these clubs, a core group of hot young players including Dizzy Gillespie, saxophonist Charlie Parker, and pianist Thelonious Monk were defining a challenging new style of jazz called *bebop*.

John Birks "Dizzy" Gillespie (1917-1993)

Like many jazz heroes including Louis Armstrong, Gillespie came up through the ranks of the big bands. In fact, big band connections gave him a direct link to Armstrong and Roy Eldridge, his immediate ancestors as leading improvisers on trumpet. In 1937, Gillespie replaced Roy Eldridge in Teddy Hill's band. Hill had taken over Luis Russell's ensemble, which Russell had inherited from King Oliver in 1929 — giving Gillespie a direct tie to Oliver, and through Oliver to Armstrong, who started out in Oliver's band.

Armstrong had earlier elevated trumpet to the status of a lead solo instrument, and he vastly expanded its improvisational repertoire. But Gillespie was the player who blew apart all preconceived notions of how trumpet, or jazz in general, should be played — and how jazz players should look and act.

In fact, Gillespie's appearance, augmented by a goatee, beret, stylish clothes, and mannerisms that included his hip lingo and the oddly bent bell of his horn, helped as much as his musical genius to gain him attention in some circles. But apart from fashion, he played a vital role in developing bebop, which was named after the sound of its speedy improvisations.

Gillespie's entry into the scene

Born in South Carolina in 1917, Gillespie (see Figure 9-2) was raised in a musically-inclined family. His dad was a musician who introduced his nine children to various instruments. Dizzy started on trombone, but switched to trumpet at 15. His dad paid for private lessons, and in 1937, still only 20, Gillespie toured Europe (and made his recording debut) with Teddy Hill's band. He joined vocalist Cab Calloway's orchestra in 1939, but he was something of a wiseacre, and he left the band after an altercation with the bandleader over a spitball thrown by someone else, but blamed on Gillespie. During the 1940s, Gillespie played in the big bands of Benny Carter, Charlie Barnet, Lucky Millinder, Earl Hines, Duke Ellington, and Billy Eckstine.

Gillespie's early influence was trumpeter Roy Eldridge, but by the mid-'40s, teamed with saxophonist Charlie Parker, Diz left behind his traditional roots. Gillespie's innovations (like Parker's) are tremendously important: He played with dizzying speed; his signature sounds include dramatic dives from high notes to low ones, and mixtures of perfectly clear notes and intentionally slurred sounds; complex new methods of improvisation involving fresh chord combinations for old songs, and new numbers composed over the chords of familiar popular songs. He incorporated new rhythms including Afro-Cuban and Latin influences, and created big band arrangements using his new ideas. His arrangements were purchased by Woody Herman, Jimmy Dorsey, and other bandleaders. And last, but not least, Dizzy Gillespie filled the role, literally, as a cultural ambassador — during the 1950s, the U.S. State Department sent Gillespie and his multi-racial band on goodwill tours to Asia, Europe, and Latin America, and he later toured the world with his United Nations Orchestra.

Figure 9-2:
Dizzy
Gillespie
(photo:
Everett
Collection).

The impact of Bird and Diz

The chemistry between Gillespie and Parker is what really set the jazz world on its ear. They got to know each other in Harlem clubs and around New York's vibrant 52nd Street jazz scene. They played together for the first time in earnest in pianist Earl Hines's band beginning in 1942, and with vocalist Billy Eckstine's band in 1944. Unfortunately, the ban on recording (prompted by a musicians' union strike over royalties) from 1942 to 1944 meant that most of this music never made it to vinyl.

So it wasn't until 1945 that Bird and Diz made their first recordings together. The songs they teamed on during this period, such as "Salt Peanuts," "Shaw Nuff," "Hot House," "Dizzy Atmosphere," and "Groovin' High," are still considered bebop's all-time classics. Introduce yourself to Gillespie with *Dizzy Gillespie/1940–1946* (Epm/Musique), *Dizzy Gillespie, Vol. 6/1945–1946* (Masters of Jazz); and, for a sweet and spicy taste of his big band music, *Complete RCA Victor Recordings/1937–1949* (BMG/RCA).

By 1945, Gillespie's bebop style was in full gear. He transformed standard tunes into subtle and complex modern jazz tunes featuring his wildly imaginative improvisations. He wrote several songs (including "Hot House," "A Night in Tunisia," "Groovin' High," and "Salt Peanuts" that defined bebop in their intricacy and eclectic borrowings from earlier jazz.

Bird and Diz At Carnegie Hall (Roost), recorded in the fall of 1947, is another fine example of vintage bebop, all the more intense because this live session includes assorted shouts and murmurs from the audience and band members as songs and solos pick up steam. "A Night In Tunisia," "Dizzy Atmosphere," "Groovin' High," and "Salt Peanuts," all originals by Gillespie, are included on the *Carnegie Hall* CD. And Parker's "Relaxin' At Camarillo" gets an especially spicy treatment with a full orchestration driven by a Latin beat.

Gillespie ages elegantly

The best artists mature, and while Gillespie made important breakthroughs during the 1940s, his most refined playing may have come during the 1950s.

"That's my favorite period, trumpetistically speaking," Faddis says. "There comes a point with Louis Armstrong, Roy Eldridge, and Dizzy, when they got older, they matured, and even though they could not technically do the things they could do when they were young and innovative, for me, that maturity and choice of notes and emotional depth can outweigh those innovations." Faddis's favorite Gillespie recording from this period is the 1963 *Something Old, Something New* (Verve).

Fats Navarro (1923-1958) and Clifford Brown (1930-1956)

Trumpeters Fats Navarro and Clifford Brown both had potential on the order of Dizzy Gillespie's talent. In fact, many jazz fanatics believe recordings by Navarro from the late '40s, and by Brown from the mid-'50s, surpass the work of any other jazz trumpeters from those periods. Navarro and Brown were both technically awesome, but without Gillespie's showiness, and with more subtlety and feeling. Both played in the trumpet's mid-range, and were equally adept at ballads and high-speed bebop numbers.

Sadly, Navarro died in 1950 of tuberculosis and drug addiction at age 26; and in 1955, Brown passed away at 25 in an auto accident. For two artists whose careers ended prematurely, both trumpeters left an impressive volume of recorded material.

Essential Navarro includes *Fats Navarro, Vols. 1-3*, released by Blue Moon; *Fat Girl — The Savoy Sessions;* and *Fats Navarro and Tadd Dameron* (Blue Note). On *Fats Navarro, Vol. 1*, the trumpeter has the benefit of an all-star mid-'40s cast, including saxman Sonny Stitt, pianist Bud Powell, and drummer Kenny Clarke.

The Best of Clifford Brown (Blue Note) gives a good introduction to this talented trumpeter. *Brownie: The Complete EmArcy Recordings* (PGD/Verve) is a more extensive collection of music.

The Beginning and the End gives you early and late Brown, with a Latin flair, and thanks to the innovation of 33$^1/_3$ rpm vinyl replacing older 78s, the songs "Walkin'" and Gillespie/Paparelli's "A Night In Tunisia" were allowed to stretch to more than 11 minutes during those sessions, with plenty of Brown's precisely polished sound. His "A Night in Tunisia" in particular, is as swinging and interesting as Gillespie's many versions.

Brown's solos are packed with long and beautiful improvised lines that span several measures, but they are so carefully constructed that you will stay engrossed all the way through. Along with Gillespie, Navarro and Brown exploded previous notions of how trumpeters should play. They interpreted standard tunes in fresh ways, and they improvised with original voices and innovative harmonies.

Jazz's Coolest Trumpeter: Miles Davis (1926-1991)

Miles Davis was born Alton, Illinois, in 1926, and he grew up in St. Louis, where his dad, a dentist, supported his son's efforts on trumpet beginning at at age 9. At 18, Davis went to New York to attend the prestigious Julliard School of Music, but the year was 1944 — the beginning of bebop — and Davis spent most of his time hanging out in 52nd Street clubs, listening to Charlie Parker, Dizzy Gillespie, and other legends.

He was playing with Parker by 1945 — his laid-back, slurry sound made an interesting match with Parker's manic saxophone. By 1947, Davis was a speedy and confident player in Parker's group, but he soon headed away from bop. Davis's playing from the 1950s forward was markedly minimalist in comparison to the many notes-per-second playing of the beboppers.

Davis's vast impact on jazz

Davis (see Figure 9-3) was not a technical giant like Dizzy Gillespie, Clifford Brown, or Fats Navarro, but he had other strengths that make him equally vital as a modern jazz trumpeter. Mainly, he was a visionary leader who gave gifted players the room to be creative. Through the years, members of Davis's various bands have included pianists John Lewis, Red Garland, Horace Silver, Chick Corea, Walter Bishop, Joe Zawinul, Keith Jarrett, Bill Evans, and Herbie Hancock; saxophonists Lee Konitz, Jackie McLean, Gerry Mulligan, Cannonball Adderley, John Coltrane, and Wayne Shorter; guitarists John McLaughlin and John Scofield, as well as a slew of gifted and relative unknowns; drummers Kenny Clarke, Art Blakey, Philly Joe Jones, Billy Cobham, Jack DeJohnette, and Tony Williams; and bassists Paul Chambers, Percy Heath, Ron Carter, and Marcus Miller. That's a treasure trove of valuable jazz talent.

Figure 9-3:
Miles Davis
(photo:
Everett
Collection).

By the time Davis died in 1991, he had been an important contributor to 1940s bebop; a founder of the laid-back 1950s style known as *cool;* one of the few jazzmen to successfully employ lavish orchestrations, on albums from *Birth of the Cool* (Capitol) to *Sketches of Spain* (Columbia), and a brave pioneer in combining jazz with other elements including rock, funk, and even hip-hop. Perhaps his single most important contribution was his controversial ability to constantly innovate, explore, and push jazz into new directions and subgenres. Purists feel that he sold out jazz by going electric during the mid-'60s, and by blending jazz with other music. But in terms of creativity, his music stands up as some of jazz's most adventurous.

Davis's recordings

Begin your explorations of acoustic Miles with the 1959 album *Kind of Blue,* (Sony) which includes the legendary John Coltrane on saxophone. Almost completely improvised, these five songs nonetheless have a simple power and beautiful melodies that make them seductive and easy to listen to.

The steady thunk-thunk-thunk of Paul Chambers' bass and Jimmy Cobb's drums serve as friendly landmarks. Davis's solos — compared in album notes by pianist Bill Evans to the precise strokes of Japanese watercolors — are warm, muted, and melancholy. Long solos by saxophonists Coltrane and Cannonball Adderley stretch the music's boundaries without breaking from the basic beat and chords.

Essential Miles albums include:

- ✔ *Birth of the Cool,* (Capitol) with arrangements by Gil Evans and a nine-piece band including Gerry Mulligan, Lee Konitz, Kai Winding, and J.J. Johnson, which helped launch the laid-back West Coast *cool jazz* style of the 1950s.

- ✔ *Round About Midnight,* (Sony) also including Coltrane, and with tight ensemble playing on tunes including "Bye Bye Blackbird."

- ✔ All of the mid-'50s cool-mood albums on Original Jazz Classics: *Cookin', Workin', Steamin', Relaxin'* — "Oleo," from *Relaxin'* is included on the *Jazz For Dummies* CD.

- ✔ *Sketches of Spain,* (Sony) the ultimate in orchestrated Miles, with an assist from Gil Evans.

- ✔ *Miles In The Sky,* (Sony) austere mood music.

- ✔ And for a taste of electric Miles: *In A Silent Way, Bitches Brew, A Tribute to Jack Johnson, Get Up With It* (for its intensity), and *Amandla.* (Warner).

The Other Legends

From the late '40s forward, dozens of other trumpeters made key contributions to the evolution of the trumpet in jazz. Some of them are legendary for their emotional impact, some for their technique.

Chet Baker (1929-1988)

Though a longtime heroin addict, Baker never failed to come up with at least one or two emotionally charged solos at any given recording session, and he helped define the cool California sound of the 1950s. Check out *Chet Baker/ Verve Jazz Masters* (Verve), *The Legacy, Vol. 1* (Enja), and *The Art of the Ballad* (Prestige). And for a peak deep into his soul, try *The Best of Chet Baker Sings: Let's Get Lost,* (Capitol/Pacific Jazz).

Lester Bowie (born 1941)

Best of the *avant garde* trumpeters, Bowie sketches spare, impressionistic pieces with impressive grace. He also makes performing a visual art by using tribal makeup and costumes. Start with *The Great Pretender,* (ECM), a wild, sometimes humorous romp from Dixieland to the lunatic fringe, but don't miss Bowie as a part of the innovative Art Ensemble of Chicago, one of the leading groups on jazz's cutting edge during the 1970s and 1980s.

Tom Harrell (born 1946)

Troubled by manic depression, Harrell moves and speaks with difficulty. But when he puts a trumpet or flugelhorn to his lips, magic happens. Harrell is a serious modern bebopper with roots in the 1940s and 1950s, and he writes fine original tunes. Check him out on *Sail Away* (Contemporary) and *Up-swing* (Chesky).

Freddie Hubbard (born 1938)

A top hard-bopper during the 1950s and 1960s, Hubbard reached new listeners with bright, funky electric jazz during the 1970s. On both trumpet and flugelhorn, Hubbard, who has played with saxmen Eric Dolphy, Sonny Rollins, John Coltrane, and Ornette Coleman, and with bebop trombonist J.J. Johnson, has a warm, lyrical sound. Sample some early unplugged Hubbard on *Open Sesame* (EMD/Blue Note) and *Ready for Freddie* (EMD/Blue Note), and dip into his lighter 1970s bag on *Red Clay* (CTI) and *First Light* (CTI).

Lee Morgan (1938-1972)

Best known for his soulful jazz album *The Sidewinder* (EMD/Blue Note), Morgan was a top trumpeter associates with hard bop, the gritty, bluesy jazz of the '50s and early '60s. A graduate of Dizzy Gillespie's Big Band and Art Blakey's Jazz Messengers, Morgan made many fine albums through two decades. Among the best are *Dizzy Atmosphere* (Original Jazz Classics), *Candy* (EMD/Blue Note), and *Search for the New Land* (EMD/Blue Note).

Woody Shaw (1944-1989)

Shaw is perhaps the most underappreciated of contemporary trumpeters. His albums can be difficult to find, but are worth the search so that you can hear one of the few players who merged 1950s *hard bop* (the later stage of bebop) with more abstract and *avant garde* ideas. *Blackstone Legacy* (Contemporary) and *Lotus Flower* (Enja) are good albums for an introduction to Shaw's playing.

Clark Terry (born 1920)

Told of his own awesome technique, Dizzy Gillespie once singled out flugelhorn specialist Terry as an example of a player even more technically gifted. Terry, who influenced Miles Davis during the 1940s, played in the big bands of both Basie and Ellington, and continues to make exciting music. A genuine living legend, Terry wows fans when he solos by alternating between a trumpet in one hand and a flugelhorn in the other. Try *Duke with a Difference* (Original Jazz Classics), *The Happy Horn of Clark Terry* (GRP/Impulse!), and *To Duke and Basie* (Enja). Also hear Terry play "In Orbit" from the *Jazz For Dummies* CD.

Too much talent, too little space

Trumpet is one of the mainstay instruments of jazz and the field of excellent players is vast. Here are a few:

- **Donald Byrd (born 1932).** A chameleon who has played trumpet in many jazz styles, Byrd was a leader in the 1970s and 1980s at fusing jazz with other musics including soul and funk. Catch him on *Byrd in Flight* (EMD/Blue Note), *A New Perspective* (EMD/Blue Note), and *Chant* (EMD/Blue Note).

- **Kenny Dorham (1924–1972).** Top '50s hard bopper, and among the leaders at bringing new rhythms to jazz. Check out *Afro-Cuban* (EMD/Blue Note).

- **Art Farmer (born 1928).** Sweet and fat, Farmer's sound on flugelhorn has been one of jazz's most distinctive voices since the 1950s. Get *Farmer's Market* (Original Jazz Classics), *Meet the Jazztet* (Original Jazz Classics), and *Something to Live For: The Music of Billy Strayhorn* (Contemporary).

- **Blue Mitchell (1930–1979).** Another soulful 1950s-era hard bopper, Mitchell played with saxophonist Cannonball Adderley, pianist Horace Silver, and other notables. Get your hands on *Big Six* (Original Jazz Classics) and *Blue Soul* (Original Jazz Classics).

- **Shorty Rogers (1924–1994).** A vital force in California during the 1950s as a trumpeter and bandleader, Rogers helped invent the laid-back *cool* sound. Try *Short Stops* (Bluebird) and *The Swinging Mr. Rogers* (Atlantic).

- **Charles Tolliver (born 1942).** One of the most melodic trumpeters of the 1960s and 1970s, Tolliver plays jazz rooted in bluesy 1950s hard bop. Hear him on *The Ringer* (Freedom) and *Live at Slugs, Vol. 1* (Strata East). You can hear his version of an updated, hard-hitting big band sound on his early '70s albums *Music, Inc. Big Band* and *Impact* (both on Strata-East).

Young Brass: A New Generation of Jazz Trumpeters

Young players who, for me, pack a lot of punch, include:

- **Terence Blanchard (born 1962).** *Malcolm X Jazz Suite,* (Sony) Blanchard's powerful score for the Spike Lee movie *Malcolm X,* is a great place to start. Blanchard also scored Lee's *Do the Right Thing* and *Jungle Fever.*

- **Roy Hargrove (born 1969).** *With The Tenors Of Our Times* (PGD/Verve) pairs Hargrove with Johnny Griffin, Branford Marsalis, Stanley Turrentine, Joe Henderson, and Joshua Redman for a sharp shakedown recorded in 1993, when Hargrove was only 24.

- **Leroy Jones.** A rising trumpeter whose second album — *Props For Pops* (Sony) — adds fresh spit and polish to elements of Louis Armstrong, including such Armstrong staples as "Struttin' With Some Barbecue." Jones also pens pieces of his own.

- **Wynton Marsalis (born 1961).** Marsalis has led the way for a new bunch of young jazz players during the early 1980s. Marsalis's technique is incredible and his dedication, intense. He's a first-class classical trumpeter too. *Black Codes From The Underground,* (Sony) the spiritual *In This House, On This Morning,* (Sony) and *Citi Movement,* (Sony) his score for the ballet *Griot New York,* are excellent albums to start with. Also look for his epic three-CD *Blood on the Fields* (Sony), a tribute to African American history.

- **Nicholas Payton (born 1973).** Young and promising, part of the newest generation. Investigate him on *Payton's Place* (PGD/Verve) and *From This Moment* (PGD/Verve).

- **Wallace Roney (born 1960).** A baby Miles Davis, Roney even played with his role model at the 1991 Montreux Jazz Festival. Roney is also a promising composer. Hear him on *Misterios* (WEA/Warners) and *Village* (WEA/Warners).

Chapter 10

Vocalists: Swinging without an Axe

In This Chapter

▶ Jazz singing's roots in blues

▶ The Depression brings hardship, but some great music

▶ The golden years of swing and song

▶ Bebop influences singers

▶ Eclectic 1950s and into the modern era

The human voice and many of jazz's instruments can be thought of as cousins: Saxophones, trumpets, clarinets, and flutes are, in a sense, mechanical elaborations of the human voice. Breath rushes over reeds (vocal chords) and resonates in a chamber (the mouth and chest) to create sound. Many of jazz's leading instrumentalists even say that their goal is to play with a lyrical, singing, human quality. In turn, many singers say that they see their voices as genuine jazz instruments. And the great jazz made by vocalists with empathetic accompanists over the years illustrates the close relationship between voice and other instruments.

Early Vocalists

During the 1920s, when the first recorded jazz came out of ragtime, blues, and New Orleans parade and funeral band music, jazz/blues singers such as Mamie Smith, Bessie Smith, Ma Rainey, and Alberta Hunter delivered their songs with gusto. These early singers swung hard. They improvised melodies, harmonies, and assorted vocal sounds. And they sang with intense emotion that gave each song their personal stamp.

Rainey, Hunter, and Bessie Smith all began their recording careers in the 1920s, soon after the Original Dixieland Jass Band made the first jazz recording in 1917. The first blues vocal recording to get any recognition was made in 1920 by Mamie Smith. Earlier vocal jazz predated recording equipment, so it hasn't been preserved.

Black revues that toured the South during the 1920s helped invent the art of jazz singing. Traveling with bands of limited size, vocalists were often called upon to accompany popular singers — Ma Rainey, Bessie Smith, and Mamie Smith all participated in such shows, using a variety of vocal techniques and improvisation as they helped provide background orchestration.

Louis Armstrong was the first genuine jazz singer — his famous instrumental-style *scat* vocals (singing with made-up syllables instead of words) from the 1920s pointed the way toward Ella Fitzgerald, Jon Hendricks, and dozens of other jazz singers. One of his coolest early vocal solos comes on "Heebies Jeebies," included on the CD *Hot Fives, Vol. 1* (Sony).

Eventually, Armstrong was at least as famous for his singing as for his trumpeting. He was among the first true jazz singers to gain wide popularity. His charismatic version of "Hello, Dolly" (on the CD *Hello, Dolly!*/MCA) from the Broadway musical was a hit, and other great Armstrong vocals are his duets with Ella Fitzgerald on *Porgy and Bess* (PGD/Verve), and, for your kids, *Disney Songs the Satchmo Way* (Disney).

The evolution of jazz singers parallels the development of great instrumentalists, from integral members of bands during the 1920s to star soloists during the 1930s, 1940s, and forward. And as the solo in a performance setting came to be a central focus of jazz, the importance of an original vocal style became the defining factor for a long list of singers.

What makes a jazz vocalist?

There is much debate on what actually makes a good jazz singer, but the basic characteristics of all jazz — swing, syncopation, improvisation, and a distinctive voice (explained in more detail in Chapter 1) apply to singing as well. And that last characteristic, a distinctive voice, is the trait that really distinguishes jazz's leading vocalists.

Like all of jazz's leading players, singers are only as good as their songs. No matter how well they improvise, most all of them need the structure of a good composition as a framework for their jazz forays. Jazz's greatest singers are also great interpreters — jazz *standards,* the songs that are standard in most every jazz player's repertoire, generally have intelligent, emotional, witty lyrics that require as much dramatic ability on the part of the singer as is required of an actor playing a role.

The fine line between jazz and blues singing becomes clearer if you listen to a singer's band. Blues bands tend to stay with a simple blues format and relatively straightforward solos, while blues singers are usually distinguished more by their emotional and interpretive abilities than tremendous vocal techniques or range. Genuine jazz singers, by contrast, usually work with jazz players who push them in challenging directions. Jazz has more complex chord combinations and melodies, and jazz singers are generally a vastly more sophisticated bunch musically than their counterparts in blues.

Scat, cat

Don Redman recorded the first improvised *scat* vocal on the song "My Papa Doesn't Two Time" in 1924 (scatting is when singers improvise melodies and sounds without words).

Over the years, several singers have advanced the art of jazz vocals — the use of the term *vocals* instead of *singing* reflects the instrumental nature of their styles. They use their voices as instruments, sometimes singing words and melodies, but often improvising freely outside of conventional singing techniques.

Ella Fitzgerald was one of the first to develop a concise scat technique. Following a more conventional start in the 1930s, she began improvising on an equal footing with saxophonists, trumpeters, and other star instrumental soloists of the 1940s and 1950s.

Further validating the expanded role of voice-as-instrument, singers including Eddie Jefferson and King Pleasure sang amazing versions of jazz tunes originally recorded as instrumentals. They also found ways for singers to adopt the musical ideas of bebop instrumentalists like saxophonist Charlie Parker and trumpeter Dizzy Gillespie.

Jon Hendricks took jazz singing ever farther in the 1950s. With Lambert, Hendricks & Ross, a vocal trio, he showed how voices could carry the music, replacing instruments to a significant degree.

And as jazz grew looser, freer, and more diverse during the 1960s and 1970s, jazz singers expanded their role again. In concert, Bobby McFerrin can sound like an orchestra all by himself. And singers such as Betty Carter and Urszula Dudziak take their voices into even more exotic places, scatting like crazy, but also adding all sorts of unusual vocal sounds.

Generally, recordings made by singers are a good place for new jazz listeners to start. Lyrics add immediate impact, although some jazz vocalists use their voices as instruments and don't always sing in words.

Ida Cox (1896-1967)

Ida Cox is joined by Coleman Hawkins and other jazz notables on *Blues For Rampart Street* (Original Jazz Classics), which was recorded in 1961 but captures much of the raw power of her 1920 releases. Born in Toccoa, Georgia, Cox recorded off and on until a few years before her death in 1967. *Wild Women Don't Have the Blues* (Rosetta) is another strong collection, recorded in 1961.

Alberta Hunter (1895-1984)

Alberta Hunter sang great jazz and blues through six decades. Some of her earliest music is on the *Complete Recorded Works 1–4* series (Document), and she's also in fine form on *Amtrak Blues* (Sony) — one of several great recordings she made during a final prolific period.

Ma Rainey (1886-1939)

Blues-based singer Ma Rainey was backed by top players including Louis Armstrong and Coleman Hawkins, and her music can be caught on a few different CD re-issues of her 1920s recordings, as well as the more recent *Ma Rainey* (Milestone).

Jimmy Rushing (1903-1972)

Jimmy Rushing was Bessie Smith's male counterpart during the 1920s and 1930s. Born in Oklahoma City in 1903, Rushing sang with a style that is similar to Bessie Smith's earthy, blues-influenced soul, but he also took singing several measures in a jazz direction. He sang with Walter Page's Blue Devils and Bennie Moten's band during the 1920s and 1930s — adding vocals to these precursors of big band swing. More importantly, Rushing sang with Count Basie's band through the late '30s and early '40s, and his bluesy voice was a perfect fit with the Basie band's driving, rootsy brand of big band jazz. Check out *Essential Jimmy Rushing* (Vanguard) and Basie's *The Complete Decca Recordings* (GRP). Also look for *Swings The Blues* (Louisiana Red Hot Records), a digitally cleaned-up collection of recordings Rushing made between 1924 and 1930.

Bessie Smith (1894-1937)

"Downhearted Blues," Bessie Smith's first recording, made in New York in 1923, definitely has a blues feel, but it has elements of jazz, too. The connection to jazz becomes stronger when Smith is backed by top jazz players such as Louis Armstrong, whose elegant cornet improvisations support Smith's vocals on the classic "St. Louis Blues."

Numerous multi-CD sets of Smith's music are available, but a great place to begin is with *Bessie Smith: The Collection* (Columbia), a single CD that includes 16 of her best songs recorded between 1923 and 1933.

Elements of Smith's blues-influenced technique show up years later in the music of several jazz singers. Each time Smith repeats a musical phrase, it comes out slightly different than the time before, with different inflections, slightly different notes, and lyrics sung with different emphasis. She also bends notes and slides from one to another. And, of course, her music always has syncopation and swing.

Mamie Smith (1883-1946)

Usually thought of as a blues singer, Mamie Smith's 78 rpm record of "Crazy Blues" and "It's Right Here For You," recorded in 1920, sold two million copies(!) and opened the recording industry to black singers. Her best music from the 1920s is compiled in the series *Complete Recorded Works, Vols. 1-4* (Document).

Smith began her career as a vaudeville singer and dancer, but she also sang with several top-notch jazz players, including trumpeter Bubber Miley, saxophonist Coleman Hawkins, and band leader Lucky Millinder.

Sippie Wallace (1898-1986)

Texas-born Wallace was a blues singer who added her vocals to 1920s jazz in Chicago. Blurring the boundary between blues and jazz, she played and recorded with trumpeter Louis Armstrong, cornetist King Oliver, and pianist/band leader Clarence Williams. Wallace is an important figure in jazz for showing how singers could give jazz tunes a bluesy feel. Have a listen to *Complete Recorded Works, Vols. 1* and *2* (Document).

Sweet Depression-Era Singers

Perhaps when a country bottoms out emotionally, it needs glib, innocuous music to soothe its senses. Maybe that's why the late '20s and early '30s were marked with a crew of male and female crooners who offered a calming contrast to the raw, gut-wrenching jazz/blues of Bessie Smith and her contemporaries in the early 1920s.

Personally, I prefer a straight shot of mid-'20s blues/jazz to the fluffier stuff that followed, but Depression-era singers opened new emotional and musical territory to subsequent generations of jazz vocalists.

Connie Boswell (1907-1976)

Paralyzed by a childhood accident, Connie Boswell didn't let her wheelchair keep her voice from soaring. Some of the Boswell Sisters' music sounds a little sappy today, like something out of an old Shirley Temple movie. But their musicianship is impeccable.

All three sisters played instruments, and their vocal harmonies together are as delicate and intricate as a handmade quilt. If you want to impress your friends, casually let them know that the Boswells recorded a song called "Rock and Roll" in 1934, 20 years before Bill Haley and the Comets sang "Rock Around the Clock."

"Rock and Roll" and other vintage Boswell classics from the 1930s are included on the carefully annotated *That's How Rhythm Was Born* (Legacy/Sony), which includes their silky smooth versions of several Broadway show tunes, mostly recorded with the Dorsey Brothers Orchestra.

Bing Crosby (1904-1977)

Bing Crosby became a famous movie star, but he also had some legitimate jazz pipes. He wasn't an improviser or scat singer, but he swung his way through some great songs in front of big bands beginning during the 1920s with Paul Whiteman's orchestra.

The quantity of Crosby's music available today is major and ranges from his famous Christmas and Irish songs, to his best performances with big bands. Look for anything he did with Paul Whiteman, Duke Ellington, Jimmy Dorsey, and Louis Jordan. He may not have the vocal chops of a Jon Hendricks or Betty Carter, but it's tough to beat Crosby for a warm, emotional touch.

Annette Hanshaw (1910-1985)

Annette Hanshaw was one of the first singers of her era to reach a wide audience via the new medium of radio. Among her peers, Hanshaw had the hardiest jazz ties, recording with both Tommy and Jimmy Dorsey, trombonists Jack Teagarden and Miff Mole, guitarist Eddie Lang, and many other top players. Amazingly, Hanshaw made all her important music by 1934, when she dropped out of jazz at the age of 23. Her best music is available now on CD.

The Girl Next Door (Rounder) includes some of Hanshaw's best singing between 1927 and 1932. You may also want to pick up *Lovable & Sweet* (ASV/Living Era) and *Twenties Sweetheart* (Jasmine).

Ethel Waters (1896-1977)

Acclaimed as a blues singer during the early 1920s, Ethel Waters went on to broader success singing jazz and popular music and starring in Broadway musicals. Her finest vocal recordings beginning in 1921 are included on a series of CDs on the Classics label. Jazz players backing her on these sessions include pianists Fats Waller and James P. Johnson, clarinetist Benny Goodman, Duke Ellington's orchestra, and Jimmy (clarinet and sax) and Tommy (trombone) Dorsey.

Waters sings a light, lyrical antithesis of early blues on *Ethel Waters* (Laserlight), backed by husband Eddie Mallory's band, Benny Goodman's orchestra, Duke Ellington, and other jazz giants.

Golden Years of Swing and Songwriting

Great songwriters of the 1930s and 1940s such as George and Ira Gershwin, Cole Porter, Harold Arlen, Richard Rodgers and Lorenz Hart, Jerome Kern, and Johnny Mercer guided jazz singers in a lighter direction, and the singers connected with a broader audience. Never before had there been so many great singers and so many great songs.

As composers created a songbook of American classics, singers became interpreters of catchy lyrics and great melodies that have become staples of the basic jazz repertoire. For most of these singers, the jazz notion of improvisation came more in the realm of *interpretation* of a song rather than some kind of abstract invention, placing their personal signature on each tune with each special voice and personal phrasing.

In front of the big bands of the 1930s and 1940s — the swing era — singers scaled new heights of popularity and creativity. Whereas singers had sung an occasional number with jazz ensembles of the late 1920s, during the swing era, several bands were built around singers, in the same way that great band leaders such as Duke Ellington and Count Basie composed and arranged music for their best soloists.

Billie Holiday (1915-1959)

Although the swing era had dozens of great singers, for my money, Billie Holiday outsang them all. She wasn't the most technically adept, but the raw emotions of her difficult life charged her music with electrifying power.

Whereas Bessie Smith and other early jazz singers were rooted in blues, and subsequent singers of the early 1930s took a lighter, lyrical approach, Billie Holiday was the ultimate combination of swinging, blues-influenced power and delicate, ethereal sound. She both stretched and condensed the tune's phrasing to suit the moment, to suit her feeling.

A child of a troubled family who later became a teenage prostitute, Billie Holiday found her calling when producer John Hammond found her singing in a Harlem club and eventually teamed her with pianist/band leader Teddy Wilson. Wilson, trumpeter Buck Clayton, and saxophonist Lester Young were among Holiday's natural soulmates. Her voice made an especially good match with Young's lush, lyrical tenor sax.

Some of Holiday's best performances are from the 1930s, when she wrote "Strange Fruit," a sad commentary on Southern lynchings — "strange fruit" being the hanging bodies of murdered African Americans. She also made many fine recordings during the 1940s, generally in lighter, more luxuriously produced sessions featuring strings, backup vocalists, and more elaborate arrangements. In the end, almost every Holiday album is worth owning — even her final recordings from the late 1950s, when her ravaged voice packed a tremendous emotional whollop.

The CD boom has brought elaborately packaged multi-CD sets of Holiday's music, but a good affordable primer to her music is *Billie Holiday's Greatest Hits* (Decca), including several of her signature songs from the 1940s. Also excellent is the multi-volume *Quintessential Billie Holiday* (Columbia) series, which thoroughly documents her singing from 1936 to 1942.

Helen Forrest

I'm head over heels in love with Helen Forrest's voice. She has an innocence and emotional transparency that is irresistible. Smooth and swinging, Forrest combines the rhythmic hipness of the great jazz/blues women of the 1920s with a soft, warm sound reminiscent of Billie Holiday with the rawness removed. In fact, Forrest replaced Holiday in Artie Shaw's band, and also sang with big bands led by Benny Goodman and Harry James. In all three bands, the arrangements of love songs such as "All The Things You Are," "I've Heard That Song Before," and "Do I Love You" put Forrest in the front, reminding me of soft velvet linings that showcase her diamond of a voice.

Other key big band swing singers

Big band swing boomed during the 1930s and early 1940s, and most of the top big bands included singers. Swing reached a mass audience via radio and records, and singers provided an immediate human connection to the music for many listeners. While many of the great big band vocalists were not improvisers, they had distinctive voices and strong abilities to interpret the era's great songs, many of which eventually became jazz standards.

Ivie Anderson (1905-1949)

Ivie Anderson is best known as a prominent member of Duke Ellington's orchestra beginning in 1931. Signature songs for Anderson included "Stormy Weather" and "It Don't Mean a Thing." Anderson was both a great interpreter of popular songs, and an inventive jazz improviser. Some of her best singing is on *Ivie Anderson (1932–42)* (Best of Jazz).

Mildred Bailey (1907-1951)

With Paul Whiteman's band, with husband Red Norvo (the vibraphonist), and often on radio, Mildred Bailey had a delicate voice and a solid sense of swing. Following early hits with "Rockin' Chair" and "Georgia On My Mind," Bailey recorded with the bands of Benny Goodman, Ellis Larkins, and Teddy

Wilson until the mid-'40s. Many of her best performances were for Columbia (now Sony), but albums on other labels have also been re-released on CD. These include *American Legends Vol. 4* (Laserlight) and *Forgotten Lady* (Jazz Archives).

Doris Day (born 1924)

Think of Doris Day and you probably think of movies she made with Rock Hudson. But before that, Day was a formidable vocalist — for a brief time with Bob Crosby, and then with Les Brown. Compared with Helen Forrest, Day's voice is clear and sweet but slightly sandpapery.

Day gives each word a subtle emotional spin, and each line dissolves into her delicate vibrato. Don't miss the CD *Doris Day with Les Brown* (Columbia), a 16-song testimonial to this other Doris Day. The band swings, the arrangements on songs including "I'll Always Be With You" and "The Last Time I Saw You" are crafted carefully and beautifully around Day.

Billy Eckstine (1914-1993)

Deep and drowsy, Billy Eckstine's wavery baritone is charming in a big way. Perhaps because of his sizeable reputation as a band leader, Eckstine's prowess as a jazz singer goes under-appreciated. His rich tone and smooth sense of romance remind me of saxophonist Ben Webster's ways with a ballad.

Everything I Have Is Yours (Verve) catches Eckstine during the late '40s and early 1950s singing a portfolio of great songs, at a time when the swing era had given way to what some called the *sing era* — great singers singing great pop songs. On this recording, several songs feature Eckstine with Woody Herman's band; on other numbers, he's joined by understated pianist George Shearing's group, and by Sarah Vaughan and the Metronome All Stars.

Slim Gaillard (1916-1991)

One half of the famous Slim and Slam duo, Slim Gaillard played a mean guitar and had a warm, light-hearted vocal style. He sang wildly funny songs like "Flatfoot Floogie," "Laughin' In Rhythm," and "Serenade to a Poodle," but he was also a serious jazz musician. Some of his best music is on *Slim & Slam* (Affinity).

Judy Garland (1922-1969)

Shortly after she visited Oz, still in her early teens, Judy Garland recorded several tunes backed by a full orchestra, and 22 of them are on *The Young Judy Garland* (ASV). Garland's "Embraceable You" is a medium-tempo tear-jerker, as she wrings extra emotion from it by sliding from phrase to phrase and singing slightly behind the beat. Other songs, such as a stiff, clunky "Stompin' at The Savoy" with Bob Crosby's band, don't work so well, but you need to have some Garland in your collection of swing-era vocalists.

Louis Prima (1911-1978)

Louis Prima's high, hoarse voice swings through 16 songs on *The Best of Louis Prima* (Summit). Sailing lightly above the orchestra, Prima dips and soars in quirky flight patterns that bring a Louis Armstrong-like charm to standard songs such as "Stardust," as well as several Prima originals. Prima is almost as much vaudeville and theater as he is jazz, but his music has warm appeal, and it swings like crazy. Made in 1934 and 1935, these recordings also feature top players such as trombonist George Brunis and guitarist George Van Eps.

Maxine Sullivan (1911-1987)

Married to bandleader John Kirby in 1938, Maxine Sullivan recorded some of her best music with his band. She also made great music during the 1950s, especially with former members of Kirby's band such as trumpeter Charlie Shavers and clarinetist Buster Bailey, and even into the 1960s, 1970s, and 1980s (she died in 1987). Sullivan's gentle, lilting voice, with its faintly wavering vibrato, was the perfect instrument for beautiful ballads.

Sullivan was especially good at singing Kirby's jazzified versions of traditional songs such as "Loch Lomond," "Red River Valley," and "Molly Malone" ("Cockles and mussels, alive, alive-o"). Typical of top jazz singers, Sullivan had a narrow vocal range, but infused her songs with wonderful depths of sweet and sad emotion. Check out *Maxine Sullivan/1937–38* (Classics) and *Maxine Sullivan/1938–41* (Classics).

Singers Go Bebopping

The evolution of jazz singing matched the music's overall development: from the blues-steeped 1920s through the sweet-but-naive early '30s, into 1930s and 1940s swing. When Dizzy Gillespie, Charlie "Yardbird" Parker and other rising jazz giants were playing speedy bebop during the mid-'40s, they set the stage for a freer approach to jazz singing. Legendary singers such as Ella Fitzgerald and Sarah Vaughan matured with bebop, making music that utilized its more complex chord changes and fast, quirky melodies — and scat-singing over bops breakneck tempos.

The advent of the $33^1/_3$ rpm long-play record further freed jazz musicians by allowing them to stretch songs to longer lengths than the old 3-minute 78 rpm format. Finally, the extended improvisations that had previously been available to listeners only in live settings could be captured in a studio.

Like the instrumentalists, vocalists in the bebop scene didn't sing a song the same way twice, and they didn't sing the same musical passage the same way twice within a single performance of a song. They stretched single words over several notes, improvised strings of notes as sounds without words, and "traded licks" with fellow players.

Ella Fitzgerald (1917-1996)

Born in 1917, Ella Fitzgerald was discovered by a buddy of bandleader and drummer Chick Webb when she took top honors in a singing contest at Harlem's Apollo Theatre. Under Webb's guidance, she became a queen of swing during the songwriting boom of the 1930s. Thanks to a career that eventually stretched into the 1980s, she was also in prime position to draw inspiration from the 1940s beboppers. (See Figure 10-1.)

Ella Fitzgerald had a 1938 hit with "A-Tisket, A-Tasket," as part of Chick Webb's ensemble, and she recorded several other vintage swing tunes with the group. When the diminutive drummer passed away in 1939, Fitzgerald stayed on to lead his ensemble through two more years. Her earliest vocals have an innocent, sweet charm that sometimes goes overboard into childish cuteness. But as she grew out of the cuteness in later years, it was this same sweetness that helped her connect with both jazz fans and a broader mainstream audience. Most of the songs she sang between 1935 and 1941 are available on the Classics label: several CDs, dozens of songs.

By the early 1940s, Fitzgerald used her voice as a true jazz instrument. She toured with Dizzy Gillespie's big band during the mid-'40s and added bebop-inspired scat solos to her performances. Unlike earlier swing singers, Ella

Figure 10-1:
Ella
Fitzgerald
(photo:
Everett
Collection).

made a marked move from gifted interpreter to true virtuoso. She was a creative improviser who traded licks on a level with fellow musicians and placed her personal imprint on a song with an impressive array of skills.

The War Years (GRP/Decca) catches Ella Fitzgerald in transition between 1941 and 1946. Material ranges from standards to more progressive jazz tunes, and she sings in various small groups that give her plenty of room to move and groove. Recordings for Verve and Decca during the late '40s and '50s document her golden years. Beginning in 1956 for Decca, she recorded dozens of great songs by top songwriters including Irving Berlin, Cole Porter, Richard Rodgers and Loren Hart, Harold Arlen, Jerome Kern, George and Ira Gershwin, and Johnny Mercer. Her energy level is mellower, but her sound is subtler, and she brings emotional depth to beautiful and romantic lyrics.

Ella Fitzgerald died in 1996, and she left a vast catalog of great recordings spanning six decades. By the mid-'70s, she was still in fine form, although her abilities tapered during the 1980s. Visit your local music store. Let instinct guide you. Anything on the Classics, Decca, and Verve labels is more than decent, and much of her later music on Pablo is also strong.

Eddie Jefferson (1918-1979)

In 1949, Jefferson put words to "Parker's Mood" and showed how a singer could handle a jazz song with the same musical nuances as any other instrumentalist. Jefferson was an innovator in vocal improvisation. During solo sections, he experimented freely with all sorts of sounds in a non-verbal style that became known as *vocalese*. Jefferson also penned lyrics for the song "Moody's Mood for Love," eventually recording with saxophonist James Moody, and Jefferson also collaborated over the years with top jazz players including saxophonists Coleman Hawkins and Richie Cole. Check out Jefferson's *Letter from Home* (Original Jazz Classics) and *Body and Soul* (Original Jazz Classics).

King Pleasure (1922-1981)

Pleasure had hits with "Moody's Mood for Love" and "Parker's Mood," and he developed his own version of vocalese around the same time as Jefferson — during the early '50s. Like Jefferson and other inventive jazz singers, Pleasure used his voice as a versatile instrument when he played with leading jazz instrumentalists such as saxophonists Teddy Edwards and Harold Land. Get your hands on *King Pleasure Sings with Annie Ross* (Original Jazz Classics) and *Moody's Mood for Love* (EMD/Blue Note).

Sarah Vaughan (1924-1990)

Sarah Vaughan has the jazz singer's essential gifts in abundance: a fine voice with a phenomenal range, and the ability to spark a song's lyrics to life with her personal emotional stamp. Her voice rivaled the voices of the world's finest singers, even in opera. It spanned more than four octaves and was capable of infinite subtleties.

Born in Newark, New Jersey, Vaughan joined pianist Earl Hines's band in 1943. She first recorded with Billy Eckstine's group in 1944 (alongside Charlie Parker and Dizzy Gillespie), quickly establishing herself as a premier vocalist. She worked magic with the era's catchy popular songs, but she also swung alongside horns, drums, basses, and pianos on the hippest bebop numbers.

Sarah Vaughan really lifted jazz vocal expression to new heights. Her use of improvisation went beyond just interpreting melodies and lyrics, like the swing-era singers before her did. She ventured into genuine spontaneous solos, as well as different deliveries of a song each time and variations on its melody and chords. Her playful twists emphasize a song's lyrics, and her *scat* singing (wordless improvisation) is fantastic — she easily swaps lines with leading instrumentalists.

Vaughan also developed a recognizable sound all her own. Her throaty, smoky low end covers a tenor sax's territory, but she also handles high passages with silky sophistication. When you listen to her in small group settings, notice how her voice is at home keeping company with a range of instruments, from bass on up to trumpet and high-pitched flute. And in keeping with her expressiveness, she makes subtle use of *dynamics* (changes in volume) and *space* (best defined as the number of instruments playing at once, which can serve to emphasize or de-emphasize her voice).

Like fellow musicians who came of age during bebop's infancy, Vaughan explored new combinations of notes and chords. She placed freshly improvised vocal lines over old chord changes. Compared with the swing singers of the 1930s and early '40s, Vaughan is light-years ahead in musical sophistication.

Sarah Vaughan (EmArcy) is only one of many great CDs capturing her career. Recorded in 1954, this set captures much of what makes this lady a legend among jazz fanatics. Joined by stellar sidemen such as saxophonist Paul Quinichette, trumpeter Clifford Brown, flutist Herbie Mann, and drummer Roy Haynes, Vaughan delivers gorgeous versions of nine songs, including what must rank among the finest performances of the standards "Embraceable You," and "April in Paris."

Divine Sarah (Mercury) from 1946–47 includes early versions of "Body and Soul" and "Tenderly," her first hit song. *Columbia Years 1949–1953* (Columbia) covers more great tunes, from Fats Waller's "Ain't Misbehavin'" to "Black Coffee," with saxophonist Budd Johnson and trumpeter Miles Davis along for the ride. *Complete Sarah Vaughan on Mercury, Vol. 1* (Mercury) has some of her best mid-'50s music, with both small groups (including trumpeter Clifford Brown) and big bands.

Sarah Vaughan/This Is Jazz 20 (Columbia/Legacy) is an excellent collection containing mostly music she made in 1949 and 1950, but also tunes she recorded during the 1970s and 1980s. In later years, her voice retained most of its original pliability and beautiful tone. In addition to great jazz standards, this CD also has Vaughan swaying through a couple of romantic Brazilian tunes. And her soaring, spectacularly wavering improvised finale to "My Man's Gone Now" could have come from one of the world's great opera stages.

Vaughan's recording career stretched into the 1980s (she died in 1990), and most of her albums rank among the best-ever jazz vocal recordings. Of course, Vaughan's vintage years (1940s and 1950s) are also thoroughly documented by many beautiful boxed CD sets (mostly on Mercury) that include detailed texts about her music. Her later recordings from the 1970s and 1980s (on Pablo) are equally fine, displaying a seasoned singer with a voice aging as elegantly as the finest wine.

Eclectic 1950s

Instrumental jazz splintered during the 1950s — see Chapter 4 for the details. Hard bop was the hippest 1950s jazz: dark, urban, brooding. But it mostly appealed to instrumentalists, and singers didn't follow that line much. Instead, they continued to swing, or they built upon the freeform improvising skills inspired by Charlie Parker, Dizzy Gillespie, and other 1940s beboppers.

Jon Hendricks (born 1921)

Among jazz singers who came on the scene during the Eisenhower years, Jon Hendricks is perhaps the most gifted and under-appreciated. As part of the vocal trio Lambert, Hendricks & Ross, he helped advance the art of jazz vocals into the space age. The group's nimble, complex harmonies and swinging rhythms have, in my opinion, never been topped. And the trio's hip bebop interpretations of all sorts of popular songs inspired dozens of singers to follow, including Al Jarreau, Bobby McFerrin, The Manhattan Transfer, and even Bette Midler.

Hendricks was born in Newark, Ohio, in 1921. By the time I found out about him, he was teaching jazz at the University of California at Berkeley and playing the lead in *Evolution of the Blues,* a theatrical history of African American music. Teamed with Dave Lambert and Annie Ross, Hendricks spearheaded the trio's vocal versions of Count Basie's music. Together, they created an orchestra of sound, only without the orchestra.

The trio recorded into the early 1960s; Hendricks kept going into the 1990s. Hendricks sings like a saxophone player — he improvises fresh melodies, adds unexpected sounds, and never sings a song the same way twice. He is also a lyricist who has put words to great jazz including Basie's. If you're into vocals, you must have at least one album by the trio or Hendricks solo — preferably a few.

From the threesome, try *Sing a Song of Basie* (GRP/Impulse!) and *Lambert, Hendricks & Ross* (Columbia). From the solo Hendricks, look for *Freddie Freeloader* (Denon), with Bobby McFerrin, Al Jarreau, George Benson, and Manhattan Transfer; and *Boppin' at The Blue Note* (Telarc), with a host of guests including Wynton Marsalis, Benny Golson, and Red Holloway.

Other jazz singers from the late 1940s and 1950s

Many other singers found their own niche in and among the vibrant and splintering jazz scene of the late 1940s and 1950s. This era was a time when a definite vocal style that could be comfortably called mainstream wasn't firmly in place as in years before, and as a result, singers, like the instrumentalists of the time, sought to define their own styles.

Chet Baker (1929-1988)

Best known as a trumpeter, Chet Baker was also a singer with a pure emotional power that defied his limited vocal range. Baker's tortured, whispery voice gives a ragged, heart-rending edge to great tunes such as "My Funny Valentine" and "Time After Time." Check out *The Best of Chet Baker Sings: Let's Get Lost* (Capitol/Pacific Jazz).

June Christy (1925-1990)

Succeeding Anita O'Day in Stan Kenton's orchestra, June Christy sang her way into the 1950s with a gentle sound synonymous with the cool style prevalent on the West Coast during those years. Start with her *Something Cool* (Capitol) album.

Nat King Cole (1919-1965)

I'm in love with his music. Nat King Cole shapes lyrics like a woodsmith sanding a delicate carving of a songbird. With his clear enunciation and irresistible charm, Cole found his way to the hearts of an ethnic rainbow audience. He was the first black singer to host his own TV program, was an amazing pianist, and has more than two dozen albums to his credit. Born in Montgomery, Alabama, he grew up in Chicago and launched his career in Los Angeles in the 1940s. For simplicity and elegance, try *The Trio Recordings* (Laserlight).

Dizzy Gillespie (1917-1993)

Famous as a trumpeter, Gillespie could also scat like crazy, often with a sense of humor as big as his trademark puffed-out cheeks. Some of his spunky vocals are included on the album *Dee Gee Days* (Savoy).

Peggy Lee (born 1920)

An early '40s hit singer with Benny Goodman, Peggy Lee scored 1950s pop-jazz hits with "Black Coffee," "Fever," and other tunes. Take a sip of *Black Coffee* (MCA/Decca), an album recorded during the mid-'50s that includes Lee's duet with Bing Crosby.

Carmen McRae (1920-1994)

Launching her career with Benny Carter's big band during the 1940s, Carmen McRae grew into a first-rate jazz singer who wrings subtle nuances of meaning from lyrics with her versions of great songs. "Here to Stay" (GRP) represents vintage 1950's McRae, *The Great American Songbook* (Atlantic) and *Carmen Sings Monk* (Novus) are a couple of more recent gems.

Helen Merrill (born 1930)

Helen Merrill bebopped alongside saxman Charlie Parker and pianist Bud Powell before launching a solo career that began during the 1950s and extended into the 1990s. Classics include *Helen Merrill with Clifford Brown* (EmArcy), *You've Got a Date With The Blues* (Verve), and *Collaboration* (EmArcy), with arrangements by Gil Evans.

Anita O'Day (born 1913)

Man, can this woman sing. Drummer Gene Krupa was first to find out, and when she joined his band for two years beginning in 1941, she developed a special chemistry with the resident trumpeter of Krupa's band: Roy Eldridge. O'Day went on to Woody Herman's big band before going solo and making several fine albums of her own during the 1950s, 1960s, and 1970s. You know a singer is hot when she can give a fresh twist to timeworn standards such as "Honeysuckle Rose," "A Nightingale Sang in Berkeley Square," "I Can't Get Started," and "Time After Time," as she does on *This Is Anita O'Day* (Verve).

Dinah Washington (1924-1963)

Grounded in gospel, Alabama-born Dinah Washington's jazz singing mixes loose, blues-tinged swing with a high, clear tone, and a special way with lyrics. She honed her sound in vibraphonist Lionel Hampton's band during the mid-'40s and eventually traded licks with trumpeters Clark Terry and Clifford Brown, and other jazz giants. Catch Washington's prime 1940s and 1950s recordings for Mercury, re-released on several CDs. Check out *Dinah '63* (EMD/Blue Note), *Dinah and Clifford* (Jazz Hour), and *Dinah in the Land of Hi-Fi* (PGD/Verve).

Frank Sinatra (1915-1998)

Frank Sinatra was vermicelli-thin when he stepped in front of Tommy Dorsey's band in 1940 and began working his magic. For many Americans, Sinatra was synonymous with the 1950s and 1960s. His singing, a combination of regret, nostalgia, warmth, and optimism, captured the mood of an era of economic prosperity and space exploration, as well as the threats of atomic warfare and communism.

Sinatra exemplified the soul-over-sensational school of jazz singing, which places emotional impact above technique. Within his limited, mellow vocal range, Sinatra put genuine heart into melodies and lyrics, and you could feel deep degrees of sadness, loss, loneliness, and hope in his songs. Sinatra wasn't big on improvisation, but to me, what made him a jazz singer was the many subtle emotional and musical shadings he brought to a tune.

Nearly all Sinatra's albums from the 1950s are top-drawer, but I'm especially fond of his 1957 *Come Fly with Me* (Capitol). Although much of this music is available on CD, you should track down a few albums on vinyl, if only to hang their great covers on your wall.

From among later Sinatra albums, try *Sinatra/Basie* (Reprise), *Francis Albert Sinatra and Antonio Carlos Jobim* (Reprise), *Francis A. Sinatra & Edward K. Ellington* (Reprise), as well as numerous boxed CD re-issue sets that began hitting stores in the late 1980s.

Brazilian Flavors

Combining elements of jazz with South American flavors, Brazilian singers are among my favorite all-time jazz musicians. Latin rhythms make the music interesting and engaging; a Brazilian sense of romance and optimism comes through the music. Some of my favorite Brazilian singers are:

✔ **Astrud Gilberto (born 1940).** She helped launch the early 1960s Brazilian craze for the rest of the world with the song "Girl From Ipanema" and recorded several albums of great music.

✔ **Joao Gilberto (born 1932).** Former husband of Astrud Gilberto, he and she played with U.S. saxman Stan Getz during the early 1960s and helped spread Brazilian bossa nova to the United States and beyond. Gilberto's voice, songwriting, and guitar are warm and sunny and perfect for spring mornings.

✔ **Antonio Carlos Jobim (1927–1994).** Good singer, great songwriter. Among his hits are "Desafinado," "Girl From Ipanema," and "Wave."

✔ **Milton Nascimento (born 1942).** Jazz is only one of Nascimento's many flavors, but for pure spirit, he's well worth a listen.

Other Brazilian singers worthy of your ears: Dori Caymmi, Gilberto Gil, Joao Bosco, Elis Regina, and Gal Costa.

Into the Modern Era

During the 1960s, while progressive new styles of instrumental jazz developed, vocalists mostly refined the art of singing a great song — adding subtleties of interpretation, as well as a variety of improvisational styles. This trend continues today, with up-and-coming singers such as Dianne Reeves, Kurt Elling, and Diana Krall working to refine their deliveries of great songs within a fairly traditional musical context.

Fringe dwellers and others

These singers, though still staying closer to tradition than their instrumental contemporaries, all experimented with going *out there* a bit. Their adventurous styles are all worth a listen.

Betty Carter (born 1930)

Probably the most awe-inspiring and far-out improviser among living female jazz singers, Betty Carter uses a song as a framework for soaring scat-singing that often leaves a familiar melody far behind. She's a powerhouse live, as you can hear on *At the Village Vanguard* (Verve), a great 1970 performance that includes her version of "Body and Soul." Also catch *The Carmen McRae/Betty Carter Duets* (Verve).

Urszula Dudziak (born 1943)

Urszula Dudziak, a Polish-born singer, made some of the most innovative vocal music during the 1970s, captured on a few recordings including *Urszula* (Arista). Along with Flora Purim, she utilized raw shrieks and cries straight out of the wilds to add emotional electricity to her songs.

Abbey Lincoln (born 1930)

Feeling a song deeply, Abbey Lincoln has done great things with lyrics and melodies, from the 1950s into the 1990s. Her 1961 *Straight Ahead* (Candid) is highly recommended — it has plenty of great singing and features sidemen such as saxophonists Coleman Hawkins and Eric Dolphy.

Flora Purim (born 1942)

With her husband, percussionist Airto Moreira, as well as keyboard player Chick Corea, Flora Purim sang some of the best Brazilian jazz of the 1970s, on albums under Corea and Moreira's names. The title track from her own *500 Miles High* is guaranteed to launch you into orbit, with Purim's voice soaring over the instruments.

More in the mainstream

Staying closer to home, and truer to the melodies of the songs they perform, the singers in the following sections tend to emphasize the traditions of interpretation and subtle improvisation in their styles.

Mose Allison (born 1927)

Not the most naturally gifted of jazz singers, Mose Allison has nonetheless moseyed to the top of the jazz heap with his laid-back drawl, dry sense of humor, and quirky piano solos. He's the epitome of 1950s cool, still moving ahead in the 1990s. *Greatest Hits* (Original Jazz Classics) makes a great first venture into Mose-land.

Shirley Horn (born 1934)

Born in 1930, Shirley Horn did some of her best singing during the 1980s. In between sensitive interpretations of great jazz songs, Horn adds inventive piano solos. Try *Close Enough For Love* (Verve), as well as her other albums on Verve.

Mel Torme (born 1925)

Famous as "The Velvet Fog," Mel Torme is a perfectionist whose soothing voice brings new meaning to jazz's great songs. (See Figure 10-2.) He sang with Artie Shaw's band, and is also a published novelist. Torme recorded a couple of dozen great albums, all worth owning. For starters, try *Fujitsu-Concord Festival* (Concord), a 1990 recording that finds him in peak form.

Nancy Wilson (born 1937)

I love lesser-known heroes, and Nancy Wilson is a *monster* (that's a good thing in jazz circles). Soft or strong, depending on the mood, her voice is a sweetly expressive instrument that she uses for major impact on albums including the fine 1961 *Nancy Wilson/Cannonball Adderley* (Capitol).

Voices for the Future

Wynton Marsalis spearheaded a traditional jazz revival during the 1980s, as the so-called *Young Lions* came on the scene playing unplugged, serious jazz in the manner of heroes such as Charlie Parker, Miles Davis, Dexter Gordon, and Art Blakey. In the 1990s, a similar movement is picking up speed with a new generation of jazz singers. Like the great big band singers of the late '30s and early '40s, the new crew is going for great songs sung with great emotion and distinctive style rather than far-out improvisation.

Figure 10-2:
Mel Torme
(photo:
Everett
Collection).

Here are a few more names that belong, eventually, in your collection:

- ✔ **Karrin Allyson.**
- ✔ **Kurt Elling (born 1967).**
- ✔ **Nnenna Freelon.**
- ✔ **Diana Krall.**
- ✔ **Kevin Mahogany (born 1958).**
- ✔ **Kitty Margolis (born 1955).**
- ✔ **Dianne Reeves (born 1956).**
- ✔ **Dennis Rowland.**
- ✔ **Cassandra Wilson (born 1955).**

Part III
Keyboards

In this part . . .

In Part III, I take you through the history of jazz piano and the various styles of great jazz pianists. Check out the early jazz piano of Scott Joplin's Ragtime and the Swing of Jelly Roll Morton. Discover other great jazz pianists like Duke Ellington and Thelonious Monk, who added their own distinctive sound to jazz music. You can also find out about cool jazz piano and the Latin connections as well as current piano greats like Keith Jarret and Herbie Hancock.

This part also includes some basic organ information. Find out how this instrument evolved from being played only in church to bringing a soulful and sexy sound to jazz. And of course you can read about the great early jazz organists like Count Basie to current greats like Lonnie Smith.

Chapter 11

Piano and Other Keyboards: Black and White Keys to Jazz

· ·

In This Chapter

▶ The role of the piano in jazz

▶ "Maple Leaf Rag" and other early jazz piano

▶ The formative swing years

▶ Bebop pianists

▶ Pianists with polish

▶ Electric keyboards

▶ Current players who keep the future bright

· ·

Sit back and listen. A right hand flits through melodies and sparkling improvisations, while a left pumps out chords and bass note patterns, adding deep-voiced harmonies and occasional melodies. Together, two hands create a symphonic array of sounds. Piano is the most versatile of jazz instruments — a veritable orchestra of possibilities.

Under the hands of players such as Scott Joplin, Jelly Roll Morton, and Fats Waller, piano was also one of jazz's founding instruments. Due to its delicate sound, it had trouble standing out as an improvising voice in large ensembles. But with the advent of small jazz groups during the 1920s and 1930s, the piano took a higher profile.

A few years later, Bud Powell and Thelonious Monk were prominent pianists in bebop in the 1940s. During the 1950s, Bill Evans, Dave Brubeck, Ahmad Jamal, and other ebony and ivory men and women played a more laid-back style called *cool*.

Cecil Taylor, Horace Tapscott, and Don Pullen teetered on the brink of chaos, keeping pace with the 1960s *avant garde*. And in the 1970s, Herbie Hancock and Chick Corea plugged in synthesizers and electric pianos as Miles Davis and assorted boundary-breakers took jazz in new electrifying directions.

Piano — the ultimate solo

Through the history of jazz, pianists pushed ahead alongside their peers on other instruments as the music moved into new phases. But for me, given the piano's delicate, lyrical sound, the ultimate jazz piano music is solo — when a player takes his art to the all-encompassing limit, filling all the roles traditionally filled by four or five musicians in a group.

The Rise of Ragtime: "Maple Leaf Rag" And Other Early Jazz Piano

As I explain in Chapter 2, ragtime isn't even considered jazz by some musical historians; to others, ragtime is but one facet of the overall genre. Either way, no one can deny that ragtime piano is important enough to jazz to be part of any discussion of jazz piano.

Scott Joplin (1868-1917)

Born in Texarkana, Texas, Scott Joplin came of age as a musician in St. Louis, and later in Sedalia, Missouri. He was a composer who drew from many sources and wrote both jazz pieces and ragtime operas including

Treemonisha. His music spills over from jazz into various categories and shows the connection between early jazz and the methodical structure of classical music. My local music superstore even keeps most of Joplin's CDs in its "Classical" section.

Joplin's "Maple Leaf Rag," written during the 1890s and preserved today through recordings of player piano rolls that he made, is the song most people think of when they imagine the earliest jazz, though he also wrote several other rags. Driving chords and bass notes blend with a light, swinging melody to give this piece its jazz flavor.

Ragtime is what Joplin's music was called, and it's a good name, because the "time," or beat, is ragged. While Joplin's left hand keeps a steady pace, his right hand sometimes strays from the beat while playing melodies to give it its signature sound. You can hear accents placed in unusual places, instead of on the beat — a technique known as *syncopation,* and a common characteristic of jazz, as I cover in Chapter 1.

Although Joplin was never recorded, pianists including Dick Hyman (who has also recorded the piano music of James P. Johnson, Jelly Roll Morton, and Fats Waller) have released their versions of his music. While these are subjective interpretations as far as tempos and dynamics are concerned, they offer a more realistic idea than mechanical player piano rolls of what Joplin's music really sounded like.

Joplin's pieces are composed all the way through, with room for interpretation on the part of the pianist, but not any significant improvisation. Joplin's rags qualify as an early form of jazz more because of their loose, rolling rhythms.

"He wasn't improvising at all," says pianist Dick Hyman, who coordinates jazz for Woody Allen's movies, and who has recorded the music of several jazz pianists, including Joplin and Morton. "But matters of interpretation are something every pianist thinks about. Joplin's tempos have one familiar aspect. On a great many pieces he wrote 'not too fast,' and on others, 'slow march tempo.' This is very inexact, but the only thing one could gather is that even in his time, people were beginning to play various rags too fast for his taste. My own performance of 'Maple Leaf Rag' is perhaps faster than he would have played it, but at a tempo that I prefer. Composers don't always know the best pace for their music."

Hyman's *Scott Joplin: Piano Works 1899–1904* (RCA) offers an excellent introduction to Joplin's music, as interpreted by an excellent player. *The Elite Syncopations* (Biograph) album captures Joplin himself on recordings made from player piano rolls.

James P. Johnson (1894-1955)

Joplin's ragtime had a different flavor from the music that pianist James P. Johnson wrote and recorded during the mid-'20s. Best known for composing "The Charleston," Johnson, like Joplin, was a songsmith with big ambitions who penned musicals such as *Running Wild* (which introduced "The Charleston"), as well as large-scale works like "Harlem Symphony" and "Symphony in Brown."

Johnson's soulful, swinging piano style is rooted in blues: he backed vocalists Bessie Smith and Ethel Waters, and composed a blues opera. But Johnson is best known as a pianist in the rag-like style called *stride,* so called for the left hand's galloping strides between bass notes.

Compared with Joplin, Johnson was a major improviser, and he influenced pianists including Duke Ellington and Fats Waller. The CD *Running Wild/ 1921–1926* (Tradition) is a solid summation of Johnson's abilities both as composer and player.

Others from the early ivory front

When I was in college, I was lucky enough to hear Eubie Blake, one of jazz's early heroes. Blake died just after his 100th birthday in 1983, having seen the history of jazz practically from the start. Blake was slim and smiled while he played, and I can still see his long, slender fingers leaping large distances over the keys.

Joplin and Johnson were prominent pianists during jazz's formative years, while Blake made his living writing Broadway musicals. But by the late 1960s, as blues-based rock sparked renewed interest in early blues and jazz, Blake found himself touring the country as a living jazz legend who could bring the early music to life from personal experience.

Recorded in 1969, when Blake was a wee lad, *The 86 Years of Eubie Blake* (Columbia) is a sweet slice of vintage jazz.

Early jazz also has countless heroes whose music was never captured on recordings. Buddy Bolden's band, formed in New Orleans in 1895, is considered by many to be the first jazz band — yet they never recorded. Around the same time, ragtime pianist Tony Jackson played New Orleans bars and bordellos with such prominent peers as trumpeter Bunk Johnson, and later led a band of first-rate players including trumpeter Freddie Keppard and soprano sax/clarinet master Sidney Bechet. Jackson was also a songwriter whose tunes "Pretty Baby," "The Naked Dance," and "Michigan Water Blues" were put to vinyl during the 1930s by pianist Jelly Roll Morton, whose playing drew from Jackson's.

Formative Swing Years

Jazz legends always seem to have great nicknames, and Thomas Wright Waller and Ferdinand Joseph Lemott were among the first with fun nicknames.

Waller was a whale of a man, so it's obvious where "Fats" came from. During his early years, Lemott (also known as Morton) played in New Orleans bordellos. Like Fats, Ferdinand was a world-class womanizer (and a pool hustler and pimp) who apparently earned his nickname.

Given that all good jazz must swing with loose, steady rhythms and serve up fresh helpings of improvisation, Jelly Roll Morton and Fats Waller were the two pianists who pointed the way toward modern jazz piano.

Earl "Fatha" Hines (1903-1983)

Hines made his first recordings in 1928 and his last in 1978. He was a leading swing era player and band leader who recorded with trumpeter Roy Eldridge, drummer Elvin Jones, saxophonist Coleman Hawkins, and, late in his career, vibraphonist Lionel Hampton.

Listening to just a little of Hines's music, you can recapture the coming of age of jazz piano, in both ensemble and solo settings. Hines probably made more solo recordings than any pianist of his era, and these sessions are especially solid examples of the piano's growing role as one of jazz's most versatile improvising instruments.

Beginning in 1926, Hines was a member of Louis Armstrong's bands (including the legendary Hot Five in 1928), top groups with roots in the traditions of early New Orleans. In Hines's playing with these groups, you can hear the influence of early ragtime and stride pianists such as James P. Johnson and Jelly Roll Morton. But by the mid-'30s, on both his solo and group albums, Hines was already cultivating a much freer and inventive style.

For a broad sampling of Hines, get ahold of *An Introduction to Earl Hines* (Best of Jazz). This CD takes you from 1927 to 1942, from "Weary Blues" (with clarinetist Johnny Dodds' Black Bottom Stompers) to the dashing "The Earl" (with an orchestra) to Hines's fine solo version of the popular song, "On The Sunny Side Of The Street." On this last song, his playing runs from early ragtime — the rolling left-hand chords — to meandering, modern improvisations that use the song as a framework for various flights of fancy, including daring right-hand runs up and down the keys.

Other essential Hines recordings include *Earl Hines (1937–1939)* (Classics), *Indispensible Earl Hines, Vol. 1 and 2* (with his orchestra, on RCA), and *Spontaneous Explorations* (Contact) from 1964-1966. Also check out Hines's recordings of the music of Duke Ellington, Hoagy Carmichael, George Gershwin, and W.C. Handy, from the early 1970s.

Jelly Roll Morton (1890-1941)

Morton's bad boy image was completed by a diamond inlaid in one front tooth (pay your dues, Mick Jagger). He played ragtime with a swinging spirit, and he improvised more beginning in the mid-'20s than earlier pianists. He was also a consummate composer and bandleader; recordings he made in Chicago in 1926 and 1927 with his Red Hot Peppers practically sweat with swing.

Along with trumpeter Louis Armstrong, Morton had a very large impact on jazz during the 1920s. His bands included red hot players such as clarinetists Johnny Dodds, Omer Simeon, and Barney Bigard, as well as banjo/guitar man Johnny St. Cyr, trombonist Kid Ory, and drummer Baby Dodds — many of them cohorts of Armstrong too.

Several CDs capture Morton from the 1920s, but the essential discs in your quest for jazz enlightenment are the Library of Congress Recordings, made by historian Allan Lomax in 1938. These recordings include a mix of Morton talking about the early years of jazz and playing the early music. Now they're available in complete form for the first time: Four CDs from Rounder Records take the full measure of Morton's piano playing, as well as his re-creations of early New Orleans jazz and lascivious barroom tunes.

Also check out Morton's track "Thirty-fifth St. Blues," included on the *Jazz For Dummies* CD.

Fats Waller (1904-1943)

Fats Waller, a student of James P. Johnson, took jazz piano another step toward the modern era with his free and melodic improvisations. By the mid-'20s, Waller was a pianistic force in his own right, and by the early '30s, he had left a legacy of great jazz piano (and organ) solos and original compositions including "Honeysuckle Rose" and "Ain't Misbehavin'" (the title song from Waller's full-length musical). Waller also had charisma on the order of Louis Armstrong. Like Armstrong, he was a spirited singer and actor who played in movies including *King of Burlesque* and *Hooray For Love*.

He made hundreds of records with legends like Fletcher Henderson (whose band played several Waller tunes), Jack Teagarden, Clarence Williams, as well as blues diva Alberta Hunter.

Waller was more ambidextrous than Morton; he could do more inventive things with both hands at the same time. His version of "St. Louis Blues" from the double-CD *Turn On The Heat: The Fats Waller Piano Solos* (Bluebird) is a prime example. After stating the familiar melody once, Waller, who was limited to three minutes per song by the old 78 rpm record format, immediately begins improvising. Not only does his right hand — traditionally taking the melody and the more aggressive improvisation — invent ideas all around the melody and add light, delicate flourishes, but his left hand roams through several interesting improvisational accompaniments, ranging from big, chunky chords in the ragtime tradition to bass notes played in a hip tango rhythm.

Breakin' The Ice (Bluebird), a two-CD set of recordings from 1934 and 1935 by Waller and his six-piece band Rhythm, show this light but bright side of the man.

Other pioneers, from ragtime to swing

Though Waller and Morton were the most prominent, quite a few other pianists had a role in the move from ragtime to swing.

Count Basie (1904-1984)

The famous leader, gave piano a fresh twist in his big bands, holding back, adding a few tasteful flourishes to season his orchestras' rhythm section. Inspired by ragtime and stride pianists such as Fats Waller and James P. Johnson, Basie played piano in Walter Page's Blue Devils and Bennie Moten's big band before fronting his own jazz orchestra beginning in the mid-'30s. *Count Basie and the Kansas City 7* (MCA) catches Basie during the early 1960s in a small ensemble that leaves room for him to stretch out on piano. Other solid Basie piano: *Blues by Basie* (Sony), *Basie Jam Vol. 2* (Original Jazz Classics), *Kansas City 7* (Original Jazz Classics), and *88 Basie Street* (Original Jazz Classics).

Nat King Cole (1919-1965)

Famous during the 1950s as a pop singer and barrier-busting black TV show host, Cole was also a phenomenal pianist. His 1940s music is bebop-hip, and *Nat King Cole Meets the Master Saxes* (Spotlite) includes collaborations with jazz giants Lester Young and Dexter Gordon.

Dorothy Donegan (born 1924)

She didn't hit her stride on piano until the 1990s, when Chiaroscuro had the good sense to get this grandmotherly master into a studio for a series of recordings. Her style draws from jazz's earliest history — stride, boogie woogie, swing, bop, and her live performances came with vaudevillian antics for dramatic emphasis. Although her music didn't get attention until later in her life, Donegan was in two movies alongside bandleader Cab Calloway: *Sensations of 1945* and *Sensation Hunters.* Introduce yourself to her with *Explosive Dorothy Donegan* (Audiophile), *I Just Want to Sing* (Audiophile), and *Live at the 1992 Floating Jazz Festival* (Chiaroscuro).

Duke Ellington (1899-1974)

Best known as a bandleader and composer, Ellington was also a superb pianist — all alone, or in groups of various sizes and styles. Born in 1899, Ellington came of age as a ragtime/stride pianist and contemporary of James P. Johnson. Eventually, though, his playing evolved into the modern era to an extent that his jagged solos fit comfortably alongside *avant garde* saxophonist John Coltrane during the 1960s. For a sample of Ellington on ivories, check out *Piano Reflections* (Capitol), *The Pianist* (Original Jazz Classics), and *Duke Ellington & John Coltrane* (Uni/Impulse!).

Jay McShann (born 1916)

McShann was among the first band leaders to spot the raw talent of his fellow Kansas City jazzman saxophonist Charlie "Yardbird" Parker, adding Bird to his band during the late '30s. McShann also played bluesy swing piano, captured on recordings such as *McShann's Piano* (Capitol) and *Confessin' The Blues* (Classic Jazz), the latter with guitarist T-Bone Walker along for the ride. McShann continued to make good jazz into the 1990s.

Mary Lou Williams (1910-1981)

Had she been born 50 years later, in more liberated times, Williams would surely have received attention on a par with her male peers. Beginning in the late '20s, she was one of jazz's top pianists. Like other piano masters including Duke Ellington and Earl Hines, her playing evolved as jazz came of age. Over a career that covered five decades, Williams went from boogie-woogie, blues, and stride to more intricate and abstract improvisations on classic swing and bebop tunes. Try *Mary Lou Williams/1927–40* (Classics), *First Ladies of Jazz* (Savoy), and *Live At The Cookery* (Chiaroscuro).

Jimmy Yancey (1894-1951)

He was playing hip jazz/blues/boogie in Chicago years before it became a throbbing center for jazz, and his multi-volume series for the Document and Storyville labels offer ample samples of his brainy improvising. Check out *Jimmy Yancey Vol. 1/1939–1940 and Vol. 2/1939–1950* (Document).

The Boogie Men

Meade "Lux" Lewis (1905–1964), Albert Ammons (1907–1949), and Pete Johnson (1904–1967) were three kings of boogie-woogie piano beginning in the 1920s. The style became popular following a live radio broadcast of all three from Chicago's Sherman Hotel in 1939, and the boogie beat was also picked up by bluesmen including John Lee Hooker and 1960s rock bands such as Canned Heat. Think of *boogie-woogie* as a good way of describing the pianist's left and right hands tossing rhythmic pairs back and forth. Check out boogie's leading pianists on Lewis' *Boogie & Blues* (Topaz) and *Meade Lux Lewis/1939–1954* (Story of Blues); Ammons's *Albert Ammons/1936–1939* (Classics/Qualiton), *Albert Ammons/1939–1946* (Classics/Qualiton), and *Boogie Woogie Man* (Pearl Flapper); and *Pete Johnson/1938–1939*, *Pete Johnson/1939–1941*, and *Pete Johnson 1944–1946* (all on Classics/Qualiton).

Flying Next to Bird: The Bebop Pianists

In the 1940s in New York City, the new *bebop* style of jazz — named after the sound of its breathtakingly fast melodies — was beginning to cook (see Chapter 4). Thelonious Monk and Bud Powell were leading bebop pianists, but others including Barry Harris, Hampton Hawes, and John Lewis also had their hands in the music.

Barry Harris (born 1929)

Never accorded the amount of attention showered on Bud Powell and Thelonious Monk, Harris humbly chalked up a solid string of fine bop recordings through five decades beginning in the 1950s. Seasoned in hometown clubs in Detroit backing trumpeter Miles Davis, saxophonist Sonny Stitt, saxophonist Lester Young, and others when they swung through the Motor City during the 1940s, Harris became a vital part of New York's 1960s jazz scene and continued to make great music into the 1990s. Give him a listen on *Barry Harris at the Jazz Workshop* (Original Jazz Classics), *Chasin' the Bird* (Original Jazz Classics), *Luminescence* (Original Jazz Classics), *Live at Maybeck Recital Hall/Vol. 12* (Concord), as well as on Sonny Stitt's *Tune Up!* (Muse) and *Constellation* (Muse).

Hampton Hawes (1928-1977)

Initially a young bebop lion, Hawes made good music into the 1970s, when he was one of the few members of the Old Guard to experiment with electric jazz. In the 1940s, Hawes played with bop saxmen Dexter Gordon and Wardell Gray, and transitioned into bluesier hard bop during the 1950s, recording several solid albums as a leader. Catch his Bud Powell-inspired style on *All Night Sessions!, Vol. 1, 2, 3* (Original Jazz Classics), *Four! Hampton Hawes!!!* (Original Jazz Classics), *The Seance* (Original Jazz Classics), *Blues for Bud* (Black Lion), and *Live at the Jazz Showcase in Chicago* (Enja).

John Lewis (born 1920)

A versatile and talented musician, Lewis has been a top pianist since the 1940s and is also a composer whose ear for exotic melodies and harmonies places him on a par with the best classical composers. Lewis swung with saxmen Lester Young and Coleman Hawkins, bopped with trumpeter Dizzy Gillespie and saxman Charlie Parker, chilled out on trumpeter Miles Davis's landmark *Birth of the Cool* (Capitol) album, and was the leading creative force in the Modern Jazz Quartet, one of jazz's most inventive small groups for more than 20 years beginning in 1952.

Go get Lewis's *Grand Encounter* (Pacific Jazz), *Wonderful World of Jazz* (Atlantic), and *Midnight in Paris* (EmArcy), as well as the MJQ's *Django* (Original Jazz Classics), *Fontessa* (Atlantic), and *Third Stream Music* (Atlantic) — *third stream* refers to 1960s efforts to fuse jazz and classical music, in which Lewis was a prime player.

Thelonious Monk (1917-1982)

Fractured chord combinations and off-kilter melodies lend Monk's playing a quirky charm. Combining wild imagination with a dark sense of humor that runs through most of his music, Monk (shown in Figure 11-1) is my favorite

Figure 11-1:
Thelonious
Monk
(photo:
Everett/CSU
Archives).

jazz pianist for pure originality. Embedded within his "Sweet and Lovely," for instance, is "Tea For Two," and he often reworked older tunes into new ones, such as the way "I Got Rhythm" became the basis for his own "Rhythm-a-Ning."

Whether making his own music or reworking classic jazz tunes such as "I Should Care" or "Willow Weep For Me," Monk is able to communicate oceans of emotion with only a few moves. Witness his playing on the Blue Note recordings from the 1940s, reissued on vinyl during the 1960s, and again on CD during the 1990s as *The Complete Blue Note Recordings* (Blue Note), a must-have set. His later *London Collection* (Black Lion) recordings are just as vital as his earliest albums.

Bud Powell (1924-1966)

If Monk was an odd individualist, pianist Bud Powell came closest of any ivoryman to the kind of definitive bebop creativity Charlie "Yardbird" Parker achieved on his saxophone. Parker's thing was the wildly improvised melodic *line,* a string of single notes stretching for several minutes. Powell, too, pursued full-tilt melodic invention, with his right hand doing most of the work, spinning improvised lines as his left hand marked time with chords and bass notes.

One of a handful of regular pianists who frequented New York City's 52nd Street scene during the mid-'40s, Powell was a vital force in bop's invention — he was a fast, fluid, cerebral player who meshed well with Parker, trumpeter Dizzy Gillespie, drummer Kenny Clarke, and other bop giants. By most estimates, Powell was the definitive bop pianist in a group that also included Thelonious Monk, Dodo Marmarosa, Hampton Hawes, and Al Haig.

Powell's impressive output includes *The Amazing Bud Powell Vols. 1, 2, 3* (EMD/Blue Note), *The Ultimate Bud Powell* (PGD/Verve), *Best of Bud Powell* (EMD/Blue Note), *Bud Plays Bird* (EMD/Blue Note), *Jazz at Massey Hall, Vol. 2* (Pablo), *A Portrait of Thelonious* (Sony), *Writin' For Duke* (Mythic Sound), and *The Complete Essen Jazz Festival Concert* (Black Lion) with bebop legends Oscar Pettiford on bass and Kenny Clarke on drums.

Cool, Hard Bop, and Beyond

Bebop eventually fractured into the *cool jazz* sound, a laid-back West Coast version of bebop, and *hard bop,* the East Coast evolution. Various pianists explored these sounds on into the 1950s.

Dave Brubeck (born 1920)

Beginning in the 1950s, pianist Dave Brubeck offered a brainy alternative to mellow *cool jazz* and driving *hard bop*. Brubeck, schooled in both the jazz and classical genres, plays music that bridges the gap. Although best known for the song "Take Five" (written by Brubeck's saxophonist, Paul Desmond), Brubeck's playing on albums such as *Time Out* (Sony), *Jazz Goes To College* (Sony), *Blue Rondo* (on Concord, with his sons), and *All the Things We Are* (Atlantic) reminds me of Picasso's art: quirky, asymmetrical, and brooding.

Brubeck also writes religious music, and he is one of the few players to fuse jazz with classical strings in a compelling way, as on *Brubeck Plays Bernstein* (Sony). Not only is Brubeck an inventive player and composer, he's an excellent human being whose warmth comes across particularly well in his live performances.

Kenny Drew (1928-1993)

Drew was one of hard bop's best pianists, (his son, Kenny Drew, Jr., is one of the most promising pianists of the 1990s). Drew tickled ivories with saxmen Charlie Parker, Coleman Hawkins and Lester Young, as well as other jazz greats, and recorded more than a dozen solid albums as a leader. *Pal Joey* (Original Jazz Classics) and the later *For Sure* (Xanadu) are among Drew's solid performances.

Bill Evans (1929-1980)

For pure emotional power, it's hard to beat Bill Evans, a member of Miles Davis's late '50s sextet that also included saxophonists John Coltrane and Cannonball Adderley. During the 1960s and 1970s, Evans went on to record several albums as a leader before he died in 1980.

Sunday at the Village Vanguard (Original Jazz Classics) and *Waltz for Debby* (Original Jazz Classics) catch Evans in his prime. Other vital titles for your collection are *Undercurrent* (EMD/Blue Note), a duet with guitarist Jim Hall, and *Conversations With Myself* (PGD/Verve), an introduction to Evans going it solo.

Tommy Flanagan (born 1930)

Jazz's unsung marathon man, Flanagan has been a hot pianist since his 1957 *The Cats* (Original Jazz Classics) recording with John Coltrane, and he has made some of his hottest music during the 1990s. Check out *Beyond The Bluebird* (Timeless), too.

Ahmad Jamal (born 1930)

Whether on conventional or electric piano, Ahmad Jamal — like Miles Davis — made masterful use of space to frame his musical ideas. In Jamal's music, what he doesn't play is often as important as what he does play. Several of his 1950s recordings are first-rate, including *Ahmad Jamal at the Pershing* (Argo), which includes his signature tune, "Poinciana."

Jamal's 1972 *Freeflight* (Uni/Impulse!) album, recorded live at the Montreux Jazz Festival, was one of my first jazz piano records — it's been reissued on CD and is still one of my favorites. Consisting of only four songs (including fellow pianist Herbie Hancock's beautiful "Dolphin Dance"), this album is a prime example of Jamal's extended lyrical improvising.

Wynton Kelly (1931-1971)

Cool and/or bebopping, Kelly played on some of trumpeter Miles Davis's best 1950s albums including *Kind of Blue* (Columbia), and you can also catch his tasteful, laid-back piano on solo recordings including *Smokin' at the Half Note* (Verve), with guitarist Wes Montgomery.

Les McCann (born 1935)

A lot of us were into acid rock or heavy metal when Les McCann and Eddie Harris captured our ears with their famous 1969 album, *Swiss Movement* (Atlantic). McCann's friendly jazz caught the attention of listeners of many stripes. Bluesy and funky, it was upbeat and danceable. McCann was also among the first pianists to try a variety of electric keyboards and synthesizers, but his best stuff is on acoustic piano. *Les McCann Anthology: Relationships* (Rhino/Atlantic) offers a double-CD dip into early (1960s) McCann.

Marian McPartland (born 1920)

A fine pianist who deserves attention more on a par with her male peers, McPartland has been making consistently solid jazz rooted in swing and bop since the late '50s. Most of her several dozen CDs are worthwhile additions to any jazz piano-lover's collection. Best bets include *Marian McPartland* (Jazz Alliance), *Plays the Music of Billy Strayhorn* (Concord), *Plays the Music of Mary Lou Williams* (Concord), *Piano Jazz: McPartland/Hinton* (Jazz Alliance), *Plays the Benny Carter Songbook* (Concord), *In My Life* (Concord), *Live at Maybeck Recital Hall, Vol. 9* (Concord), *Piano Jazz: McPartland/Blake* (Jazz Alliance), *Piano Jazz: McPartland/Konitz* (Jazz Alliance), and *Piano Jazz: McPartland/Coltrane* (Jazz Alliance).

You can also catch Marian McPartland on her syndicated National Public Radio show *Piano Jazz,* on which she spends an hour interviewing, showcasing, and sometimes doing a duet with a jazz pianist.

Dodo Marmarosa (born 1925)

Barney Kessel is my favorite bebop-era guitarist, and the little-known Marmarosa was Kessel's frequent bandmate during the 1940s and 1950s. Marmarosa made few recordings of his own — try *Dodo Lives* (Pearl) and *Up in Dodo's Room* (Jazz Classics). He played with big bands including Gene Krupa's and Artie Shaw's, and he added hot licks to recordings by saxophonists Lester Young, Charlie Parker, and Gene Ammons. Also hear him on *Complete Charlie Parker on Dial* (Jazz Classics).

George Shearing (born 1919)

Ranging from swing to Latin, bebop, cool, and classical, Shearing's piano playing is complex, subtle, and spectacular. The quintet Shearing formed in 1949 sparked some great interplay between his piano and Marjorie Hyams's vibes. Hear Shearing on *The London Years/1939–1943* (Hep), *Lullaby of Birdland* (Verve), *Blues Alley and Jazz* (Concord), and *My Favorite Things* (Telarc).

Horace Silver (born 1928)

Drummer Art Blakey is commonly associated with the Jazz Messengers, but Silver was the legendary group's co-founder, and he was an important figure in 1950s hard bop. Silver launched his career in 1950 in saxophonist Stan Getz's band and played with saxmen Lester Young and Coleman Hawkins, and bassist Oscar Pettiford before fronting the Messengers with Blakey during the mid-'50s. Silver is also a prolific arranger/composer, and was among the first jazz players to bring soul and funk flavors into the music.

Horace Silver and the Jazz Messengers (EMD/Blue Note) is one of the classics of 1950s Hard Bop, but most any of Silver's albums for Blue Note from the 1950s and 1960s are vital. Also get *Finger Poppin'* (EMD/Blue Note) and *Song for My Father* (EMD/Blue Note).

Billy Taylor (born 1921)

Taylor has been a doubly strong force for the cause of jazz. Since the 1950s, he's been a swinging player in a latter-day bop style and was a leader in bringing Latin elements into jazz through recordings with percussionists Chano Pozo and Candido. In the name of keeping jazz alive for generations to come, Taylor helped start the *Jazzmobile* program to bring music to New York City kids. Also in the name of education, he has hosted radio and television programs (and now a Web site at `www.town.hall.org/Archives/radio/Kennedy/Taylor`).

Top Taylor CDs include *Billy Taylor Trio* (Prestige), *Billy Taylor Trio with Candido* (Original Jazz Classics), *My Fair Lady Loves Jazz* (Impulse!), *Solo* (Taylor Made), and *Homage* (Uni/GRP), a collaboration with the Turtle Island String Quartet.

Bobby Timmons (1935-1974)

Another seldom-heard-but-great player, Timmons was a Jazz Messenger and member of Cannonball Adderley's group who wrote important tunes for both bands. His playing could be funky or as fleet as vintage 1940s bebop. Timmons passed away in his thirties, but he left some great jazz including the 1960 *This Here Is Bobby Timmons* (Original Jazz Classics).

Lennie Tristano (1919-1978)

Ornette Coleman and John Coltrane are the famous figureheads of jazz's *avant garde,* but in 1949, on the songs "Intuition" and "Digression" — found on *Crosscurrents* (Capitol) — Tristano played spacey, meandering improvisations that were ten years ahead of their time. Tristano also played in the cool style associated with such collaborators as saxophonists Warne Marsh and Lee Konitz, and he stirred up the jazz scene during the early 1960s with *overdubbed* piano parts (at the time, overdubbing was taboo) on the album *Requiem* (Atlantic).

Randy Weston (born 1926)

Rooted in Africa, Weston's playing has a power that harks back to jazz's original sources. Born in Brooklyn, Weston composes and plays provocative, richly textured jazz that incorporates African rhythms he assimilated during lengthy stays in Morocco.

In the 1950s, Weston, who has been inspired by Duke Ellington and Thelonious Monk, played bluesy hard bop as leader of his own small groups. He has also arranged and recorded music with sizeable jazz ensembles. Hear his eclectic brand of music on *Jazz a la Bohemia* (Original Jazz Classics), *Tanjah* (Verve), *Carnival* (Freedom), *African Sunrise* (PGD/Verve), *Splendid Master Gnawa Musicians of Morocco* (PGD/Verve), *Earth Birth* (PGD/Verve), *Perspective* (Denon), and *Marrakech in the Cool of the Evening* (PGD/Polygram).

Overdubbing and a bit on recording technology

Overdubbing is a technique that allows musicians to add parts to a recording — sometimes laying additional parts over their own initial parts, other times going back to re-record a passage. Early tape recorders had as few as four tracks, meaning there was room for four distinctive musical parts that could each be individually added or replaced. Newer digital technology allows for dozens of tracks — one musician can sound like an entire orchestra.

Early jazz was recorded live in the studio. The music was put to tape in a single *take*. Some newer jazz utilizes overdubbing to add parts . . . or to replace parts a musician is not satisfied with. Correcting mistakes by overdubbing is somewhat taboo: Because of jazz's spontaneous, improvisational nature, many "old school" musicians feel that genuine jazz occurs when players invent great music together on the spot without resorting to overdubbing.

Latin Piano Connections

Although trumpeter Dizzy Gillespie was among the first to utilize Latin rhythms in a major way, Latin jazz had a particularly hot spell during the 1950s and 1960s, when players including saxman Stan Getz, vibraphonist Cal Tjader, and percussionists Tito Puente and Mongo Santamaria made some wonderful music. Although not as well known as some bandleaders and horn players, pianists played a vital part during this prime time for Latin jazz. Several fine pianists today continue the Latin/jazz connection.

Eliane Elias (born 1960)

A Brazilian-born pianist who grew up in the 1960s hearing Antonio Carlo Jobim's bossa novas and recordings by American jazz pianists Art Tatum, Bud Powell, Wynton Kelly, Erroll Garner, Bill Evans, and Herbie Hancock, Elias launched her career in the U.S. in the 1980s. She's played bebop-inspired jazz as well as freer music with players including bassist Marc Johnson. Look for *Eliane Elias Plays Jobim* (EMD/Blue Note), *Fantasia* (EMD/Blue Note), *Solos & Duets* (EMD/Blue Note), *The Best of Eliane Elias* (Denon), and *The Three Americas* (EMD/Blue Note).

Eddie Palmieri (born 1936)

He grew up in New York hearing pianists Thelonious Monk and McCoy Tyner, but Palmieri has made his own freer forms of Latin jazz since the 1950s. Palmieri is a seasoned jazz pianist with a handful of great recordings to his name, including *Mozambique* (Tico), *El Sonido Nuevo* (Verve) with vibraphonist Cal Tjader, and *Sun of Latin Music* (Coco).

Hilton Ruiz (born 1952)

An excellent pianist whose eclectic jazz includes Afro-Cuban and Latin elements, Ruiz is a young player who has already made several good albums, including *Cross Currents* (Stash), *El Camino/The Road* (Novus), *A Moment's Notice* (Novus), *Rhythm in the House* (Uni/Rmm), and is also part of the all-star Afro Blue Band, whose 1996 album is titled *Impressions* (Milestone).

Bebo (born 1918) and Chucho Valdes (born 1941)

Cuban-born Bebo Valdes was a 1940s and 1950s master of Cuban jazz. Beginning in the 1960s, his son Chucho led some of Cuba's hottest jazz bands, including Orquesta Cubana de Musica Moderna and Irakere, which included saxophonist/clarinetist Paquito D'Rivera and trumpeter Arturo Sandoval. While the use of Latin rhythms by American jazz players is well documented, Latin musicians like Bebo and Chucho Valdes living outside the U.S. — who originated historically significant jazz of their own — are not often mentioned. Get *Bebo Rides Again* (Messidor) and Chucho's *Lucumbi: Solo Piano* (Messidor) and *Solo Piano* (Blue Note).

Timeless Classics

Jazz has some of the most advanced musicians on the planet. Not only can they play with speed and dexterity, but much of the time, they are making up the music as they go. When it comes to finicky technique, Oscar Peterson and Art Tatum were jazz's consummate craftsmen, but several of their peers from the 1940s forward also earn "timeless classics" status — for the epic sweep of their careers and music.

Erroll Garner (1921-1977)

Erroll Garner is often identified as a bebopper through his late '40s association with bebopper saxman Charlie Parker. In truth, Garner was a more middle-of-the-road pianist than other bebop pianists such as Bud Powell or Thelonious Monk. He was more meticulous and extremely tasteful in his playing.

Best known for composing the song "Misty," Garner sounds deceptively simple, due to the shimmering beauty of his playing and his subtle ways with famous ballads by composers such as George Gershwin and Jerome Kern. Yet his rhythmic variations, the way he let his left and right hands dance to different drummers, plus the fresh ways in which he combines chords and melodies, made him as much of a genius as any jazz pianist.

Body and Soul (Columbia) gives an excellent entree to Garner and includes his version of that famous song, as well as his interpretations of "The Way You Look Tonight," Fats Waller's "Honeysuckle Rose," "I Can't Get Started," and "Summertime." Monk may be maniacal, Powell the baddest bebopper, and Hines a heroic ironman, but Garner's playing is more . . . elegant than any of them, just like his immaculately coiffed hair.

Oscar Peterson (born 1925)

Montreal-born Peterson is a solid, silky smooth player with an encyclopedic grasp of jazz piano. He utilizes ragtime and stride piano elements dating back to James P. Johnson, Jelly Roll Morton, and Fats Waller, but his music is much more subtle and complex. Some of the pieces from his *Jazz Masters 16* (Verve) CD serve as a good introduction to Peterson, and recall the mood of 1920s, but his playing is vastly advanced.

Peterson's rapid right-hand runs up and down the keys are so smooth, it's difficult to appreciate how tough and quick they really are. His left hand pumps out ragtime's relentless, rolling rhythms, but with countless variations. Peterson is also a consummate accompanist. For years, he was the house pianist for the Verve label, recording with legends ranging from saxmen Lester Young and Coleman Hawkins to singers Billie Holiday and Ella Fitzgerald.

Essential Peterson includes *The Complete Young Oscar Peterson* (BMG/RCA), *At Zardi's* (Pablo), *Oscar Peterson Plays Count Basie* (PGD/Verve), *At the Stratford Shakespearean Festival* (PGD/Verve), *My Favorite Instrument* (PGD/Verve), *Tracks* (PGD/Verve), *The Trio* (Pablo), *The More I See You* (Telarc), and *Oscar Peterson Meets Roy Hargrove and Ralph Moore* (Telarc).

Art Tatum (1909-1956)

Equally polished, but more aggressive than Peterson in his attack, was Art Tatum, a partially blind, self-taught pianist whose recording career lasted from the 1930s through the 1950s (he died in 1956). He made the most of all 88 keys, playing killer chord combinations and gorgeous improvised melodies, so that "Willow Weep For Me," "Night And Day," "Love For Sale" and other popular tunes took on a degree of complexity more common to classical compositions. Try *Tatum's Piano Starts Here* (Sony), *Classic Piano Solos* (GRP), *Art Tatum Solo Masterpieces, Vols. 1–8* (Pablo), *The Tatum Group Masterpieces, Vols. 1–8* (Pablo), and *20th Century Piano Genius* (PGD/Verve). And don't forget Tatum's "Danny Boy" on the *Jazz For Dummies* CD.

McCoy Tyner (born 1938)

In my teens, I was fortunate enough to be at San Francisco's Keystone Korner nightclub when pianist McCoy Tyner recorded a portion of his live *Atlantis* (Milestone) album. It remains one of my all-time favorites.

More than any pianist, Tyner — who came to fame as a sideman to saxophonist John Coltrane — attacks the piano with awesome percussive force. Pounding out chords with his left hand and powerful, speedy runs with his right, Tyner is one pianist who comes close to Coltrane's raw energy and mystical power. Pick up *The Real McCoy* (EMD/Blue Note), *Sahara* (Original Jazz Classics), *Echoes of a Friend* (Original Jazz Classics), *Enlightenment* (Milestone), *Trident* (Original Jazz Classics), *Tribute to John Coltrane* (Impulse!), *Infinity* (Impulse!), and Coltrane's *A Love Supreme* (Impulse!).

Wide Open Places the Piano's Been

Piano can change colors like an exotic animal in camouflage mode. Given 88 notes and two healthy hands, a pianist — more than any other instrumentalist — can put all sorts of chords and melodies together. He or she can give a song simple solo treatment, or weave many elements together into a complex orchestral tapestry. Because of its musical range, piano is the most popular solo instrument in jazz, yet it is also used as a leading instrument in big bands.

Here are some pianists who have adapted the piano to suit wildly different personal visions of jazz, from light, lyrical extended improvisation, to brash and brutal free jazz.

Muhal Richard Abrams (born 1930)

In the realm of abstract jazz, the Chicago-based AACM (Association for the Advancement of Creative Musicians) has been a focal point. Abrams was one of its founders during the mid-'60s. Although much of his music is free and experimental, he has also played with familiar jazz heroes including saxophonists Sonny Stitt and Dexter Gordon, and drummer/bandleader Max Roach. Whether solo or in charge of a full jazz orchestra, Abrams has been responsible for some of jazz's most innovative music, and still has plenty of fire left. Hear him on *Levels and Degrees of Light* (Delmark), *Afrisong* (Navigation), *Rejoicing with the Light* (Black Saint), *Blues Forever* (Black Saint), *The Hearinga Suite* (Black Saint), and *Think All, Focus One* (Black Saint).

One man's favorites

I asked Dick Hyman, a formidable pianist who has scored several Woody Allen movies, to name his favorite jazz pianists.

"Personally, I think Art Tatum was the greatest," Hyman said. "He was the consummate technician, harmonist, creator of improvised melodies, he swung, and he was a great soloist. His Decca album that includes 'Tea For Two' is a personal favorite.

"I find Lennie Tristano to be underappreciated. Tristano stretched the boundaries. He pushed harmonies farther, and he used counterpoint and odd scales. He was very much a pioneer in freeform jazz during the late 1940s. He reintroduced collective (group) improvisation in his music, and I especially like "Intuition," an improvised piece.

Paul Bley (born 1932)

Bley's approach is free and unstructured, but gentler and more melodic than percussive *avant garde* jazz pianists such as Marilyn Crispell and Cecil Taylor. Bley's career has been long and prolific, beginning in the early 1950s, extending into the 1990s, and producing several dozen great albums, including the 1972 *Open For Love* (ECM).

Marilyn Crispell (born 1947)

A first lady of abstract jazz, Crispell has one of the biggest backlogs of recorded experimental jazz, beginning with her 1982 *Spirit Music* (Cadence), and continuing through the present. She's a hard-hitting heavyweight (musically, that is) when she attacks a keyboard.

Herbie Hancock (born 1940)

Catching the tale end of cool jazz/hard bop when he came into jazz during the early '60s, Hancock grew into one of jazz's most lyrical, inventive pianists. Hancock has some of the spare, melodic sensibility of 1950s pianist Bill Evans or swing saxophonist Coleman Hawkins (early in his career, Hancock played with Hawkins), but his sound is distinguished by a funkier, bluesier vibe.

From the start of his career, Hancock played with an economy and grace beyond his years. His albums *Takin' Off* (Blue Note), *Empyrean Isles* (Blue Note), and especially *Maiden Voyage* (Blue Note) capture a mature player, composer, and improviser — in his early twenties! His song "Watermelon Man" from *Takin' Off* was a hit, and Hancock originals including "Dolphin Dance" have become a part of the jazz player's standard songbook.

A part of trumpeter Miles Davis's superb mid-'60s group beginning in 1963, Hancock played piano, and later electric piano and synthesizer, on the classic Davis albums *Sorcerer* (Sony), *Seven Steps to Heaven* (Sony), *The Complete Concert: 1964* (Sony), *E.S.P.* (Sony), *Complete Live at the Plugged Nickel* (Sony), *Miles Smiles* (Sony), *Nefertiti* (Sony), and *Miles in the Sky* (Sony).

And when Davis ventured farther into electric jazz-rock-funk in the late '60s, Hancock played a vital role, helping Davis produce dreamy, electrifying music on *In a Silent Way* (Sony).

During the acoustic jazz revival of the early '80s brought on by a group of younger players led by trumpeter Wynton Marsalis, Hancock was in the thick of things again. With trumpeter Freddie Hubbard replacing Miles, Hancock led the productive *VSOP* reunion of Davis's mid-'60s quintet including drummer Tony Williams, bassist Ron Carter, and saxophonist Wayne Shorter.

Meanwhile, Hancock kept his hand in eclectronica, assimilating 1970s funk, 1980s disco, and 1990s hip-hop into his music. His albums *Mwandishi* (WEA/Warner Brothers), *Head Hunters* (Sony), *Thrust* (Sony), and *Dis Is Da Drum* (PGD/Polygram) all had hot spots. His song "Rock-It" from his album *Future Shock* (Sony) was a crossover jazz/hip-hop hit that even made it to MTV while never giving the impression that Herbie sold out.

Following his electric jazz/rock run during the 1970s and 1980s, Hancock (shown in Figure 11-2) returned to his acoustic roots. Although he still plugs in and synthesizes from time to time, he has trained his talents on unplugged jazz, like *The New Standard* (PDG/Verve) and the excellent *1+1* (Verve), a spare, moody collaboration with saxophonist Wayne Shorter.

Andrew Hill (born 1937)

A reservoir of jazz piano's history, Hill combines elements of stride, swing, bop, and newer free jazz. Saxophonists Lee Konitz, Eric Dolphy, Sam Rivers, Joe Henderson, and Rahsaan Roland Kirk have been among Hill's henchmen, which gives some idea of his range. Sample him on *Black Fire* (Blue Note), *Point of Departure* (Blue Note) with saxmen Eric Dolphy and Joe Henderson, *Verona Rag* (Soul Note), *Spiral* (Freedom) with saxophonist Lee Konitz, and *But Not Farewell* (Blue Note) with rising young saxman Greg Osby.

Figure 11-2:
Herbie
Hancock
(photo:
Everett
Collection).

Abdullah (Dollar Brand) Ibrihim (born 1934)

South Africa-born Ibrihim brings rich-multicultural influences to his music, ranging from African folk to Fats Waller, Duke Ellington, bebop, and assorted world rhythms. Hot Ibrihim recordings include *Anatomy of a South African Village* (Black Lion), *Reflections* (Black Lion), and *Round Midnight at the Montmartre* (Black Saint). Music stores often have his music filed under his previous name "Dollar Brand."

Keith Jarret (born 1945)

Like Ahmad Jamal, Keith Jarrett makes his music into extended meditations. Keith Jarrett's electric piano floored listeners on trumpeter Miles Davis's jazz-rock recordings from the early 1970s, but Jarrett went on to become a premiere soloist and pioneer of introspective playing that inspired subsequent "new age" musicians. Jarrett's *Koln Concert* (ECM) album from 1975 is my all-time favorite of his, with endless solos that never become boring. Jarrett made several albums on ECM, a label known for brainy, meditative, and *third stream* (imbued with heavy classical influence) jazz. Most of his other ECM efforts are also worth owning.

Don Pullen (born 1941)

Pullen is one of the most aggressive pianists, but also one of the most thoughtful. His solos combine fragments from blues, funk, and bebop, and he's done some of his best work with jazz's experimenters including bassist Charles Mingus, flute and saxophone player Sam Rivers, and *avant garde* baritone sax player Hamiett Bluiett. Pullen's *Solo Piano Album* (Sackville) is a great solo piano album, and he's still going strong in the 1990s.

Horace Tapscott (born 1934)

One of jazz's more seasoned players, Tapscott made great music during the 1950s with trumpeter Don Cherry and saxophonist Eric Dolphy before launching his solo career with the 1969 *West Coast Hot* (Novus). He's played with top beboppers, but also with saxman Arthur Blythe, clarinetist John Carter, and other musicians from jazz's cutting edge.

Cecil Taylor (born 1929)

Picture Jackson Pollock in action, spattering paint on a giant canvas, and you get some idea of the pure power of *avant garde* jazz pianist Cecil Taylor. Dreadlocks flying, fingers launching a nuclear attack on the keys, sitting, standing, sitting, standing, Taylor turns piano playing into an athletic event. His solo pieces are wild freeform excursions in sound; his music is an acquired taste, but it grows on you. Approach his albums in search of raw feelings or imaginary images, instead of familiar romantic melodies, and you come away highly enlightened. Still in prime form, Taylor has made more than two dozen albums since his first in 1955; most every one of them is a provocative, inspiring work of art. *Unit Structures* (Blue Note) is a classic Taylor recording that demands to be in every jazz collection.

The ultimate test: Solo piano

Going solo is the jazz player's ultimate test, and for solo piano, you can't beat Concord Jazz's series of recordings made at Maybeck Recital Hall in Berkeley, California — actually a cozy living room in a house designed by Bay Area architect Bernard Maybeck during the 1920s. Among the many (often under-appreciated) pianists showcased in these carefully recorded live sessions (with a small audience): Mike Wofford, Hank Jones, Jessica Williams, John Hicks, Ellis Larkins, Gene Harris, and Buddy Montgomery.

Keys with a Cord

Plugging in during the mid-'60s, pianists began to shape new jazz sounds. Initially, their electric efforts consisted primarily of electric piano. On albums with trumpeter Miles Davis such as *In A Silent Way* and *Bitches Brew,* pianists Joe Zawinul, Chick Corea, and Herbie Hancock explored new electronic horizons.

In the 1970s, all three pianists graduated to synthesizers, and all used them to produce what is, in my opinion, more complex, imaginative music than today's lighter, radio-friendly "contemporary jazz" keyboard players. Zawinul's albums as co-leader of the group Weather Report (especially the albums *Mysterious Traveller* and *Black Market,* both on Columbia), Corea's recordings with Return to Forever (particularly *Light As A Feather* on Polydor and *Romantic Warrior* on Columbia), and Hancock's releases with his band the Headhunters (try *Headhunters* and *Thrust,* both on Columbia) all stand the test of time. Both Zawinul and Hancock were adept at adding synthesized textures without getting sappy.

Other electric jazz keyboard players of note include Joe Sample (formerly of the Crusaders), Russell Ferrante (the Yellowjackets), and Les McCann, who began his career as a serious acoustic jazz pianist during the 1950s and 1960s before moving to electric keyboards in the 1970s.

Today's Prime Pianists

Jazz piano's keys are in good hands with today's young players. Here are a few who have already made some great music, and who still have the potential to make a lot more:

- ✔ **Kenny Barron (born 1943).** A humble master of 1950s-era hard bop, Barron is still in his prime. For a breathtaking sample, try *Live at Maybeck Recital Hall, Vol. 10* (Concord) — Barron all by his lonesome, making magic.

- ✔ **Joanne Brackeen (born 1938).** Comfortable playing driving hard bop or spacier free jazz, Brackeen has been making great music since recording her first solo album, *Snooze* (Choice) in 1975. More recent efforts showcase her light, fleet touch on spacier jazz.

- ✔ **Cyrus Chestnut (born 1963).** Hot on Mulgrew Miller's heels, Chestnut is an even younger turk showing early promise on provocative acoustic jazz albums such as *Revelation* (Atlantic Jazz).

- ✔ **John Hicks (born 1941).** I love the passion in Hicks's playing, particularly on his *Live at Maybeck Recital Hall, Vol. 7* (Concord) album, a masterpiece of solo piano. Hicks was a member of drummer Art Blakey's Jazz Messengers during the early 1960s, and has since made several recordings of his own. He has also played freer jazz with saxophonists Arthur Blythe and David Murray, both members, at times, of the experimental World Saxophone Quartet.

✔ **Kenny Kirkland (born 1955).** Rising to prominence during the 1980s alongside Branford and Wynton Marsalis, Kirkland (like Branford) played with Sting. Kirkland is best known as a sideman, but his own *Kenny Kirkland* (GRP) is solid jazz.

✔ **Mulgrew Miller (born 1955).** One of the Young Turks who hit the jazz scene during the 1980s, Miller is an aggressive, hard-driving pianist whose music swings hard. A Jazz Messenger during the mid-'80s, Miller has since made several good albums of his own, including *Hand in Hand* (Novus) with seasoned support from saxophonist Joe Henderson and trumpet player Eddie Henderson, as well as *With Our Own Eyes* (Novus), with his own hot, young trio.

✔ **Marcus Roberts (born 1963).** An impressive composer and player, Roberts shows a lot of maturity for a young player, opting for tasteful restraint instead of flamboyant *showboating*. Initially contemporary in his approach, Roberts has dedicated himself in recent years to expanding the potential of the ragtime and stride piano styles popularized by Jelly Roll Morton and Fats Waller during the 1920s and 1930s. *Blues For The New Millenium* (Sony) is Roberts' imaginative, engaging update of rootsy blues.

✔ **Renee Rosnes (born 1962).** Playing driving unplugged jazz with top guns such as saxophonists Wayne Shorter and Joe Henderson, trombone player J.J. Johnson, and flute/sax player James Moody, was a warmup for the emergence in the 1990s of Rosnes's own full-blown career. She's released a string of solid albums on the trusty Blue Note label.

✔ **Gonzalo Rubalcaba (born 1963).** Born in Havana, Cuba, Rubalcaba brings authentic Afro-Cuban flavors to his jazz. Some of the best music of his young career has been made with a boost from bassist Charlie Haden, such as *The Blessing* (Blue Note).

✔ **Jacky Terrasson (born 1966).** On recordings such as *Jacky Terrasson,* (Blue Note) this young pianist displays impressive range, from a relentless pounding left hand reminiscent of McCoy Tyner to a dexterous right hand that runs from lyrical to wild and free. Terrasson's powerful live performances are legendary. Don't miss him if he comes to town.

✔ **Cedar Walton (born 1934).** Another seasoned master, Walton is another important alumnus of Art Blakey's Jazz Messengers (circa 1960s) who carried their bluesy, hard-driving spirit forward into the 1970s, 1980s, and 1990s. He hit a zone during the 1980s, recording almost a dozen great albums.

✔ **Can't fit 'em all, but . . .** there are many more names to watch for as you cruise your local music store in search of pianistic inspiration: Jaki Byard, Roger Kellaway, Bill Cunliffe, Steve Kuhn, Billy Childs, Mike Garson, Geri Allen, and Benny Green.

Chapter 12

Organists: Cool, Laid-Back Peacekeepers

In This Chapter

▶ Organ's split personality

▶ Early jazz organ

▶ The 1960s groove — jazz organ's heyday

▶ Keepers of the cool blue flame: Jazz organ today

Sacred and profane — that's one way to view the organ's evolution as a jazz instrument. Pipe organs, originally created for spectacular European cathedrals, eventually became fixtures in early American movie theatres, where African American musicians, including Fats Waller and Count Basie, often played them with bravado. Then, during the 1960s, electric organs became centerpieces in some very sexy soul-jazz.

In their construction, pipe organs bear obvious similarity to the human voice: Their sound comes from wind rushing through tubes. And the organ is actually as much a wind instrument as a member of the keyboard/piano clan — it has a keyboard, but the sound quality and way it is produced is similar to many horns and flutes. Later electric organs like the venerable Hammond B-3 use electronic circuits to create the sound. Thanks to foot-pedaled bass notes, a good organist can, by himself, cover all the elements of a small jazz group: bass, rhythms and chords, and melodies, and improvisations.

Partly because of its sound and partly because of its presence in churches, organs first met the hands of African American musicians during Sunday services. From there, it wasn't much of a leap to Fats Waller — legendary pianist and jazz's first important organist. Due to its wailing sound and lethargic key-action compared with piano, the organ is particularly well-suited to slower, bluesy jazz . . . and in fact, some of the coolest organ music is blues.

Organ-ically speaking: A few basics

The earliest organs were gigantic church pipe organs, which used a system of bellows to move air through pipes to get their sound. These organs, because of their mechanical guts, take up a large space and are not at all suitable for traveling musicians.

The organs that became popular for jazz were primarily electric, and use electronic circuits to produce their sound. This method of sound production allows the organs to be much smaller and made it possible for musicians to take the organ out of the church and into clubs.

The Hammond B-3 is the most familiar organ in music — for blues, jazz, and rock, the Hammond B-3 is the classic instrument. It offers several different instrumental sounds from two keyboards and a set of foot pedals, arranged like another keyboard for the player's feet, for bass tones.

The main differences between electric organ and piano are

✔ An organ has 61 keys while a piano has 88 keys.

✔ Many organs have a set of foot pedals for bass notes.

✔ On an organ, notes can be held indefinitely whereas on a piano, they eventually die out.

✔ The keyboard *action* is slower — keys react less quickly to the player's touch.

✔ Electric organs have a variety of built-in sounds, and most include a vibrato feature that makes notes waver (like an opera singer). The vibrato is produced by a spinning *Leslie* — a horn-like element that rotates at variable speeds in its enclosure.

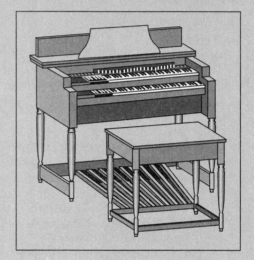

Early Jazz Organ

Jazz piano grew out of turn-of-the-century ragtime — Scott Joplin, and, a few years later, James P. Johnson, Fats Waller, and the rest of the ragtime/stride stylists, as I cover in Chapter 11. Jazz organ had other origins. Although it's a rare and somewhat unusual instrument in jazz, a couple of its early innovators were famous jazz figures better known for other musical achievements.

Count Basie (1904-1984)

And as if he isn't awe-inspiring enough for all his other contributions to jazz, Count Basie was also an early jazz organ pioneer. Basie, however, played the more practical electric organ — portable and more responsive to the touch than the ponderous and ecclesiastic pipe organ. Basie recorded only rarely with organ, and songs on which he plays organ are tucked between other cuts on piano-based albums, including *Satch and Josh* (Pablo), his collaboration with paramount pianist Oscar Peterson.

Fats Waller (1904-1943)

Fats Waller was best known as a pianist, composer, and band leader . . . but he also had a passion for organ that began in his teens when he played the instrument at Sunday Baptist services in Harlem.

By the 1920s, Waller was playing organ in theaters, and in the 1920s and 1930s he made organ recordings, including spirituals (such as "Sometimes I Feel Like a Motherless Child") and blues ("St. Louis Blues" and other songs). He also had an organ at home that he used both for playing and composing, and there's also a famous story of Waller sitting down and coaxing booming chords and soaring high notes from the Notre Dame's pipe organ during a swing through France . . . what a combination!

Fats Waller in London (Disques Swing) includes Waller's organ solos on several gospel tunes. *Fine Arabian Stuff* (Muse) is Waller playing spirituals on piano and organ, around 1939. *Fats at the Organ* (ASV/Living Era) is an unconventional but provocative presentation of Waller's organ skills — some of his player piano rolls, put through a pipe organ.

Other early jazz organists

Other early jazz players to sit down at the organ include

- **Milt Buckner (1915–1977).** A pianist and organist, Buckner recorded several albums that show off his soulful, bluesy organ. Buckner launched his jazz career as a pianist and arranger for McKinney's Cotton Pickers during the 1930s, played the same role with band leader Lionel Hampton, and led a variety of bands on his own. Get a copy of *Milt Buckner* (Progressive).

- **Wild Bill Davis (1918–1995).** Although some of his best recordings came during the 1960s, Davis was an early explorer of jazz organ. Between 1951 and 1955, Davis recorded several jazz/blues tunes on the

Okeh label — extremely tough to come by. Among his best 1960s recordings are several collaborations with saxophonist Johnny Hodges, a fixture in Duke Ellington's orchestra during the 1930s, 1940s, and 1950s. On CD, check out *In Atlantic City* (RCA) and *Con Soul and Sax* (RCA).

✔ **Glenn Hartman.** Seldom recorded, and unlisted in most books, Hartman was among the first jazz organists to record with the distinctive-sounding Hammond organ, in 1939. His 78 rpm records include *Upright Organ Blues* and *Who?*. Hartman set the stage for Wild Bill Davis in the 1940s and Milt Buckner in the 1950s.

✔ **Chester Thompson.** Organ was seldom heard — but not altogether absent — in those mid-'40s days when saxophonist Charlie Parker and trumpeter Dizzy Gillespie were inventing their furiously fast bebop. *Takin' Off* (Delmark) catches Thompson at that time, with Parker, saxophonist Dexter Gordon, and other biggies of bebop.

Other than these few early jazz organists, the instrument didn't play much part in the music as it evolved from big band swing through bebop and then on to 1950s hard bop and cool jazz. But the bluesy/cool/bop sound of trumpeters Miles Davis and Clifford Brown, drummer Art Blakey, guitarist Kenny Burrell, saxophonists Lou Donaldson and Ike Quebec, and, on piano, Horace Silver, Bobby Timmons, Ramsey Lewis, and others, set the stage for the organ's 1960s prime in groove-jazz.

The 1960s Groove

The 1960s were when organ jazz really started to come of age. Jimmy Smith set the pace, and the organ hit a high point as a jazz instrument during the late 1950s and 1960s. Combining the organ's bluesy sound, jazz's emphasis on improvisation, and assorted flavors from funk and soul, many players made some great music.

A "must" Web site for organ freaks

If you want to expand your explorations of organ, and you're a Net-surfer, visit the great site at www.theatreorgans.com/grounds. Dedicated to the Hammond B-3 organ — its history in jazz, characteristics, and a gargantuan list of B-3 players — it's a fascinating place to spend an hour or two. Hammond fanatic Gilles Bacon put up the page and oversees it as a nonprofit labor of love. A section on new albums is particularly useful.

You can also use the links to click over to www.theatreorgans.com, where you find extensive information and amazing color photos of vintage theatre organs — original organ training grounds of Fats Waller and his pupil, Count Basie.

Jimmy Smith (born 1925)

Jimmy Smith (see Figure 12-1) is the player who put the organ in jazz in a big way. Born in Norristown, Pennsylvania, Smith started out on piano but switched to organ a few years before his first recording sessions in the mid-1950s. Beginning in the late 1950s, Smith, a bluesy organist and tap dancer whose nimble feet did a great job on the organ's bass pedals, began a series of collaborations with jazz players that stretched into the 1990s and eventually included both small ensembles and unusual combos of Smith's organ with big bands.

Figure 12-1:
Jimmy
Smith
(photo:
Everett
Collection).

Although Smith's beloved Hammond B-3 had various instrumental effects, he usually stayed with a full, recognizable, straight-ahead organ sound, and he improvised graceful lines of melody in a manner similar to great jazz saxophonists Charlie Parker and Lester Young.

Greatest Hits, Vol. 1 teams Smith with trumpeter Lee Morgan, Lou Donaldson on alto sax, Stanley Turrentine and Tina Brooks on tenor sax, Kenny Burrell on guitar, Art Blakey on drums — plus other solid jazz musicians. The music is more blues and gospel than jazz, but intricate improvisation — a hallmark of good jazz — is found on several cuts. *Standards* (Blue Note) finds Smith with Burrell again, in a trio tackling popular tunes from the jazz repertoire such as "Bye Bye Blackbird," "I Didn't Know What Time It Was," and "Mood Indigo."

Later albums like *Crazy! Baby* (Blue Note), *Back at the Chicken Shack* (Blue Note), *Jimmy Smith Plays Fats Waller* (Blue Note), and *The Dynamic Duo* (Verve), with cool jazz guitarist Wes Montgomery, showcase Smith stretching out in more jazzified fashion, improvising freely, playing jazz standards, spicing up his basic blues with jazzier chords and melodies.

Smith's blues-based playing is so inventive when it comes to varied rhythms, chords, and improvisations that he is highly regarded among jazz players and critics. Throughout his career, he has often played jazz venues and has usually recorded with leading jazz players. Yet his instrument's religious roots are never far away, especially on slower tunes where Smith's sustained quivering chords, with the Leslie sending the vibrato sound into the heavens, call to mind the uplifting aura of a gospel service.

Bill Doggett (born 1916)

Philadelphia-born, Doggett's early career as a pianist mixed jazz (with Lucky Millinder's band) with blues (with Johnny Otis) and R&B (with the Ink Spots). He took up the organ when he replaced Wild Bill Davis in singer Louis Jordan's band in 1948. Doggett fronted his own bands during the 1950s through early 1990s, sometimes playing jazz, other times veering into various spots on the funk-soul-blues spectrum. *Everybody Dance to the Honky Tonk* (King) is a solid set from 1956, and a fresh foursome of Doggett CDs hit music stores in 1994, led by *Dance Awhile with Doggett* (King).

Johnny "Hammond" Smith (born 1933)

With a nickname like that, you know Smith is serious about his Hammond B-3. Inspired by Wild Bill Davis, Johnny "Hammond" Smith has recorded some of jazz's best organ music. Try *Talk That Talk, The Stinger,* and *Soul Talk* — all on Prestige.

Charles Earland (born 1941)

Perhaps no 1960s groove-jazz player has enjoyed more of a mid-'90s renaissance than "The Burner," Charles Earland, a saxophonist-turned-organist whose music can be found on assorted compilations playing tribute to the acid jazz forefathers. Earland's *Black Talk* (Original Jazz Classics) is rife with funky rhythms. The music's high funk-factor is particularly impressive considering the absence of a bassist — Earland's nimble feet lay all those cool bass lines on the organ's pedals. Earland's hip, up-tempo version of "Aquarius" is a period-perfect highlight. Tenor saxman Houston Person, another popular 1960s groover revisited by 1990s acid jazz buffs, is in fine form, blowing up a soulful storm.

In the late 1990s, Earland's still got the goods, and newer recording technology makes his organ ring through bright and clear on albums, including the 1997 *Blowing the Blues Away* (High Note). Promising young players such as tenor saxophonist Eric Alexander and trumpeter James Rotundi fuel Earland's fire as he works through tunes ranging from the title track (by hard bop pianist Horace Silver) to pianist Herbie Hancock's "Dolphin Dance."

Richard "Groove" Holmes (1931-1991)

Holmes hit his groove during jazz organ's heyday, collaborating with several top jazz musicians during the early 1960s. Whether playing chords while others soloed, or soloing himself, Holmes was a soulful organist with a jazz pianist's technical finesse. Born in Camden, New Jersey, Holmes developed a tasteful, wailing style that emphasized the organ's ability to stretch notes indefinitely. Not nearly as prolific as fellow organist Jimmy Smith, Holmes nonetheless earns a ranking near the top of 1960s jazz organists with the high quality of his recordings.

Groovin' with Jug (Capitol/Pacific Jazz) teams him with tenor sax titan Gene Ammons in a swinging live session at the Black Orchid nightclub in Los Angeles. On the cut "Hittin' the Jug," and throughout this album, it's plain to hear how "Groove" earned his nickname. *Blue Groove* (Prestige) is a tighter mid-'60s studio session that includes bassist Paul Chambers (who played famously with trumpeter Miles Davis and saxophonist John Coltrane), drummer Billy Higgins, and underappreciated guitarist Pat Martino. Intertwining lines of melody carried by Holmes and his top-notch teammates soar above a bed of simmering rhythms driven forward by Holmes' swinging chords. This is the best Holmes album for genuine jazz fans who want to hear what the organist can do with a group of jazz giants.

Jazz fans (especially guitar fanatics) will also love *After Hours* (Pacific Jazz), which teams Holmes with jazz guitarists Joe Pass and Gene Edwards in a hard-driving quintet. Soloing prodigiously, Holmes is an endless font of hot organ licks — and a cool sidekick for Pass and his fleet bebopping guitar improvisations. In CD form, this album includes several bonus tracks not offered with the original vinyl LP.

"Brother" Jack McDuff (born 1926)

Good jazz organ is timeless, and McDuff's made solid music since the 1950s, with a career revival in the late 1980s resulting in fresh recordings, including *The Re-Entry* (Muse), with Houston Person blowing up a soulful storm on tenor saxophone. McDuff's vintage stuff, such as the 1961 *The Honeydripper* (OJC) — one of many albums reissued on CD — is also awesome.

Jimmy McGriff (born 1936)

A protégé of Jimmy Smith and Richard "Groove" Holmes (he later recorded with Holmes), this guy's a sweetheart who once sent me a Christmas card with a keyboard of some sort on the front. McGriff's upbeat outlook comes through in his mighty, funky soul-jazz sound, captured on several fine Milestone CDs from the 1980s, as well as the 1994 *Right Turn on the Blues* (Telarc).

Don Patterson (born 1936)

Mining the soul jazz/hard bop vein in the late 1960s wake of Big John Patton and others, Patterson played delicate, finely crafted solos on recordings into the next decade. *Dem New York Blues* (Prestige) and *These Are Soulful Days* (Muse) are among his best efforts.

Big John Patton (born 1935)

A genuine native Kansas City jazzman (like saxophonist Charlie Parker), Patton matched Larry Young in prolific output on Blue Note during the early 1960s. Patton recorded with saxophonist Lou Donaldson, guitarist Grant Green and other cool "groove" jazz players who have enjoyed a late 1990s comeback as part of the advent of acid jazz.

Sun Ra (1914-1993)

One of jazz's most colorful fringe figures, Sun Ra is best known as the leader of his Arkestra, which, beginning in the 1950s, made some of the coolest, oddest jazz ever. Ra, who said he was from another galaxy, played a variety of keyboards, including organ. Start with *Cosmic Tones for Mental Therapy* (Evidence), which features Ra's "astro space organ" — whatever that is.

Shirley Scott (born 1934)

A jazz organist who grooves as well as Groove Holmes, Scott has a distinctive minimalist style. Whether playing behind another soloist, or soloing herself, Scott has subtle ways of combining rhythms, chords, and melodies with beboppish intricacy. Scott made close to a dozen great albums in the early 1960s, most of them on Prestige.

And she's still making great music. Her 1996 *A Walkin' Thing* (Candid) features baby-faced players including trumpeter Terell Stafford and tenor saxman Tim Warfield (who does a great imitation of the saxophone style of

Ben Webster). Fueled by Scott's laid-back sense of swing, this quintet makes some fine jazz — on new tunes, and on chestnuts like saxophonist Benny Carter's title track, and Irving Berlin's "Remember."

Lonnie Smith (born 1953)

Another 1960s-era soul-jazzer, Smith (not to be confused with keyboardist Lonnie Liston Smith) added shades of blue to recordings with trumpeter Lee Morgan and saxman Lou Donaldson. *Think* (Blue Note) is one of his best efforts.

Larry Young (1940-1978)

Young combined Jimmy Smith's cool soulful vibe with frenetic, freeform moods, melodies, and harmonies inspired by saxman John Coltrane and the early-'60s *avant garde*. Young played with trumpeter Miles Davis and drummer Tony Williams's band Lifetime. He also made a string of solid mid-'60s recordings for Blue Note, working out with legends like drummer Elvin Jones, saxman Sam Rivers, and vibraphonist Bobby Hutcherson. Among them, *Unity* (Blue Note) is a great one for starters.

Keepers of the Flame: Jazz Organ Today

The advent of synthesizers during the late 1970s and 1980s put a variety of new toys in a keyboard player's hands. But in keeping with renewed 1990s interest in authentic acoustic jazz, a handful of keyboard players are keeping the organ alive as a vital jazz instrument.

Joey DeFrancesco (born 1971)

An organist since boyhood, DeFrancesco toured with Miles Davis and made his first recordings while still in his teens. In the 1990s, he's the best known young jazz organist, adding his Hammond B-3's soulful vibe to a series of solid jazz sessions, including *Where Were You?* (Columbia), with saxman Illinois Jacquet and bassist Milt Hinton plus a pair of Young Turks: trumpeter Wallace Roney and saxophonist Kirk Whalum.

Also catch DeFrancesco going Hammond-to-Hammond with B-3 master Jack McDuff on *It's About Time* (Concord), and teaming with his father and mentor Papa DeFrancesco on *All in the Family* (HighNote), alongside sizzling soul jazzers Houston Person (saxophone) and Melvin Sparks (guitar).

DeFrancesco must sleep in the studio — he's also on several 1990s albums with guitarist John McLaughlin, one of which, *After The Rain* (Verve), also features powerhouse drummer Elvin Jones. If that isn't enough, he's also part of the all-star cast on *Bongo Bop* (Hip Bop), grooving alongside drummer Idris Muhammad and other first-rate jazz players.

Barbara Dennerlein (born 1964)

Dennerlein's German, but she has an all-American feel for the Hammond B-3. In a career that's produced about an album a year since 1984, Dennerlein's established herself as a genuine jazz organ force. *Straight Ahead* (Enja) features her in a quartet that also includes talented trombonist Ray Anderson. Anderson turns up again, along with groovin' drummer Dennis Chambers, to spur Dennerlein ahead on her *That's Me* (Enja) CD.

Larry Goldings (born 1968)

Goldings, also a pianist, has made some great jazz organ recordings, including an exploration of Latin rhythms on *Caminhos Cruzados* (Novus/RCA), with a cameo by young saxman Joshua Redman, and *The Intimacy of the Blues* (Verve), with saxophonist David "Fathead" Newman and bassist Bill Stewart.

Greg Hatza

A longtime pianist urged by Joey DeFrancesco to return to organ, Hatza responded in 1995 with *The Greg Hatza Organization* (Palmetto), a rousing Hammond B-3 romp through tunes by trumpeter Dizzy Gillespie, saxophonist John Coltrane, and others, with fellow organist Joey DeFrancesco and other talented bandmates along for the ride.

John Medeski (born 1965)

He's one-third of Medeski, Martin, and Wood, one of the hippest things to happen to jazz organ in the 1990s. Working laid-back grooves labeled "acid jazz" by fans too young to remember the 1960s and 1970s, this trio reminds me of *Bitches Brew*-era Miles Davis, but with spacier special effects. Medeski is a master of Hammond B-3, but his schtick also includes assorted techno tricks. *Shack-man* (Gramavision) is some of the coolest road music I've ever heard, and MMW also lends vital support on guitarist John Scofield's 1998 release *A Go Go* (PGD/Verve). For a trio of young guys, these musicians are masters of understatement, letting their grooves play out naturally, without overflexing their improvisational muscles.

Part IV
Percussion

By Rich Tennant

In this part . . .

In Part IV, you can discover the anchor of a great jazz band, the drummer. Find out about the simplicity of the jazz drum kit. You can read about the great drummers beginning with Baby Dodds and Jo Jones, to Buddy Rich and Chick Hamilton. You also can discover *avant garde* drummers such as Elvin Jones and head straight into the power of electric jazz and rock fusion with drummers like Bill Cobham and Tony Williams.

In this part, you can also find out about the vibraphone and its great players. Discover how the vibraphone became a part of jazz in the early years with players like Lionel "Hamp" Hampton. And find out how it evolved to the contemporary vibes of Spyro Gyra's Dave Samuels.

Chapter 13

Drummers: Swingin' through Time

In This Chapter

▶ Early jazz drummers drive the beat

▶ Drummers grow more adventuresome

▶ Buddy Rich and Louie Bellson swing the big bands

▶ Kenny Clarke, Max Roach, and Art Blakey keep the bebop beat

▶ *Avant garde* drummers loosen up

▶ Jazz-rock drummers tap new power

*S*wing is the pulse of all great jazz — it's that loose-but-relentless forward momentum of the music, rooted in rhythm sections of basses, drums, pianos, and guitars, but carried by all the players. A good drummer is a jazz band's glue. While bass players (or tubas or trombones in early jazz bands) anchor the beat, the drummer has a multi-purpose role: Utilizing his bass drum pedal, he can emphasize the beat, but he can also embellish it with accents, or bass drum *kicks*. Using an array of drums, cymbals, and accessories, he fills in with accents, flourishes, rolls, cymbal crashes, and rhythmic combinations.

Great drummers help make great jazz bands. Seated behind horns, given fewer solos than most of their bandmates, drummers can seem anonymous. And yet, drummers are the catalysts who move the music ahead, keep it swinging, and interact with various lead soloists, spurring them on to new creative highs.

Early Jazz Drummers

Cornetist Buddy Bolden and others led groups in New Orleans that played the music that would later be called jazz. Based on early photos, Bolden didn't have a regular drummer. But the band's rhythmic variety set the pace for jazz to come. Much of the music had a basic one-two beat or one-two-three-four beat rooted in the bass drum. Other pieces, however, were waltzes and *quadrilles* (French square dancing songs in a variety of rhythmic patterns).

The exact sound of early jazz is described in assorted writings, but not preserved on records. Jazz was not recorded for the first time until the late teens, and extensive recording didn't take place until the mid-'20s — when jazz bands fronted by hot players such as trumpeters Louis Armstrong and King Oliver and clarinetists Johnny Dodds and Sidney Bechet were powered by jazz's first percussion powerhouses.

The evolution of the drum kit

Early jazz drummers played primitive drum sets, sometimes as simple as a snare drum, cymbal, and cowbell or assorted small percussion instruments. But by the time Baby Dodds hit the stage and studio with King Oliver in 1923, he was using an early version of today's jazz set: a bass drum struck by a foot pedal (first manufactured by Ludwig in 1910), snare drum, *choke cymbal,* and rack of wood blocks and other small percussion accessories. The bass drum was large — 28 inches in diameter — a holdover from the large marching band drums. A drummer would accent key moments in the music by striking the cymbal, then quickly *choking* it with his hand to emphasize this rapid crash. *High-hats* — stands with two cymbals clapped together by a foot pedal — didn't become commonplace until the 1930s.

Pictures document the evolution of the drum set through jazz's history. Bass drums became much smaller, compact enough for easy travel but still capable of producing big sound. Snare drums, originally made from bent, laminated wood, have been mostly steel since the 1960s, producing a much crisper, louder sound.

Whereas early jazz drummers relied mainly on snare and bass drums—the basic drums of marching and funeral bands — later drum sets began to utilize a variety of *tom-toms* — sometimes one or more smaller ones mounted on the bass drum, as well as one or more *floor toms* resting on legs.

Along with snare drums and bass drums, cymbals are the jazz drummer's essential tools — even more prevalent as basic timekeepers than any of the drums. As jazz has matured, the quality and variety of cymbals available increased dramatically. Whereas an early jazz drummer may have relied upon one cymbal, or a high-hat, jazz drummers beginning in the 1930s often had a high-hat and at least two other cymbals.

But compared with drummers playing other types of music — especially rock, where many of today's drummers have monstrous sets of a dozen drums and a dozen or more cymbals — most jazz drummers since the 1940s have stayed with a fairly standard set-up: bass drum (see the figure), snare drum, floor tom, mounted tom on bass drum, high-hat, and two or three other cymbals.

Baby Dodds (1898-1959)

Dodds was jazz's first important drummer, playing on several early and innovative jazz recordings. Although the music Dodds (brother of clarinetist Johnny Dodds) made with King Oliver and later Louis Armstrong and Jelly Roll Morton is well documented on recordings, his drums are often faint or inaudible due to primitive recording techniques. In some early jazz, drummers including Dodds had minimal parts, and on certain tunes, they didn't play at all.

Dodds was an exuberant drummer — sometimes too exuberant. Even on recordings, you can sometimes catch a bass drum kick, sudden snare drum flourish, or cymbal crash that is too strong for the music. By taking risks and playing with personality, though, Dodds inspired jazz drummers to break away from the steady old rhythms of New Orleans marching and funeral bands.

The strength of his playing is evident from the length and variety of his career. His legacy from the 1920s is large. Hear him on Armstrong's *Hot Fives and Hot Sevens, Vols. 1 and 2* (JSP), with King Oliver's Creole Jazz Band on *King Oliver/1923* (Classics) and *King Oliver/1923–26* (Classics), and on Jelly Roll Morton's *Birth of the Hot* (BMG/RCA). Listen for the big beat Dodds puts down on Morton's famous version of "Black Bottom Stomp" on this last CD.

By the 1940s, when jazz had evolved significantly from his earliest years, Dodds was still playing and recording New Orleans-style jazz with his brother Johnny, the clarinetist, as well as with clarinetist Jimmie Noone, trumpeter Bunk Johnson, and others.

Even though his early recorded legacy is scant, Dodds developed some key methods of modern jazz drumming. The pedal let him keep solid, steady time on the bass drum. He supplemented the bass drum with faster rhythmic patterns on snare drum — increasingly, the snare became the primary drum in jazz ranging from swing to bebop. Dodds tuned his drums to go with the other instruments, which lent his playing a melodic element. And, like other players in small and large modern jazz groups, he improvised, playing off his bandmates, responding to and supporting their solos, contributing short solo breaks of his own.

Zutty Singleton (1897-1975)

Zutty Singleton was Baby Dodds' counterpart during the 1920s, and he played with several of the same people. But where Dodds had taken short drum solos, only a few beats long, Singleton extended the duration and dynamic range of drum solos, and was among the first jazz drummers to use wire brushes to add new color.

Although Dodds can barely be heard on recordings from the mid-'20s, Singleton's drum parts with band leaders such as Armstrong and Morton come through clearer due to better microphone placement. Singleton's strongest playing was with Armstrong during the 1920s, and his most famous moment comes on Armstrong's recording of the song "A Monday Date" (On *Hot Fives and Sevens Vol. 3*/Sony) as Armstrong urges Singleton, "Come on Zutty, whip those cymbals Pops!"

Singleton played and recorded until a few years before his death — with trumpeter Roy Eldridge, clarinet/sax player Mezz Mezzrow, clarinet/sax player Sidney Bechet, and famous band leaders Lionel Hampton and Jack Teagarden.

Paul Barbarin (1899-1969)

Not as famous as Dodds or Singleton, Barbarin played with several of the greats during the 1920s through 1950s, including clarinetist Sidney Bechet, trumpeters Red Allen, Freddie Keppard, King Oliver, and Louis Armstrong, and band leader Luis Russell. Partly due his long career, Barbarin, more than any other early jazz drummer, became a polished soloist. Catch him on his own on *And His New Orleans Jazz* (Atlantic).

Cozy Cole (1906-1981)

Cole launched his career with pianist Jelly Roll Morton, and later became one of the top swing drummers of 1930s and 1940s. Cole's drums supplied rhythmic juice in bands led by Cab Calloway, saxophonist Benny Carter, and mid-career Louis Armstrong. He also played with vibraphonist Lionel Hampton, pianist Earl Hines, and trumpeter Dizzy Gillespie, giving him as broad a stylistic reach as any jazz drummer. Hear him on *Cab Calloway/1939–1940* (Classics) and on *Cozy Cole/1944* (Classics).

Dave Tough

Working his way into jazz during the 1920s, Tough played in Chicago with saxophonist Bud Freeman, guitarist Eddie Condon, and sax/clarinet player Frank Teschemacher. Tough went on to power bands led by Tommy Dorsey, Bunny Berigan, Benny Goodman, Jack Teagarden, and Woody Herman. Tough was a humble but hard-swinging player well suited to big bands, also known as a sensitive accompanist to soloists. Hear him on *Tommy Dorsey/1936-1938* (Jazz Archives), *The Indispensable Artie Shaw/1944–1945* (BMG/RCA), and on Woody Herman's *Thundering Herds* (Sony).

Modern Colorists

Drummers in early jazz bands from the teens and 1920s chugged ahead at consistent 1-2-1-2-1-2, or 1-2-3-4-1-2-3-4 pace, laying down a solid foundation without venturing away much from the basic beat. But as the jazz of Louis Armstrong, King Oliver, and Jelly Roll Morton gave way to big band swing during the 1930s, and the fast, frenzied bebop during the 1940s, drummers grew more adventurous.

Big Sid Catlett, Chick Webb, and Jo Jones built upon the earlier playing of Dodds and Singleton. Using sets stripped of superfluous knick knacks such as whistles, bells, and ratchets, they streamlined modern drumming to bass drum, tom toms, snare drum, high-hat, and a few cymbals. They produced subtly colored supporting rhythms for increasingly subtle music. They also advanced the art of the drum solo to new levels of rhythmic and melodic complexity.

Chick Webb (1909-1939)

Tiny and bent by a deformed spine, Chick Webb made a big smash on drums. In New York during the mid-'20s, he was the battery in the Harlem Stompers, a band that included saxophonists Benny Carter and Johnny Hodges. More importantly, during the mid-'30s, Webb was among the first drummers to front a band, with a fast and flamboyant style that utilized the whole drum kit. After he added Ella Fitzgerald on vocals, the group had hit songs including "A-Tisket, A-Tasket."

Webb was way ahead of his drumming peers. He tuned his drums for melodic effect. His bass drum, for instance, was often tuned to the standup bass's G string, which at times let Webb and his bassists really lock in on the beat. Webb's nimble right foot produced shifting bass-drum accents. And foreshadowing Jo Jones and others, Webb used both sticks and wire brushes, and he mastered a full array of cymbal sounds: crashes, soft swishes, and abrupt *chokes* dating back to Baby Dodds. Combining cymbals, snare, and his other drums, Webb invented endless combinations that emphasized a song's shifting moods and rhythms. He was fast and explosive and a marvel to watch, a technician as well as a crowd-pleasing showman.

Check Chick out on *Chick Webb/1929–1934* (Classics), on *Chick Webb/1935–1938* (Classics), and on *Standing Tall* (Drive Archive), with Ella Fitzgerald.

Gene Krupa (1909-1973)

Growing up in Chicago, Krupa heard Baby Dodds and Zutty Singleton in local clubs, and was especially impressed by Dodds' playing. Inspired also by Chick Webb, Krupa developed a combustible style of his own that became the driving force of Benny Goodman's big band in 1935. With his whirling sticks, sweat-soaked suits, and bangs that flopped around as his head bobbed to his flashy solos, Krupa was a cocksure showman.

Ultimately, he and Goodman butted heads, and Krupa formed his own band in 1938, eventually adding trumpeter Roy Eldridge and singer Anita O'Day as co-stars. (Goodman still respected Krupa's talent, and the two played together again during the 1940s.)

Krupa brought drums into the spotlight. Mixing charisma, good looks, and great technique, he proved that drum solos could keep an audience excited and add valid musical variety to recordings. Like other great jazz drummers, Krupa not only kept swinging good time, but he embellished basic rhythms elaborately, and he was the catalyst behind explosive moments in Goodman's band and others.

Hear Krupa on *Gene Krupa/1935–1938* (Classics), on *Gene Krupa & Buddy Rich* (Verve), on *Uptown* (Columbia), and on the famous *Benny Goodman Carnegie Hall Concert* (Columbia).

Jo Jones (1911-1985)

Following the peak years of Dodds, Singleton, Webb, and Krupa, drummer Jo Jones added new elegance, subtlety, and rich musicality to his craft.

Born in Chicago in 1911, Jones (like Big Sid Catlett, Buddy Rich, and Louie Bellson) began his career as both a drummer and tap dancer, which gave him a broad experience of rhythmic possibilities. Jones was one of bassist Walter Page's famous Blue Devils in Oklahoma City during the late '20s at a time when red-hot regional territory bands tore up Midwest jazz clubs with all-night jams (see Chapter 3). Jones joined Count Basie's big band in 1935 and made his mark as a great jazz drummer with the Count for the next 13 years. He spurred on great soloists such as saxophonists Lester Young, Lucky Thompson, Herschel Evans, and Buddy Tate, and trumpeter Harry "Sweets" Edison to some of their best improvisations.

On high-hat alone, Jones could outswing just about any drummer. With a full array of cymbals, he was a smooth, subtle timekeeper who made an audience's fingers snap. Add in a full set of drums, and Jones became jazz's leading all-around rhythm machine, the first to utilize all the tonal colors of the set in fresh combinations. Jones could solo better than the best, but was a humble team player too — a counterpart to the showier styles of Webb and Krupa.

"Papa Jo Jones was very musical and he played with a lot of swing," says top-notch jazz drummer Jack DeJohnette. "He was very innovative, a very fresh drummer, very critical of other drummers. But he was also very supportive, and a beautiful human being. I knew him up until the time he died."

Smooth cymbal work, *polyrhythmic* (more than one steady rhythm at once, also sometimes called *cross rhythmic*) playing, drums tuned to melodic perfection, subtle support of a song's underlying rhythms and the rhythmic inventions of the other players' solos — these are Jones' contributions to the art of jazz drumming. Using his high-hat as a focal point, Jones lifted the drummer's rhythmic center from bass drum to a higher, lighter plateau, lending the music a looser feel that left more latitude for a band's leading improvisers. Using his hands, feet, and all of his drums and cymbals, Jones helped jazz drumming evolve from its early 1-2-3-4 groove into an infinite variety of possible rhythmic patterns that embellished the main beat, the music, and the lead soloists.

Although any of the Basie band's recordings with Jones on drums are important exhibits of his mastery, one CD stands out as my all-time favorite example of vintage Jones — and of modern jazz drumming: *The Essential Jo Jones* (Vanguard). I think that this CD has on it the most polished jazz drumming ever. Recorded in the 1950s by producer John Hammond as part of a multi-album project documenting leading jazz legends, the album opens with "Shoe Shine Boy," showcasing Jones as he forcefully swings an all-star band with a Rolls Royce rhythm section of Count Basie on piano, Freddie Greene on guitar, and Walter Page on bass. Jones' wire brushes swish over cymbals and snare on the sweet jazz standard "Lover Man" before he sweeps into "Georgia Mae" (his own composition) with a scaring splash of high-hat. Several ballads show his soft touch, and songs such as "Little Susie," with Jones' swinging solo introduction, illustrate his feel for the call-and-response of African drumming, where drummers answer each other's statements in an ongoing percussive dialogue.

Listen closely, and you'll be fascinated by how Jones holds the music together. During solos he switches back and forth between swinging the rhythm section and supporting soloists by responding to every nuance of their improvisations. And his brushwork is phenomenal, adding new shades to the music.

Buddy Rich (1917-1987)

As a young man, Buddy Rich was also a tap dancer and singer. He launched his career as a drummer in big bands led by trumpeter Bunny Berigan, clarinetist Artie Shaw, and trombonist Tommy Dorsey during the late '30s and '40s, and recorded with saxophonist Charlie Parker and other bebop-style innovators of the 1940s and 1950s. Beginning in the 1960s, he led his own big bands.

To get a sense of how much drumming progressed technically over the years, listen to *Krupa and Rich* (Verve), recorded in 1955, when Krupa was 46 and Rich was 38. Krupa sticks mainly with cymbal/snare/bass drum patterns. Rich uses his whole set, drumming up overlapping waves of rhythm.

"Gene Krupa was a solid drummer who swung, and he had a melodic sense and a rhythmic sense," says top jazz drummer Jack DeJohnette. "Buddy was a technical genius. His technique surpassed his ability to swing. Both were great drummers."

You can judge with your own ears whether or not Rich swung as hard as Big Sid Catlett or Jo Jones, but he was undeniably a master of rhythmic variety. His 1965 album *Mercy Mercy* (World Pacific), recorded live in Las Vegas, shows how closely Rich connected with the sections in his big band. His intricate idea of a song's rhythmic layers is audible on the song "Channel 1 Suite." Sometimes he ties accents on his snare and cymbals to bass patterns played by piano, basses, and trombones, other times he links his playing to subtle accents in other sections. The "Suite" is also exemplary because it passes through several moods, allowing Rich a chance to shine at fast and slow tempos, in fiery passages, and through soft, romantic sections that show his sensitive side.

For a searing example of Rich's roots in tap dancing and theatrical drama, check out the album *This One's for Basie* (Verve) including a snare drum explosion that ignites the song "Down For Double," and a swinging version of the Basie band's signature "Jumping At The Woodside," driven by Rich's drums.

Louie Bellson (born 1924)

Louie Bellson is among the most versatile big band drummers. Like Rich, Bellson was a product of the swing and bop eras of the 1940s and 1950s. He energized ensembles led by Benny Goodman, Tommy Dorsey, Harry James, and Duke Ellington, and he also wrote songs for Ellington. His light touch on cymbals and snare shows his sensitivity, but he can also play with explosive power and rhythmic complexity that rank him among the top all-time jazz drummers.

Polywhat?

Polyrhythms are one key piece of evidence for jazz's roots in African culture, and you can find polyrhythm as a key component of most African drumming traditions. Polyrhythm is very difficult to understand if you don't already play music, but I'll give it a try anyway. Imagine you have a song with accents that fall on the beat (the tune "Mary Had a Little Lamb" works as an example).

Then you take a tune with accents that fall more randomly ("Take Me Out to the Ball Game" works here) and lay it over "Mary Had a Little Lamb." What you end up with is 6 beats crossing with 4 beats over each measure, resulting in a composite rhythm — that's *polyrhythm,* or as some call it, *cross rhythm.*

In a polyrhythm, the beats of the two rhythms being crossed sometimes coincide, other times they are syncopated (fall at different points). The result is a complex rhythm with both components still discernible from the overall rhythm.

Bellson was among the first jazz drummers to play a set with two bass drums — many electric jazz and rock drummers now use these expanded sets. The way Bellson carefully tunes his drums places him in a line of melodic drummers stretching back through Jo Jones and Chick Webb.

Bellson is still going strong, and his 1996 CD *Their Time Was The Greatest* (Concord), a tribute to 12 of his favorite all-time jazz drummers, is an essential addition to the "drummers" section of any good jazz collection. Bellson is all over his set on "Liza," a tribute to Chick Webb, with a short but rousing solo that exhibits his Webb-like sense of melody and rhythm. "24th Day" evokes Big Sid Catlett's warm, bright swing, "Brush Taps" recalls some of Jo Jones' delicate playing on high-hat and with wire brushes, "Well Alright Then" honors Max Roach's pure combustible power, and "It's Those Magical Drums In You" brings back Krupa's light melodic touch, with carefully tuned drums. Bellson also brings back the bold Afro-Cuban rhythms of Art Blakey (on "Acetnam") and the cool California swing of vintage-1950s Shelly Manne on "Our Manne Shelly."

Among important earlier recordings by Bellson: *Prime Time* (Concord Jazz), *Side Track* (Concord Jazz), *Classics in Jazz* (Music Masters), and *Live From New York* (Telarc).

Bop and Post-Bop Drumming

Bebop's advent during the 1940s, and elaborations on bop during the 1950s, opened new possibilities to jazz players. Not only was the music sometimes blazingly fast, but it was much more complex than what had come before in terms of harmony, melody, and rhythmic combinations. Almost at the same time as they were developing bop, trumpeter Dizzy Gillespie and a few other players began bringing Latin influences into their music through associations with musicians such as band leader Machito, Cuban composer/arranger Mario Bauza, and Cuban percussionist Chano Pozo.

In the realm of drums, the music's new, broader outlook meant that its timekeepers needed to become more versatile. In this post-war period of tremendous innovation in jazz, several drummers helped make some wildly inventive new music.

Kenny Clarke (1914-1985)

In the early 1940s when trumpeter Dizzy Gillespie and saxophonist Charlie Parker created their blindingly fast bebop, Clarke frequently kept the pace as the drummer. Making increased use of cymbals and snares, which could be used most effectively to produce light, fast rhythms, he helped the new music flow smoothly. Clarke worked closely with bassists to put down a solid rhythmic foundation, but he also cemented the music together, filling gaps between horn parts with loose, swinging rhythmic combinations and surprisingly placed accents.

Clarke's *Bohemia After Dark* (Savoy) shows how subtle and effective a drummer he was. His soft, quick swishes on cymbals and high-hat are straight from the Jo Jones school of modern drumming. His ear for various rhythmic possibilities is impressive. Sometimes, he drives the music stride for stride with the bassist and the pianist's left hand. Other times, he plays counterpoint to the soloists, spurring them forward with snare drum rolls and bass drum kicks, responding to their accents with punches of his own. Clarke's sense of time is also what makes him innovative. He doesn't always play in neat groups of two or four beats, like early jazz drummers with the bands of Louis Armstrong or King Oliver, and he doesn't always emphasize the same beats. Instead, Clarke goes with the flow of the music, adding accents where appropriate, letting his *phrases* (rhythmic groups) fall as they will.

Clarke spent most of the last 30 years of his life in France (he died in Paris in 1985) and played on dozens of sessions with both beboppers and more traditional players including Louis Armstrong, Benny Carter, Sidney Bechet, and Coleman Hawkins. He also played on four songs on trumpeter Miles Davis's 1949 *Birth of the Cool* (Capitol) album, a key recording in the evolution of the laid-back cool style played in California during the 1950s.

Although some of Clarke's strongest playing is on other players' sessions, he also made several solid albums as a leader, including *Kenny Clarke All-Stars* (Savoy) and *Kenny Clarke Meets the Detroit Jazzmen* (Savoy).

Art Blakey (1919-1990)

More than any drummer of the 1940s and 1950s, Art Blakey took a genuine interest in authentic African music and its rhythms and even visited Africa in 1949. Along with his inventive drumming in some of the best 1950s hard bop — the successor to bebop — Blakey experimented with assorted international rhythms in his music.

Early in his career, during the 1940s, Blakey played a few times with bebop saxophonist Charlie Parker. Later he helped launch the Jazz Messengers with pianist Horace Silver in 1953 and took over as leader in 1956. Through four decades, Blakey's Messengers made dozens of recordings of excellent music, and Blakey became unofficial "dean" of his definitive "grad school" for rising young players. Pupils included saxophonists Wayne Shorter and Bobby Watson, trumpeters Freddie Hubbard and Lee Morgan, trombonist Curtis Fuller, pianists Cedar Walton, Joanne Brackeen, Wynton (trumpet) and Branford (saxophone) Marsalis, and the list goes on. . . .

On their debut recording, *Horace Silver and the Jazz Messengers* (Blue Note), Blakey swings the band relentlessly forward, punctuating solos by saxman Hank Mobley and trumpeter Kenny Dorham with rimshots (lightning cracks on his snare drum's steel rims), rolls, cymbal crashes, and simmering high-hat. Two hands and two feet sound, at times, like four independent players. Check out Blakey's short, sweet introduction to "Hippy." (By the way, during the 1960s, *hippy* applied to revolutionaries, but in the 1950s jazz world, it was a derogatory term that implied a phony attempt at hipness.)

Blakey's playing is always highly musical, not just rhythmic. His drums are tuned so that whether he's playing behind soloists or soloing himself, the sounds from his set come together in melodic phrasings. And like Kenny Clarke, Blakey shifted primary timekeeping duties from bass drum up to snare and cymbals, providing a looser, more fluid sound.

Blakey's talents are readily apparent on numerous CDs, but some of my favorite Blakey moments include:

✔ *Buhaina's Delight* (**Blue Note**). Crisp rolls and precise cymbal work on the song "Bu's Delight" and the rhythmic complexity of his drums on an amazing remake (actually two versions) of "Moon River" from this CD make for an excellent listen.

✔ *A Jazz Message* (**MCA-Impulse!**). Latin cross currents leading into "Cafe" on the Art Blakey Quartet album, with Sonny Stitt blowing up a storm on sax.

✔ *Orgy In Rhythm, Vols. 1 & 2* (**Blue Note — Japanese import**). A provocative blend of primal percussion, with Sabu Martinez on bongos, timbales, and vocal chants, Jo Jones and Specs Wright on drums and timpani, Art Taylor on drums, Herbie Mann adding flute sounds redolent of tropical rain forests, plus additional congas, timbales, and percussion including tree log. Blakey even takes a turn on vocals, leading a Swahili chant on "Toffi."

Max Roach (born 1924)

Max Roach was a mainstay of 1940s bebop and *hard bop* — its 1950s cousin. Roach recorded dozens of albums with Charlie Parker, Dizzy Gillespie, Charles Mingus, Bud Powell, and Sonny Rollins, and has make a tremendous range of music utilizing unconventional instrumentation over the course of a career that is still going strong.

Some of Roach's best early drumming is included on *The Smithsonian Collection of Classic Jazz* (Smithsonian) available in its original form on vinyl, and in an expanded and updated version on CD. On this CD set, Roach's simmering cymbals drive Charlie Parker's breathtaking alto sax solo on

"Embraceable You," and the drummer's own dazzling solo carries the song to its frenetic climax. On a slower version of "Embraceable You," Parker gives it a mellower reading, with Roach trading his sticks for wire brushes.

My favorite among Roach's earliest solo recordings is *Max Roach Plus Four* (EmArcy), which showcases his drums behind the blazing horns of trumpeter Kenny Dorham and tenor saxman Sonny Rollins. Roach was recovering from the death in a car crash a few months earlier of his bandmate Clifford Brown, the gifted trumpeter who died in 1956 at age 25. Roach's relentless rhythms help the horn players build volcanic solos that boil over the heat of his driving drums.

More than other drummers of his generation, Roach was also open to the *avant garde. One in Two, Two in One* (Hat Hut) is his 1979 duet with far-out saxophonist Anthony Braxton, and the 1979 *Historic Concerts* (Soul Note) album teams him with free-jazz pianist Cecil Taylor. Several of Roach's albums from the 1960s and 1970s were inspired by social/political events in Third World countries.

Over a career now in its sixth decade, Roach has made more than 40 recordings as a leader, and nearly all of them are worth adding to your collection. Music on his 1991 *To the Max* (Blue Moon) is an eclectic blend of jazz players with vocal chorus, orchestra, and M'Boom, Roach's percussion group. As does Blakey, Roach conveys a rich sense of jazz's African roots — the rhythms, the group improvising, the spiritual aura, the provocative patterns of shifting and overlapping rhythms. Each of the two CDs in this set ends with an inspired solo by Roach.

Other excellent Roach includes *Deeds, Not Words* (Original Jazz Classics), *Freedom Now Suite* (Columbia), *Percussion Bitter Suite!* (Impulse!) and *Easy Winners* (Soul Note), as well as Charlie Parker's *Jazz at Massey Hall* (Original Jazz Classics).

Others from '50s and '60s

Along with the more well-known drummers of the time, these players had a significant impact on jazz drums in the 1950s and 1960s:

- ✔ **Chico Hamilton (born 1921).** Vastly under-appreciated, Hamilton was a solid drummer and visionary bandleader who brought new sounds (and hot young players) into jazz. Hamilton played with top musicians from disparate styles of jazz: swingers such as Count Basie and Lester Young, 1950s cool and hard bop mainstays including saxophonist Gerry Mulligan and flutist Charles Lloyd, *avant garde* innovators like saxophonist Arthur Blythe, even jazz-rock fusion players including guitarist Larry Coryell. Get hold of Hamilton's *Man from Two Worlds* (Uni/ Impulse!), *My Panamanian Friend* (Soul Note), and *Transfusion* (Studio West).

✔ **Philly Joe Jones (1923-1985).** Not to be confused with Jo Jones, Philly Joe entered jazz playing bebop in Philadelphia clubs with trumpeter Fats Navarro and saxman Dexter Gordon, in New York with trumpeter Dizzy Gillespie, saxophonist Charlie Parker, and pianist Tadd Dameron, and became a leading hard bop drummer of the 1950s. Jones set the cool pace on classic albums by trumpeter Miles Davis such as *Cookin'* (Original Jazz Classics), *Workin'* (Original Jazz Classics), and *Steamin'* (Prestige). Also hear Jones on his own albums *Drums Around the World* (Original Jazz Classics), *Showcase* (Original Jazz Classics), and *Mo' Joe* (Black Lion).

The Avant garde

Jazz loosened up during the 1960s and 1970s, and when players such as John Coltrane and Ornette Coleman began blowing freeform hurricanes of sound, a number of drummers added fire to their storms. New jazz fans may not find abstract jazz as immediately satisfying as more structured styles, but dedicated listening pays off by provoking a whole new realm of emotions and perceptions.

Elvin Jones (born 1927)

Elvin Jones, little brother of famous jazzmen Hank Jones (piano) and Thad Jones (trumpet), was immortalized by his prominent part in Coltrane's innovative recordings on the Impulse! label in the mid-'60s.

Sometimes, on ballads, Jones played straightforward accompaniment on cymbals and snare, in the spirit of Jo Jones (no relation). Other times, on fast numbers, Jones swung the music forward with a drumming style rooted in Blakey and Roach, but with added punch: stronger bass drum kicks, splashier cymbal crashes, speedy rolls that cut across Coltrane's lines, and other combinations that threaten to veer out of control along with Coltrane's saxophone.

Coltrane's lengthy improvisations are the stuff of legend. On recordings, some of them last for 20 or 30 minutes or more; in person, he was known to blow for hours, until he had exhausted a song's creative possibilities. Jones's focus and power are apparent in the way he stays with Coltrane no matter where the saxophonist goes. Jones's feel for Coltrane's wild solos is uncanny; you can hear how he spurs the saxophonist on to higher and higher levels of creativity.

Jones also fronted his own sessions over the years, with players including his brothers as well as former Coltrane sideman and pianist McCoy Tyner, saxophonist James Moody, and rising young players including trumpeter Nicholas Payton, saxman Joshua Redman, and trombonist Delfeayo Marsalis.

But Jones's later recordings, to me, don't match the best of the 1940s through 1960s in imagination, improvisation, intensity, and intuitive interplay between musicians.

If you ever have a chance to catch Jones live, don't miss him. His solos are still superhuman. I love it when jazz drummers like Jones pull more sound from a small set than rock-and-rollers get from drum kits two or three times the size.

Ronald Shannon Jackson (born 1940)

Drummer Ronald Shannon Jackson merges the dexterity of Jo Jones or Art Blakey with the pure power of great rock drummers such as Led Zeppelin's John Bonham, Cream's Ginger Baker (who also plays jazz), and the Who's Keith Moon.

Born in 1940, Jackson broke into jazz during the 1960s with bassist Charles Mingus, alto saxman Jackie McLean, pianist McCoy Tyner and other established greats, but ventured into abstract jazz as a drummer in bands fronted by saxophonists Albert Ayler and Ornette Coleman and pianist Cecil Taylor. Jackson's own groups have included guitarist Vernon Reid from the rock group Living Colour, and offer an eclectic mix of musical influences including funk, rock, and blues. Check out his albums *Eye on You* (About Time) and *Mandance* (Antilles).

Fusing to Funk and Rock: Tapping New Power

Trumpeter Miles Davis plugged in his horn and utilized bands of electric musicians during the 1960s, giving birth to a new generation of electric jazz-rock players including keyboardists Chick Corea, Herbie Hancock, and Joe Zawinul, saxophonists Wayne Shorter and Gato Barbieri, guitarists John McLaughlin and Al DiMeola, and bassists Stanley Clarke and Alphonso Johnson. Supplying the rhythmic punch behind them all were drummers such as Billy Cobham, Alphonse Mouzon, and Tony Williams, many of whom moved on to prolific solo careers.

Billy Cobham (born 1946)

Cobham played briefly with pianist Horace Silver and cut his earliest records with Miles Davis and with John McLaughlin's Mahavishnu Orchestra. Live, he's a wonder to behold, one of my all-time heroes. I caught him behind a gigantic drum set in San Francisco during the early '70s, around the time of his debut solo album, *Spectrum* (Atlantic). I dare you to listen to the title cut and stay in your seat.

Blurring above an array of tom toms, Cobham's sticks made sounds with a speed and intensity beyond anything heard before from a jazz drummer. Laying down a steady backbeat straight out of funk, he shifted with blinding dexterity into all manner of rhythmic combinations. It's mind-blowing to ponder what he might come up with on a live date if he could travel back in time to take the stage with Charlie Parker or Dizzy Gillespie.

Alphonse Mouzon (born 1948)

Alphonse Mouzon was the percussive force behind the first version of Weather Report and in guitarist Larry Coryell's Eleventh House — both important bands of the fertile 1970s era of electric jazz-rock fusion. Mouzon has since led several sessions of his own, with varying degrees of success. But during the 1970s, those of us who loved fusion liked Mouzon almost as much as Billy Cobham.

Tony Williams (1945-1997)

A Miles Davis "find," Williams was still in his teens when he first played with the famous trumpeter. He was a vital member of Davis's mid-'60s Quintet and stayed with the trumpeter through his transition into electric jazz-rock. Williams provided the rhythmic juice on such unplugged early 1960's albums by Davis as *Sorcerer* (Columbia) and *Seven Steps to Heaven* (Columbia), as well as early electric outings including the meditative *Filles De Kilimanjaro* (Columbia) and *In a Silent Way* (Columbia).

Meanwhile, Williams's own group Lifetime was another one of the leading ensembles from the early '70s era of electric jazz-rock, with Williams providing the punch on both drums and vocals. *Emergency* (Polydor) is one of Lifetime's best albums. Also, try *The Best of Tony Williams* (Blue Note), *Foreign Intrigue* (Blue Note), *Angel Street* (Blue Note), and *Tokyo Live* (Blue Note).

In the tradition of earlier drummers such as Chick Webb, Jo Jones, and Art Blakey, Williams was a rhythmic genius whose presence inspired Davis and his groups, as well as many other players with whom he created good jazz: saxophonists Eric Dolphy, Sam Rivers, and Jackie McLean, pianist Herbie Hancock, bassists Ron Carter and Stanley Clarke, vibraphonist Bobby Hutcherson, guitarists George Benson and John McLaughlin (a member of Williams' group Lifetime), and others.

Jack DeJohnette (born 1942)

A last and prolific alumnus of Davis's band is Jack DeJohnette, another dark horse favorite of mine for his humility, polish, versatility, and consistent high quality.

DeJohnette has drummed it all. Rising from roots in Chicago rhythm and blues, DeJohnette broke into jazz during the 1960s with saxophonist Jackie McLean, and vocalists Abbey Lincoln and Betty Carter, and has also played with a roster of all-stars ranging from pianists Thelonious Monk and Bill Evans, to saxophonist Stan Getz, and trumpeter Miles Davis.

A list of DeJohnette's more than 20 recordings as a leader includes a couple of the top all-time drum-based albums: *Special Edition* (ECM) and *Album, Album* (ECM). DeJohnette's 1997 *Oneness* (ECM) is an intriguing collaboration with percussionist Don Alias that reflects DeJohnette's new commitment to music as meditation on a Higher Power.

Other excellent jazz drummers

The following are some other young, mature, and late-great forces to reckon with:

- **Roy Haynes (born 1926),** is a master force with Thelonious Monk, Charlie "Bird" Parker, Pat Metheny, Miles Davis, Bud Powell, Eric Dolphy, Wardell Gray, Lennie Tristano, Stan Getz, Rahsaan Roland Kirk, and others. I love small groups where players have lots of room to move. Metheny's *Question and Answer* (Geffen), a 1990 trio album, teams Haynes with guitarist Pat Metheny and bassist Dave Holland for some edgy improvisational jazz.

- **Shelly Manne (1920–1984).** He's the captain of cool 1950s California jazz: drummer, band leader, and frequent Downbeat poll winner (*Poll Winners* CDs, on Original Jazz Classics label, with drummer Barney Kessel); owner of Shelly's Manne-Hole night club.

- **Jeff "Tain" Watts (born 1960).** Best known as the powerhouse drummer in bands fronted by brothers Branford and Wynton Marsalis, Watts is also (as of 1998) a TV regular. You can catch him as a member of the house band on *The Tonight Show with Jay Leno*.

- **Other greats:** Shadow Wilson, Roy Brooks, Louis Hayes, Al Foster, Billy Higgins, Jake Hanna, Victor Lewis, Ralph Penland, Billy Hart, Mickey Roker, Grady Tate, Jimmy Cobb, Danny Richmond, and Barry Altschul.

Chapter 14

Vibraphonists: Jazz's Musical Rhythm Makers

In This Chapter

▶ Vibes claim a place in modern jazz

▶ The 1960s produce good vibes

▶ A connection between pop and jazz

*V*ibraphone just may be the ultimate jazz instrument. Marrying melodic capability with percussive power, the instrument slips easily between rhythmic and lyrical roles. Vibraphone, often just called *vibes,* can also add piano-like chords, but with an echoey, ringing sound that gives depth to the music. Although somewhat rare, vibes have been used in dramatic ways since the 1920s: Lionel Hampton's vibes were a driving lead voice in his big bands; Milt Jackson's vibes added a fresh dimension to bebop; Cal Tjader fused vibes with Latinized versions of great jazz tunes; and vibraphonist Gary Burton has made some of the most provocative and subtle jazz, often in duo or small-group settings.

Early Vibraphonists

Big bands were in full swing by the mid-'30s, and Red Norvo was the first xylophonist/vibraphonist to lead one. Building from the loose, swinging New Orleans jazz made by bandleaders Louis Armstrong, King Oliver, Jelly Roll Morton, and others during the 1920s, big band swing was distinguished by new sophistication. Songs written especially for these orchestras made imaginative use of various sections, pitting sharp trumpets against soft saxophones, letting other instruments soar with a melody or trade impro-vised solos.

Good vibes

A vibraphone (*vibes* for short) is a member of the percussion family, and its relatives include marimba, xylophone, and glockenspiel. All have bars laid out like a piano's keys, which the player strikes with mallets. While marimba and xylophone both have bars made of wood, vibes use bars made of metal — aluminum alloy on the latest models (as a group, metal-barred instruments are known as *metal-lophones*.)

Vibes get their unique sound from motorized baffles that open and close inside resonating tubes hanging below each aluminum bar (see the figure). The baffles add a wavering (vibrato) effect that can be varied in frequency (by changing the speed of the motor that turns the baffles) to fit the mood or song. Vibes also have a pedal that allows the player to *damp* the bars, that is, to stop them from ringing after they are struck.

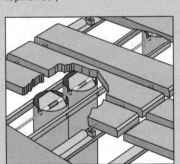

Over the years, the role of great soloists grew, and Red Norvo and Lionel Hampton helped define vibes as a lead instrument. Both were part of jazz's evolution from 1930s big band swing to 1940s bebop and the predominance of smaller groups from the 1950s forward.

Lionel "Hamp" Hampton (born 1909)

Lionel Hampton, one of jazz's all-time top vibraphonists and band leaders, launched his career during the 1920s and made his first recording (still concentrating on his other instrument: drums) in 1929. By the mid-1930s, Hampton had turned his attention to vibes and was fronting his own groups.

"The first vibes player I ever heard was Lionel Hampton," says San Diego pianist/vibraphonist Mona Orbeck, who has recorded with her husband, saxophonist Anthony Ortega. "I saw him when he first came to Norway in the fifties, with Anthony and Quincy Jones in the band. At the time I was playing classical piano, but I loved it when jazz started coming to Norway." Smitten with Hampton's swinging spirit and rapidly wavering vibrato, she was inspired to take up vibes herself, and she did after she moved to Los Angeles a short time later.

Some of Hampton's identity comes from the rhythmic variety he adds to the music — to his melodies, solos, and accompaniment of other players. When you listen to Hampton, notice how he hangs back, building anticipation, revealing his musical ideas slowly. Norvo generally stated melodic ideas directly, in predictable groups of notes, but Hampton's modern slant is apparent in the way his solos are composed of musical phrases of varying length that start and end in surprising places. His aggressive, unpredictable solos helped him fit in more naturally with beboppers than Norvo ever did.

Lionel Hampton/Greatest Hits (BMG) is a good basic collection of some of the best music Hampton made between 1939 and 1956. Hampton was one of the big band leaders who helped bring Latin rhythms into jazz; songs such as "Flamenco Soul" and "Hot Club of Madrid Serenade" are irresistible and include some of Hamp's most inspired soloing.

Through several decades, well into the 1990s, Hampton (see Figure 14-1) retained his musical abilities, continuing to perform and record. In a lasting gesture, the University of Idaho named its music school after him in 1987 perhaps the first music school to bear the name of a jazz musician.

Red Norvo (born 1908)

Red Norvo's big band showcased his xylophone (he switched to vibes in the 1940s) and vocals by his wife, Mildred Bailey. With some arrangements by Eddie Sauter (famous for his arrangements for Benny Goodman), and with tight musicianship, Norvo's band swung hip and hard.

Born in 1908 in Beardstown, Illinois, Norvo spent formative years playing xylophone in Paul Whiteman's band before heading out on his own. Norvo's evolution is well-covered by CDs. *Dance of the Octopus* (Hep) is a rousing testament to his mid-1930s innovations. *Red Norvo, Featuring Mildred Bailey* (Columbia/Legacy) includes numerous songs highlighted by Norvo's in-spired solos, with Bailey's sweet, sassy vocals as an added bonus (Norvo was married to Bailey from 1930 to 1942).

"Tea Time," a Norvo original, includes his ringing solo, with rapid runs up and down the bars, and *trilling* (alternating quickly between two or three notes) mallet rolls that accent key transitions. In addition to supple soloing, Norvo frequently allots himself the virtuoso's other main role: carrying the melody. In the context of a big band, this role was revolutionary, and really sets Norvo apart from other vibists. On "Jivin' the Jeep," it's a fresh twist to hear Norvo plunking his xylophone over a sea of swinging horns and driving bass and drums.

Figure 14-1:
Lionel
Hampton
(photo:
Everett
Collection).

During the 1940s, Norvo was among the few swing-era innovators who played extensively with new beboppers such as Dizzy Gillespie and Charlie Parker. Many couldn't keep the pace in this quick company. Norvo was fast enough, but his sensibility remained rooted in 1930s swing. When he solos alongside Gillespie and Parker on the CD *Red Norvo's Fabulous Jam Session* (Stash), his playing is nimble and melodic, and the album offers a rare and intriguing listen to jazz in a transitional stage between swing and bebop.

If you only buy one of Norvo's recordings, my recommendation is *Red Norvo Trio with Tal Farlow and Charles Mingus at the Savoy* (Savoy). I'm head-over-heels for this one — all 20 songs' worth. Norvo hits many creative highs, soloing with great imagination, speed, and fluidity, developing telepathic rapport with his bandmates. Some of the combinations he and Farlow dream up together are musical treasures. And to push this record over the top (and into any good jazz collection) is bassist Charles Mingus. His genius is obvious here, and he serves as a catalyst for the success of this cooking session; his percussive bass really drives this drummerless group.

The trio radically retools several standard jazz numbers, including "Prelude to a Kiss" (with Mingus's bowed bass), "Move," "September Song," "I'll

Remember April," "I Get a Kick Out of You," and "I've Got You Under My Skin." Hearing these songs through this group's fractured prism, you'll smile as you recognize familiar melodies recast in fresh light.

Adrian Rollini

Red Norvo is best known among early vibesmen, but Adrian Rollini was an important transitional figure between swing and 1940s bebop. Born in 1904 in New York City (he died in Homestead, Florida, in 1956) Rollini was playing piano by age 4, and by his teens teamed with Jimmy and Tommy Dorsey in a 1920s outfit called the California Ramblers. The group made several solid recordings during the 1920s, including *Hallelujah, Vol. 2* (Biograph), but the versatile Rollini was actually best known for his playing on rare bass saxophone, as on recordings he made with jazz violinist Joe Venuti during the 1930s.

In his jazz prime, Rollini recorded with Frankie Trumbauer, Bix Beiderbecke, Jack Teagarden, Bunny Berigan, and Benny Goodman. He stuck with vibes from the mid-'30s on, but his later music veered away from jazz, and into pop.

Vibes in the Modern Era

By the Modern Era, I'm referring to jazz played after the 1950s and the heyday of bebop — moving into the fractured bebop-inspired movements such as *hard bop* and *cool jazz,* and more experimentation and emphasis on the *avant garde.*

Terry Gibbs (born 1924)

Milt Jackson bridged jazz's transition between 1930s and 1940s swing, and the speedier, quirkier bebop that followed during the mid-'40s. Vibraphonist Terry Gibbs' playing isn't as diverse as Jackson's, but around 1945, Gibbs began a long reign as a leading swing-style vibesman still in action through the 1990s.

Born in New York in 1924, Gibbs played during the 1940s and 1950s in big bands led by Tommy Dorsey, Buddy Rich, Chubby Jackson, Woody Herman, and Benny Goodman. By 1959, he was fronting big bands of his own. Following several years in television (he was musical director of the *Steve Allen Show*) and as a recording studio sideman, Gibbs began a prolific second phase of his recording career in the 1980s — and went on to deliver some of his most polished performances.

Dream Band, Vol. 1 (Contemporary) catches Gibbs fronting his own 1959 group (including unsung trombone-meister Frank Rosolino), with swinging results. *Kings of Swing* (Contemporary) showcases an older, wiser Gibbs in 1991, with his frequent collaborator Buddy DeFranco on clarinet. Listening to Gibbs is like taking a trip through the early years of swing — those years during the 1930s and 1940s when legendary songwriters turned out great tunes, and great jazz players played them with the utmost feeling and finesse.

Milt "Bags" Jackson (born 1923)

Milt "Bags" Jackson, like Lionel Hampton, was a modernist — a musician who advanced jazz from its swing-era roots and into bebop and the post-World War II years of space exploration, big-finned cars, and experimentation in many art forms. Jackson constituted one-fourth of the famous and consistently excellent Modern Jazz Quartet. *MJQ,* as the Modern Jazz Quartet is known to fans, was one of the important jazz groups from the 1950s forward, putting together a string of vital jazz recordings over a span of more than 40 years. Jackson had the advantage of newer recording technology (33^{1}/$_{3}$ rpm records) that let songs break out beyond the old three-minute envelope.

"When I moved to the states from Norway in 1954, I stopped in New York and went to listen to Milt [Jackson] at Birdland," recalls San Diego vibraphonist Mona Orbeck. "And I said to myself, 'that's the nicest thing I've ever heard.' I was completely stoked, and I said, 'if it's the last thing I do, I want to learn vibes.' Milt Jackson's sound went right to my heart. I think it was his tone, with a slow vibrato, and the way he played: real bluesy, soulful, funky, true jazz."

Hitting at gut level, Jackson's sound is distinguished by his sensitive use of his instrument's adjustable vibrato — on ballads, he uses a suitable warm, wavering sound. Jackson's music has bebop's musical and rhythmic complexity and creativity. Instead of just playing a song's melody straight, Jackson and his bandmates often reinvented it, or gave it a fresh twist by teaming up in imaginative harmony.

Bags' Opus (Blue Note) is a prime example of this creativity. In a stellar sextet that includes saxman Benny Golson and trumpeter Art Farmer, Jackson does no wrong.

On "Ill Wind," a ballad with a beautiful melody written by legendary tunesmith Harold Arlen, Jackson introduces the melody before he takes off on several cycles of improvisation. While the band keeps the chord changes going, Jackson keeps the fresh improvised melodies coming, making up more imaginative material than what was originally written — genuine jazz. At the end, the song fades out beautifully in a pool of quivering vibes.

Because of the way the other players support Jackson here — harmonizing with him on melodies and supporting his solos — his vibes come off as much more effective than Red Norvo's and Lionel Hampton's were on earlier recordings. Norvo and Hampton both tried to front their bands with the other players relegated to the background, leaving less of the unified ensemble you get with Jackson, and more of a disparate "vibes plus some other players" feel.

Jackson's strength as a team player is even more apparent on the many recordings he made as a member of the Modern Jazz Quartet, under the genius of pianist John Lewis's composing and arranging (Jackson was also a prolific composer). Beginning in the early '50s, the MJQ kept a consistently creative pace over more than 40 years and several dozen albums.

Most of the MJQ's many recordings are top-notch. *Fontessa* (Atlantic) displays Lewis's intricate classically influenced composing skills, while *Third Stream Music* (Atlantic) is a sometimes-successful, always-interesting merger of jazz with classical music. *European Concert* (Atlantic) is a live 1960 date that includes plenty of Jackson's thoughtful, swinging improvisations — on tunes including his trademark "Bags' Groove."

The Best of the Modern Jazz Quartet (Pablo) CD, recorded in the mid-1980s, presents four jazzmen at the height of maturity. Jackson, John Lewis (piano), plus bassist Percy Heath and drummer Connie Kay, make some of the most meticulous jazz ever. Surprising shifts in rhythm and tempo, subtly harmonized melodies (often carried by similar-sounding piano and vibes), and a consistent sense of swing move the music relentlessly forward.

Other 1940s/1950s vibes

Here is short list of a few other players you may come across in your hunt for good vibes:

- **Teddy Charles (born 1928).** Also a pianist, Charles made his first recording during the late '40s with swing bassist Chubby Jackson's band. He also played with swing kings Benny Goodman and Artie Shaw, as well as beboppers Oscar Pettiford (bass) and Slim Gaillard (guitar). Charles was also an inventive composer/arranger. Catch him on *Coolin'* (Original Jazz Classics) and *Live at the Verona Jazz Festival* (Soul Note).

- **Tubby Hayes (born 1935).** Another multi-talented musician, Tubby Hayes applied a bebop sensibility to flute and tenor sax, as well as vibes. *New York Sessions* (Columbia) is probably his best-known album, but he also played with heavies like trumpeter Clark Terry, saxophonist James Moody, and sax/flute giant Rahsaan Roland Kirk.

- **Marjorie Hyams.** A significant swing-style vibraphonist during the mid-'40s, Marjorie Hyams played with Woody Herman's big band, as well as fronted a trio of her own. Look for her on Herman's recordings; and if you have a turntable, keep an eye out for possible rare vinyl LPs by her own small group.

> ✔ **Lem Winchester (born 1928).** This vibist grabbed attention at the Newport Jazz Festival in 1958, and made several recordings before he died in 1961 in a gun-related accident. Winchester's *Another Opus* (Original Jazz Classics) features him in a quintet that also includes Hank Jones and flutist Frank Wess.

Good Vibes in the '60s

Jazz kept pace with other arts and society in general during the 1960s. It was a time of tremendous change and experimentation — from saxophonist Ornette Coleman's free jazz to fellow saxman John Coltrane's far-out musical meditations, and trumpeter Miles Davis's coolest-of-the-cool quintet. Vibes, while never a spotlight-grabbing instrument like sax or trumpet, came along for the ride as the music evolved.

Gary Burton (born 1943)

Swimming in jazz's mainstream, as well as its abstract tributaries, Gary Burton is a creative powerhouse on vibes. Burton cut his first solo albums during the mid-'60s, and made some of my favorite jazz during the 1970s. With two (or even three) mallets in each hand, Burton plays piano-like chords and adds dense harmonies under his own melodies.

Duet albums with pianists Keith Jarrett (*Gary Burton and Keith Jarrett* on Atlantic) and Chick Corea (*Crystal Silence,* on ECM) showcased Burton's inventiveness in spare settings that leave plenty of room for improvisation.

Burton also tried his mallets at electric jazz-rock fusion during the 1960s, on albums including *Duster* (sparring with guitarist Larry Coryell). Not only did Burton import elements of rock into jazz, but he also utilized country players and sounds. One of Burton's most provocative recordings is *A Genuine Tong Funeral* (RCA), with music composed by pianist Carla Bley.

As a mentor-figure, Burton has passed the jazz torch on through his long tenure as a faculty member at Boston's prestigious Berklee School of Music. He's still making strong music on his own, including the 1998 *Reunion* (Concord) album with bandoneon (a cousin of the accordion) player Astor Piazzola — an unconventional merger of jazz with Piazzola's Argentinean tangos.

Bobby Hutcherson (born 1941)

Most prolific among vibes players whose careers took off during the 1960s is Bobby Hutcherson. Hutcherson's career stretches from the 1950s to the

1990s. Born in Los Angeles in 1941, he made his mark in jazz when he moved to New York during the early '60s. Since then, Hutcherson has played in traditional jazz settings, but he is also one of the few vibraphonists who occasionally stray into *avant garde* territory.

Compared with some of his predecessors, Hutcherson's playing can seem fast, dense, largely improvised, and tougher to follow. However, he is also a beautifully melodic player whose music captures a great range of emotions.

Some of Hutcherson's later music may appeal to jazz newbies more than his earlier, more abstract recordings. For years, Hutcherson fronted a West Coast band with saxophonist Harold Land, Jr., and their collaborations are a great way to get into Hutcherson's vibes. *Total Eclipse, Medina,* and *San Francisco* (all on Blue Note) are excellent examples of the Hutcherson/Land era.

Hutcherson's 1965 solo debut, *Dialogue* (Blue Note), is driven by the synergy between his vibes, Sam Rivers's saxophone, and Andrew Hill's piano, as they spur each other on through extended improvisations. *Components* (Blue Note), recorded in 1965 and reissued on CD, is more user-friendly. Several ballads penned by Hutcherson make this set more approachable; the music offers several warm, cozy moments, as when Hutcherson and flutist James Spaulding carry a melody together, or when Hutcherson delivers friendly, relaxed solos.

In the Vanguard (Landmark), a live mid-'80s set, also delivers a peak performance by Hutcherson, this time with bassist Buster Williams, pianist Kenny Barron, and drummer Al Foster.

Contemporary Pop/Jazz Vibes

Although some of the light "jazz" popularized by FM radio is, to most critics, neither genuine jazz nor great music, other so-called "contemporary" jazz is pleasing in its own way, if not exactly jazz. Two of the most popular pop-jazz bands of the 1980s — Spyro Gyra and Steps Ahead — featured vibes prominently. Newcomers to jazz may find this electric, percolating funk-jazz more immediately friendly than some of the harder-edged jazz made by vibraphonists such as Bobby Hutcherson and Gary Burton.

Spyro Gyra and the vibes of Dave Samuels (born 1948)

Led by saxophonist Jay Beckenstein, Spyro Gyra made challenging pop-jazz during the 1980s and early '90s. Vibraphonist Dave Samuels was instrumental in the group's sound. A protégé of Gary Burton, Samuels is a genuine jazzman who crosses into other realms.

Albums such as *Incognito* (MCA) and *Dreams Beyond Control* (GRP) show off his friendly-but-inventive sound. He teams with Beckenstein, assorted horns, or keyboards on catchy melodies, or trades improvised riffs with his bandmates. "Bahia," written by Samuels for the *Dreams* album, has a breezy, tropical sound warmed by Samuels ringing vibes. Samuels also takes a catchy, rhythmic solo that shows how Spyro Gyra can build jazzy improvisations on a friendly, funky foundation. Also check out Samuels' solo recordings, beginning with the 1977 *Double Image* (Enja).

Steps Ahead and Mike Mainieri (born 1938)

Exotic and tropical, electric pop-jazz produced by Steps Ahead beginning in 1980 is another good place to begin your explorations of vibes and improvisation. Vibraphonist Mike Mainieri is a seasoned jazz player who made music with drummer/bandleader Buddy Rich, tenor saxophonist Coleman Hawkins, and guitar man Wes Montgomery before turning to more accessible pop-jazz.

Steps Ahead's music, much of it written by Mainieri, is danceable and engaging, with Mainieri and bandmates, including saxophonist Michael Brecker, riffing over dense, funky electronic forests of sound. *Modern Times* (Elektra/Asylum) is classic Steps Ahead, with Mainieri's vibes prominently featured. Although the music crosses over from jazz into funk, Latin, and other genres, Mainieri's thoughtful improvisations qualify this stuff, in my opinion, as legitimate jazz.

From the '50s Forward: Other Happenin' Vibraphonists

Vibes has always been a fringe instrument in jazz, and less-famous players are even further on the fringe, making a significant contribution well away from the spotlight. In this section, I present a few.

Roy Ayers (born 1940)

Ayers led his own group, Ubiquity, during the late '70s prime of electric soul/ jazz fusion. Some of his CDs, on various labels, will give new jazz buffs a gentle introduction to vibes and improvisation.

Eddie Costa (1930-1962)

On *The Eddie Costa Quintet* (VSOP) album, he's in good company, including Art Farmer (trumpet), Phil Woods (alto sax), and Paul Motian (drums). Although Costa plays piano on several cuts, he shows his soft, sensitive feel for vibes on pianist Dave Brubeck's *In Your Own Sweet Way*. This album isn't worth buying just for Costa's vibes, but it is worthy for the overall strength of the music.

Victor Feldman (1934-1987)

Born in London, Feldman launched his career stateside with Woody Herman's big band during the 1950s, played with trumpeter Miles Davis, clarinetist/bandleader Benny Goodman, and alto saxman Cannonball Adderley, and was still going strong on vibes, marimba, and keyboards until his death. His *Fiesta and More!* (JVC) CD, a reissue of music from the mid-1980s, places him in a light, listener-friendly context including electric bass and synthesizers, playing mostly original music. This isn't virtuoso vibes on the order of Milt Jackson or Bobby Hutcherson, but it is pleasant, atmospheric pop-jazz. For vibes in a traditional jazz setting, try Feldman's 1955 *Suite Sixteen* (Original Jazz Classics).

Jay Hoggard (born 1954)

Listen to first-rate vibes on jazz's fringe on several discs, including *The Fountain* (Muse). Hoggard is a New York-born baby boomer who has pitted his improvising skills against far-out jazzmen such as pianist Cecil Taylor and saxophonist Sam Rivers — as well as musicians more in the mainstream, including guitarist Kenny Burrell and flutist James Newton. *Solo Vibraphone* (India Navigation), Hoggard's debut recording, is the only album I've found of a vibraphonist playing alone — this is instant total immersion in the sounds and textures of vibes. *Mystic Winds, Tropical Breezes* (India Navigation) teams Hoggard with freeform pianist Anthony Davis and others, in an electrifying session.

Gary McFarland (1933-1971)

McFarland passed away prematurely, but he had already played with Gerry Mulligan and Stan Getz in Los Angeles, and made several albums as a leader, including *Profiles* (Impulse!). Best known as a composer (Mulligan was among those who recorded his songs), McFarland was a speedy vibraphonist — at his best working in a latter-day bebop mode. He was a sympathetic sideman on albums with pianist John Lewis and singer Anita O'Day during the 1960s. On the best of his own recordings, McFarland taps the soulful, bluesy, hard-driving vibe of 1950s and 1960s hard bop.

Buddy Montgomery (born 1930)

Brother of guitarist Wes and bassist Monk, Buddy Montgomery made some of his best jazz on Wes Montgomery's laid-back 1960s albums, but he also made music of his own, including the album *So Why Not?* (Landmark). Born in Indianapolis in 1930, Montgomery is a solid composer, and has taught music to underprivileged kids and put on prison concerts. Montgomery concentrated more on piano in later years; his good vibes can be heard on *The Montgomery Brothers with Wes Montgomery* and *Shearing & Montgomery Brothers* (both on Original Jazz Classics). On piano, he also recorded one of Concord Records' critically acclaimed *Live at Maybeck Recital Hall* CDs.

Steve Nelson (born 1955)

Nelson plays good vibes with guitarist Grant Green, pianist Kenny Barron, and other jazz wheels, but also on dates of his own, including *Full Nelson* (Sunnyside). Working in a swing/bebop Milt Jackson-inspired mode, Nelson has also played a supporting role behind top hard-boppers, including saxophonist Bobby Watson — an "author's favorite."

Cal Tjader (1925-1982)

Pioneer purveyor of Latin jazz, closely linked with *cool* 1950s California jazz, Tjader was both a solid vibesman and a strong bandleader. Albums such as the 1956 *Latin Kick* (Original Jazz Classics) and the 1958 *Cal Tjader-Stan Getz Sextet* (Original Jazz Classics) catch Tjader in his prime. Tjader studied music at San Francisco State University. He stayed in the area and formed groups to play jazz with a Latin/Afro Cuban flavor.

Tjader came by his Latin leanings legitimately — playing with Latin masters such as percussionists Willie Bobo and Mongo Santamaria, pianist Eddie Palmieri, as well as Latin-loving bassist Al McKibbon. Tjader may not have been as prolific or speedy as Bobby Hutcherson or Milt Jackson, but, for his combination of musicianship and bandsmanship, he deserves to be ranked among jazz's five or six top vibraphonists. Check out Chapter 6 for a bit on Tjader's contribution to the Latin jazz scene.

Also look out for

Ray Alexander (*Cloud Patterns*/Nerus Records), Charles Dowd (on KM Records), Ed Hartman (Olympic Marimba Records), Ed Saindon (World Mallet Records), Cecilia Smith (Brownstone), and promising young German vibraphonist Matthias Lupri, a protégé of Gary Burton. And if you really want to dive deep into vibes, see the definitive list of vibraphonists on the Internet (www.shakti.trincoll.edu), which lists more than 100 players.

Part V
Strings

The 5th Wave   By Rich Tennant

OF ALL THE BASS PLAYERS THAT WORKED WITH PIANIST, BILL EVANS, THE STRANGEST WAS "GIL" MONTGOMERY, WHO ALSO DOUBLED ON CARP.

In this part . . .

In Part V, you can find out about the original bass of jazz, known as the acoustic bass, and the early jazz bassists. Discover how the bass and its great players evolved, changing the sound and style of jazz.

You can also find out about the other set of strings in jazz, the guitar. Read about the early jazz guitarists like Lonnie Johnson and discover the gypsy sound and influence of Django Reinhardt. You can find out about the beginning of the electric guitar with Charlie Christian, bebop guitarists like Kenny Burrell and Herb Ellis, and the 1950s with Wes Montgomery and T-Bone Walker. And then you can discover current great jazz guitarists like Al DiMeola and John McLaughlin.

Chapter 15

The Bassists: Boomers of the Beat

In This Chapter

▶ Early bassists keep time

▶ Jimmy Blanton redefines the role of the bass

▶ Leading bassmen take the spotlight

▶ Oscar Pettiford expands the role of the bass in jazz

▶ Charles Mingus combines sophistication and emotional power

▶ Ray Brown offers congeniality and subtle creativity

▶ The *avant garde* goes beyond bass-ics

▶ Jaco Pastorius blows audiences away with his electric bass

*O*omphing away under clarinets and cornets, tubas powered some of the earliest jazz music, made by turn-of-the-century New Orleans marching bands. But by the time of the first jazz recordings in the 1920s, tubas had dropped away like vestigial tails, sometimes replaced by trombones, but more often by basses. The bass allowed for a more percussive attack with a broader range of sounds better suited to versatile jazz ensembles.

As Armstrong and innovative soloists such as swing-era saxophonists Lester Young and Coleman Hawkins, bebop saxophonist Charlie Parker, and multi-style trumpeter Miles Davis explored new roles for their instruments, bassists advanced their art too. Although standup bass is big and cumbersome, bassists such as Jimmy Blanton, Charles Mingus, Ray Brown, Scott LaFaro, and Charlie Haden vastly extended its emotional range over the years. While basses have never equaled horns, guitars, or pianos as lead instruments for melodies and solos, they have, on occasion, succeeded in starring roles. In the hands of versatile bassists beginning with Blanton in the 1940s, a bass can beautifully carry a melody or ring out improvisations in its resonant, deep voice.

Although the bass is commonly perceived as a partner of drums in a jazz band's rhythm section, bassists and drummers really play independent but complementary parts. Together, they assure that the music's steady pulse is felt, sometimes by implication (that is, carefully placed silences or off-beat accents) as much as emphasis. Sometimes one instrument keeps the basic beat while the other embroiders it. Other times, both musicians move all around the beat. In the rhythm section, a bassist and drummer form the nucleus of the music, the solid rhythmic core around which other players build layers of improvisation.

The acoustic bass

Bass is one of jazz's oldest instruments, and the only classical string instrument to make it big in jazz (a handful of jazz musicians including Joe Venuti, Stephane Grappelli, and Leroy Jenkins have played violin). Originally named *contrabass* — named because its range is lower than the bass range of other instruments including piano.

In jazz, the instrument is commonly called "bass" . . . or "standup bass," or "upright bass." Standup? Upright? Sounds like an honest enough instrument.

Big brother among its violin siblings, the bass has a slightly different shape distinguished by sloping shoulders (other violin-family members have squarer shoulders). Instruments in this family (unlike, say, guitars) are *fretless* — the neck has no metal *frets* to aid in hitting a note accurately — which makes the instrument difficult to play well, but also affords the bassist the potential of expressive sounds such as *glissandos* produced by sliding a finger smoothly along a string, through several notes.

Basses haven't changed much since keeping the beat in classical orchestras during the late 18th and early 19th centuries. They are still made of wood (often maple for the back and sides, spruce for the top), and as the wood ages, a well-made bass's sound gets warmer and mellower. S-shaped slots (called *f-holes* — the letter "F" used to be written much more like a tall "S" with a line through the middle) on the front project sounds outward from inside the body, where they echo in the cavernous chamber as the bassist plucks (*pizzicato* style) or bows (*arco* style) the strings.

New Orleans Jazz's Early Bassists: Playing on the Beat

Standup basses aren't exactly portable, and in early jazz bands, bass parts were played by tubas and trombones — although cornetist Buddy Bolden's band, formed in 1895, included a bassist. When trumpeter/cornetist Louis Armstrong, cornetist King Oliver, and pianist Jelly Roll Morton made some of jazz's early important recordings during the 1920s, tubas or trombones were still more common than basses. But jazz is music distinguished by the strong individual voices of its players, and during the 1920s, a few bassists helped the instrument assume its primary role as a jazz band's rhythmic anchor.

Wellman Braud (1891-1966)

Born in 1891, Braud participated in the creation of jazz. In his teens, he played around New Orleans and briefly in Chicago, and by the 1920s he was in New York, where he became a vital pioneering bassist in big band swing. He was in Duke Ellington's Orchestra during the late '20s and early 1930s, and he later played with trumpeter Roy Eldridge, drummer Buddy Rich, and saxophonists Johnny Hodges and Illinois Jacquet. Hear him on *Early Ellington* (Uni/Decca), a three-CD set you should have anyway, and on many other Ellington CDs covering Braud's years with the band.

Pops Foster (1892-1969)

Pops Foster played bass during the 1910s and 1920s in several of the earliest New Orleans jazz ensembles: groups led by Armstrong, as well as Fate Marable, Kid Ory, and Luis Russell. By today's standards, though, Foster's role was relatively simple. He kept time to a 1-2 or 1-2-3-4 count, in step with the trombone. In Armstrong's group, Armstrong himself was the only player allotted significant space for *improvisation,* that is, making up new music spontaneously around a song's melody and chords.

The structure of early jazz is fairly logical. At given points in the music, the various players play notes that together form a chord — that is, they fit together in harmony around a certain note. Foster and other early jazz bassists commonly stuck to the *root* notes — the note around which chords were built by the other players. A few years later, jazz bassists began to experiment with "walking" through more diverse series of notes, often out of their traditional range.

John Kirby (1908-1952)

At a time (the 1930s) when big bands still ruled, Kirby was already fooling around with a small group that also included trumpeter Charlie Shavers and clarinetist Buster Bailey. Kirby is also noteworthy as a symbol of the bass's entry into jazz: In 1930, in Fletcher Henderson's big band, Kirby switched from tuba (the traditional low-end jazz instrument) to upright bass. Hear him on *Boss of the Bass* (Sony), as well as *John Kirby/1938–1939* (Classics), *John Kirby/1939–1941* (Classics), and *John Kirby/1941–1943* (Classics).

Walter Page (1900-1957)

Leader of the legendary Walter Page's Blue Devils, he was also a dervish of a bass player. Page didn't solo much, but he swung his band hard during the late '20s. Page was also in Count Basie's big band during the 1930s and early '40s, and during the Dixie revival of the 1950s Dixie, he toured with Eddie Condon. Hear him on Basie's *Complete Decca Recordings* (GRP), and on *Essential Count Basie, Vol. 3* (Classics).

Jimmy Blanton (1918-1942): First of the Modern Bassists

Improvisation is essential in great jazz, but prior to Jimmy Blanton, bassists weren't given much creative latitude. After Blanton showed what could be possible in the realm of improvising and carrying melodies, several generations of bassists built upon his ideas. The sound of a bass singing out lead parts is so unlike the sound of horns, guitars, or piano, that it takes some getting used to. In the same way that a horn player's breathing becomes part of the music, the sound of the bassist's fingers sliding over string, or slapping them, or plucking them, gives the instrument a tangible human quality.

Born in Chattanooga, Tennessee, Jimmy Blanton launched his career by filling a bass slot once held by Pops Foster: in Fate Marable's band aboard riverboats plying the Mississippi near St. Louis. In 1939, Duke Ellington drafted Blanton for his "Famous Orchestra," as the ensemble was frequently billed, and Ellington soon penned several tunes that maximized the bassist's burgeoning ability.

Blanton's work is preserved on Duke Ellington recordings. *Take the "A" Train: The Legendary Blanton-Webster* (Vintage Jazz Classics) showcases the bassist alongside Ben Webster's beautiful, breathy tenor saxophone in an all-star band that also includes Ellington.

On *Solos, Duets and Trios,* Blanton displays, within just four songs, all the raw tools of the modern jazz bassist. He shows his ability to carry a melody, as well as a talent for aggressive improvisation, creating new melodies using the full range of expression available on the bass. He moves up and down the length of the neck, and utilizes both *pizzicato* and *arco* techniques (see the sidebar earlier in this chapter). And his style keeps that steady swing, the loose tough-to-describe drive that makes you want to dance or snap your fingers.

"He was my idol," says bassist Chubby Jackson, a one-time member of Woody Herman's band, who caught Blanton live. "I heard him playing with Duke's band. I spent an evening watching this guy. He changed the whole conception of bass. Before that it was just thump, thump, thump, thump, and all of a sudden he started playing all over the fingerboard."

Adds Milt Hinton, a living bass legend after more than 60 years in jazz, "I heard him, I was so amazed, I says, put my bass down and burn it!" (Hinton was an important early innovator, too. His solos on tunes including "Pluckin' the Bass," with Cab Calloway's band, brought the instrument forward as a vehicle for improvisation and carrying melodies.)

Swing Bassmen

People who came out to hear the great big bands of the late '30s and early '40s expected more than music — they wanted a *show.* They loved to hear great music, but they also wanted to see gifted musicians get into the music and show it by moving around instead of standing still. Among bassists, Chubby Jackson was one who had plenty of musical talent, but who also knew how to grab an audience's attention.

Milt Hinton (born 1910)

Jazz's most durable bassist, Hinton first recorded during the 1930s, and he was still making great music well into the 1990s. Hinton has a hand on several key periods of jazz. He was a part of the 1920s Chicago scene, playing with trumpeter Freddie Keppard and others, was part of Cab Calloway's bands beginning in the late '30s, and in recent years has teamed with some of jazz's new generation. Get Hinton's *Old Man Time* (Chiaroscuro) and *Laughing at Life* (Sony). Hinton also appears on Cab Calloway's *Cab Calloway/1937–1938* (Classics) and *Cab Calloway/1939–1940* (Classics), as well as on several other Calloway recordings.

Hinton is also a fine photographer who has snapped candid shots of most of jazz's legends over the years — they're gathered together, along with the story of his life in jazz, in the book *Bass Lines* (Temple University Press).

Chubby Jackson (born 1918)

"I come from the show-off era," Chubby Jackson says. "My mom was in vaudeville and my dad was in Broadway shows. I came from the world of theater, where in order to be noticed you had to smile and shake your bum and really move around. I was the first bass player ever to use an amplifier, at Carnegie Hall in New York around 1945. With the addition of amplification, we started playing way up on the neck, because you could finally hear the high notes, and the bass became more of a solo instrument."

In 1945, Jackson won *Downbeat* magazine's poll as best bassist, and Kay (an instrument company that made, among other things, basses) made him a custom five-string bass to his specifications. On "Caldonia," Jackson recalls, "I walked way up on the (new) C string, and that was the beginning of recognition of the capability of the five-string bass." Other bassists tried five-stringers, but Jackson was the only one who stuck with it, and he made it an integral part of his electrifying stage act.

Slam Stewart (1914-1987)

As part of the famous duo Slim and Slam (with bop guitarist/humorist/ vocalist Slim Gaillard), Stewart made some hip and amusing music during the late '30s and mid- '40s, including the hit "Flat Foot Floogie." He also jammed with beboppers like trumpeter Dizzy Gillespie and Charlie Parker during the 1940s. Check him out on *Slam Stewart/1945–46* (Classics), as well as on several albums by Gaillard.

Building from Blanton: Oscar Pettiford (1922-1960)

If Jimmy Blanton brought jazz bass into the modern era, Oscar Pettiford expanded the instrument's role to encompass a symphonic array of musical roles. He also stretched the bassist's range by picking up a cello. Pettiford was a fiery, versatile innovator: player, composer, improviser, and band leader. Pettiford's 1940s recording as co-leader of a group with trumpeter Dizzy Gillespie placed him in the thick of the invention of bebop (see Chapter 4). Pettiford was also a vital part of Duke Ellington's big band from 1945 to 1948.

But Pettiford realized his full potential on several recordings he made as a leader during the 1950s. The 1957 album *Deep Passion* (GRP/Impulse!), now available on CD, is one of best bass albums ever. It points the way toward directions jazz bass players would take in the decades ahead. Pettiford composed five pieces to exploit his skills on bass and cello — an instrument seldom heard in jazz but adopted by Mr. P. with great results. A supporting cast including trumpeter Art Farmer, tenor saxman Lucky Thompson, and pianist Tommy Flanagan adds creative juice, and Pettiford even incorporated a harpist on nine cuts.

Pettiford's bass and cello are the stars here. Even in a "backing" role, his bass percolates steadily beneath the music as his fingers fly up beautiful strands of notes, into the range of a piano or horn, and then back down again. Sometimes the band breaks from its accompaniment and Pettiford's nimble hands fill the space with spontaneous melodies that elevate his instrument to the leading-role status of saxophones, trumpets, and guitars.

Born in Okmulgee, Oklahoma in 1922, Pettiford passed away too early in 1960. Listening to his impressive body of work, including about ten albums as a leader, you can only imagine what he may have done had he lived long enough to play with John Coltrane, Wes Montgomery, Herbie Hancock, Wayne Shorter, and some of the other jazz giants of the 1960s.

Big Bad Bassman: Charles Mingus (1922-1979)

More than any other jazz bassist, Mingus (see Figure 15-1) hits me at a gut level. Mingus's jazz is the most consistently powerful music I have ever heard, marrying musical sophistication with emotional power.

His recording career began during the 1940s and continued until a year before his death in 1979. Some of his best recordings are bebop dates with saxophonist Charlie Parker, pianist Bud Powell, and trumpeter Howard McGhee, and Mingus was one of the few bop-era jazz musicians who also became a vital force in *avant garde* jazz during the late '50s and '60s. Among more than 50 albums Mingus made as a leader, several are "keepers." You can also find him on sessions with trumpeter Louis Armstrong, vibraphonists Lionel Hampton and Red Norvo, and many other legendary jazz players.

His 1959 album *Blues and Roots* (Columbia) is a raw, sweaty session that includes some ultimate Mingus. You can hear him moaning and humming as he plays, channeling the creative spirit with primal power. *Mingus Ah Um* (Columbia) from the same year has a similar intensity and features some of Mingus's moody compositions, with their intricate and odd-sounding arrangements of overlapping horns.

Seldom has a jazz musician combined such intricate songwriting with loose, inspired performances by all the players. Raw, squealing horns skitter over Mingus's low, rumbling bass and seem to capture the energy and uncertainty of this era of rapid change in America. I picture towering high-rises, hustling business people with collars turned up against the cold, and steam rising from manhole covers.

Figure 15-1:
Charles
Mingus
(photo:
Fantasy,
Inc.).

The album *Mingus Mingus Mingus Mingus Mingus* (Impulse!) from 1963 opens with Mingus's bass calling out in a deep, moaning voice. Here again, and throughout this collection, are Mingus's dense, dark arrangements of horns; his playing is extremely assured as he drives his band relentlessly with a thrumming undercurrent.

Mingus's guttural hog call opens "Hog Callin' Blues" on his 1962 album *Oh Yeah* (Atlantic). Mingus is at his grittiest best on this session, which includes plenty of bass playing, but also his shouts and groans as he gooses a band that includes multi-reed master Rahsaan Roland Kirk (see Chapters 8 and 18).

And for a 1990s taste of Mingus's legacy, watch for live performances in your town by the Mingus Big Band, supervised by his widow, Sue Mingus. Or catch them on your next trip to the Big Apple.

Mr. Congeniality: Ray Brown (born 1926)

Mingus's music was dark and disturbing, but bassist Ray Brown fits seamlessly into any musical context with consummate technique and subtle creativity, playing bass with a more sunny disposition.

"He's the greatest working bass player I know," says jazz bassist Milt Hinton, who has heard the best during a career that dates back to the 1930s. "He's done more of it, and he's done it well. He's a complete bass player and a soloist."

Ray Brown began his career in the midst of jazz's most technically challenging music. During the mid-'40s, he played with saxophonist Charlie Parker and trumpeter Dizzy Gillespie in New York City during the days when they were inventing the bebop style. Brown has since recorded many albums of his own (look for titles on Original Jazz Classics, Concord, and Telarc), as well as playing alongside Ella Fitzgerald, and serving as the regular bassist in pianist Oscar Peterson's group for many years. Listening to his music, you can hear how he plays a subtle, multifaceted role: He drives the music rhythmically, but he also slides sweetly through the spaces between drums, piano, guitar, and horns. Brown plays patterns that carry key rhythms, but his melodic accompaniments support, enhance, and inspire the soloists.

For a snapshot of how much jazz bass playing progressed in the years between Blanton and Brown, get your hands on a copy of *This One's for Blanton* (Original Jazz Classics). On this CD, Brown and Duke Ellington update the piano-bass duets Blanton and Ellington recorded in 1940. Aside from the much-improved recording quality, Brown takes Blanton's raw innovation and puts polish on it. Whether walking the neck on "Do Nothin' Till You Hear From Me," going head-to-head with the Duke on "Pitter Panther Patter," carrying the melody on "Things Ain't What They Used to Be," improvising all over the instrument on every song, or simply accompanying Ellington with all manner of rhythms, chords, sassy string-bends, and sliding chords, Brown gives a masterful display.

Others from the '40s and '50s

Beginning with bebop's arrival during the mid-'40s, jazz evolved through several phases during the 1950s, including cool and hard bop. Here are a few more bassists of note from those decades.

Cecil McBee (born 1935)

Yet another bassist comfortable with one boot in hard bop and the other in *avant garde,* McBee was a powerhouse behind some of jazz's greatest innovators. Hear him on saxophonist Jackie McLean's *It's Time* (EMD/Blue Note), on saxophonist Wayne Shorter's *Etcetera* (EMD/Blue Note), on trumpeter Charles Tolliver's *Live at Slugs, Vol. 1* (Strata-East), flutist James Newton's *Luella* (Gramavision), as well as on his own fine *Compassion* (Enja) and *Flying Out* (India Navigation).

Red Mitchell (1927-1992)

Hitting the scene in big bands led by Woody Herman, Charlie Ventura, and others, Mitchell is noteworthy both for these affiliations and for several small-group projects that included leading players like saxophonist Gerry Mulligan, vibraphonist Red Norvo, even cutting-edge saxophonist Ornette Coleman. Catch Mitchell on his own *Talking* (Capri), as well as on *Gerry Mulligan in Paris, Vols. 1* and *2* (Vogue).

Beyond Bass-ics: The Avant garde

In New York lofts and other artsy settings across the country, jazz players probed new directions during the 1960s. Like other instrumentalists in jazz, bassists pushed the limits. Not only did they find ways to extend the Blanton-Pettiford-Mingus-Brown line of rhythmic complexity and improvisational innovation, but they explored abstracts approaches to playing bass that emphasized raw sounds and feelings over traditional melodies and harmonies.

Charlie Haden (born 1937)

Bassist Charlie Haden's career has covered many changes, beginning with cutting edge recordings he made alongside trumpeter Don Cherry and saxophonist Ornette Coleman beginning in 1959. Coleman's "harmolodic" approach to music provided minimal structure in terms of chords and written melodies, giving maximum freedom for improvisation.

In the late '50s, with Ornette Coleman, Haden felt for the first time that he was in a musical setting free enough to accommodate the music he heard in his head. He made several provocative recordings with Coleman, as well as later abstract jazz albums with pianist Keith Jarrett and saxophonist Jan Garbarek.

Haden's 1970 *Liberation Music Orchestra* (Impulse!) is an all-time classic of contemporary free jazz. He conceives much of his music as a vehicle for his feelings on social and political issues. Inspired by the songs of the Spanish Civil War and by Vietnam War-related conflict at the 1968 Democratic National Convention, Haden recorded this suite of music that bounces between the folksy warmth of the old Spanish songs and the Liberation Orchestra's wild, far-out playing.

Like much of the free jazz of the 1960s, this music appeals to me for the obvious virtuosity of the musicians, and the sheer power of the playing. But it is anxious, troubling music, not music I return to again and again in search of warm fuzzies. For that purpose, my favorite Haden album is the 1995 *Steal Away* (Verve), a series of duets with pianist Hank Jones. The music on this album consists of traditional African American songs such as "Swing Low, Sweet Chariot," "Wade in the Water," and "Nobody Knows the Trouble I've Seen." In their spare, earthy beauty, these songs have a sweeping emotional impact and simplicity that's often more appealing than the anarchic playing of the Liberation ensemble.

During the 1980s and early '90s, Haden used the mysterious Los Angeles of Raymond Chandler's mystery novels as the inspiration for several albums with his Quartet West. Although direct connections to the L.A. of noir novels and movies are difficult to detect, the music on CDs such as *Haunted Heart* (Verve) is solid jazz.

Niels-Henning Orsted Pedersen (born 1946)

In the technical virtuosity department, Danish jazzman Niels-Henning Orsted Pedersen has titan talents. He can run off blindingly fast improvised lines of melody with amazing clarity and nuance.

"If I really want to be truthful about it, the bass player that thrills me is Orsted Pedersen," says Chubby Jackson, bassist in Woody Herman's big band during the 1940s. "He expounds so much truth that it is unbelievable. I have a video of him with pianist Oscar Peterson, and I am in awe of the way he chooses notes and the way they all fall into line."

Trio 2 (SteepleChase), Pedersen's 1977 live recording with drummer Billy Hart and French guitarist Philip Catherine is an unsung great album of electric jazz/rock *fusion*. Pedersen's bass and Catherine's echoey electric guitar duke it out on a series of electrifying cuts with lots of clear space for improvisation. Some of Orsted Pedersen's most amazing playing is also found on the CD *Dancing on the Tables* (SteepleChase).

On both recordings, Orsted-Pedersen puts his bass through amazing work-outs. He matches guitarists Catherine and John Scofield neck-and-neck as they speed through melodies, taking the bass to new heights as a lead instrument.

Gary Peacock (born 1935)

Spanning space between traditional jazz and edgy jazz, bassist Gary Peacock has had a long and prolific career, rooted in later day bebop, but also venturing into *avant garde* areas. In the late '50s, Peacock became a part of the cool/hard bop Los Angeles scene, playing with guitarist Barney Kessel, trumpeter Shorty Rogers, and others. In New York during the 1960s, Peacock connected with pianist Bill Evans, multi-reedman Jimmy Giuffre, and cutting-edge pianist/composer George Russell.

I'm a guitar fanatic, and *Just So Happens* (Postcards), Gary Peacock's CD of duets with spacey guitarist Bill Frisell is a "desert island disc." If you have the patience to put on some headphones, lie in the dark, and listen for an hour or so, I promise expanded jazz consciousness.

Eberhard Weber (born 1940)

German-born bassist Eberhard Weber is another mainstay of the ECM label's legacy of thoughtful, meditative jazz. Weber is an imaginative composer, and you can experience the epic grandeur of his songs on *Works* (ECM), a compendium of his best music from several recordings during the 1970s and 1980s. A couple of cuts employ symphony orchestras, further blurring boundaries, or perhaps exploring the commonalities (depending on your perspective), between jazz and classical music.

Weber is also important because he was among the generation of upright bass players who doubled on electric bass — in Weber's case equipped with five strings instead of the usual four. Great CDs featuring Weber include his own *The Colours of Chloe, Fluid Rustle,* and *Pendulum,* as well as vibraphonist Gary Burton's *Ring* (all on ECM).

Connected with Current: Electric Bass

During the 1960s, electric rock-and-roll with jazzy flavors caught the attention of many jazz players. Rock musicians including Jimi Hendrix, Jack Bruce (bassist in the group Cream), Frank Zappa, and Allan Holdsworth made music with rock's intensity and volume, but also some of jazz's complexities. Early jazz bassists, led by Monk Montgomery, added electric bass to their arsenal during the 1950s.

Ron Carter (born 1937)

Carter, whose roots are deep in jazz, brought an extensive knowledge of the bassman's craft to his electric instrument — sometimes a smaller, higher pitched electric "piccolo bass."

Standup versus electric — the details

Going back to the advent of recording and microphones in the 1920s, bassists experimented with amplifying their instrument. Many standup bassists today use a *pickup* — an electronic microphone-like device attached to their instrument that picks up the vibration of the strings.

But electric basses available beginning in the 1950s added a whole new dimension to jazz. Gaining widespread use during the '60s, electric bass has similarities to acoustic bass, but also significant differences. Standup basses, as stated in the sidebar earlier in this chapter, are big, hollow-bodied wooden instruments that belong to the violin family. Electric basses, on the other hand, are much smaller, made of a solid hunk of wood, and closer cousins of the electric guitar. They have a parallel range in terms of notes, but they look like a slightly larger guitar and they are held like a guitar.

Some electric basses have frets, others don't — fretless electric basses can produce a sound more similar to acoustic basses, which also lack frets. As with standup bassists, electric bassists sometimes use instruments with additional strings. A standard bass — unplugged or electric — has four strings. Contemporary electric basses may have five or even six, giving the player much broader range and the ability to play fuller-sounding chords, as well as bass lines, melodies, and improvisations.

During the early '60s, Carter played driving acoustic jazz with drummer Chico Hamilton and multi-reedman Eric Dolphy, and later with pianists Thelonious Monk and Randy Weston. He joined Davis's quintet in 1963 and as the trumpeter music grew more raucous and electrifying, Carter played more and more electric bass.

As a member of Davis's mid-'60's quintet, Carter brought electric bass into a new era on albums such as *Miles Smiles, Nefertiti, Miles in the Sky,* and *Filles De Kilimanjaro* (all on Columbia). Marcus Miller, Michael Henderson, and other electric bassists succeeded Carter in Davis's groups, and later albums by Miles such as *On the Corner* (Sony) and *Amandla* (Warner) were dance-inducing experiments in fusing jazz improvisation with a funked-up beat.

Carter's electric bass also boosted recordings he made with Brazilian percussionist Airto Moreira (including my favorite, *Virgin Land,* on CTI). On electric bass, Carter mostly played parts similar to what he played on his standup bass, but being plugged in gave him a bolder sound. Later in his career, Carter returned to acoustic standup bass as his main instrument.

Stanley Clarke (born 1951)

Stanley Clarke, a solid acoustic bassman, pushed the limits of jazz bass playing in recordings with keyboard player Chick Corea's group, Return to Forever. On the Brazilian-flavored *Light As a Feather* (Polydor), Clarke focused on standup bass, pushing its melodic potential by pairing up with Flora Purim's vocals on long improvisations. By 1973's *Hymn of the Seventh Galaxy* (Polydor), though, Clarke was plugged in and funking along with Corea's electric keyboards and Bill Connors' electric guitar. To me, Clarke's solo recordings, including his 1974 debut, *Stanley Clarke* (Epic), never combusted like his sessions with Corea, although they contained many moments of astounding bass-ery.

Wild Man on a Mission: Jaco Pastorius

Although most of the electric bassists playing jazz during the 1960s and 1970s approached the instrument in either a conventional jazz or jazz-funk fashion, one player, Jaco Pastorius, took the instrument to entirely new places.

In his 20s, Jaco Pastorius was already taking on traits of vintage Muhammad Ali, boasting often that he was the world's best bassist. And like Ali, Pastorius backed up his mouth with some formidable displays of prowess. On his own albums and especially on recordings with the electric jazz/rock group Weather Report and with rock singer Joni Mitchell, Pastorius produced a fresh, distinctive sound that is instantly recognizable: swooping, soaring, droning strings of notes that stamped every song he played with his warm, melodic presence.

Pastorius and his band were opening a show for Weather Report when that group's founders — saxophonist Wayne Shorter and keyboard player Joe Zawinul — heard him and were blown away. From his first recording in 1974 (*Jaco,* on Improvising Artists) with guitarist Pat Metheny, until he died in 1987 after years of struggling with drug addiction, Pastorius was the most original electric bassist of his era.

Two of my favorite all-time albums show the impact Pastorius had with his powerful electric bass playing. Weather Report's *Black Market* (Sony) is a gem of electric jazz/rock fusion, and on folk/rock singer Joni Mitchell's *Hejira* and *Mingus* albums (both on Asylum), Pastorius provided long, singing lines of electric bass. His ability to fit in a variety of settings showed his versatility, and spread inventive jazz ideas to other styles of music heard by other audiences. During live performances, Pastorius blew audiences away with his wild Jimi Hendrix solo medley.

Seasoned Stalwarts

Through the 1960s and 1970s, as jazz went through electric incarnations, several longtime leading bassists stayed with acoustic bass and are still going strong today. With styles rooted in swing, cool, bebop, hard bop, and the *avant garde,* they bring a well-rounded approach to their newest music.

↙ **Charles Duvivier.** He never recorded as a leader, but over the years he was a rock-steady sideman to top players. Some of Duvivier's best playing was with pianist Oscar Peterson during the 1950s, a decade during which he also made great music with under-appreciated tenor saxophonists Arnett Cobb (including *Blow, Arnett, Blow,* on Original Jazz Classics) and Eddie "Lockjaw" Davis (such as *Smokin',* on Original Jazz Classics).

Some of Duvivier's most progressive playing was with experimental sax/flute/bass clarinet player Eric Dolphy, on the 1961 album *Magic* (Prestige), on which Duvivier at one point duels with Dolphy on bass and cello. Duvivier also plays on *The All Stars With Shorty Baker* (Original Jazz Classics), vocalist Etta Jones' *Don't Go to Strangers* (Original Jazz Classics), drummer Shelly Manne's *2-3-4* (Impulse!), saxman Oliver Nelson's *Straight Ahead* (Original Jazz Classics), saxophonist Sonny Stitt's *Sonny's Back* (Muse), and several sessions with bebop pianist Bud Powell.

↙ **Percy Heath (born 1923).** A longtime member of the Modern Jazz Quartet (MJQ), Heath is a rock-steady bassist capable of solid accompaniment and inventive solos. During the 1940s, he was present at the inception of bebop, playing alongside saxman Charlie Parker, trumpeters Dizzy Gillespie and Fats Navarro, and pianist Thelonious Monk. Most of the MJQ's many recordings are well worth the price.

↙ **Rufus Reid (born 1944).** Several of Reid's recordings as a leader are superb. Reid is a strong rhythm section anchor and an excellent improviser. He has also backed bands for saxmen Dexter Gordon and Sonny Stitt, and trumpeters Dizzy Gillespie and Art Farmer.

↙ **Miroslav Vitous (born 1947).** A former member of the electric jazz/rock unit Weather Report, album-mate of keyboardist Chick Corea, drummer Jack DeJohnette, saxophonist Wayne Shorter, and trumpeter Donald Byrd, Vitous has also recorded a number of notable solo albums, including his debut, the 1969 *Mountain in the Clouds* (Atco).

↙ **Buster Williams (born 1942).** *Something More* (In + Out) is one of Williams best recordings as a leader, but he has also played on recordings by saxmen Gene Ammons and Sonny Stitt, as well as vocalists Betty Carter, Sarah Vaughan, and Nancy Wilson.

↙ **Reggie Workman (born 1937).** Anchoring the rhythms in both hard bop and *avant garde* contexts, Workman, like his name implies, has been a workhorse bassist, teaming with countless top players from the 1950s through 1990s. He was one of Art Blakey's Jazz Messengers during the early 1960s, and he's on Coltrane's *Ole Coltrane* (WEA/Atlantic), saxophonist Archie Shepp's *Four for Trane* (GRP/Impulse!), and on *avant garde* pianist Marilyn Crispell's *Live in Zurich* (Leo).

Back to Bass-ics: Young Cats Worth a Listen

Several bassists are currently playing jazz with plenty of power, keeping their instrument alive as a vital tool for carrying melodies, improvising, and keeping steady time. The so-called *Young Turks* of jazz returned to the unplugged approach during the early 1980s, and bassists went back to standup acoustic basses, in search of soulful, earthy sounds.

Trumpeter Wynton Marsalis's second album *Wynton Marsalis* (Columbia) includes both Ron Carter and talented young bassist Charles Fambrough. Charnett Moffett and Robert Hurst played standup bass on subsequent albums by Marsalis, such as *Hot House Flowers* (Columbia) and *Black Codes (from the Underground)* (Columbia). Originally a guitarist, Hurst is an especially strong bassist. In live performances with bands led by Wynton Marsalis and his brother Branford (saxophone), Hurst attacks his instrument with percussive power, plucking out the rhythmic pulse and also playing lyrical solos.

Charles Fambrough (born 1950)

Leader on several recordings of his own, including the excellent *Blues at Bradley's* (CTI), Fambrough is a seasoned pro who first plucked a standup bass with drummer Art Blakey's Jazz Messengers. Blakey's bands were legendary for their propulsive rhythms, and for Fambrough to survive Blakey's tight playing, he had to be good. Also check out Fambrough as a sideman on CDs by Wynton and Branford Marsalis, saxophonist Kenny Garrett, trumpeter Roy Hargrove, percussionist Airto Moreira, and pianist McCoy Tyner (former pianist with saxophone giant John Coltrane).

Fambrough's solo recording *The Proper Angle* (CTI) is a searing example that includes several of his own lyrical compositions. Unfortunately, Fambrough's more recent CD, *Upright Citizen* (nuGroove), finds him fingering the strings under some exceedingly bland pop-jazz.

Christian McBride (born 1972)

By his early 20s, McBride had already played with major jazz musicians such as Bobby Watson, Benny Golson, Freddie Hubbard, and Benny Green. *Fingerpainting* (PGD/Verve) is a collection of pianist Herbie Hancock's compositions performed by McBride with fellow peach-fuzzers Nicholas Payton on trumpet and Mark Whitfield on guitar. For a more convincing earfull of what McBride can do, get *Parker's Mood* (PGD/Verve), their tribute to the legendary saxophonist Charlie "Yardbird" Parker.

Chapter 16

Guitar: Strung Out on Jazz

In This Chapter

▶ Jazz guitar before the electric era

▶ Charlie Christian and the electric guitar

▶ Django Reinhardt's Gypsy jazz

▶ An introduction to modern jazz guitarists

▶ Electric guitarists and rock-jazz fusion

▶ Fringe dwellers

Guitarists and pianists are jazz's split personalities. They play both rhythmic and melodic roles. Officially members of a jazz band's rhythm section — along with bassists and drummers — they frequently keep a low profile, pulling and pushing the music forward with rhythmic chord combinations. But guitarists and pianists can also take the lead when it comes to carrying melodies, and they can improvise alongside trumpeters, saxophonists, and other brassier bandmates.

And guitars have something in common with drums, the traditional rhythmic ringleaders. Guitars can be percussive instruments when played with a more striking, strumming motion.

Around New Orleans, where jazz was born, guitar and its cousin the banjo had been popular for years. String trios with a guitar or banjo — and with the addition of mandolin and bass — played often in African American and Creole neighborhoods. Between 1895, when, in New Orleans, Buddy Bolden formed what many historians consider to be the first jazz band, and the 1920s, when jazz proliferated and the earliest jazz recordings were made, the guitar's role in jazz was minimal. Yet Bolden's lineup in 1905 included Jefferson Mumford on guitar — in a photo of the six-piece ensemble, Mumford holds a small, conventional acoustic guitar. Whereas many early jazz bands utilized tubas to cover low bass notes, Bolden's band also had a bassist.

Guitar players often *doubled* (played both at various times) on banjo because it is louder and can be heard in settings that drown out acoustic guitar. Johnny St. Cyr often favored his banjo over a guitar on recordings he made with Louis Armstrong, Jelly Roll Morton, and others — photos from the 1920s frequently show St. Cyr with a banjo. Musicians who concentrated on banjo in early jazz bands included Bill Johnson (with King Oliver), Papa Charlie Jackson, and Harry Reser. Even Fletcher Henderson's Orchestra, a 1920s prototype for classic 1930s and 1940s big bands, often included a banjo in the guitar's eventual slot.

Whether jazz's earliest fretmen selected a banjo or a guitar, their role was predominantly rhythmic. They rarely carried a melody or soloed. Strumming chords, they helped bassists, pianists, and drummers keep the pace.

Early Jazz Guitarists

By the mid-'20s, when the earliest jazz recordings were made by bands fronted by Louis Armstrong, Sidney Bechet, King Oliver, and others, newer, louder guitars made the instrument more prevalent in jazz. By 1927, St. Cyr's banjo had given way to a guitar — a simple, small acoustic model similar to the one Jefferson Mumford played with Buddy Bolden.

As jazz rose to popularity via records and, eventually, radio, guitarists replaced banjo players as the music's primary stringmen. And Eddie Lang and Lonnie Johnson were jazz's earliest guitar virtuosos — rhythm section players, but also soloists who began to take their place alongside trumpeters, saxophonists, and other spotlight players.

Lonnie Johnson (1889-1970)

Lonnie Johnson was one of jazz's earliest guitar soloists, in bands led by Armstrong, Oliver, and Duke Ellington. Best known as a blues player (and singer), Johnson also added bluesy licks to numerous jazz recordings during the 1920s and 1930s.

Born in New Orleans in 1889, he played around Storyville, the fabled red-light district, during the early 1920s, then moved to St. Louis. Improvising short strings of single notes, Johnson was the forerunner of Charlie Christian and other jazz guitarists who took much longer, more complex solos in the single-note style.

Johnson recorded with Armstrong's Hot Five, soloing simply but with tons of spirit, as when he trades licks with Louis on "Hotter Than That." Johnson even tosses in a *string-bend* or two (bending strings by pushing them across the guitar's neck is a technique more common to blues, and later rock guitar, but also used by jazz players).

Thanks to a spate of CD reissues of vintage jazz in the 1990s, Johnson's career as both a guitarist and a blues singer is thoroughly documented. Some of his best early jazz is included on his album *Steppin' on the Blues* (Sony), as well as on Armstrong's *Hot Fives and Sevens, Vol. 3* (Columbia) CD. Johnson also sang some blues. Other fine Johnson CDs include *Completed Recorded Works, Vol. 1 (1925-1932)* (Document) and *Lonnie Johnson, Vol. 2 (1926-1927)* (Document). And if you want to sample Johnson's extensive body of blues, his music of choice after the 1930s, CDs on Document, BMG/RCA, and Original Blues Classics capture his blues guitar up through the 1960s.

Eddie Lang (1902-1933)

Lonnie Johnson's alter-ego during jazz's early years was Philadelphia-born Eddie Lang, famous for duets with violinist Joe Venuti. Lang had a deeper knowledge of music than Johnson.

Whereas Johnson's guitar playing was blues-based, Lang was more of a jazz purist. He had a larger repertoire of chords than Johnson, and his solos were more complex. Lang was much in demand — in addition to his own recordings, he worked with leading jazz bands led by Paul Whiteman, Jean Goldkette, Bix Beiderbecke, Frankie Trumbauer, and he backed a young singer named Bing Crosby.

And both together . . .

Besides being innovative jazz guitar soloists, Johnson and Lang put down some of the earliest jazz guitar duets (with Lang using the name Blind Willie Dunn), several of which are available today on CD and offer an intriguing contrast between Johnson's straightforward chords and bluesy solos, and Lang's more refined use of chords with improvised Johnson-like strings of single notes.

Catch these two together on Lang's *Stringing the Blues* (Columbia), which also includes several Lang/Venuti collaborations. *Jazz Guitar* (Yazoo) offers another good listen to Lang between 1927 and 1932. New in 1998, *The Quintessential Eddie Lang* (Timeless) gives yet another good sampling of Lang's solid contribution to jazz guitar before he died from a failed tonsillectomy at age 30 in 1932.

Other jazz guitarists made contributions during jazz's early years

Lonnie Johnson and Eddie Lang, though the easiest stars to spot, were not the only lights in the sky of early jazz:

- **Teddy Bunn (1909–1978).** A leading swing guitar slinger during the 1930s, Bunn played with clarinetists Jimmie Noone and Johnny Dodds, trumpeter Tommy Ladnier, saxophonist/clarinetist Mezz Mezzrow, and soprano sax/clarinet master Sidney Bechet. He also recorded with Duke Ellington in 1929. Some of Bunn's best playing is on *Teddy Bunn/1929-1940* (RST).

- **Al Casey (born 1915).** One of the most gifted among early guitar soloists, Casey was an innovator who mixed chords and lines of melody in his improvisations. During the 1930s and 1940s, he also played with Billie Holiday, Chu Berry, and King Curtis. Catch him on Fats Waller's *I'm Gonna Sit Right Down* (Bluebird) album, as well as his own 1960 *Buck Jumpin'* (Original Jazz Classics).

- **Dick McDonough (1904–1938).** Promising guitarist cut down by alcoholism, McDonough played with violinist Joe Venuti, the Dorsey brothers, the singing Boswell sisters. His pioneering solos used chords and melodic strings of notes. Sample his stuff on *Benny Goodman: The Early Years 1934* (Biograph), and *Bill Challis and His Orchestra* (Jazzology).

- **Oscar Moore (1921–1981).** A Texan, Moore played with singer/pianist Nat King Cole for a decade beginning in 1937. Moore used an electric jazz guitar, and though he didn't record much on his own, he was an important innovator in combining improvised single-note strings of notes with chords. Check him out on *The Oscar Moore Quartet* (VSOP), which includes his versions of popular jazz tunes such as "Love for Sale," "Body and Soul," and "April in Paris."

In the wake of Lang's death and Johnson's growing preference for blues, jazz guitarists including Carl Kress (who recorded a few duets with Lang) and Dick McDonough also made minor contributions—but they never matched Johnson and Lang's prowess as soloists, accompanists, and integral members of jazz rhythm sections.

The Parallel Reality of Django Reinhardt (1910-1953)

Meanwhile, in France, guitarist Django Reinhardt was inventing different but equally intriguing new approaches to jazz, initially on a conventional *acoustic* (non-electric) guitar. By most accounts, Charlie Christian and Reinhardt heard and knew little of each other, although they both hit their prime during the 1930s.

Reinhardt, a Belgian coming from French Gypsy roots, made some of his best music co-leading a group with violinist Stephane Grappelli. Reinhardt's sound was more European and folk-influenced than Christian's, but his contribution to jazz guitar was parallel. His sound was distinctly Gypsy, reminiscent in some ways of music one might hear at a Jewish wedding . . . yet that's oversimplifying the way he combined earthy European folk music with hot new swing in a style best described as *Django*. He made the guitar a lead instrument for carrying melodies, and for improvising. His solos were long, intricate, and beautiful — much more challenging than earlier jazz guitar solos.

"Django, in his own way, was almost as good as Charlie, but he wasn't a straight jazz player," explains leading jazz guitarist Herb Ellis. In a New York club during the 1950s, Ellis was performing one night when Reinhardt walked in. Ellis surrendered his guitar, and was knocked out by the music, which he says could be called "folk Gypsy jazz."

The inimitable power of Reinhardt's playing came partly — as it did with other great jazz players — from a soul that had struggled. Reinhardt ruined all but two left fingers in a fire during the 1920s, but he played a great guitar.

His early playing with Grappelli in their Hot Club group is captured on the *Quintet Du Hot Club De France* (Jazz Archives), and *Django Reinhardt and Stephane Grappelli* (Pearl Flapper). Countless CDs capture Reinhardt on his own, including *Django Reinhardt 1935–36* (Classics), *Django Reinhardt: The Quintessence 1934–1943* (Fremeaux & Associates), *Django Reinhardt Vol. 5/ Solo Sessions 1937/43* (Jazz Archives), *Django Reinhardt 1936–40* (Giants of Jazz), *Plays the Great Standards* (Empress/Empire), *The Best of Django Reinhardt* (EMD/Blue Note), *Django's Music* (Hep), *Djangologie/USA Vols. 1 and 2* (DRG) with saxophonist Benny Carter and Coleman Hawkins, and *The Indispensable Django Reinhardt/1949–1950* (BMG/RCA). All told, Reinhardt recorded close to 50 albums during a career that lasted from the 1920s until his death in 1953 . . . and just about all of the music can be considered essential.

Reinhardt's influence on jazz was felt far and wide. Here are some other guitarists associated with his style:

- ✔ **Oscar Aleman.** Argentinean guitarist and Django-ite who even played the same type of strange-shaped, oval-holed guitar as Reinhardt, Aleman was a first-rate swing-jazz guitarist who some say could out-Django Django. *Swing Guitar Masterpieces 1938–1957* (Acoustic Disc) takes a broad measure of the man's music in two CDs containing 52 cuts of Latinized standards, ragtime, and swing tunes. Also listen to *Stringtime in Buenos Aires* (Hot Club Records), a 1990s tribute to Aleman featuring top Argentinean guitarists.

- ✔ **Philip Catherine (born 1942).** Catherine, like Lagrene, launched his career with Reinhardt as an early inspiration. *Chet's Choice* (Enja) features Catherine with trumpeter Chet Baker during the final period of Baker's career. *Transparence* (Inak) includes the song "Rene Thomas," a tribute to another excellent Belgian guitarist. Catherine cooks with saxophonist Dexter Gordon on *Something Different* (SteepleChase) and pays homage to Reinhardt alongside violinist Stephane Grappelli, guitarist Larry Coryell, and bassist Nils-Henning Orsted Pedersen on *Young Django* (MPS).

✔ **Bireli Lagrene (born 1966).** Belgian, same as Reinhardt, Lagrene sounded like his early role model as a teenage guitar prodigy. After veering into electric jazz-rock fusion during the 1980s, Lagrene is back to straight, driving jazz in a 1950s hard bop direction. *Standards* (Blue Note) is a good CD to start with. Also check out *Live in Marciac* (Dreyfus).

✔ **Rene Thomas (born 1927).** Another Belgian-born (1927) fretman, Thomas toured Europe after the war with fellow Belgian Bobby Jaspar (flute/sax) and the Bob Shots Orchestra. Inspired by Django Reinhardt, he eventually impressed Reinhardt himself, who touted Thomas as a top talent. Thomas recorded with trumpeter Chet Baker and saxophonist Sonny Rollins during the 1950s, and made his first album as a leader in 1954. Eventually, Thomas moved to Canada and played with saxophonists Stan Getz and Jackie McLean and trumpeter Miles Davis, as well as touring and recording with Jaspar. *Guitar Groove* (Original Jazz Classics) catches Thomas in 1960 in a trio with Albert "Tootie" Heath on drums. Thomas is also on Rollins' 1958 *Brass/Trio* (Polygram). *The Italian Sessions* (RCA/Bluebird) teams Thomas with Baker and Jaspar.

AUTHOR'S CHOICE

Jazz guitar: A seventh (string) dimension

Playing the guitar is an act that marries the instrument's rhythmic and melodic sides. On the one hand, delicate fingerwork renders intricate melodies. On the other, a jazz guitarist plays chords by pushing down strings between *frets* — strips of metal across a guitar's neck — in various combinations of notes. Strumming chords with a swipe of thumb or plastic guitar pick, sometimes even tapping on the neck or body of the guitar, jazz players give their instrument a percussive power akin to drums.

A standard jazz guitar has six strings, but guitarists including Bucky Pizzarelli, John Pizzarelli (Bucky's son), Howard Alden, and George Van Eps use seven-stringers that extend the instrument's range.

Other guitarists, such as young San Francisco Bay Area phenomenon Charlie Hunter, now residing in New York, have developed even more unusual instruments. Hunter's guitar combines five strings in the guitar's standard range with three fat bass strings. This setup allows him to play the part of both bassist and guitarist — on one instrument. Hearing Hunter live and closing your eyes, you'd swear that he's two people. His sound doesn't seem possible within the limitations of two hands and ten fingers.

The Rise of Electric Guitar

In 1935, guitarist Eddie Durham played what may have been the earliest amplified jazz guitar solo. Durham had carved out the top of his acoustic guitar and inserted a pie-pan-like resonator under the strings to brighten and reflect the sound back toward the audience. On the song "Hitting the Bottle" with Jimmie Lunceford's big band, Durham soloed as Lunceford held a microphone up to his guitar, to get a new, amplified sound. Also catch 1930s-era Durham on *Lester Young — The Kansas City Sessions* (Uni/GRP), playing inventive solos that point the way toward Charlie Christian.

Guitar fanatics experimented with ways to electrify guitars during the early 1930s. Pioneering guitar inventor Les Paul even jammed a phonograph needle into the top of his acoustic guitar and got a primitive electric sound.

When the earliest electric guitars came out during the late '30s, a few savvy jazz guitarists quickly saw their potential. St. Louis-born Floyd Smith, a member of Andy Kirk's orchestra, was among the first guitarists to plug in. He played an electric guitar developed primarily for Hawaiian music, and his efforts can be heard on Kirk's recordings from the late '30s on the Classics label.

Rickenbacker produced some early electric guitars (including the famous solid-body "frying pan" guitar), but none found widespread use in jazz. Les Paul experimented with a variety of electric guitar technology during the 1930s. Other entrepreneurs also developed electric prototypes.

Lloyd Loar, a Gibson technician, began developing electric pickups during the early 1920s. He later left the company, but in 1935, Gibson introduced its ES 150 Electric Spanish model, and the floodgates were opened. A guitarist by the name of Charlie Christian bought one in 1937.

Charlie Christian (1916-1942) Plugs In

As soon as Charlie Christian plugged in his ES–150 — with an electric pickup — jazz guitar underwent a full-fledged personality change. Gibson had the mass production and marketing to make the ES–150 the first electric jazz guitar to be widely used — the first to produce a fat, resonant hollow-body sound that could be amplified to be heard in any jazz setting.

In Christian's hands, with a bold new voice, the guitar stepped out as a solo instrument that traded licks with saxes and trumpets.

Christian's early years

Born in Bonham, Texas, Christian grew up in Oklahoma City — ripe music territory during the 1920s. Situated in the heart of blues country, it was also the center of a sizzling jazz scene of competitive regional groups known as "territory bands." Although the area had no jazz guitarists for Christian to emulate, the Midwest was famous for first-class saxophonists, including Ben Webster, Lester Young, Herschel Evans, and Charlie Parker. Young's solos in particular — long, graceful, emotion-laden strings of notes — are especially evident in Christian's playing.

Christian gets his first break

In 1939 in Los Angeles, producer John Hammond persuaded band leader Benny Goodman to audition Christian. Goodman reluctantly agreed, and Christian's performance was electrifying.

The audition was revolutionary for two reasons: Christian was black and was among the first African American jazz players to integrate Goodman's once all-white band. Christian took a rip-roaring solo that spurred the band through 45 minutes worth of a song called "Rose Room." There are amazing photos of Christian and Goodman soloing head to head on stage — the palpable excitement reminds me of today's dueling rock-and-roll guitar players.

Christian was only 22 or 23 when he auditioned for Goodman. Considering that he died less than three years later of tuberculosis in New York, the volume of great jazz guitar recordings he left behind is doubly impressive. Plugged in, and with prodigious musical abilities, Christian could "blow" face-to-face with horn players, sharing the spotlight with jazz's leading improvisers in a period when all manner of fresh jazz solos were improvised.

Christian was the first jazz guitarist to take long, fluid runs up and down the guitar's neck. His solos combined melodic inventions that started in surprising places, stretched for several choruses, and ended surprisingly; complex and rapid rhythmic variations; strings bent by his left-hand fingers, blues-style, to give an effect of sliding from note to note, or hitting odd notes in between the standard notes on a piano.

"Charlie Christian was way out front, above anyone else," says guitarist Herb Ellis, a top jazz guitarist since the late '50s. "He was not the first to play an electric guitar, but he was one of the first, and he was by far the best. He played chords, but he was the first important single-note solo jazz player, and he had all the ingredients. His time was sensational; he could play the same rhythmic pattern as someone else and sound three times as good. He was so far ahead of everybody else, if he were alive today with a good rhythm section, I think we'd all be chasing him."

Listening to Christian today is still a revelation. _Live Sessions at Minton's Playhouse_ (Musidisc) catches Christian playing complex, speedy solos alongside seminal beboppers including pianist Thelonious Monk and drummer Kenny Clarke. Christian was a regular at Minton's, along with other inventors of bebop including saxophonist Charlie Parker and trumpeter Dizzy Gillespie. He was the only jazz guitar player who had a hand in the invention of bebop.

For a sampling of Christian's red-hot playing with Benny Goodman — in the clarinetist's sextet and big band — get ahold of _Solo Flight_ (Jazz Classics), a two-CD set that captures some spectacular Christian performances, including collaborations with his saxophone-playing alter-ego, Lester Young. Meanwhile, the Masters of Jazz label in 1994 issued an authoritative seven-5-CD series documenting Christian's meteoric two-year streak as _the_ genius of jazz guitar.

When you listen to Charlie Christian, pay attention to how he takes a song's melody and revamps it, and how he invents completely new melodies while the rest of the band plays the song's chords.

Sadly, a recording ban was in place from 1942 to 1944 (due to a standoff over royalties between recording companies and the American Federation of Musicians). This period also happened to be the time when fast, new complicated jazz known as bebop was in its formative stages. Christian missed out on the prime of this rising new style of jazz because he died in 1942. But his recordings attest to his genius, and to the fact that he was a prominent force, alongside other legends named trumpeter Gillespie, saxophonist Parker, and bassist Thelonious Monk, in the earlier jazz swing style and also in the emerging bebop.

Christian's contemporaries

Although Christian and his electric guitar dominated jazz guitar during the late 1930s and early 1940s, several other players deserve recognition:

- **Eddie Condon (1905–1973).** Best known as a swing band leader, Condon was also a guitarist who played with drummer Gene Krupa, clarinetist/saxophonist Frank Teschemacher, and trumpeter Jimmy McPartland in 1920s Chicago. Later, he also played in big bands led by Artie Shaw and Bobby Hackett. Not much of a soloist, he was nevertheless a decent rhythm guitarist. _Dixieland All-Stars_ (Decca) catches Condon playing with a variety of leading New Orleans/Dixieland jazz purists.

- **Freddie Green (1911–1987).** A consummate big band swing guitarist, Green spent the major portion of his lengthy career as staff stringman in Count Basie's band from the late '30s through the 1980s. Green wasn't a significant soloist, but he played acoustic jazz guitar to excellent effect as part of a series of swinging Basie rhythm section, laying down killer chord combinations in lock-step with bass, drum, and piano. The late '30s section teaming Green with drummer Jo Jones, bassist Walter Page, and of course Basie on piano, was one of the strongest. *Natural Rhythm* (Bluebird), Green's collaboration with trumpeter Al Cohn, is perhaps Green's only recording as a leader and showcases the guitarist in a small group.

- **Tiny Grimes (1916–1989).** A bluesy bebopper, Grimes was part of a mid-'40s trio with bassist Slam Stewart and pianist Art Tatum, and his own debut recording featured Charlie Parker on sax. *Tiny in Swingsville* (Original Jazz Classics) gives a good musical summary of the tall, swinging things Tiny did with an electric guitar, with an able assist from Texas saxman Jerome Richardson. *Tiny Grimes/Coleman Hawkins* (Original Jazz Classics) is the guitar player's collaboration with the great tenor saxman.

- **Les Paul.** Not only was Paul an excellent guitarist, but he was a studio wizard and guitar inventor who experimented with *overdubbing* (recording one part and then recording a second part along with the first) and early electric guitars. He eventually had one of Gibson's most popular models named for him. *The Complete Decca Trios* (Uni/Decca) finds Paul backing top singers including Helen Forrest. *The Guitar Artistry of Les Paul* (One Way Records) captures a later version of this fine guitarist. Several CDs spotlight Paul with his frequent collaborator and wife, the singer Mary Ford.

- **George Van Eps.** George Van Eps is jazz guitar's living legend, with a career that reaches back to the Dorsey Brothers Orchestra during the 1930s. He's a swing-style player, never swept away by bebop or the *avant garde*. Van Eps favors melodic solos that include liberal use of chords interspersed with single-note lines of melody. Van Eps invented the 7-string jazz guitar, which allowed him to add his own bass lines to songs. He played with bands led by Benny Goodman and Ray Noble during the 1930s, and he's still going strong in the 1990s, recording several collaborations with younger guitarist Howard Alden. A good way to get into Van Eps, and to hear two generations collide, is to get *Hand-Crafted Swing* (Concord), his collaboration with Alden.

- **Chuck Wayne.** Wayne was a member of saxophonist Joe Marsala's house band at New York City's Hickory House during the mid-'40s — jam sessions that sometimes hinted at saxophonist Charlie Parker and trumpeter Dizzy Gillespie's full-blown bebop. Wayne's important guest spots included guitar parts on Dizzy Gillespie's "Groovin' High," and he was singer Tony Bennett's musical director during the mid-'50s. Wayne eventually recorded with clarinetist Barney Bigard, saxophonist Lester Young, and bassist Slam Stewart. *Tasty Putting* (Savoy), with Wayne and saxophonist Zoot Sims, offers a good sampling of Wayne's jazz guitar. Also check out *Jazz Guitarist* (Savoy).

Bebop Guitarists

Although guitar didn't play a central role during the bebop era, a handful of guitarists were a part of the scene in New York City, jamming at clubs around 52nd Street in New York City during bebop's formative years.

Kenny Burrell (born 1931)

Bluesy, soulful, smooth as satin, Kenny Burrell's sound is the epitome of elegance. Whether playing '50s hard bop or other varieties of cool jazz later on, Burrell is a thoughtful improviser who also lends sensitive support to bandmates.

Over five decades, Burrell has made tens of good albums, including some excellent Latin jazz. Check out any of the following: *All Night Long* (Original Jazz Classics), *Kenny Burrell & John Coltrane* (Prestige), *Midnight Blue* (Blue Note), *The Best of Kenny Burrell* (EMD/Blue Note), and *Ellington Is Forever Vol. 1 and 2* (Fantasy).

Burrell is an active force for the advancement of jazz, as a music professor at the University of Southern California. Meanwhile, he's still playing strong, as on the 1998 *Laid Back* (32 Jazz), with tunes ranging from "Groovin' High" to "In The Still of the Night."

Bill DeArango

Rarely captured on records, DeArango was, by some accounts, one of the best bebop guitarists. Playing alongside Parker, Gillespie, vibraphonist Milt Jackson, and other jazz legends, DeArango improvised solos of impressive originality. Check him out on *Dizzy Gillespie 1945–46* (Classics), which catches DeArango (with Diz) in his prime, just two years before he abandoned jazz for good.

Herb Ellis (born 1921)

Like Burrell, Ellis is a smooth master of 1950s-based bop and swing. Breaking in with trombonist Jimmy Dorsey's big band during the mid-'40s, Ellis first made a significant mark as part of pianist Oscar Peterson's mid-'50s trio. He has also backed Ella Fitzgerald and toured with the Great Guitars (also including Charlie Byrd and Barney Kessel). Recommended albums: *Nothing But The Blues* (PGD/Verve), *Roll Call* (Justice), and *Texas Swings* (Justice), which gives a taste of Ellis's roots in the Lonestar State.

Barney Kessel (born 1923)

Among guitarists whose careers began in the 1940s during the bebop era, I think Barney Kessel came closest on guitar to the levels of creativity achieved by saxophonist Charlie Parker, trumpeter Dizzy Gillespie, and pianist Thelonious Monk. Kessel actually considers himself an all-around musician and composer who draws from many styles of jazz. He could play fast like Parker and Gillespie, and he was also extremely creative when it came to harmonies and mixing chords with unusual single-note strings of improvised melody.

I was fortunate enough to catch Kessel live during the early '90s, in peak form just before a stroke took away his playing capacity. Even in his sixties, he was sensational: fast and fluid, but with an economy of motion and melody that comes only with maturity. In an interview, Kessel recalled his earliest experiences of fledgling electric guitar.

"I first saw/heard an electric guitar in 1926, in Muskogee, Oklahoma, my hometown," says Kessel, who was 14 then. "It was an all-white band and the guitarist had an electric guitar. I had also heard one on the radio, with Bob Wills and the Texas Playboys, a country band. I was drawn to the sound because I could be heard better. The mikes in those days weren't very good. I first played an electric guitar when I was 14. I asked my mother to buy me one, and she did. It was a National guitar, and she paid $150 for both the guitar and amplifier. I was playing with Ellis Ezell's band, all black except for me, and on the marquee advertising our shows, it said 'featuring Barney Kessel's electric guitar.'"

"The first guitarists I listened to were Eddie Lang, Carl Kress, and then George Barnes and Tony Mottola," says Kessel. "None of them, in my opinion, were jazz players. Then in jazz I was influenced by George Van Eps, Allan Reuss (with Benny Goodman's band), and Bus Etri (with Charlie Barnet's band). Then comes Charlie Christian."

Like Christian, Kessel, in his solos, combined rapid and melodic strings of notes with carefully placed chords. But chords, and the rhythmic patterns he created with them, were more central to Kessel's improvisations. His solos are subtle, thoughtful, and full of emotion.

Kessel can be heard and seen alongside saxophonist Lester Young in the famous 1944 short film *Jammin' The Blues,* available as part of the *Lester Young: Song of the Spirit* video. As a studio musician, he's also on the soundtracks of four Elvis Presley movies, among other jobs. Kessel played with the big bands of Charlie Barnet, Artie Shaw, and Benny Goodman during the mid-'40s, but his best music is on his own recordings, beginning during the late '50s.

My favorite Kessel albums include the *Poll Winners* (Original Jazz Classics) series — all-star sessions spanning the years from 1957 to 1975 — as well as *Red Hot and Blues* (Contemporary), Kessel's last studio recording before he had a stroke. As a guitarist and guitar fanatic, I am in love with Kessel's pure, distinctive tone. Although he has endorsed various guitars, he always favored a vintage Gibson with a pickup (and sound) similar to Christian's.

Guitar in the '50s and Forward

In the years following bebop, and as bebop as a movement in jazz began to splinter into *hard bop* and *cool jazz,* a few guitarists held forth with unique styles and new blends of influences.

Wes Montgomery (1925-1968)

One of the coolest jazz guitarists during the 1950s and 1960s was Wes Montgomery, who grew up in Indianapolis and first made his mark as a jazz player during the late '50s in San Francisco, pointing the way toward the bluesy, soulful sound of 1960s jazz.

Montgomery's signature sound involves the use of a technique guitar players refer to as *octaves.* This term refers to a way of playing melodies and solos by using pairs of notes an octave apart. It gives each note — two different Cs played in unison, say, or two Ds — added depth, almost as if two guitars were playing at once.

Two of Montgomery's best albums are *The Incredible Jazz Guitar of Wes Montgomery* (Original Jazz Classics) and *The Wes Montgomery Trio* (Original Jazz Classics). The first captures Montgomery playing straightforward jazz in a quartet of top jazzmen. The second album places him in a trio powered by Melvin Rhyne's organ — it's a mellow, bluesy setting perfectly suited to Montgomery's laid-back, melodic style.

In my opinion, Montgomery was the first of a series of gifted jazz guitarists who unfortunately had their sound watered down by producers and/or record labels in search of broader audiences. Although Montgomery's popularity peaked during the 1960s, I don't find the later albums of this period as satisfying as his earlier material. String sections dilute the guitarist's role, and he seems restrained by the pop context. But he did put a pleasing spin on popular tunes.

Check out Wes's tune "Tune Up" on the *Jazz For Dummies* CD for a taste of his early guitar genius.

Aaron "T-Bone" Walker

T-Bone Walker was the first guitarist to span the space between blues and jazz, on dozens of vinyl sides recorded during the 1940s and 1950s. He influenced dozens of jazz players — including Wes Montgomery. Walker was friends with Charlie Christian and preceded Christian as guitarist in the Lawson-Brooks band in Texas.

The Complete Imperial Recordings (EMI) is a two-CD set that runs the range of vintage Walker from the 1950s. Several songs utilize a jazz horn section, and Walker also turns in some rousing vocals. If you like jazz, but you also like to boogie, T-Bone's your man.

Other cool axmen, '50s forward

Wes and T-Bone weren't the only guys picking out jazz butter in the post-bebop years. Many other guitarists from the time deserve mention — and a listen.

Tal Farlow (born 1921)

Launching his career as a late '40s bebopper, Farlow played with vibraphonists Red Norvo and Marjorie Hyams before settling into a relaxed-but-fleet groove during the 1950s, when he made cool jazz and played with clarinetist Artie Shaw and his Gramercy Five. Check out Farlow on *Autumn in New York* (Verve), *The Return of Tal Farlow* (Original Jazz Classics), and *Cookin' on All Burners* (Concord).

Grant Green (1931-1979)

Enjoying a late '90s revival thanks to the acid jazz scene, Green was the original soul-jazz-groove guitarist beginning in the 1960s. Improvising melodic lines more reminiscent of saxophonists than guitarists, Green played with bluesy, melodic beauty. Dial him in on *Green Street* (Blue Note), *Complete Blue Note with Sonny Clark* (Blue Note), *Best of Grant Green Vols. 1 and 2* (Blue Note), and on *Idle Moments* (Blue Note), spurred by vibraphonist Bobby Hutcherson and saxophonist Joe Henderson.

Joe Pass (1929-1994)

For me, the ultimate solo jazz guitar album is Joe Pass's *Virtuoso* (Pablo). Pass, who died in 1994, plays with great passion that comes across through his sensitive use of contrasts: loud/soft, fast/slow, as well as happy/sad combinations of notes. When Pass's fingers speed up and down the neck, it's for expression, not for show. Where appropriate, he also presents melodies in simple, unadorned fashion.

Many classic jazz tunes are included on *Virtuoso,* songs that have been played over the years by giants such as Charlie Parker, John Coltrane, Miles Davis, and many others. Their titles include "Night And Day," "Stella By Starlight," "How High The Moon," "Cherokee," and "All The Things You Are."

In Pass's hands, these pieces become much more than nostalgic jazz artifacts. They are warm and personal, brought to life by a player with a big heart and towering technique, but also a level of improvisational genius attained by only a handful of players in jazz's history. The fact that Pass had enough confidence to leave a few tiny bloopers intact only adds to this music's allure.

Gabor Szabo (1936-1982)

Born in Hungary, Szabo brought bebop roots forward into the mid-'60s jazz/ rock fusion he played with bands led by drummer Chico Hamilton as on *Man from Two Worlds* (GRP). Also check out Szabo's own *The Sorcerer* (Impulse!).

Heroes of the Electric Guitar

If you're like me and were weaned on rock-and-roll during the 1960s, you'll love the guitarists who fused jazz with rock to help make new music called *fusion,* so-named because it fused the sounds of rock and jazz.

Derek Bailey (born 1932)

Working the fringes, British-born Derek Bailey does electrifying things with electric guitar, teaming with American free jazzers such as trombonist George Lewis, bassist Dave Holland, and way-gone saxophonist/composer John Zorn. Check out Bailey's *Solo Guitar* (Incus) and *Wireforks* (Shanachie).

Larry Coryell (born 1943)

When I was 18, guitarist Larry Coryell's music with his group, the Eleventh House, lured me deeper into jazz. *Introducing Larry Coryell and the Eleventh House* (Vanguard) is still a good album. Coryell was among the pioneering jazz guitarists during the mid-'60s birth of electric jazz/rock fusion, which combined a driving beat and wailing electric guitar with much of jazz's musical subtlety and complexity. In drummer Chico Hamilton's band Free Spirits (try *The Dealer* on MCA/Impulse!), and later with flutist Herbie Mann (*Memphis Underground* on Atlantic), as well as on his own albums, Coryell was an electrifying player. Coryell is also a fine acoustic guitarist, as on *Together* (Concord) his 1985 duet album with the late guitarist Emily Remler.

Al DiMeola (born 1954)

Al DiMeola's solo recordings — on both acoustic and electric guitars — are awesome, although he sometimes lets technique take precedent over emotional nuance. His 1976 *Land of the Midnight Sun* (Columbia) is a sizzling trip on electric guitar, and his 1993 *Heart of the Immigrants* (Mesa) is a strange and wonderful collaboration with Dino Saluzzi on *bandoneon* (an accordion-like instrument).

John McLaughlin (born 1942)

Like saxophonist John Coltrane, guitarist John McLaughlin views music as a spiritual experience. Although McLaughlin (see Figure 16-1) is a serious player who can hold his own in many settings, he made some of his most exciting music during the early 1970s as the leader of a band called Mahavishnu Orchestra.

McLaughlin played electric guitar on trumpeter Miles Davis's 1969 *Bitches Brew* (Columbia) album, an all-time electric jazz classic. Then he formed Mahavishnu Orchestra, and their albums *Inner Mounting Flame* and *Birds of Fire,* both on Columbia, are electrifying examples of McLaughlin's brainy composing and fiery, soulful improvising. You should also try McLaughlin's acoustic guitar albums, including his recordings with percussionist Trilok Gurtu, and *Passion, Grace and Fire* (Columbia), with fellow fretters Al DiMeola and Paco De Lucia.

Pat Metheny (born 1954)

Though Pat Metheny plays great in a straight acoustic jazz context, his electric music incorporating guitar synthesizer is equally intriguing. The albums *Still Life (Talking)* and *Letter From Home,* both on Geffen, remind me of Ennio Morricone's scores for those Sergio Leone "spaghetti westerns." For me, this music provokes panoramic visual images.

Lee Ritenour (born 1952)

Lee Ritenour has an ear for a happy melody and an obvious love of the late great Wes Montgomery. During the 1990s he was the guitarist in the light-jazz band Fourplay, with Bob James (keyboards), Nathan East (bass), and Harvey Mason (drums). On his own, Ritenour has made some lackadaisical music, as well as livelier recordings including *Wes Bound* (GRP) and *Larry & Lee* (GRP), which teams him with Carlton, his successor in Fourplay.

Figure 16-1:
John
McLaughlin
(photo:
Everett
Collection).

Terje Rypdal (born 1947)

On the forefront of jazz/rock/electronic fusion, Rypdal creates highly
original musical atmospheres. Introduce yourself to his music (he also plays
saxes and flute) on *Works* (ECM), and on the 1997 *Skywards* (BMG/ECM).

John Scofield (born 1951)

Some of Scofield's best playing is on pianist Herbie Hancock's 1996 album,
The New Standard (Verve). Scofield gets a moist, dreamy sound on "Norwe-
gian Wood," the old Beatles' song. He and Hancock rework the song's
melody with alluring jazz variations. Also check out Scofield's 1998 *A Go Go*
(PGD/Verve), a bluesy grooving session teaming the guitarist with young
acid-jazzers Medeski, Martin and Wood.

A few more

Guitar is personal fascination, and I could list great albums into infinity. But I
wind up this section by mentioning a few more of my favorite players.

✔ **George Benson (born 1943).** George Benson had a history much like Montgomery's. A fine pure jazz player during the mid-'60s, Benson eventually became famous by switching to a simpler pop style and concentrating on his singing. The albums *Bad Benson* and *Benson Burner,* both on Columbia, were ones that helped hook me on jazz in my teens.

✔ **Joshua Breakstone (1955).** Working a cool, laid-back groove, Breakstone's a tasteful baby-boomer guitarist who has made several good albums, including *Evening Star* (Contemporary) and *Let's Call This Monk* (Double Time).

✔ **Lenny Breau (1941–1984).** A little-known but talented jazz guitarist, Lenny Breau died at 43 in 1984 and left only a few recordings, including *Live At Bourbon St.* (Guitarchives), a two-CD set that showcases his whirlwind technique.

✔ **Bruce Forman (born 1956).** A latter-day bebopper, Forman's made some exciting music during the 1980s and 1990s with bandmates including saxophonist Richie Cole and bassist Buster Williams. *Forman on the Job* (Kamel) is one of his best efforts.

✔ **Peter Leitch (born 1954).** Under-appreciated Canadian guitarist who has turned out several find latter-day bebop albums including *Red Zone* (Reservoir), *Mean What You Say* (Concord), *Duality* (Reservoir), and the 1997 *Up Front!* (Reservoir).

✔ **Pat Martino (born 1954).** Sidelined by a brain aneurysm in 1980, Martino taught himself how to play all over again. Earlier recordings like *East!* (Original Jazz Classics) and *Consciousness* (Muse) are excellent, as is Martino's post-trauma *All Sides Now* (BMD/Blue Note), released in 1997.

✔ **Emily Remler (1957–1990).** One of the few female jazz guitarists, Remler chalked up a 10-year string of consistently solid albums before she died in 1990 at age 32 after struggling with a heroin addiction. All of her recordings on Concord are first-rate, including *Take Two* and *Transitions.*

✔ **Some gifted newcomers:** Among young guitarists, I think that a few of the most promising are Mark Whitfield, Nels Cline, Ron Affif, and Jimmy Bruno.

Part VI
More Brass and Reeds

The 5th Wave · By Rich Tennant

MEMORABLE JAM SESSIONS: THE NIGHT CHARLIE PARKER ASKED SPIKE JONES TO SIT IN ON AH-OOOGAH HORN.

In this part . . .

In Part VI, you can find out about the clarinet, the main instrument of vintage jazz. Read about its great players like Johnny Dodds and Benny Goodman. Discover the flute and its evolution through the music. And read about the great flutists from Albert Socarras to Herbie Mann, to present players like James Newton and Dave Valentin.

And don't forget about the trombone. In this part, you can find out how the trombone held the anchor spot in the early jazz bands until the bass came along. Discover the great early trombonists such as Kid Ory and the slidemen of Swing like Jack Teagarden to current players like Steve Turne and Delfeayo Marsalis.

Chapter 17

Clarinetists: Leading Licorice Men

In This Chapter

▶ The clarinet in New Orleans

▶ Benny Goodman and Artie Shaw bring together clarinet and swing

▶ Clarinet plays a subtle role in bebop

▶ Clarinet finds a place in electric and abstract jazz

Clarinets conjure visions of vintage jazz. No longer the hippest of jazz instruments, the *licorice stick*, as the hepcats call it, was once jazz's leading tool and reigned as a supreme force. In the hands of men such as Sidney Bechet, Jimmie Noone, Johnny Dodds, Benny Goodman, and Artie Shaw, it was a sort of magic wand waved by jazz's leading sorcerers. Clarinet has an aura of mystery, a mesmerizing, snake-charming sound. In early New Orleans jazz bands, the clarinet cut boldly through big ensembles to play a leading role in the music's evolution.

With a wide range and big distinctive sound in low, medium, and high ranges, the clarinet is an ideal jazz instrument. Even early jazz bands, beginning with Buddy Bolden's, included a clarinet or two. In the years when jazz was born in New Orleans, clarinets rivaled cornets and trumpets as the predominant lead instruments, carrying melodies and improvising with a powerful, sexy tone.

Trumpet/cornet players such as Bolden, Louis Armstrong, King Oliver, and Freddie Keppard were among jazz's early heroes. Matching them note for note, as can be heard on jazz recordings from the 1920s, were equally gifted clarinetists. Clarinetists remained among jazz's leading legends through the big band swing era, but with the emergence of trumpet- and saxophone-dominated bebop around 1945, clarinets faded from popularity. Goodman, Shaw, Bechet, and others continued to make great music for several years, but few new clarinetists emerged with equivalent high profiles.

The clarinet: Details

Clarinets resemble oboes and soprano saxophones, but clarinets are distinctive in both construction and tone. Oboes and clarinets are made of hardwood, usually *grenadilla,* while saxophones are brass. Oboes have a small double reed that lends a whinier, more exotic sound. Clarinets and saxophones have a larger single reed that requires more respiratory strength but yields a bigger tone.

The alto clarinet has a wide range and big tone that make it well suited for jazz, but it is perhaps the most difficult to master among woodwind instruments. Fingerings are more complex than for saxophone or oboe.

In addition to the alto clarinet favored by most jazz clarinets, some jazz musicians play bass clarinet — larger, more cumbersome, and with a fuller, deeper tone. Bass clarinetists are rare in jazz. Clarinetists including Harry Carney, Omer Simeon, Benny Goodman, and Buddy DeFranco made some limited use of the instrument. (See the figure in this sidebar.)

But with the advent of *avant garde,* free jazz, and fusion during the 1960s, more players turned to bass clarinet in search of fresh sounds. (See the figure in this sidebar.) Among those participating in the contemporary clarinet boom are Gunter Hampel, David Murray, Roscoe Mitchell, Hamiett Bluiett, and Bennie Maupin.

Alto clarinet

Illustration courtesy of: Yamaha Corp. of America, Band and Orchestra Division

Bass clarinet

Even though saxes and trumpets remained jazz's predominant lead instruments through the 1950s and 1960s, a few innovative clarinetists came along — most notably Buddy DeFranco and Eddie Daniels. When jazz players began to experiment with *avant garde* and free jazz during the 1960s and 1970s, a few more new clarinetists brought this instrument's distinctive sound back to jazz once again in new contexts.

Clarinets in New Orleans

Early jazz in New Orleans didn't feature extended solos, but in terms of carrying melodies and standing out in a crowd of instruments, clarinets kept a high profile. Several New Orleans clarinetists were among the most important figures in early jazz. While they weren't major band leaders or prolific composers, the clarinetists helped pioneer the idea of the gifted soloist for whom a band's music might be custom tailored.

Sidney Bechet (1897-1959)

Bechet was perhaps the baddest of them all, *cutting* the others to shreds one night in Chicago during the 1930s — cutting contests were extended jams that lasted until one soloist had technically KO'd the others. Bechet played both clarinet and soprano saxophone, but the clarinet was his primary instrument.

Born in New Orleans, Bechet was the first great jazz soloist to record (even before Armstrong), and his career lasted until a few years before his death in 1959 in Paris — like many American jazz musicians, Bechet became a hero in Europe even though he was barely appreciated in his own country. Bechet had jazz's basic elements in abundance: *swing,* that loose, relentless driving rhythm; and a gift for *improvisation,* or the spontaneous invention of melodies around a song's chords and/or tune. And his French and African ancestry virtually embodied the varied roots of jazz.

Many of Bechet's earliest recorded clarinet solos were on blues tunes: backing blues singer Rosetta Crawford in 1923, and as a member of pianist Clarence Williams' New Orleans bands of the mid-'20s. Blues included collective improvisation among musicians, particularly horns, who improvised frantically as a team. Bechet invented lyrical melodies that wrapped around melodic lines played by trombones and trumpets in early bands. It's sheer nirvana when these bands are blowing up a full head of steam. Frequently, he soloed alone during breaks in the music, the space around his sound heightening the drama of his spontaneous creations.

Early New Orleans jazz was also bawdy barroom music. Bechet's clarinet playing from the mid-'20s, with its wildly expressive crescendos and sensuous quivers called *vibrato,* conjures visions of smoky late nights in Storyville, the city's old red-light district. Although Benny Goodman played clarinet a few years later with impressive technique, I much prefer the earthy, soulful sound of Bechet and his peers.

If you want to start with one CD of Bechet's music, I suggest *Centenary Celebration — 1997: Great Original Performances 1924–1943* (Louisiana Red Hot Records) due to the variety of music and the high quality of the sound. Older music on this CD, including "Mandy Make Up Your Mind," benefits from an electronic sprucing up that cleaned away crackles and hiss.

Bechet's 1940 version of "Indian Summer" on the *Centenary* CD is a *tour de force* of expressive clarinet, with a small group that, surprisingly, includes drummer Kenny Clarke, who went on to be a prime timekeeper during the bebop years. Earl Hines's "Blues In Thirds" gets great treatment from a trio including Hines on piano, Baby Dodds on drums, and Bechet on clarinet — so few players, so much sound. Finally, for a glimpse of Bechet on the cutting edge of the technology of his time, check out "Blues of Bechet," on which he *overdubbed* (added additional parts by recording new tracks alongside the original tape) all parts including clarinet, tenor and soprano saxes, and piano.

The *Centenary* set shows just how big Bechet was among early jazz masters. All in all, it's a five-star set (on a scale of five). Key elements of his music are

- ✔ Full, clear, beautiful tone.
- ✔ Sexy vibrato.
- ✔ Thoughtful storytelling.
- ✔ Swing (his music's loose but steady rhythmic momentum).
- ✔ Long improvised lines.
- ✔ Phenomenal dexterity, even at high speed.
- ✔ Great songwriting.

An Introduction to Sidney Bechet/His Best Recordings 1923–1941 (Best of Jazz) is another good collection of his early music. *Sidney Bechet 1923–1936* (Classics Records) is another collection of vintage Bechet that offers some of the same songs as *An Introduction to Sidney Bechet,* but other tunes, too. I'm in love with Bechet's version of "Summertime."

Once you get to listen to a little Bechet, you'll want a lot more. Also, locate a copy of his book *Treat it Gentle: An Autobiography* (Da Capo), which is about as close as you'll get to first-hand experience of the early New Orleans jazz life.

Red-Hot Henchmen: Johnny Dodds and Jimmie Noone

Bechet's partners in taking New Orleans jazz, via clarinet, to new levels were Johnny Dodds and Jimmie Noone, who left several significant recordings of their own.

Johnny Dodds (1892-1940)

Dodds' sinewy improvised lines put the zing in 22 tunes on *An Introduction to Johnny Dodds/His Best Recordings 1923–1940* (Best of Jazz). Dodds plays with bands led by Louis Armstrong, King Oliver, and Jelly Roll Morton, but my favorite tunes are the ones in which he fronts The Black Bottom Stompers. "Come On And Stomp, Stomp, Stomp" and "Joe Turner Blues" swing especially hard, and Dodds displays a great deal of finesse on both numbers, whether playing the melody, soloing, or improvising tightly together with the other horns.

Jimmie Noone (1895-1944)

An Introduction to Jimmie Noone (Best of Jazz) is a companion CD to the *An Introduction to Johnny Dodds* volume, and is devoted to this other great New Orleans clarinetist. Noone doesn't play as wild and free as Bechet and Dodds, but his smooth, fluid technique gives him a sound of his own as he fronts his Apex Club Orchestra. Noone's playing is so polished that he makes it sound easy when he delivers speedy solos on songs such as "I Know That You Know," and more relaxed, romantic improvisations on "Sweet Sue, Just You." Considering that many of these recordings were made during the mid-'20s, Noone's arrangements were especially advanced, pointing the way toward subtle arrangements utilized by Duke Ellington and others.

Swinging Licorice: Big Band Clarinet

Big bands were in full swing during the 1930s, and two top clarinetists, Benny Goodman and Artie Shaw, fronted two of the top swing bands.

Benny Goodman (1909-1986)

Goodman was born in 1909 in Chicago. He was playing professionally by the time he was 14, and recorded for the first time as a member of Ben Pollock's band in 1926. He first gained national notice from performances on the national *Let's Dance* radio program. Goodman's groups were known for tight arrangements (especially by Eddie Sauter), and Goodman was known for his smooth, polished playing and an exacting, clean tone. As he became famous, Goodman hired leading African American jazz artists to join his previously all-white band, including vibraphonist Lionel Hampton, pianist Fletcher Henderson (also an excellent arranger), guitarist Charlie Christian, and pianist Teddy Wilson, at a time when jazz bands were mostly segregated.

Documented by dozens of recordings, Goodman's career lasted until shortly before his death in 1986.

I think that the hottest of all Goodman recordings is *Live At Carnegie Hall* (Columbia), a two-CD set that documents a monumental occasion: the first time jazz was presented at the famous New York City concert hall. With ringers on hand from the bands of Basie and Ellington, the music soars; you can hear the crowd cheering its approval. Gene Krupa's drumming is a revelation in the powers of percussion to swing a band, with solid snare socks and bass bombs punching up the music (and the audience).

As a sign of the times, Goodman's Carnegie Hall concert was important for one other reason: It marked the beginning of jazz's transition out of dance halls and clubs and into concert venues, from music for dancing and partying to a more challenging, intellectual music for listening.

Over the years, Goodman had the good sense to break smaller groups off from his big band for the sake of recording. Several of these sessions produced great music. What would you expect from combos composed of players like Charlie Christian on guitar, Teddy Wilson on piano, Harry James on trumpet, Lionel Hampton on vibes, and Gene Krupa on drums?

Artie Shaw (born 1910)

For overall impact, Benny Goodman and his groups are tough to beat, but Artie Shaw, the other great clarinetist of the 1930s and 1940s, brought together equally tight bands and solid arrangements, and he was a first-rate clarinet player, too. Shaw's touch was subtler and more expressive than Goodman's, as on the popular Cole Porter tune "Begin the Beguine," included alongside several other prime Shaw pieces on *Artie Shaw: Greatest Hits* (RCA). To me, Goodman was a great showman and highly technical player with phenomenal speed and dexterity. Shaw, on the other hand, played far fewer notes, but got much more emotional mileage out of them.

Just about any of Shaw's music on the Bluebird and RCA labels is worth owning, and his 1950's *Last Recordings* (Music Masters) series shows that he never lost his expressive touch. Shaw was also a prose writer, and his musings, if you can find them in print, capture much of the swinging energy of the 1930s and 1940s.

Other important big band clarinetists

Another essential clarinet album is the 1997 *Pee Wee Russell/Jazz Original* (GRP), a compilation of several fine performances recorded between 1938 and 1944. Russell's playing is relaxed and confident, warm and easy to enjoy.

Bandmates such as saxophonist Bud Freeman, guitarist/leader Eddie Condon, trombonist Jack Teagarden, pianist Fats Waller, drummer Zutty Singleton, and bassist Bob Haggart give this CD both musical and historical value. A pleasant surprise is Teagarden's earthy blues vocal on "Serenade To A Shylock." Only one minor drawback: The older cuts come with a fair amount of hiss, perhaps because they were recorded directly from old vinyl, or because the original recordings just weren't that clean.

If you get deep into clarinet music, you'll also want to investigate Kenny Davern, Ken Peplowski, Bob Wilber, Woody Herman, Peanuts Hucko, and Pee Wee Russell, all top players during the early 1940s.

Bebop: Clarinet Eases from the Spotlight

Charlie Parker, Dizzy Gillespie, Thelonious Monk, Bud Powell, Kenny Clarke, and other key players concocted fresh energy and critical controversy with the frenetic music they made at Minton's Playhouse in New York City, and you would think that clarinetists would want to pop in. However, for some reason, even though clarinet players could play plenty fast, clarinetists didn't really catch on to bebop — at least not with the same force and popularity Goodman and Shaw gave big band swing — however, there were a few.

Joe Marsala (1907-1978)

And although it would be easy to assume, based on recordings and writings, that clarinet didn't play much of a part in bebop, that is not a wholly accurate assumption. In fact, a clarinet player named Joe Marsala, who made a name for himself in the years just prior to the explosion of bebop, had a large influence on the bebop sound, though some people may not think of him as a member of the bebop movement.

"Joe Marsala started Dizzy off when he was 18," says clarinetist Bobby Gordon, who is a former member of the Marty Grosz Orphan Newsboys band and has made several excellent recordings of his own on the Arbors label. "They made a bebop record of 'My Melancholy Baby' and 'Cherokee' on the Black and White label, before Dizzy and Charlie started playing together. Joe Marsala was the first bebopper — on clarinet. He's kind of hard to find. He's an obscure artist. He also had one of the most innovative bands in New York, at the Hickory House, with his wife, Adele Girard, on harp. They were making music in the 1930s that sounded like bebop just beginning."

Some of Marsala's best music is included on *Joe Marsala 1936–1942* (Classics).

Jimmy Hamilton (born 1917)

Jimmy Hamilton is one of my unsung clarinet heroes. Best known as a member of Duke Ellington's Orchestra, Hamilton combined bebop's speed and complexity with some of the laid-back *cool* jazz style popularized by saxophonist Stan Getz, bandleader Gerry Mulligan, trumpeter Chet Baker, and others in California during the late 1940s and 1950s. Reissued on CD in 1997, Hamilton's *Sweet But Hot* (Drive Archive) album is a fine set that even your jazz-buff friends have probably never heard. Hamilton is joined by top players including Clark Terry on trumpet and Oscar Pettiford on bass. The music swings with the spirit of Goodman and Shaw, but it has a more modern feel thanks to Hamilton's fresh clarinet.

Licorice Virtuosity: Buddy DeFranco and Eddie Daniels

Some artists simply defy category. That's the case with Buddy DeFranco and Eddie Daniels, clarinetists who take their instrument to new heights.

Buddy DeFranco (born 1923)

Compared to Eddie Daniels, DeFranco is the more seasoned player. Born in Camden, New Jersey (site of the nation's first drive-in movie theater) in 1923, he played in bands led by drummer Gene Krupa, saxophonist Charlie Barnet, and trombonist Tommy Dorsey during the 1940s, and later led his own bands. Technically, DeFranco is a marvel, making fast, intricate solos sound easy.

DeFranco made many good albums as a leader over the years, and much of this music is included on *The Complete Verve Recordings of Buddy DeFranco and Sonny Clark* (Mosaic), teaming him with the bebop pianist. Some of his best playing, though, has come in the group he often co-led with vibraphonist Terry Gibbs. An example of his best work is the 1991 *Kings of Swing* (Contemporary). Some vintage DeFranco has been re-released on CD, one of my favorite specimens being the 1974 *Free Fall* session, which includes DeFranco's own four-part "Threat of Freedom" suite. Here, in 12$^{1}/_{2}$ minutes, he exploits his instrument's full range of moods and textures, from sensuous and slow, to a fast beboppish climax with some spirited improvising from DeFranco, bassist Victor Sproles, and pianist Victor Feldman.

Eddie Daniels (born 1941)

Another clarinetist who has scaled the heights of speed and innovation is DeFranco's younger counterpart, Eddie Daniels. Born in New York City in 1941, Daniels is — next to Sidney Bechet — my personal favorite licorice stickman. Schooled at prestigious Juilliard and capable in both the jazz and classical idioms, Daniels bridges the two musical forms in his playing. He swings with the best jazzmen, but he also has a soft, light touch and gentle vibrato (wavering sound) that lend his music an appealing emotional side lacking in some swing and bebop.

On the 1997 *Beautiful Love* (Shanachie) CD, Johann Sebastian Bach's "Awakening" becomes a jumping off point for some spirited jazz, and other material ranges from Erik Satie's familiar "First Gymnopedie" to Sergey Rachmaninoff's "Love's Journey" and several songs written by Daniels, including a waltz (a song style based on groups of three beats rather than the two- or four-beat patterns more common to jazz) and "A Take On Five" (inspired by saxophonist Paul Desmond's five-beats-per-measure piece, "Take Five," made famous by pianist Dave Brubeck) that put a fresh rhythmic spin on jazz.

Daniels's stuff is what I would call *heavy headphone music,* the deep sort of stuff you want to hear on a wet winter day by the fire. For listeners with a deep love of classical music, *Beautiful Love* is the perfect clarinet recording.

During the late '80s and early '90s, Daniels recorded for GRP, the label that capitalized on the popularity of light pop-jazz. This period of Daniels' career is summarized on *Collection* (GRP), ten of his best songs from that era. His improvising is some of the most inventive I've heard on clarinet, combining the complexity and speed of the best bebop with a funky feel provided by electric bass, Latin percussion, and Daniels' rhythmic adroitness.

Electric and Abstract Licorice

Compared with its golden years of the 1930s and 1940s, the clarinet has fallen out of favor in jazz, but it hasn't dropped completely out of orbit. The Electric jazz and *avant garde* jazz movements, both of which began during the 1960s, both had capable clarinetists as part of them.

Overall, though, the clarinet has been scarce in electric jazz, and it has also played only a minor part in *avant garde* jazz. Multi-instrumentalist Roscoe Mitchell has contributed some clarinet to the Art Ensemble of Chicago's urgent, jagged jazz. *Avant garde* saxman Anthony Braxton has also made limited use of the clarinet on several albums beginning in the 1970s.

Alvin Batiste (born 1937)

One of the more prolific clarinetists from jazz's cutting edge is Alvin Batiste (with a last name like that, you'd guess he was born in New Orleans, and you'd be correct). Even if you have a limited budget, try to add Batiste to your collection. He's the most original player to come along in years.

Evan Christopher (born 1970)

Finally, keep an eye on California prodigy Evan Christopher, a promising twenty-something whose debut solo album, *Classic Jazz Classics* (Stick), includes his versions of vintage tunes such as "Struttin' With Some Barbecue," "St. James Infirmary," and "Honeysuckle Rose."

Bennie Maupin (born 1940)

Bass clarinetist Bennie Maupin played an important part on trumpeter Miles Davis' innovative *Bitches Brew* (Columbia) album, which hailed a new era of electrified jazz in 1969. Maupin's clarinet is a haunting, probing presence that darts in and out of Davis' dense music. Maupin was also a member of Herbie Hancock's electric jazz/rock group the Headhunters during the early '70s, and his own *The Jewel in the Lotus* (ECM) album extends the spacey, electric music he made with Hancock.

Bob Mintzer (born 1953)

On another electric front, Bob Mintzer, also a bass clarinetist, added a jolt of vitality to the electric pop-jazz group the Yellowjackets during the early '90s. Albums such as *Green House* (GRP) and *Like a River* (GRP) show off his searing improvisations.

Chapter 18

Flutists: Mellow Pipers of Jazz

. . . .

In This Chapter

▶ Exploring the ancient origins of the modern flute

▶ Jazz flute in the 1950s

▶ Extending jazz's boundaries through flute

▶ Flute fusion: a merging of jazz, classical, pop, and funk

. . . .

Reedy and delicate-sounding, the flute has been a fringe instrument, played well by only a handful of musicians during each of jazz's stylistic phases, and players don't agree about the instrument's appropriate role.

"It can be played with just as much guts as a saxophone," says James Moody, a leading saxophone and flute player since the 1940s.

"The flute is not a major jazz instrument," counters jazz flutist/saxophonist Lew Tabackin. "It never was and it never will be. It's not a major classical instrument, either. A lot of that has to do with its dynamic limitations. You pick up a tenor sax or a trumpet; you've got it — you just play. You don't even need a mike. With flute, no matter how hard you try, it's tougher to be heard."

Still, the flute's ethereal sound is one of the most distinctive in jazz. A mouthpiece unlike that of any other wind instrument lets a flutist blend chanting, humming, and other vocal sounds into his or her flute-playing, and to make shrill, distorted shrieks and cries utilizing a technique called *overblowing*. In the hands of James Newton, Hubert Laws, or Prince Lasha, the flute makes a lush, exotic addition to jazz's garden of sounds.

One word of caution: Getting a concentrated sample of great jazz flute music is nearly impossible. Probably half of jazz's top flutists play other wind instruments, including saxophones, and these players seldom make recordings that focus solely on flute. More commonly, these *doublers* — players who double on flute and other instruments — include a flute tune or two on their albums. Only a handful of flutists — including Herbie Mann, Frank Wess, Hubert Laws, Holly Hofmann, Rahsaan Roland Kirk, Charles Lloyd, Sam Most, Jeremy Steig, Buddy Collette, Lloyd McNeil, and James Newton — have made recordings primarily devoted to flute.

The flute through the ages

Flutes sound ancient and mysterious — in fact, they are pictured in primitive drawings dating back thousands of years. But the essential breakthrough for future jazz players came in 1850, when Theobald Boehm redesigned the instrument with larger holes that produced a bigger sound. The larger holes made it impossible for players to use their fingers to cover the holes, so Boehm also added keys to control padded hole covers — and the modern flute (see the figure) was born as a member of the wind instrument family.

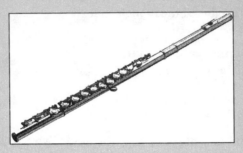

Early Jazz Flute

The first jazz recordings made in the 1920s by Louis Armstrong, King Oliver, and other band leaders didn't utilize Theobald Boehm's silver pipe. (See the sidebar "The flute through the ages.") Unlike the clarinet or trombone, which went through waves of popularity over the years, the flute has kept a consistently elusive profile in jazz. However, a few early players made excellent use of the instrument. It was difficult to play loud enough to be heard in live context with the amplification technology of the time, but in studios where the first major jazz was recorded during the 1920s, flutists could step closer to the microphone to enhance their sound.

Albert Socarras: The first jazz flutist on record

Albert Socarras was the first to record jazz flute. Like many other jazz flutists, Socarras was a *doubler* — he played saxophone and clarinet, too. Socarras played flute on several songs recorded by Clarence Williams's big band in 1929, and his solo on "Have You Ever Felt That Way" included on *Clarence Williams 1929* (Classics) is the earliest example of flute improvisation I've found.

"Have You Ever Felt That Way" is an upbeat number led by Williams' *stride* piano (see Chapter 11 for further details on stride piano) and "de-de-de-doo" vocal improvisations. After cornetist Ed Allen's raunchy solo, Socarras comes trilling in, delivers a nimble, inventive solo, and pauses as Williams calls out, "Everybody in the cycle now, everybody in the cycle" and takes his piano break. Socarras then returns for another burst of invention. While his moment in the spotlight lasts only 30 seconds or so in this three-minute song, it's enough to show that he was a capable improviser as creative as horn players, pianists, and vocalists — the common leading sounds of his day. Socarras pointed the way toward jazz's great flute virtuosos, who didn't come along until the 1950s.

Wayman Carver (1905-1967)

Improvisation is an essential element of jazz, and the second flute solo of note was recorded in 1933 by Wayman Carver with Spike Hughes's big band on the song "Sweet Sue." Hughes's version of the song is hard to find, but Carver repeated his performance with drummer Chick Webb's orchestra in 1937, available on the CD *Chick Webb-Ella Fitzgerald/The Quintessence* (Fremeaux & Associates). "Sweet Sue, Just You," as Webb's version is titled, makes a great vehicle for the virtuosity of both Wayman Carver and Chick Webb, whose wire brushes whip the music with a relentless rhythm reminiscent of a tap dancer.

Carver's performance here is all the more significant because the song is structured to showcase his flute. Carver and clarinetist Chauncey Haughton team up on the song's opening, introducing the melody at breakneck speed. Together, their instruments sound almost like an accordion. On a tune that could almost be a German beer-hall polka, the mood is an odd folk/jazz mix of music, rhythms, and improvisation.

Lasting a mere 25 seconds, Carver's solo is nonetheless a more polished turn in the spotlight than Socarras's 1929 flourish with Williams's band.

Fifties Flowering: Frank Wess & Co.

As bebop hit during the mid-'40s, flute was seldom seen . . . or heard. Perhaps because the sound of the flute is so lush and soft, and because much of bebop has a harder edge, flute never played a prominent part in bebop.

Not until the 1950s did modern flutists emerge, led by Frank Wess. Like beboppers trumpeter Dizzy Gillespie and saxophonist Charlie Parker, Wess and some of his peers brought new sophistication to their instrument. They played songs that utilized more complex harmonies and melodies. At times, they played much faster, and they vastly extended the flute's emotional range by creating a fresh palette of sounds and tones.

Buddy Collette (born 1921)

Like James Moody and many other flute players, Buddy Collette doubles on saxes and flute; and like Moody, Collette has a sixth sense for the flute.

Collette's 1956 *Man of Many Parts* (Contemporary) is one of his best efforts as a leader and includes exquisite tenor saxophone as well as some sensuous flute. He wrings great emotional range from his flute. "Ruby" is a lovely ballad that features a warm, breathy tone sweetened by gentle vibrato. "Frenesi" opens with a light, nimble duet between Collette and bassist Gene Wright. But "Jungle Pipe" is this album's hot spot, a freeform improvisation featuring Collette with guitarist Barney Kessel and pianist Ernie Freeman. Here, Collette cuts loose with some long, fluid, mesmerizing lines of melody that evoke primal, tropical visions.

Unlike doublers who play flute only occasionally, Collette has a soft spot for it and uses it often. He has made some of his best music with it. *Buddy's Best* (Dootone) catches Collette on sax and flute in 1957, in a quintet that includes Gerald Wilson on piano. "My Funny Valentine" has been done countless times by dozens of players, but Collette's version here is slow, sweet, and seasoned by his sexy, lyrical sound. When he hits the familiar melody's high notes in his clear, singing tone, it's pure nirvana. And Collette is particularly mesmerizing on his own composition "Blue Sands," with its haunting eastern melody carried by Collette's softly wavering flute.

Herbie Mann (born 1930)

From his RayBans to his goatee, the young Herbie Mann was the coolest of the cool 1950s flutists. Thanks to his graceful ways with simple melodies, Mann helped raise awareness of jazz flute during the 1950s and 1960s. He became a popular figure in clubs and concert venues, releasing albums including his 1962 *Do the Bossa Nova with Herbie Mann* (Atlantic) that tied in with one wave of the occasional Latin fascination that periodically sweeps the United States.

But Mann (see Figure 18-1) is a serious jazzman. His cool bebop side is amply displayed on several albums, including *Just Wailin'* (Prestige), music he made in the mid-'50s in a sextet including guitarist Kenny Burrell and tenor saxman Charlie Rouse. This is some solid jazz, but having top-notch side-men does not necessarily play in Mann's favor: They take so many good solos that the album becomes more of a showcase for this all-star band than for Mann.

Other early Mann you should hear includes *Flute Souffle* (Original Jazz Classics), *Herbie Mann* (Verve), and *Flute, Brass, Vibes and Percussion* (Verve). More recent recordings include the 1997 *America/Brasil* (Lightyear Entertainment), a CD of Brazilian-flavored jazz from a week of performances at the Blue Note in New York City.

Figure 18-1:
Herbie
Mann
(photo:
Everett
Collection).

Frank Wess (born 1922)

Like explorers Lewis and Clark, Frank Wess led the way into uncharted
territory. Also a fine saxophonist, Wess has been one of jazz's most prolific
flutists, using the instrument on several albums. He played flute with Count
Basie's band during the late '50s and early '60s, and you can hear him on
various recordings from that period. But for a concentrated collection of
Wess's flute, look for several albums under his own name.

Going Wess (Town Crier), released in 1993, is an all-time top album by Wess,
placing his flute alongside Bobby Forrester's organ and Clarence "Tootie"
Bean's drums. To me, the flute, with its delicate sound, usually does best in
such spare settings. The song "Antiqua," with its medium-tempo Latin beat,
is a great showpiece for Wess's flute. He swings hard, and he plays extremely
creative, carefully articulated solos that show how far he advanced the
flutist's technique.

Wess is still making great music, and his output includes several other good
titles, some of them quite unconventional in their instrumentation. Some of
Wess's best playing, for instance, is on jazz harpist Dorothy Ashby's *In a
Minor Groove* (Prestige) — what a great combination. *Trombones and Flute*

(Savoy) is exactly what the title implies: an extended workout by Wess with four trombonists including Benny Powell and Jimmy Cleveland, recorded in 1956. And *Opus in Swing* (Savoy) is another recording from the same year that puts Wess with Burrell, Green, bassist Eddie Jones, and bebop drummer Kenny Clarke.

The '60s and '70s: Jazz Flutists Follow Different Paths

Jazz fractured into several camps during the 1960s and 1970s (see Chapter 5). Some players attempted mergers of jazz with other genres such as funk and rock; others opted for a lighter, commercial sound; and many stayed with the straight-ahead acoustic jazz format of the 1950s and 1960s. Flute players were a small group during this era, and the styles and flute playing vary widely.

Two Wizards: Rahsaan Roland Kirk (1936-1977) and Yusef Lateef (born 1920)

On the more experimental and forward-thinking side of the 1960s and 1970s are two musicians who deserve special attention for their multiple talents: Yusef Lateef and Rahsaan Roland Kirk. Both have made fine flute music, but both have also utilized a variety of unconventional instruments in jazz, from Lateef's *Chinese globular flute* and *bamboo flute,* to Kirk's *nose flute* and sax-like *stritch* and *manzello.* Both musicians hit their creative prime during the mid-1950s and kept a vital creative pace over several decades and numerous recordings that vastly expanded jazz's cross-cultural range — as well as the sonic range of woodwind players.

Rahsaan Roland Kirk's rootsy range

By now, Kirk's technical tricks are the stuff of jazz legend. He used *circular breathing,* by which he could hold a note indefinitely, using air from his puffed up cheeks while he refilled his lungs through his nose. He often played two or three horns at once, and was a master of the nose flute, which initially seems odd, but in his hands made stunning sounds. Kirk's special creativity and his confidence in his creative vision are evidenced by the fact that almost from the start of his career, he always led his own bands. He never did extended tours of duty as a sideman, as did most other jazz players in their early years.

Almost everything Kirk recorded beginning with *Early Roots* (Bethlehem) in 1956 is worth owning. Use your instincts to help you select his music for your collection.

A Kirk solo is a comprehensive course in jazz improvisation. Sometimes he plays around with a song's melody, sometimes he follows the chords. Other times he makes up fresh music on the spot, inventing melodies, veering off in surprising directions, quoting fragments of other songs, repeating riffs until he has explored numerous variations, or running with various patterns just for their rhythmic force. One minute, he's dialed into the driving power of bass and drums, the next he's flying free alongside his fellow windborne friends before coming back down to blow guttural blues.

A good place to start with Kirk is the two-CD issue *Does Your House Have Lions: The Rahsaan Roland Kirk Anthology* (Rhino), a collection of music he originally recorded for Atlantic between 1961 and 1976. Beautifully packaged, with a slick booklet and great photos, this set is a keeper that you will return to again and again.

Yusef Lateef casts a wide net

Yusef Lateef grew up in Detroit and began his career the old-fashioned way: He earned his reputation in bands led by Lucky Millinder and trumpeters Oren "Hot Lips" Page, Dizzy Gillespie, and Roy Eldridge. Later, Lateef played with bassist Charles Mingus, trumpeter Donald Byrd, and saxophonist Cannonball Adderley, but by 1957, he headed recording sessions of his own.

A *doubler,* equally at home on saxes, oboe, and flutes, Lateef brought new sounds into jazz in his use of unusual wind instruments, and the way he combined elements of blues, jazz, gospel, classical, and assorted exotic musics from abroad.

"Brother Yusef had a beautiful sound," says saxophonist/flutist James Moody. "His sound knocked me out, boy. He could play the changes, but his sound was a sound I just loved."

Moody's reference to "changes" describes Lateef's technical finesse, his ability to invent intricate improvisations around a song's chord changes. But it is Lateef's distinctive tone on flute that is instantly recognizable: lush and full and with a gently wavering vibrato that adds depth.

Like Rahsaan Roland Kirk, Lateef made much of his best music for the Atlantic label; also like Kirk, a good place to start listening to Lateef is a double-CD reissue of his Atlantic music. The CD is titled *Every Village Has A Song* (Rhino/Atlantic) that documents his evolution from 1949 to 1976.

As with Kirk, most everything Lateef touched turned into musical gold, so almost any album of his will give good listening. From his experiments fusing jazz with African and Middle Eastern sounds (don't miss the leaky balloon squeaks and 7-Up bottle blowing that accompany him on *The Sounds of Yusef Lateef,* on Prestige) to his hot early 1960s Impulse! recordings and his 1990s releases on his own YAL label, you pretty much can't go wrong.

Contemporary Crosswinds

Of course, the influence of electricity and 1970s-era mergers of jazz with other musics wasn't lost on flute players. They soul jazzed and funk jazzed, and they plugged into amplifiers. They produced lighter commercial jazz, or more challenging music that drew from jazz's various periods.

Prince Lasha (born 1929)

Prince Lasha is among jazz players who pushed the boundaries of jazz far out during the 1960s. A *doubler* on flute and saxes, Lasha's recorded legacy is small but essential to an appreciation of the flute's full range.

If you are up for a challenge, take on *Firebirds* (Contemporary). A quintet fronted by Lasha and saxophonist Sonny Simmons shreds its way through five extended songs of freeform jazz. For a pure, raw creative jolt, Lasha's playing on this recording is the equivalent of an 8-ounce shot of pure wheat grass juice.

Hubert Laws (born 1939)

Some of the best flutery in contemporary times comes from crossovers between classical, jazz, pop, funk, and other genres. Case in point: Hubert Laws, who made excellent mid-'70s albums including *The Rite of Spring* for CTI Records, the decade's dominant pop-jazz label. Merging classical and jazz influences, Laws played lyrical melodies and long improvisations that I remember listening to for hours during some dark nights of my stormy teen years.

And on *In The Beginning* (CTI), a gem among Laws' early recordings, Laws shows he is not only among the most lyrical flutists, but he is a thoughtful arranger, too. He gets able assists from sidemen such as bassist Ron Carter, drummer Steve Gadd, percussionist Airto Moreira, and Hubert's brother Ronnie on tenor sax — as well as a string section of violin, viola, and cello.

Flute into the Present

Flute continues to be something of a fringe instrument in jazz, but a few players are pushing the instrument to new heights.

James Newton (born 1953)

Now in his prime, James Newton has already played some of jazz's best flute. As with Rahsaan Roland Kirk and Yusef Lateef, Newton gives the instrument a broad organic range and incorporates a variety of breathing and vocal sounds with his playing. His distinctive tone is especially strong on high notes, which he plays with clear, vibrato-less purity.

If you are relatively new to jazz, be patient . . . Newton's music is dense, intricate, and potentially daunting for newcomers, but pays off with tremendous emotional and musical range.

For a comprehensive understanding of the way Newton hears jazz, get a copy of *The African Flower* (EMD/Blue Note) where he serves as both band leader and virtuoso musician interpreting the music of Duke Ellington and Billy Strayhorn with an all-star ensemble. From the spare beauty of his flute on "Fleurette Africaine" to the thumping rhythms and dense swirling sounds that support Newton's trilling, soaring flute on "Virgin Jungle," he delivers an exotic array of musical colors. And Newton's "Sophisticated Lady" is a solo *tour de force,* a one-man reinvention of one of Ellington's classic songs.

In recent years, Newton has matured into an artist of epic ambitions, as evidenced on the 1986 *Romance and Revolution* (EMD/Blue Note) and the 1994 *Suite For Frida Kahlo* (Audioquest), a forest of sounds as mysterious as the late painter herself. Assisted by top Southern California players, including free jazz trombonist/electronic artist George Lewis, Newton orchestrates a free-blowing *tour de force.*

Lew Tabackin (born 1940)

In the category of flute players who stuck to straight-ahead acoustic jazz, my favorite flutist is Lew Tabackin, also a fine saxman and former big band leader with Toshiko Akiyoshi. On flute, Tabackin is one of the few musicians to take extended solos on long, largely improvised songs that allow room for him to explore the instrument's range of moods and sounds.

Tabackin is my choice for an underrated flutist who does marvelous things with the instrument. His 1994 album *Live At Vartan* (Vartan Jazz) includes a 12-minute version of the song "Pyramid," with Tabackin stretching out over spare, Latin rhythms. When he finds a good riff, he's not afraid to repeat it with slight variations until he has explored its full potential.

He's also in fine form on the earlier *I'll Be Seeing You* (Concord Jazz) album, turning in fine improvisations on John Coltrane's "Wise One," on Toshiko Akiyoshi's "Chic Lady," and on Duke Ellington's "Lost In Meditation." Tabackin is a master of the flute's full range of sounds: speedy, beboppish lines; *overblowing* to produce warped, whistling sounds; and spare, simple tones that strike the right mood for slow- and medium-tempo ballads.

Dave Valentin (born 1954)

Of all the artists who combine musical influences with electronic experimentation and commercial success, the leader is Dave Valentin. He has managed to gain a fairly wide audience through frequent radioplay, without sacrificing creativity.

If you only buy one album by Valentin, make it *Live at the Blue Note* (GRP), a rousing performance that ranges from Valentin's exotic flute on "Cinnamon & Clove" (written by Brazilian singer Milton Nascimento) to his energized playing on the up-tempo, electric-bass-powered "Footprints" (written by saxophonist Wayne Shorter). He also records a fine solo reading of "Mountain Song," and a moody interpretation of percussionist Mongo Santamaria's "Afro Blue."

Other flutists of note

Thankfully for fans of jazz flute, several talented players are poised to take jazz flute into a new millennium:

- ✔ Joe Farrell (born 1937).
- ✔ Sonny Fortune (born 1939).
- ✔ Holly Hofmann.
- ✔ Steve Kujala.
- ✔ Byard Lancaster (born 1942).
- ✔ Sam Rivers (born 1930).
- ✔ Bud Shank (born 1926).

Chapter 19

Trombonists: Sliding to the Beat

● ●

In This Chapter

▶ Tailgaters and their trombone style

▶ Early improvisers: Kid Ory and company

▶ Swingin' slidemen

▶ J.J. Johnson and other bebop bosses of the 'bone

▶ After J.J. Johnson: Modern trombonists

● ●

*E*arly jazz trombonists were called *tailgaters,* and the name comes from the instrument's cumbersome character. When horse-drawn wagons carried jazz bands through the streets of New Orleans, trombonists hung their horns out the back so they wouldn't bonk anyone with their long brass tubes and slides.

Key elements characterize the playing of the early New Orleans tailgaters. These sounds really defined the role that trombone was to play, and continues to play in the jazz ensemble. To me, some of these devices aren't much different than what a great singer does with his or her voice in order to add emotional nuances. If you listen carefully, these characteristics of jazz trombone tip you off and let you instantly pick out the trombone from the other horns:

  ✔ Glissando, or a smooth slide, through a string of notes that sounds, at times, like an elephant braying. This technique is what most people recognize as "that trombone sound." (The term is Italian, as are many musical terms — purists may refer to more than one glissando as *glissandi.*)

  ✔ Vibrato, a wavering sound (and another Italian word) often kept up through the entire length of a note or phrase, adding dynamic detail. The term literally means "with vibration," and after you can recognize the use of vibrato, you can understand why. Vibrato is a technique you commonly hear vocalists using.

  ✔ Steady playing on the beat. Trombone lends itself well to playing lower in pitch than other horns, and so often picks up the rhythm section (bass and drums) function of playing strictly with the beat of the song.

Variations on the trombone

When I talk about jazz trombone, I'm referring mainly to the classic slide trombone, although a handful of jazz players have utilized *valve trombone*. All brass instruments work in essentially the same way. The player can create different pitches by varying the vibrations of his lips in combination with varying the length of the brass tubing through which the lip vibrations carry. Slide trombone uses a slide to vary the length of tubing, whereas valve trombone — like its cousin horns including trumpet — has valves that route air through various lengths of brass tubing and help produce different notes. Important valve trombone players include Juan Tizol (with Duke Ellington's big band) and Bob Brookmeyer, who played with California *cool* jazzmen Gerry Mulligan and Jimmy Giuffre during the 1950s, and has also recorded several solid albums of his own including *Bob Brookmeyer Small Band, Vols. 1 and 2* (Gryphon).

✔ Bright solos that incorporate glissandos, as well as a wah-wah sound produced with various types of mutes and plungers placed over or inside the horn's bell. Mutes were especially popular with early New Orleans and subsequent swing-era trombonists — as well as trumpeters.

✔ Improvising collectively with other horns — mainly cornet or trumpet, as well as clarinet, a member of the woodwinds family — to create the classic New Orleans sound of loosely overlapping, intermingling, melodies.

Early Trombonists: Beatkeepers and Improvisers

In early New Orleans bands led by Buddy Bolden, King Oliver, Louis Armstrong, and Jelly Roll Morton, trombonists, along with tuba players, took roles that would later be filled by bassists, anchoring the music's bottom end, pushing the beat with help from the banjo or guitar player's strummed chords.

"In some of the early Dixieland bands, the trombone served a similar function (playing low, rhythmic bass notes) to the tuba, then Kid Ory and others developed the *tailgate style,* with growls and slurs — glissandos, sliding from one to another," says David Wilkens, a trombonist who wrote a history of jazz trombone as part of his doctoral degree program at Ball State University in Indiana. "Trombone is the only horn that can do that, so early jazz players took advantage of this quality to create their sound."

Although not the stars of early jazz groups, trombonists were highly visible and flamboyant players. Even though they plodded away beneath the higher sound of other instruments, keeping time to a regular 1-2, or 1-2-3-4, count, they used an occassional glissando (see the signature sound list in the preceding section) to punctuate transitions in the music.

Kid Ory (1886-1973)

Kid Ory had a hand in the creation of some of the earliest jazz. In New Orleans, where jazz grew out of marching parade and funeral bands, Ory was an early master of the dramatic tailgate style — playing flamboyant, improvised bass lines that served as the music's solid foundation.

Introduce yourself to jazz trombone by listening to Kid Ory on some of the famous songs recorded by trumpeter Louis Armstrong's Hot Fives and Hot Seven bands in the 1920s. Much of this music is included on albums under Armstrong's name, but also on many history-of-jazz anthologies.

Ory's own bands during the teens featured early jazz legends like clarinetists Jimmie Noone and Sidney Bechet. During the 1920s, he was frequently featured with pianist Jelly Roll Morton, trumpeter Louis Armstrong, and cornetist/band leader King Oliver (Ory played on several of their early jazz recordings made in Chicago).

During the New Orleans revival of the 1940s and 1950s, Ory enjoyed a major comeback, performing and recording often as a band leader. Catch him during this period on *Kid Ory/1944–1945* (Good Time Jazz), *King of the Tailgate Trombone* (American Music), and *Kid Ory's Creole Jazz Band/1954* (Good Time Jazz).

Ory's playing is simple but majestic on such popular Armstrong tunes as "Struttin' With Some Barbecue" (from *Louis Armstrong Hot Fives and Sevens/Vol. 3* on Sony). On this tune, Ory improvises a few catchy phrases before gracefully bowing out with a few slides through several notes (glissandos) that give the song some of its party spirit.

On the cumbersome trombone, Ory was first and best at proving that this sizeable horn could be used for improvising quick lines of melody — that it could become a valid creative counterpart to the trumpets of Louis Armstrong and King Oliver, and the clarinets of Jimmie Noone, Sidney Bechet, and Johnny Dodds.

Around the same time as Armstrong's important early jazz, Jelly Roll Morton's Hot Peppers made music that to me sounds, well, *hotter,* utilizing some of the same players including Kid Ory on trombone. *The Birth of the Hot* (Bluebird) CD is also recorded better than some of Armstrong's early music.

Ory gives a funeral-dirge introduction to "Dead Man Blues," a wailing march that gives some sense of the early New Orleans funeral and marching bands that led to early jazz. Then he launches into a series of slides that shove the song on its way. On "Smoke House Blues," Ory turns in a simple but strong solo that slides loosely to the beat. For pure oom-pah timekeeping, check out Ory on "Steamboat Stomp," which evokes images straight out of Mark Twain, or "The Pearls," a minimal arrangement that gives his trombone a more prominent rhythmic role.

You can also hear Ory on King Oliver's *Okeh Sessions* (EMI), on Louis Armstrong's famous *Hot Fives, Vol. 1* (Sony/Columbia), one of the hottest jazz recordings of the 1920s, and on *Kid Ory/1944–1945* (Good Time Jazz).

Other early titans of trombone

Ory was the leading trombonist in the teens and 1920s, but others made major contributions to the evolution of early jazz and the trombone's role around the same time. Although there weren't trombonists who soloed on the order of trumpeter Louis Armstrong or clarinetists Sidney Bechet and Bix Beiderbecke, these trombonists advanced the role of their instrument:

- **George Brunies (1902–1974)**
- **Honore Dutrey (1894–1935)**
- **Charlie Green (1900–1936)**
- **Jimmy Harrison (1900–1931)**
- **J.C. Higginbotham (1906–1973)**
- **Charlie Irvis (1899–1939)**
- **Miff Mole (1898–1961)**
- **Roy Palmer**

Swingin' Slidemen

During the 1920s, big bands led by Fletcher Henderson, Duke Ellington, Luis Russell, Ben Pollack, and others (see Chapter 3) played jazz related to the small-group jazz of King Oliver, Louis Armstrong, and Jelly Roll Morton (see Chapter 2). But sophisticated compositions and arrangements, and a steady supply of gifted young players, refined the music into the more subtle and sophisticated big band swing of the 1930s and 1940s, with horn sections playing off rhythm sections, and songs arranged to showcase a growing number of capable soloists — including trombonists.

On a song such as "Oh Baby" by Henderson's band (hear it on *A Study in Frustration* on Sony), Charlie Green has a fast and complicated part. He also takes a solo nearly as nimble as the one played by tenor saxophonist Coleman Hawkins.

In the mid-'30s, tuba player John Kirby switched to stand-up bass, freeing trombones from their tailgater role as rhythm-keepers to become a more integral part of melodies, harmonies — and the soloing action. More and more, trombone solos were sandwiched between solos by saxophonists and trumpeters, hailing the passing of the tailgate era and the arrival of the trombone as an instrument capable of taking the spotlight.

Jack Teagarden (1905-1964)

Prominent as a big band leader during the 1940s, Teagarden wielded a mean trombone. He was also an excellent singer, and Teagarden brought a singer's sense of melody to his trombone. Teagarden wasn't a flashy player, but as a soloist he had an understated maturity that helped elevate the trombone to new status as a more versatile instrument in big band ensembles — and as a leading instrument for solos, alongside saxes, trumpets, and clarinets.

Before he organized his own big band, Teagarden had years of solid journeyman experience in 1920s and 1930s jazz groups led by Eddie Condon, Red Nichols, Louis Armstrong, and Paul Whiteman. Although his career lasted through the advent of fast, furious bebop during the mid-'40s, Teagarden wasn't a bebopper. Instead, he was a master at playing fluid melodies and inventing long, lyrical solos in the early New Orleans and swing styles of jazz.

Check out Teagarden on *That's a Serious Thing* (Bluebird), *Jack Teagarden/ 1934–1939* (Classics), and *Jack Teagarden and His All-Stars* (Jazzology).

Duke Ellington's heavies

Duke Ellington was notorious for writing music around his gifted band members. Several songs featured soloists including trombonists.

One great collection of early Ellington is *Duke Ellington/The Quintessence* (Fremeaux & Associates). Trombonist Tricky Sam Nanton checks in with a melodic solo on "East St. Louis Toodle-oo," takes a long, throaty break on "Jubilee Stomp," and makes a wailing, muted contribution to W. C. Handy's

"Yellow Dog Blues." A trombonist — probably Nanton — also plays sexy solos utilizing some sort of mute (a device cupped over the horn's bell and wiggled slowly for a "wah-wah" sound) on "Daybreak Express" and "Blue Light."

As a testing and development ground for new trombonists, Ellington's orchestra produced a phenomenal number of great players beginning in the 1930s:

- **Lawrence Brown (1907–1988).** Through the 1930s and 1940s, Brown was a fixture in Ellington's trombone section — a smooth, lyrical contrast to the brash sounds of Nanton and Jackson.

- **Buster Cooper (born 1929).** An Ellington trombonist during the 1960s, Cooper had a distinctively sharp, biting, bluesy attack.

- **Tyree Glenn (1912–1974).** In Ellington's late '40s orchestra, Glenn (who also played solid if not innovative vibes) often utilized a plunger-produced "wah-wah" effect reminiscent of his predecessor, Tricky Sam Nanton.

- **Quentin Jackson (1909–1976).** One of Ellington's 'bones during the 1940s and 1950s, Jackson picked up where Nanton left off, advancing the plunger "wah-wah" solo into jazz's bebop years.

- **Tricky Sam Nanton (1904–1946).** Known for using a rubber plunger in the bell of his horn to produce a "wah-wah" sound, Nanton produced solos with a singing vocal quality, almost as if Louis Armstrong were singing without words. Nanton was with Ellington in the 1920s, 1930s, and 1940s.

- **Juan Tizol (1900–1984).** A master of the seldom-heard valve trombone (with finger-operated valves instead of a slide), Tizol added Latin flavors to Ellington's orchestra during the 1930s and early 1940s, and again in the early 1950s. Tizol was more of an ensemble player than a soloist.

- **Britt Woodman (born 1920).** With Ellington during the 1950s, Woodman, who was inspired by bebop trombonist J.J. Johnson, helped produce the surging horn-section cross currents that characterized the band, and he was a regular soloist on several of the band's signature songs, including "One O'Clock Jump" and "Things Ain't What They Used to Be."

Other kings of swing trombone

While bebop, a relentless, speedy, brash new form of jazz, was being invented (see Chapter 4), there was still a strong audience for big band swing.

Vic Dickenson (1906-1984)

One of the most durable among trombonists who began their careers during the 1930s, Dickenson started out in bands fronted by Benny Carter, Count Basie, and others, and continued playing early New Orleans-style jazz and swing into the 1970s. *The Essential Vic Dickenson* (Vanguard), *Gentleman of the Trombone* (Storyville), and *Breaks Blues and Boogie* (Topaz) are good starters.

Tommy Dorsey (1905-1956)

Dorsey and his clarinet/sax-playing brother Jimmy helped popularize big band swing with the bands they led together and individually. Tommy Dorsey was also one of the top swing-era trombonists. With his sweet tone, warm ways with a melody, and fluid improvising skills, he was one of the most advanced players of the 1930s and 1940s. Hear him on *Music Goes Round and Round* (Bluebird), the multi-volume *Complete Tommy Dorsey* series (Bluebird), and *Yes, Indeed!* (Bluebird).

Benny Morton (born 1907)

Playing with big bands led by Fletcher Henderson, Don Redman, and Count Basie, recording with legends like saxophonist Benny Carter and pianist Teddy Wilson, Morton was one of the strongest swing-era trombone soloists. Listen to him on *Don Redman/1933–1936* (Classics), and on cornetist Ruby Braff's *This Is My Lucky Day* (Bluebird).

Dickie Wells (1907-1985)

Wells's solos were distinguished by a strong vibrato (wavering sound), imaginative rhythmic combinations, and his wry sense of musical humor. A 1930s mainstay of big bands led by Fletcher Henderson and Teddy Hill, Wells was in Count Basie's big band from 1938 to 1945, and again from 1947 to 1950. Wells continued to play vintage swing with trumpeter Buck Clayton and others into the 1950s. Start with *Dickie Wells in Paris* (Prestige) and *Essential Count Basie, Vol. 2* (Columbia).

Trummy Young (1912-1984)

Young was a major force on trombone with pianist Earl Hines's late '30s big band, and with Jimmy Lunceford's orchestra during the late '30s and early '40s. He also played occasionally with beboppers during the mid-'40s, and he was a member of Louis Armstrong's All-Stars through the 1950s and early '60s. Young is known for his smooth, flamboyant solos, and for an occasional humorous vocal, as on the hit song "Margie" with Lunceford. Catch him on multi-CD sets devoted to both Lunceford and Hines on the Classics label, as well as on *Jimmie Lunceford/The Quintessence* (Fremeaux & Associates), where he takes great solos on songs including "Annie Laurie." Also hear Young on Armstrong's *The California Concerts* (GRP) and *Armstrong/Ellington: Together for the First Time* (Roulette).

Bebop Bosses of the 'Bone

Nimbler and easier to play fast, trumpets and saxophones were the obvious tools for bebop. But, even though the cumbersome trombone seemed an unlikely vehicle for the fleet new music, a new generation of trombonists led by J.J. Johnson came along and proved they could fit bebop to their 'bones.

J.J. Johnson (born 1924)

Playing the demanding, fast licks required of bop on a trombone is like teaching an elephant to tap dance — but dance these guys do. Beginning with Johnson, trombonists found ways to get around on their horns with the agility and expressiveness of trumpeters and saxophonists.

Johnson, shown in Figure 19-1, paid journeyman dues in Benny Carter and Count Basie's big bands during the mid-'40s, and by 1946, he was a regular 52nd Street clubmate of the beboppers, and the first trombonist to play super fast without tripping all over himself. Johnson joined Parker, trumpeter Miles Davis (on Davis' quintessential *Birth of the Cool* album, on Capitol), and Oscar Pettiford to make some of the best jazz of the late 1940s and early 1950s. However, Johnson's definitive recordings came when he fronted his own ensembles.

I think that Johnson's two CDs for Blue Note, *The Eminent Jay Jay Johnson, Vols. 1 and 2,* recorded in 1953 and 1955, are the two most amazing jazz trombone recordings of all time. They catch Johnson playing with his characteristic greatness, and they prove that he was also a fine composer who knew how to showcase himself and his bandmates.

A new style for trombone

Johnson immediately made 1920s and 1930s trombone techniques, such as long slides (glissandos) and heavy vibrato, seem outdated. Of course, having superhuman sidemen helps, such as drummer Kenny Clarke and trumpeter Clifford Brown (on *The Eminent Jay Jay Johnson, Vol. 1,* on Blue Note); and pianist Horace Silver, bassists Charles Mingus and Paul Chambers, pianist Wynton Kelly, and tenor saxman Hank Mobley (on *The Eminent Jay Jay Johnson, Vol. 2,* on Blue Note).

Dating back to the tailgate trombonists of jazz's early years, the big unwieldy horn sometimes seems more of a musical oddity than a legitimate creative force. But Johnson made it a facile tool for improvisation. His long solos on songs such as "Capri" (on *The Eminent . . . Vol. 1*) are studies in grace and subtlety. Although he was a cohort of the beboppers and could play fast, Johnson was also sensitive to a song's nuances. On a number like "Lover Man" (also on *The Eminent . . . Vol. 1*) made famous by singer Billie Holiday, Johnson plays the melody in soft, mellow fashion, each note as gently rounded as some of trumpeter Miles Davis's 1950's solos. Johnson's improvisations on these slow numbers are delicately crafted variations that grow organically around the melody and chords.

On *The Eminent Jay Jay Johnson Vol. 2*, "Old Devil Moon" is especially cool. It kicks off with drummer Kenny Clarke's sizzling high-hat, picks up steam with Johnson playing the jaunty melody over Sabu's simmering congas, and comes to a shimmering climax during Johnson's sensuous solo. Johnson's

Figure 19-1:
J.J.
Johnson
(photo:
Everett
Collection).

laid-back reading of "Time After Time" on *The Eminent/Vol. 2* is my favorite interpretation of this slow, blue ballad — along with trumpeter Chet Baker's heart-rending vocal version.

Johnson also recorded numerous other albums that showcase his virtuosic trombone. *Trombone Master* (Sony), *Proof Positive* (GRP/Impulse!), *Things Are Getting Better All The Time* (Original Jazz Classics), and *Standards: Live at the Village Vanguard* (Antilles) are all excellent — the newer albums also benefit from improved recording techniques.

Johnson also teamed with fellow trombonist Kai Winding during the mid-'50s, but to me, their recordings, such as the fairly famous early '50s album *Jay and Kai* (Savoy), don't pack as much grace and power as Johnson's *Eminent . . .* albums on Blue Note. Their collaborations do, however, showcase Johnson's fine writing abilities. He penned 11 of 12 tunes on *Jay and Kai,* creating beautifully harmonized melodies for the two trombones to play together.

Johnson's still smooth

To subsequent generations of trombonists, Johnson is godly. In his sixth decade of musicmaking, he continues to make good music. On the Grammy-nominated *J.J. Johnson/The Brass Orchestra* (Verve) he is joined by younger trombone disciples including Robin Eubanks and Steve Turre.

Johnson's rich compositions show that he has lost none of his flair for overlapping trombone lines supported by subtle big band section arrangements. "Canonn For Bela" (also nominated for a Grammy) shows that Johnson can compose a minimalist modern piece, and that he has an ear equal to great classical composers including Bartok, presumably the Bela honored by this song.

Kai Winding (1922-1983)

Kai Winding moved fluidly between 1940s bop and 1950s cool. During the late '40s he played with Benny Goodman's band, and with Stan Kenton's unconventional swing orchestra, known for unusual harmonies and melodies. Winding also played bebop with pianist Tadd Dameron and others.

In 1949, Winding was a part of trumpeter Miles Davis' ensemble on the 1949 album *Birth of the Cool* (Capitol). Catch Winding in his prime on *Kai Winding Solo* (Verve) and *Boy Next Door* (Jazz Time). Also check out Winding's album *Live in Cleveland Ohio June 1957* (Status), with special guests including fellow trombonist Carl Fontana. Going deep into the trombone's full-bodied potential, this CD has harmonies among four horns: Winding's and Fontana's trombones and tromboniums (a mellow marriage of trombone and *euphonium* — a tuba-like instrument), as well as Wayne Andre's trombone and trombonium and Dick Lieb's bass trombone and trombonium.

Post-Eminent Trombones (After J.J. Johnson)

As jazz evolved through 1950s cool and hard bop, 1960s *avant garde*/free jazz, 1970s electric jazz-rock and jazz-funk fusions, and the acoustic jazz revival of the 1980s and 1990s, a few trombonists played vital parts. As with other instruments during these phases of jazz history, trombonists advanced their instrument by making it a more prominent player of melodies and solos.

Ray Anderson (born 1952)

Ray Anderson's a fine composer and improviser. Generally speaking, I believe that less is always more, and Anderson's 1987 album *It Just So Happens* (Enja) utilizes spare instrumentation that leaves plenty of room for his warm, romantic melodies. Like J.J. Johnson, Anderson can also swing hard, extending the energy stirred up by Johnson and the beboppers of the 1940s. Bassist Mark Dresser's inventive swooping bass lines make an excellent foil for Anderson's horn.

Curtis Fuller (born 1934)

If you love soul and blues, you'll love Fuller, one of the most soulful jazz trombone players. Beginning in the 1950s, Fuller played with several of jazz's giants: guitarist Kenny Burrell, multi-woodwind genius Yusef Lateef, Dizzy Gillespie, and Art Blakey. Catch Fuller on *Curtis Fuller with Red Garland* (Blue Note). Unlike many trombonists, Fuller also stood out as a leader. See for yourself on *Blues-Ette* (Savoy), *The Curtis Fuller Jazztette* (Savoy), and *Blues-Ette, Part 2* (Savoy).

George Lewis (born 1952)

On freeform jazz's cutting edge, Lewis has put the trombone to some of the most provocative uses in jazz. During the 1970s he collaborated with *avant garde* players such as saxophonists Anthony Braxton and Roscoe Mitchell, drummer Barry Altschul, and trumpeter Lester Bowie. Beyond jazz, Lewis has also used electronics and computers in experimental music he makes with *avant garde* musicians such as John Zorn. Strap yourself down, then take a listen to Lewis's *Homage to Charlie Parker* (Black Saint) and *Voyager* (Avant).

Albert Mangelsdorff (born 1928)

A German-born trombonist who played bebop during the 1950s, Albert Mangelsdorff eventually explored more abstract jazz forms. *Three Originals* (MPS), a two-CD set of music from the 1970s through 1990s, makes my list of a half-dozen must-have trombone albums.

Grachan Moncur III (born 1937)

A pioneer in utilizing trombone in *avant garde* jazz, Moncur played with hard boppers like trumpeter Lee Morgan and saxophonists Sonny Rollins and Jackie McLean during the early '60s. He was also in far-out saxman Archie Shepp's band. Not often recorded on sessions of his own, Moncur has made them count. Get *Evolution* (Blue Note), *Some Other Stuff* (Blue Note), *New Africa* (Actuel), and *Echoes of a Prayer* (JCOA).

Roswell Rudd (born 1935)

Honing his chops on New Orleans-style jazz during the 1950s, Rudd broke out with some of the wildest free-jazz trombone beginning in the 1960s. He collaborated with saxophonist Archie Shepp (check out *Four for Trane* on Impulse!), and recorded several intriguing albums of his own, including *Everywhere* (Impulse!) and *Regeneration* (Soul Note).

Steve Turre (born 1948)

You've probably caught him on the late-night comedy show *Saturday Night Live* playing either trombone . . . or *conch shell* (the shell of a large sea snail). Turre is an accomplished player, capable of dexterous bebop-style improvisations. He's also a talented composer and arranger who knows how to play the big sound of his horn off of other horns, the rhythm section (drums, bass, and piano), and, on some songs on his excellent 1991 album *Right There* (Island/Antilles), even violin and viola.

A handful of others

A few more trombonists who have made an impact in J.J. Johnson's wake:

- ✔ **Slide Hampton (born 1932).** Hampton's evolved with the music, beginning as a 1950s hard bopper, playing in bands led by Lionel Hampton and Woody Herman, also in groups with trumpeter Freddie Hubbard and some other famous trombonists. Hear several masters of trombone together on *World of Trombones* (Black Lion), also check out Hampton's *Roots* (Criss Cross).

- ✔ **Wayne Henderson (born 1929).** A soulful hard bopper, Henderson played rhythm and blues in Texas during the 1950s before joining the electric jazz-funk Jazz Crusaders, later known as simply the Crusaders. *I* (Chisa) and *Second Crusade* (Chisa) are among their best from the 1970s. The Crusaders gained popularity during the late 1970s — but Henderson left the band in 1975.

- ✔ **Delfeayo Marsalis (born 1965).** Brother of the famous Wynton (trumpet) and Branford (saxophone), son of noted New Orleans pianist Ellis Marsalis, Delfeayo is one of the most promising young trombonists. *Pontius Pilate's Decision* (Novus) was a solid debut, and he's growing on newer releases including *Musashi* (Evidence).

- ✔ **Bill Watrous (born 1939).** A seasoned big band player (Maynard Ferguson, Woody Herman), Watrous also led big bands of his own in the 1970s at a time when they were few and far between. Watrous is a technical master equally adept at speedy bop and slow ballads. Hear him on *Manhattan Wildlife Refuge* (Columbia), *Tiger of San Pedro* (Columbia), and *Bone-Ified* (GNP).

Part VII
The Part of Tens

"Funny—I just assumed it would be Carreras, too."

In this part . . .

Congratulations. If you've made it to this section, you're no neophyte. You're well on your way to being a bona fide jazz buff! Here are details on 10 great jazz labels — imprints known for releasing consistently first rate music. So when you go shopping, even if you don't know exactly what you want, you have some idea where to look for quality.

In this part, you can check out some of the hot cities that have great jazz clubs for the live experience. And you can discover all kinds of great resources to absorb more information about jazz, including books, magazines, moves, and Web sites.

Chapter 20

Ten Trustworthy Jazz Labels

In This Chapter

▶ Old standbys

▶ A couple of off-the-beaten path choices

This list is by no means a complete one, but it includes a few essential labels as well as a couple of important smaller players. As you build a jazz collection and gain a knowledge of the music's history, you may want to spend time perusing the catalogs of these labels. Record labels are often run by one or two dedicated fans who, because of their taste, lend an overall feel to the recordings the label represents. You may find that one or two labels in particular consistently give you what you crave.

Most larger labels have Web sites that list their titles and give you a chance to order a catalog. Many of these sites are multimedia events, with plenty of photos, samples of music, and artist bios, and I've included the address where applicable.

BMG Classics/RCA/Bluebird

Web site: www.classicalmus.com/bmgclassics/index.html.

RCA has a big backlog of vintage jazz, both under its own name, and in the form of music licensed from vintage Bluebird and the newer Novus label. Pianists Jelly Roll Morton and Fats Waller and clarinetist/band leader Artie Shaw are among the jazz legends on Bluebird, while RCA's treasure trove of CD reissues includes music by saxophonists Sonny Rollins and Gerry Mulligan, pianist/big band leader Duke Ellington, trumpeter Dizzy Gillespie, and many other greats.

Black Saint/Soul Note

Web site: www.blacksaint.com

A leader in free and *avant garde* jazz, this Italian label has released fringy jazz by the World Saxophone Quartet, saxophonist/bass clarinetist David Murray, saxophonist Hamiett Bluiett, composer George Russell, and others. Both labels are well represented on the Web site with great info on artists and albums.

EMD/Blue Note Records

Web site: www.bluenote.com

Founded in 1939 by Alfred Lion, Blue Note has a long, illustrious track record when it comes to delivering blue chip jazz. The label has also closely kept to Lion's original mission of capturing the essential "impulse" of "hot jazz or swing" — not its "commercial adornments." Lion's earliest recordings were of pianists Albert Ammons and Meade Lux Lewis. Blue Note later recorded clarinetist Sidney Bechet, pianist Earl Hines, and guitarist Charlie Christian, before taping beboppers such as pianist Tadd Dameron, trumpeter Fats Navarro, and pianists Bud Powell and Thelonious Monk. Blue Note hit a high mark during the 1950s and 1960s with drummer Art Blakey and the Jazz Messengers, saxmen James Moody, Dexter Gordon, and Sonny Rollins, pianist Horace Silver, trumpeters Miles Davis and Clifford Brown, and countless others. Revived and restored to its original mission in 1985, Blue Note has developed new talents such as singers Kurt Elling and Cassandra Wilson.

Concord Jazz

Web site: www.aent.com

Based in the San Francisco Bay Area, Concord was launched in the early 1970s by founder Carl Jefferson after he had produced several successful Concord Jazz Festivals. Guitarists Herb Ellis and Joe Pass were first to record for the label, which now counts more than 200 artists including trumpeter/band leader Maynard Ferguson, singer Mel Torme, bassist Ray Brown, pianists Marian McPartland, Dave Brubeck, and George Shearing; and guitarists Jim Hall, Howard Alden, and George Van Eps. Younger Concord stars include saxophonists Chris Potter and Jesse Davis. One of Concord's most vital efforts has been the *Live at Maybeck Hall* solo piano series, which has so far recorded more than 40 of jazz's best pianists. Concord Picante, the label's Latin division, offers music by percussionists Tito Puente and Poncho Sanchez and vibraphonist Cal Tjader, and others.

Fantasy

Web site: www.fantasyjazz.com

Fantasy's massive collection of great jazz includes music on Pablo, Prestige, Milestone, Riverside, and Original Jazz Classics. Most every major player throughout jazz's sweeping history has good stuff under the Fantasy umbrella: trumpeters Louis Armstrong and Chet Baker, pianists Jelly Roll Morton and Bill Evans, cornetist Bix Beiderbecke, band leader/pianist Duke Ellington, guitarists Joe Pass and Django Reinhardt, saxophonists Lester Young, Coleman Hawkins, Cannonball Adderley, and Eric Dolphy, singers Ella Fitzgerald and King Pleasure, and bassist Oscar Pettiford. Fantasy has released some great boxed sets on individual musicians, as well as Riverside's thorough three-CD *History of Classic Jazz*. Fantasy also owns rights to some great 1950s jazz recorded on Debut, the company founded by bassist Charles Mingus and drummer Max Roach.

Uni/GRP/Impulse!

While Impulse! definitely has much of Coltrane's finest music, the label is also well stocked with plenty of other great jazz from the 1960s forward, including some of the more experimental sounds. Impulse! artists include saxophonists Coleman Hawkins and Archie Shepp, pianist Cecil Taylor, band leader/pianist Duke Ellington, saxophonist/composer Oliver Nelson, saxophonist Pharoah Sanders, and trombonist Curtis Fuller.

During the 1980s, GRP was the most prominent label for lighter contemporary jazz from artists including pianists Chick Corea and Dave Grusin, and the electric fusion band Yellowjackets, and it also has a long list of players working in more traditional jazz modes, such as trumpeter Arturo Sandoval and singer Diane Schuur. Uni/GRP also owns Arista/Freedom's vast *avant garde* jazz catalog: saxophonists Anthony Braxton and Archie Shepp, pianist Cecil Taylor, and others. And the company also has Argo/Cadet's 1950s/ 1960s jazz recordings, including drummer Max Roach, pianist Barry Harris, and saxophonists Gene Ammons and James Moody.

Rhino Records

Web site: www.rhino.com

This whopping resource of reissues includes music by saxophonists Ornette Coleman, John Coltrane, and Rahsaan Roland Kirk, singer Mose Allison, drummer Art Blakey, vibraphonist Gary Burton, trumpeter Don Cherry, saxophonist/clarinetist/band leader Jimmy Dorsey, pianist/band leader Duke Ellington, and trumpet/flugelhorn player Art Farmer.

Sony/Columbia

Web site: www.sony.com

One of the heavies almost from the beginning of jazz, Columbia recorded countless legends, from singer Bessie Smith to band leader Clarence Williams, trombonist/band leader Jack Teagarden, vibraphonist Red Norvo, band leader/clarinetist Benny Goodman, pianist/band leader Count Basie, and pianist/band leader Duke Ellington. Much of Columbia's solid jazz has been reissued in the form of elegent multi-CD boxed sets. Sony also has the contemporary Noptee division, which has recorded new young players like trumpeter Leroy Jones.

Ubiquity

Web site: www.ubiquityrecords.com

Hip music including acid jazz (by original groovemasters from the 1960s and 1970s, as well as new young players) and Latin jazz. Ubiquity also issues the Cubop series highlighting the Cuban-bebop connection. Ubiquity's compilations are a great way to score some rare tracks and get a taste of some fantastic artists before committing to entire albums.

PGD/Verve/Polygram

Web site: www.verveinteractive.com

Another giant among jazz labels, Verve has a monster catalog that is thick with phenomenal jazz, primarily from the 1950s forward. Trumpeters Louis Armstrong and Dizzy Gillespie and saxophonists Charlie Parker, Lester Young, Benny Carter, Jackie McLean, Joe Henderson, and Cannonball Adderley all have titles on Verve, as do trumpeter Dizzy Gillespie, pianists Bud Powell, Tommy Flanagan, and Chick Corea, singers Betty Carter and Shirley Horn, guitarists John McLaughlin and Wes Montgomery, and drummer Art Blakey. Verve has an excellent array of greatest hits-type CDs for many artists, as well as some amazing multi-CD boxed sets.

Chapter 21

Catching Real Live Jazz

● ●

In This Chapter

▶ Cruising the clubs from New Orleans to New York, and the other side of the Atlantic as well

▶ Making the most of your club visit

● ●

A jazz music collection is crucial to get a feel for the music, and Appendix A in this book is devoted to building a quality jazz library. But jazz is best experienced live — no question about it. Jazz is most powerful when you can hear it, see it, and feel it bouncing through a club and colliding with your body. When players get in the zone with their instruments, often expressing themselves more clearly and fluently than if they were speaking to you, the experience is magic.

Making the Most of Your Club Visit

All jazz clubs were not created equal. Although you can have a great jazz experience by improvising upon arriving in a city, you should do some advance work if you really want to enjoy a first-rate live jazz experience.

Call ahead and find out whether you'll need to buy tickets in advance. Find out if seats are reserved, and if so, how far in advance you need to purchase tickets in order to get good seats. Also find out if the show on the evening you want to go out is jazz at all — many clubs book a few different styles of music.

Try to find out about any details that could make some tables better than others. For example, sitting near the bar can be distracting, what with all the glasses and silver clicking. (All that kitchen sound is kind of cool in the background, and it's part of the charm of live recordings, but you don't want any major clatter spoiling the quieter numbers.) Sound quality to the sides of the stage can be uneven compared to out front, but side seating may be desirable if you're going to hear a pianist and the house piano is situated on one side of the stage.

When you get to town, scope out local magazines and newspapers. If you are a business traveler making reservations well in advance, find out whether your hotel's concierge can procure tickets, or at least suggest a club. Also place a call to your destination's tourism office. Every city has one, and they should be able to tell you immediately what are the one or two hottest clubs for big-name jazz players, and for top local bands.

And one more of Dirk's Rules of Clubbin'. . . or, Ear. If you can only catch a portion of an evening's music, try to make it a later portion. Time and again, when I've stayed for a whole evening of jazz somewhere, the best moments come at least midway into the night, after the musicians are loose and sweaty and have built a rapport with the crowd. Many, many times, a significant part of the first set is stiff and uninspired.

Hittin' the City Scene

Some cities have more vital jazz scenes than others. If you are a traveling jazz fan, make it a point to check out live jazz when you're on the road. Different cities have entirely different personalities associated with their jazz scenes.

New Orleans is where it all began, but New York is where most of the heavies hang today. Urban blues was born in Chicago, the same town where Benny Goodman grew up and began his career. Kansas City, Missouri, is the heart of old big band territory and Charlie "Yardbird" Parker's birthplace. Beat poets and 1950s West Coast jazz hipsters made their mark in San Francisco. And across San Francisco bay, Oakland has long been a great place for blues, and is now the home of what may be the nation's plushest jazz venue.

Other cities such as Portland (Oregon), Las Vegas, Boston, Baltimore, Seattle, Denver, Detroit, Washington D.C., Miami, Toronto, Atlanta, Minneapolis, St. Louis, Cleveland, Philadelphia, Nashville, and Austin are all good places to hear live jazz.

Of course, you can find fine live jazz everywhere, from Paris to Tokyo, to London, Berlin, and Rio de Janeiro. Europeans and Japanese seem to appreciate U.S. jazz much more than Americans do. Many famous U.S. players have found their audiences overseas, and, as a result, moved their homes abroad to be closer to the action.

Here, then, are some top places for jazz — along with a few of their venues — listed in alphabetical order, so there's no bickering about who came first or last and why.

Clubbing on the Internet

Jazz info on the Web seems to grow practically by the hour.

Use a Web browser to search for "Jazz" sites and you'll hit a veritable Cotton Club full of hot listings with club information. Here are a few of them:

Earshot Jazz: Seattle-based Web site tells you all you wanted to know about jazz in this Pacific Northwestern city. You'll find club and concert info, as well as links to other great regional jazz sites on the Net. www.accessone.com/earshot

Hard Bop Café: Clearly, Canadians love their jazz as much as anyone in the world. This Web site has listings for cities across Canada, as well as tons of photos and information on legendary jazz musicians and their music. www.mbnet.mb.ca/~mcgonig/hardbop.html

Jazz Clubs: An essential stop on your cyber search for cool clubs, this Web site provides dozens of links to local and regional sites related to jazz clubs. www.dialspace.dial.pipex.com/jazz/links_cl.htm

Jazz in France: Headed for Paris? Don't go before you check out yet another of Europe's authoritative Web sites on jazz. Here you'll find club, festival, and concert listings—for France and the rest of Europe. You'll also find lots more about French and European jazz players and their scene. www.jazzfrance.com/US/

Jazz Italia: Italians are as hip to Monk as anyone on the planet. For proof, check out the lineup of clubs and other jazz info at this site. www.insinet.it/jazz/index.html

JazzNet: Cool site dedicated to jazz in Southern California, this place has club and concert listings, as well as current news about players and links to a bunch of other great jazz sites. www.dnai.com/~lmcohen/

JazzWeb: The Dutch are a cultured bunch too, as one visit to their JazzWeb site will show you. Here is a thorough list of clubs and concerts, as well as tons of other useful information about jazz in The Netherlands . . . and jazz in general. www.huizen.dds.nl/~toetsie/ukindex.html

Oz-Jazz Worldwide: Australians bop too, as you'll find on this extensive Web site, with lots of news, clubs, concerts, and links to other great jazz information sources. www.magna.com.au/~georgch/

Twin Cities Jazz: One of the more authoritative regional sites, this one has thorough listings of jazz and blues clubs and concerts, as well as news information on area jazz musicians. www.mtn.org/TCJS

World Wide Jazz Web: A great site to visit if you're a genuine globetrotter. This site links you to extensive jazz and entertainment sites all around the world. www.xs4all.nl/~centrale/region.html

For all these clubs, I've provided a phone number (which I hope is still in service by the time you read this book). In any case, make sure to call ahead to see who's playing and what time the music begins. Showing up at a club expecting live music and finding none, or finding that the music is something you had no intention of sitting through, is a real drag. Also, new clubs open all the time. If none of my suggestions pan out, be sure to check the local paper (especially the free ones which tend to have very complete entertainment listings) in whatever city you find yourself looking for a night on the town.

Boston

Collegiate types have always been hip to jazz. Perhaps that's why Boston, the ultimate college town, has one of the country's strongest jazz scenes. Living legends such as pianists Kenny Barron and Jaki Byard and drummer Billy Hart turn up at the Regattabar, and several other area venues regularly present jazz:

- **Acton Jazz Café, 452 Great Road, phone 978-263-6161.** This club is open Wednesday through Sunday starting at 5:00 p.m. Acton Jazz Café hosts jazz nightly starting with piano Wednesday through Sunday from 6:00 to 8:00 p.m., with a band after that. Friday and Saturday shows start at 9:00 p.m. and on Sunday run from 8:00 to 10:00 p.m. Also of note is that this is a non-smoking establishment and all ages are welcome.

- **Johnny D's Uptown Restaurant & Music Club, 17 Holland Street, phone 617-776-2004.** Johnny D's is open 11:30 p.m. to 1:00 a.m. during the week and 9:00 p.m. to 1:00 a.m. on weekends. Jazz shows start nightly at 9:45 p.m.

- **Regattabar, Charles Hotel, 1 Bennett Street, 3rd floor, Cambridge, MA, phone 617-661-5000.** This club is open Tuesday through Saturday with shows Tuesday through Thursday at 8:30 p.m. and Friday and Saturday at 8:00 and 10:00 p.m.

- **Ryles Jazz Club Inman Square, 212 Hampshire Street, Cambridge, MA, phone 617-876-4330.** On the Web: www.rylesjazz.com. Ryles Jazz Club is open Tuesday through Sunday and features a jazz brunch Sunday from 10:00 a.m. to 3:00 p.m.

- **Sculler's Jazz Café, Doubletree Guest Suites Hotel, 400 Soldiers Field Road, phone 617-562-4111.** On the Web: www.scullersjazz.com. The Sculler's Jazz Café features live jazz shows Tuesday through Thursday starting at 8:00 and 10:00 p.m., Sunday at 7:00 and 9:00 p.m. and Friday and Saturday at 8:00 and 10:30 p.m.

- **The Tam, 299 Harvard Street, phone 617-277-0982.** This venue is open Monday through Saturday with live music from 8:30 p.m. to 12:30 a.m., and Sunday 7:30 to 11:30 p.m. The Tam also features a jazz brunch on Sundays from 10:00 a.m. to 3:30 p.m.

- **Wally's Café, 427 Massachusetts Avenue, phone 617-424-1408.** Wally's is open seven days a week from 11:00 a.m. to 2:00 a.m. Shows begin nightly at 9:00 p.m. Wally's also features a Sunday afternoon jam session starting at 3:30 p.m.

Chicago

The Windy City helped jazz gain national attention, serving as a center for performing and recording beginning in the 1920s, when Louis Armstrong and other legends made their first records there. Chicago has a booming jazz scene these days, with leading clubs including:

- **Andy's, 11 East Hubbard, phone 312-624-6805.** Andy's is open Monday through Friday for live jazz from 12:00 to 2:30 p.m. and 9:00 p.m. to 1:00 a.m. Friday night features blues from 9:00 p.m. to 1:30 a.m. and Saturday live jazz goes from 6:00 p.m. to 1:30 a.m. On Sundays, top 40 is featured after 6:00 p.m.

- **The Cotton Club, 1710 South Michigan Avenue, phone 312-341-9787.** The Cotton Club features piano jazz during Wednesday Happy Hour and live jazz Friday and Saturday starting at 10:30 p.m. and on Sundays at 12:00 p.m.

- **The Green Mill, 4802 North Broadway, phone 773-878-5552.** The Green Mill is open 12:00 p.m. to 4:00 a.m. most days and Saturday 12:00 p.m. to 5:00 a.m. Live jazz is featured Fridays from 9:00 p.m. to 4:00 a.m. and Saturdays 8:00 p.m. to 5:00 a.m.

- **Jazz Showcase, 59 W. Grand, phone 312-670-2473.** Jazz Showcase shows are at 9:00 and 11:00 p.m. Friday and Saturday, 4:00, 8:00, and 10:00 p.m. on Sunday, and 8:00 and 10:00 p.m. Tuesday through Thursday.

- **Joe's Be-Bop Café & Jazz Emporium, 600 East Grand Avenue (Navy Pier), phone 312-595-5299.** Joe's summer hours are 11:00 a.m. to 12:00 a.m. nightly, shows starting at 7:30 p.m. In the winter, hours are from 11:00 a.m. to 9:00 p.m. nightly, with shows starting at 6:00 p.m.

- **La Perla del Mediterraneo, 2135 South Wolf Road, Hillside, phone 708-449-1070.** La Perla is open daily and features live jazz Friday and Saturday nights starting at 8:30 p.m.

- **The Note, 1565 North Milwaukee Avenue, phone 773-489-0011.** The Note is open 8:00 p.m. to 4:00 a.m. daily, Saturday until 5:00 a.m. Features big band on Wednesday nights starting at 9:30 p.m. and tenor saxman Von Freeman on Sundays at 9:30 p.m. Call ahead for the rest of the week's schedule.

- **Velvet Lounge, 2128 and 1/2 South Indiana, phone 312-791-9050.** The Velvet Lounge features shows at 9:30 p.m. to 1:00 a.m. Thursday through Sunday.

Cleveland

Rock-and-roll stole the music show in Cleveland when the I.M. Pei-designed Rock and Roll Hall of Fame and Museum opened not long ago. But this city also has jazz at venues including:

- ✔ **The Bop Stop, 1216 W. 6th Street, phone 216-664-6610.** On the Web: www.imperium.net/~sduncan/. The Bop Stop features jazz during the week from 9:00 p.m. to around 2:00 a.m. except on Mondays when the jazz starts at 8:30 p.m. On weekends jazz begins at 10:00 p.m. Closed on Wednesdays.

- ✔ **Savannah Bar & Grille, 30676 Detroit Road, Westlake, phone 216-892-2266.** Open seven days a week from 1:00 a.m. to 2:30 a.m. Shows begin at 9:00 p.m. on weekdays, 10:00 p.m. on weekends.

And if you make it over to Toledo, check out

- ✔ **Rusty's Jazz Café, 2202 Tedrow/Jazz Avenue, phone 419-381-9194.** On the Web: www.primenet.com/~bnoodles/Rusty's/. Rusty's is open daily from 4:00 p.m. to 2:30 a.m. on weekdays, 7:00 a.m. to 2:30 p.m. on Saturday and Sunday. The club features jazz weekdays at 9:00 p.m. with big bands on Tuesdays from 8:00 to 10:00 p.m. Weekend jazz is featured from 7:00 p.m. to 2:00 a.m. According to the Web site, Rusty's is the third-oldest jazz club in the United States.

Denver

John Elway and that gargantuan new international airport get more than their fair share of attention, but Denver's a happening place for jazz, with more music per capita than many larger cities. Vartan's is one of Denver's top jazz clubs. My friends Charles McPherson (the Charlie Parker-inspired saxophonist) and his son and drummer Chuckie, are among leading players who have recorded Live At Vartan's albums.

The Denver Post is the major local newspaper, a source of information about local jazz and jazz clubs. *Westword* is the alternative weekly, available free at local stores and other businesses — and a good place to hunt for local jazz clubs.

These clubs supply live jazz:

- ✔ **1515 Market Grille, 1515 Market St., phone 303-571-0011.** Top local jazz players, Friday and Saturday, 9 p.m. to 1 a.m.

- ✔ **Bourbon St. Pizzabar and Grill, 10158 S. Parker Rd., Parker, phone 303-805-7683.**

- **Cotton Club, 1401 17th St., phone 303-297-8663.** Live jazz Fridays through Sundays.

- **Rodney's, Tamarac Square, 7777 E. Hampden Ave., phone 303-750-7722.** Jazz Thursday through Saturday nights.

- **Roundup Grill, Main Street at Highway 73/74 junction, Evergreen, 303-674-3173.** Jazz Thursday nights, 6:30 to 9:30.

- **Trios, 1155 Canyon Blvd., Boulder, phone 303-442-8400.** Locally and nationally known jazz players various nights.

- **Vartan's, 18th and Broadway, downtown Denver, phone 303-399-1111.**

- **Walnut Brewery, 1123 Walnut St., Boulder, phone 303- 447-1345.** Live jazz Friday and Saturday nights.

Los Angeles

Jazz has this East Coast/West Coast thing going on: New York supposedly has the energy, California is allegedly mellower dating back to the *cool jazz* played by Chet Baker, Gerry Mulligan, and Stan Getz at places like the Lighthouse in Huntington Beach. The best way to decide for yourself is to check out the scene.

Thanks in part to gregarious young guitarist Kevin Eubanks, leader of *The Tonight Show* with Jay Leno band, and his bandmates, L.A. has a fairly strong youth movement in jazz. It also offers good clubs such as:

- **Atlas Supper Club, 3760 Wilshire Boulevard, phone 213-380-8400.** The Atlas Supper Club is open Monday through Saturday and hosts live music starting at 8:00 p.m. weekdays and 9:00 p.m. weekends. The club presents a mix of music, including jazz, so call for a schedule.

- **The Baked Potato, 3787 Cahuenga Boulevard, phone 818-980-1615.** The Baked Potato is open daily and features jazz nightly from 7:00 p.m. to 2:00 a.m.

- **Catalina Bar & Grill, 1640 North Cahuenga Street, Hollywood, phone 213-466-2210.** This club features jazz daily at 8:30 and 10:30 p.m. during the week and on Sunday at 7:00 p.m. and 9:00 p.m.

- **JAX Bar & Grill, 339 North Brand Street, Glendale phone 818-500-1604.** JAX is open daily and features jazz every night starting at 9:00 p.m.

- **The Metro Lounge at Lunaria, 10351 Santa Monica Boulevard, phone 310-282-8870.** The Metro Lounge is open Tuesday through Saturday from 5:30 p.m. to 1:30 a.m. and has jazz shows Tuesday through Thursday at 9:00 and 11:00 p.m., Friday and Saturday at 9:30 p.m., 11:00 p.m., and 12:15 a.m.

✔ **World Stage, 4344 Degnan Boulevard, phone 213-293-2451.** World Stage features live music on Friday and Saturday nights with shows starting at 9:45 p.m. and 11:30 p.m. The club books mostly jazz, but call ahead for the schedule to be sure.

Montreal

To the north of the United States lies the vast country and jazz scene of Canada. Montreal in particular hosts a flourishing array of clubs:

✔ **L'Aire Du Temps, 409 St. Francois X Coin St. Paul, phone 514-842-2003.**

✔ **L'Autre Bar, 278 Rue Laurier West coin Parc, phone 514-278-1519.**

✔ **Balattou, 372 St. Laurent, phone 514-845-5447.**

✔ **Le Café Campus, 57 Prince-Artur East, phone 514-844-1010.**

✔ **Isart, 263 St. Antoine West, phone 514-393-1758.**

✔ **Jazzons, 300 Ontario Street, phone 514-843-9818.**

✔ **Lion D'Or, 1676 Ontario East, phone 514-598-0790.**

✔ **Resto-Bar Biddle's Jazz, 2060 Rue Aylmer Street, phone 514-842-8656.**

✔ **Salle Du Gesu, 1200 Rue Bleury Street, phone 514-861-4378.**

✔ **Upstairs Jazz Bar, 1254 Mackay Street, phone 514-931-6808.**

New Orleans

This is a small sampling of what is available in New Orleans. Don't forget the huge New Orleans Jazz and Heritage Festival every April.

✔ **Café Brasil, 2100 Chartres Street, phone 504-947-9386.** This club is open seven days a week from 6:00 p.m. to 4:00 a.m. with jazz shows starting at 8:00 p.m.

✔ **Maison Bourbon, 641 Bourbon Street, phone 504-522-8818.** Maison Bourbon is open during the week from 2:30 p.m. to 12:15 a.m. and on weekends from 3:30 p.m. to 1:15 a.m. Live jazz is featured all night starting on the half hour.

✔ **Preservation Hall, 726 St. Peter Street, phone 504-522-2841.** This venue is open 8:00 p.m. to 12:00 a.m. seven days a week with jazz nightly. Call for a schedule.

✔ **Snug Harbor, 626 Frenchman Street, phone 504-949-0696.** Snug Harbor is open seven days a week from 5:00 p.m. to 2:00 a.m. with jazz shows starting nightly at 9:00 p.m. and 11:00 p.m.

✔ **Tipitina's, 501 Napolean at Tchoupitoulas, phone 504-897-3943.**
Tipitina's is open daily and features mostly jazz. Shows start Monday
through Wednesday at 9:00 p.m., Thursday at 9:30 p.m., Friday and
Saturday at 10:30 p.m., and Sunday from 5:00 to 9:00 p.m.

New York City

Famous clubs from jazz's 1940s bebop prime, such as Monroe's, the Savoy,
the Spotlite, the Three Deuces, the Downbeat, and the Onyx, are long gone.
But the Big Apple still offers more good live jazz on an off night than most other
cities on a red-hot Saturday. Check listings in *New Yorker* magazine or the
Village Voice for extensive choices. Or check out these renowned venues.

✔ **Birdland, 315 W. 44th St., phone 212-581-3080.** They'll serve you
dinner, but more importantly they'll serve you some of the world's
finest live jazz.

✔ **Blue Note, 131 W. Third St., phone 212-475-8592.** On the Web:
www.bluenote.net. Coolest name for a venerable old jazz club that
presents nothing but first-rate music.

✔ **Carlyle Hotel, Madison Ave. at 76th St., phone 212-744-1600.**

✔ **Iridium, 44 W. 63rd St., phone 212-582-2121.** Catch a living legend
every Monday night when guitarist and electric-guitar co-inventor Les
Paul holds forth. Top jazz talent is featured on other nights.

✔ **Jazz Standard, 116 E. 27th St., phone 212-576-2232.** More great jazz by
top players.

✔ **Knitting Factory, 74 Leonard St., between Broadway and Church,
phone 212-219-3055.** Hotbed for far-out New York loft jazz, this place
presents players on the cutting edge, some of the country's top *avant
garde* and free jazz.

✔ **Lenox Lounge, 288 Malcolm X Blvd. (Lenox Ave.), between 124th and
125th, phone 212-722-9566.**

✔ **Smalls, 183 West 10th. Street, phone 212-929-7565.** Smalls is open
seven days a week from 10:00 p.m. to 8:00 a.m.

✔ **Sweet Basil, 88 Seventh Ave. S., at Bleecker St., phone 212-242-1785.**

✔ **Tavern on the Green, West 67th Street and Central Park West, phone
212-873-3200.**

✔ **Village Vanguard, 178 7th Avenue South of 11th Street, phone 212-
255-4037.** Open seven nights a week, this club is the most famous in the
world for live jazz recordings.

✔ **Zinno, 126 West 13th Street, phone 212-924-5182.** Jazz nightly as well
as during Sunday brunch.

Oakland (California)

Clint Eastwood first heard Charlie "Yardbird" Parker here in the 1940s. More recently, Oakland vaulted itself to the top tier of the national jazz scene a couple of years ago when it opened the richly appointed jazz club, Yoshi's, down by the bay in Jack London Square — with more than $1 million contributed by city government. For local listings, pick up the independent weekly *S.F. Bay Guardian*.

- ✔ **Alice Arts Center, 1428 Alice Street, phone 510-238-7219.** This venue is open Monday through Friday and features shows from 8:00 to 10:00 p.m.

- ✔ **Claremont Resort and Spa, at the corner of Ashby and Domingo Avenues (you can't miss it), phone 510-549-8576.** The Terrace Lounge, open daily, is the jazz spot at this gorgeous historic hotel.

- ✔ **Clem Daniels End Zone, 1466 High Street, phone 510-536-9332.** The End Zone is open seven days a week from 11:00 to 2:00 a.m. and 6:00 to 10:00 p.m. on Sundays. The club holds weekly jams led by bop saxman Vince Wallace.

- ✔ **Jupiter, 2181 Shattuck Avenue, fine brew, occasional jazz, phone 510-843-8277.**

- ✔ **Kimball's East, 5800 Shellmound, Emeryville, lots of live music including frequent jazz, phone 510-658-2555.**

- ✔ **Mr. E's, 2284 Shattuck Avenue, phone 510-848-2009.** Latin percussionist Pete Escovedo's (father of singer and percussionist Sheila E.) new Berkeley club is a definite "must."

- ✔ **Yoshi's Japanese Restaurant and World Class Jazz House, 510 Embarcadero West, phone 510-238-9200.** On the Web: www.yoshis.com. Yoshi's is open daily with shows starting at 8:00 p.m. and 10:00 p.m. and a special 2:00 p.m. matinee on Sundays for kids. With several top San Francisco jazz clubs (including the famous Keystone Korner) long gone, Yoshi's has become the region's leading showcase for world-class jazz. Yoshi's also prepares top-notch sushi — if you want raw fish with your hard bop, Yoshi's is it.

Philadelphia

Coltrane came of age musically in Philadelphia, and has always been a vital place for jazz and blues. Nationally known acts turn up at these venues:

- ✔ **Ortlieb's Jazzhaus, 847 N 3rd Street, phone 215-922-1035.** Ortlieb's is open seven days a week from 6:00 p.m. to 1:00 a.m. weekdays, 6:00 p.m. to 2:00 p.m. weekends, and 5:00 p.m. to 1:00 a.m. on Sundays. Shows run Sunday through Thursday from 8:30 p.m. to 12:30 a.m. and Friday and Saturday from 9:30 p.m. to 1:30 a.m.

- **Theatre of the Living Arts, 334 South St., phone 215-336-2000.** A leading Philly venue for big-time jazz.

- **Zanzibar Blue, 305 S 11th St (Spruce/Pine), phone 215-829-0300.** On the Web: www.zanzibarblue.com.

Here are some other jazz clubs worth visiting:

- **Chris' Jazz Café, 1421 Sansom Street, phone 215-568-3131.** This club is open Monday through Saturday with live music on Monday and Tuesday from 8:00 p.m. to 12:00 a.m. and Wednesday through Saturday from 9:00 p.m. to 1:00 a.m.

- **Dock Street Brewing Company, 2 Logan Square (18th and Cherry), phone 215-496-0413.** This venue hosts several kinds of live music Friday and Saturday from 9:00 p.m. to 1:00 a.m. As always, call ahead for details.

- **Pompano Grille, 701 East Passyunk Avenue, (5th and Bainbridge), phone 215-923-7676.** This scene is open daily from 4:00 p.m. to 2:00 a.m. and features live music Friday and Saturday night between 9:00 p.m. and 10:00 p.m. The music is mostly jazz or latin jazz.

- **Slim Copper's Lounge, 6402 Stenton Avenue, phone 215-224-0509.** Slim Copper's is open daily from 10:00 p.m. to 2:00 a.m. and features jazz on Fridays from 7:00 to 11:00 p.m. and Mondays from 6:00 to 10:00 p.m.

- **Temperance House, 5 South State Street, Newtown, phone 215-860-0474.** The Temperance house features jazz on Friday and Saturday from 9:00 p.m. to 1:00 a.m. and hosts Dixieland jazz Sundays from 12:00 to 4:00 p.m.

San Francisco

If you visit San Francisco, pick up a copy of the weekly *S.F. Bay Guardian* for club listings. These venues offer some good jazz:

- **Cafe du Nord, 2170 Market Street, phone 415-861-5016.** This venue hosts jazz and blues with live music seven days a week, 9:30 p.m. to 1:30 a.m., and Saturday and Sunday afternoons 4:00 to 8:00 p.m. as well.

- **Elbo Room, 647 Valencia St., phone 415-552-7788.** The Elbo Room is open seven days a week from 5:00 p.m. to 2:00 a.m. and shows usually start between 10:00 and 10:45 p.m.

- **New Orleans Room, at the Fairmont Hotel, California and Mason Streets, phone 415-772-5000.** This venue hosts jazz from 8:30 p.m. to 12:30 a.m. nightly.

- **Pearl's, 256 Columbus Avenue, phone 415-291-8255.** Monday through Thursday 9:00 p.m. to 1:00 a.m., Friday and Saturday until 1:30 a.m.

Toronto

Canada's a cosmopolitan place, complete with live jazz. Many Canadian cities have good jazz clubs, but Toronto's a leader.

- ✔ Bar Italia, 584 College Street, phone 416-535-3621.
- ✔ C'Est What?, 19 Church Street, phone 416-867-9499.
- ✔ College Street Bar, 574 College Street, phone 416-533-2417.
- ✔ Gate 403, 403 Roncesvalles Avenue, phone 416-558-2930.
- ✔ Montreal Bistro & Jazz Club, 65 Sherbourne Street, phone 416-363-0179. On the Web: www3.sympatico.ca/mcmurrich/montreal/montrieal.htm.
- ✔ N'Awlins Jazz Bar, 299 King Street West, phone 416-595-1958.
- ✔ The Rex Jazz & Blues Bar, 194 Queen Street West, phone 416-598-2475.
- ✔ Reservoir Lounge, 52 Wellington Street East, phone 416-955-0887.
- ✔ Silver Dollar Room, 484 Spadina Avenue, phone 416-975-0909.
- ✔ Top O' the Senator, 249 Victoria Street, phone 416-364-7517.

Chapter 22

Resources for Further Jazz Enlightenment

• •

Books

The All Music Guide to Jazz, edited by Michael Erlewine, Vladimir Bogdanov, Chris Woodstra, and Scott Yanow. The authoritative guide to recorded jazz, reviewing more than 13,000 albums. In my opinion, the best reviews are written by Yanow, whose goal is "to collect every good jazz record ever made." Yanow's writing is incisive, his ear unerring.

American Musicians: 56 Portraits in Jazz, by Whitney Balliett. Published in 1978, Balliett's initial survey of top jazz players — out of print, but worth hunting for in used bookstores.

American Musicians II: Seventy-Two Portraits in Jazz, by Whitney Balliett. More great writing on jazz musicians from the gifted *New Yorker* magazine writer.

American Singers, by Whitney Balliett. Balliett, longtime writer for the *New Yorker* magazine, profiles 27 of jazz's leading vocalists. Balliett is such a solid and sensitive writer that his essays attain a literary quality seldom found among music scribes.

Louis Armstrong: A Cultural Legacy, by Mark H. Miller. Assembled by top writers and academics, this book takes a broad view of Armstrong and his music, examining it within the context of African American culture.

Louis Armstrong: An Extravagant Life, by Laurence Bergreen. A thick and thorough account of Armstrong's music, passions, and personality quirks.

The Autobiography of Miles Davis, by Quincy Troupe. Getting inside Davis's head, Troupe, a renowned poet, puts Davis's story down on paper in language that rings true to the brooding, colorful personality of one of jazz's great trumpeters.

Bass Line, by Milt Hinton and David Berger. Jazz aficionados know that Hinton is one of the music's most prolific and inventive bassists, with a career spanning seven decades. This book proves that he is also an excellent photographer. These black-and-white photos capture dozens of jazz greats in private, behind-the-scenes moments that only a fellow jazzman would be privileged to observe.

Sidney Bechet: The Wizard of Jazz, by John Chilton. Chilton takes a close look at the great reedman's life, music, and jazz scenes in New Orleans and Paris.

Beneath the Underdog, by Charles Mingus. Wild, colorful, possibly part figment of the great bassist's imagination, this is nonetheless an all-time literary classic of jazz — loaded with sweat, tears, passion, sex, and the struggles of one of the 20th century's most inventive jazzmen.

Bird: The Legend of Charlie Parker, by Robert Reisner. Passionate, colorful memories of Parker and his music, from dozens of folks who heard and/or knew Parker.

Bird Lives! The High Life & Hard Times of Charlie (Yardbird) Parker, by Ross Russell. Russell, who also produced some of Parker's best recordings (on for the Dial label), shares an insider's view of Parker.

Bird's Diary, by Ken Vail. Some fascinating details about Parker's prodigious, 10-year-long creative prime.

The Birth of Bebop, by Scott DeVeaux. Containing more details than most beginning jazz listeners will comprehend, this is an eventual essential in your library if you pursue and in-depth knowledge of jazz. DeVeaux, a music professor at the University of Virginia, gives one of the most thoughtful social, musical, historical, and theoretical accounts of this vital form of jazz.

Celebrating Bird: The Triumph of Charlie Parker, by Gary Giddins. Focusing on music (instead of Parker's self-destructive habits), this book is an in-depth look at the man who some say was jazz's greatest creative force.

Coltrane: Chasin' the Trane, by J.C. Thomas. A sensitive chronicle of the life of the late great jazz saxophonist. Thomas's biography includes comments from several of Coltrane's contemporaries, as well as insightful sections from various letters.

Django Reinhardt, by Charles Delaunay. Who better to tell the story of the great Belgian gypsy guitarist (whose career was based in France) than one of France's leading jazz critics?

Drummin' Men, by Burt Korall. They keep the beat and move the music, and if you want to learn a bunch about top timekeepers and lesser known legends of drums, this is the book for you. Korall is a jazz drummer whose writing keeps you spellbound.

Early Jazz: Its Roots and Musical Development, by Gunther Schuller. Schuller, who has written several excellent books analyzing jazz, gives one of the most thorough accounts of jazz's birth. His cool, logical dissection of the music rings true and accurate.

Encyclopedia of Jazz, by Leonard Feather (and co-authors). This work spans several volumes covering various periods. Feather, a musician and composer who was one of the first to write intelligently about jazz, was also among the first to publish authoritative reference books on the music.

Good Morning Blues: The Autobiography of Count Basie, by Albert Murray. Detailed chronicle of this top big band leader and pianist.

The History of Jazz, by Ted Gioia. The newest "must" for your history section, Gioia's version of the music's development is thoughtful, detailed, and extremely well written.

In Search of Buddy Bolden, by Donald Marquis. Beginning in the 1890s in New Orleans, trumpeter Bolden led what many historians say was the first jazz band. Marquis's book is a fascinating look at Bolden and his music, and at New Orleans during jazz's formative years.

Jazz Anecdotes, by Bill Crow. A funny, wild, provocative collection of short stories about jazz's great players, grouped under headings such as "Prejudice," "Louis Armstrong," and "The Word 'Jazz'."

Jazz: Its Evolution and Essence, by Andre Hodeir. A "must" among four or five books you should have in your collection covering the history of jazz.

The Jazz Makers, by Nat Shapiro and Nat Hentoff. Top writers profile top jazz musicians. A solid resource for rounding out your knowledge of jazz's players and their music.

The Jazz Musician: 15 Years of Interviews/ The Best of Musician Magazine, by Mark Rowland and Tony Scherman. Great profiles of, and interviews with, top jazz players, well written by musicians and other writers with solid knowledge of jazz.

Jazz: New Perspectives on the History of Jazz, edited by Nat Hentoff and Albert J. McCarthy. A collection of good essays by top writers including Hentoff and Gunther Schuller.

Jazz Portraits, by Len Lyons and Don Perlo. Well-written profiles of more than 200 leading jazz musicians, giving insight both to their lives and to their individual contributions to the music.

The Jazz Word, by Dom Cerulli, Burt Korall, and Mort Nasatir. Fine writing about jazz, including several articles written by musicians. Published in 1960, the book takes a rigorous look at several players and styles, with a degree of detail and critical insight not often found today.

A Lester Young Reader, by Lewis Porter. A collection of colorful stories of the legendary saxophonist, his music, and his troubled life.

The New Grove Dictionary of Jazz, edited by Barry Kernfeld. The Big Daddy of them all, this monster from Grove Press is the authoritative source of basic info on jazz and its players.

Pres: The Story of Lester Young, by Luc Delannoy. A detailed account of the saxophonist's life, loves, music, and self-destructive habits.

Satchmo, by Gary Giddins. A well-written account of Louis Armstrong's life and music, plus dozens of great photos of Armstrong.

Singing Jazz: The Singers and Their Styles, by Bruce Crowther and Mike Pinfold. A useful, detailed history of jazz's great vocalists.

The Story of Jazz, by Marshall W. Stearns. Another "must" for your "overall history of jazz" selection, Stearns's book is a classic that traces the music's development from Africa through bebop (it was first published in 1956).

The World of Earl Hines, by Stanley Dance. British-born Dance is one of jazz's leading scribes, and here he serves as a medium, letting the great pianist tell his own story.

Magazines

Downbeat. Jazz's oldest magazine has recently hit hard times. It's thin and extremely dated in terms of graphic design, but it still contains some of the best writing on jazz.

Jazz Times. Thick and prosperous-looking, *Jazz Times* counts internationally renowned jazz writer Stanley Dance among its contributors (he's a book editor and writes features). Along with well-written profiles of musicians and news items, the magazine includes dozens of CD reviews each month.

Jazziz. The slickee of jazz pubs — too slick for some purists — this magazine nonetheless contains lots of well-written profiles of jazz players, as well as CD reviews that can help you decide what to buy next.

Just Jazz Guitar. Glossy, thick quarterly dedicated to jazz axmen. Short on good writing, but long on great guitar tales, as well as ads for exotic handmade jazz guitars.

Tower Pulse. Sure, it's a P.R. piece for the giant music store chain, but the magazine pays respected music journalist's to speak their minds. This publication, available for free at Tower stores, is a useful resource in keeping tabs on new jazz recordings.

Television/Videos

Many of these videos can be mail ordered from The Jazz Store (Web site: www2.thejazzstore.com).

A Great Day in Harlem. Documentary that gives a behind-the-scenes look at the making of the famous 1958 Esquire magazine portrait of 57 jazz greats by photographer Art Kane.

Anatomy of a Murder. Duke Ellington penned the music for this mystery movie.

Art Blakey: The Jazz Messenger. Inside look at one of jazz's top drummers, also a mentor to countless younger players; includes old footage and interviews with peers, including Dizzy Gillespie.

Barney Kessel In Concert. A compendium of 30 years of performances by the master of bebop jazz guitar.

Ben Webster: Brute and the Beautiful. In-depth look at the great tenor saxman, whose hushed, whispery tone gave ballads amazing power.

Benny Goodman: Adventures in the Kingdom of Swing. A look at the great clarinetist/big band leader.

The Benny Goodman Story. Comedian Steve Allen is also a jazz fanatic; he plays the famous bandleader in this 1955 dramatization of Goodman's life. Good entertainment, not so good as history or at capturing Goodman and his music.

BET. Black Entertainment Television, a cable channel, features regular programming on jazz.

Billie Holiday: The Many Faces of Lady Day. A look at the gifted and tragic jazz diva.

Billy Eckstine/Dizzy Gillespie: Bebop Big Bands. Forties footage of two hard-driving big bands in action, led by a pair of bebop pioneers.

Bird. Director Clint Eastwood's look at the life of Charlie Parker, with the legendary saxman played by Forrest Whittaker, and with musicians including Bird-disciple Charles McPherson adding some new Bird-like music. Worth a look, but not completely faithful to history — Dirty Harry and Forrest don't, in my estimation, capture the true essence of the man and his music.

Bix: Ain't None of Them Play Like Him Yet. The title comes from a quote by Louis Armstrong. This video covers the life and music of early jazz cornetist Bix Beiderbecke, who achieved mythical status due to the fact that he lived hard, played hard, and died at 28 — having already made a major contribution to the music.

Blow Up. An artsy black-and-white British flick from the 1960s, with David Hemmings playing a photographer who solves a murder by *blowing up* — that is, enlarging — one of his photos. With a score by jazz pianist Herbie Hancock.

Cab Calloway and Friends 1935-1950. The "Hi-De-Ho" man in action with Milt Hinton, Doc Cheatham, Chu Berry, Tyree Glenn, and other legends from jazz's golden years.

Cannonball Adderley/Teddy Edwards. Footage of two jazz masters from the 1962 "Jazz Scene USA" series.

Cecil Taylor: Burning Poles. Great introduction to the *avant garde* jazz pianist.

Celebrating Bird: The Triumph of Charlie Parker. Based on the book by Gary Giddins, this high-quality documentary includes interviews with Bird's female entourage as well as numerous musicians who knew him and played with him — plus great footage of the bebop giant making some hot music.

Charlie Christian: Solo Flight. The story of jazz's first great guitar soloist — the only drawback is that the video includes there are no performance clips.

Club Date. Taped in the studios of public television station KPBS in San Diego, these shows had a strong national run during the late 1980s and early 1990s, and resumed production in 1997. Although the pseudo-club studio setting doesn't capture the vibe of the real thing, "Club Date" represents one of the few significant efforts being made to capture jazz's living legends making their music.

The Cotton Club. Francis Ford Coppola's spectacular musical set in Harlem during its swing-jazz heyday, when stylish patrons hit the neighborhoods hippest clubs to hear the hottest jazz being made by African American players.

Count Basie: Swingin' The Blues. Video about the legendary pianist/big band leader includes performances from the 1930s.

Dizzy Gillespie: Jivin' In Bebop. Vintage footage of the trumpeter during his hipster days.

Duke Ellington: On The Road. The title says it all.

Elevator to the Gallows. Dramatic movie directed by Frenchman Louis Malle — with a haunting soundtrack by Miles Davis.

Eric Dolphy: Last Date. Dolphy's final performance in June 1964, before he died too early — in his 30s. The saxman/flutist is joined by Buddy Collette, Jaki Byard, and others.

Elvin Jones: Different Drummer. A look at the powerful drummer who powered some of saxophonist John Coltrane's best performances.

Gene Krupa: Jazz Legend. Lots of performance footage is included in this profile of the charismatic jazz drummer.

The Gene Krupa Story. Movie dramatization of the great drummer's life and music, released in 1959 with actor Sal Mineo playing Krupa.

The Glenn Miller Story. Worth seeing if only because it stars Jimmy Stewart as the big band leader who disappeared in a plane over the English Channel in 1944.

Great Guitars: The Jazz Guitar Supergroup. Barney Kessel, Herb Ellis, and Charlie Byrd team up to make some rare music not available on CD. A must for guitarists, as the video gives a close look at the fingerwork of these seasoned jazz players.

Harlem Harmonies (Vol. 1 & 2). Duke, Cab, Louis Jordan, Noble Sissle, and other leading jazzmen in action.

Harlem Jazz Festival. This 1955 blowout featured Cab Calloway, Lionel Hampton, Count Basie, Duke Ellington, and other famous players.

Illinois Jacquet: Texas Tenor. Profile of one of jazz's under-sung heroes, featuring his famous solo on Lionel Hampton's "Flying Home."

The Jazz Singer. The first movie to use sound, it stars the white Al Jolson in blackface, capturing the spirit of the times, but not the true spirit of genuine 1920s jazz.

Jazzball. Performance footage of Artie Shaw, Duke Ellington, Louis Armstrong, Gene Krupa, and others.

John Coltrane: The World According to John Coltrane. Profile of the mystical sax legend, directed by *The New York Times* music critic Robert Palmer.

Kansas City. Those who view this Robert Altman film expecting epic treatment of Kansas City's legendary "territory" band scene of the 1920s and 1930s will be disappointed. But the soundtrack album contains some great music by top players including several of jazz's Young Lions.

Lady Sings The Blues. Diana Ross as Billie Holiday in this musically decent dramatized version of the great singer's life. Ross's portrayal of the singer as weak and dependent is considered by many people to be way off the mark, but the film has one of Ross's best performances as an actress nonetheless.

Lester Young: Song of the Spirit. Interviews and rare footage are included in this profile of the troubled and talented tenor saxman.

Let's Get Lost. A gritty documentary about jazz trumpeter Chet Baker that follows him during the late phase of a life troubled by chronic heroin addiction. Although the emaciated Baker is a sorry sight, his soul, charisma, and musical genius come across, even in his final months.

Louis Armstrong: Satchmo. Includes rarely seen home movies of Armstrong relaxing, as well as performances, TV appearances, and interviews.

Mambo Kings. Latin jazzmaster Tito Puente makes a cameo in this excellent dramatization of Latin jazz and culture — a movie with a genuine plot, great acting, and interesting characters (mainly two brothers who lead a hot Latin big band), as well as mucho fine music.

Minnie the Moocher. Cab Calloway leads viewers on a tour of Harlem, reminiscing about the budding jazz scene of the 1930s and 1940s, with performance footage of Duke Ellington, Fats Waller, Louis Armstrong, and others.

Mo' Better Blues. A hip, lively movie by director Spike Lee, starring Denzel Washington as a jazz musician.

Mystery, Mr. Ra. A video portrait of a jazz interloper — Sun Ra claimed he came from outer space, and his music was plenty spacey. Surprisingly, he began his career in Fletcher Henderson's big band, and that's only one of the revelations about the *avant garde* keyboardist.

Nat King Cole: Unforgettable. Portrait of the great crooner — who was also a first-rate pianist.

Oscar Peterson: Life of a Legend. Performance footage, plus coverage of a Peterson family reunion.

Piano Legends. An insider's look at several great pianists, hosted by pianist Chick Corea.

Reed Royalty. Great men of woodwinds, from Sidney Bechet to Ornette Coleman, and several in between.

Round Midnight. Saxophonist Dexter Gordon stars in this dramatization of the life of a jazzman, dedicated to Bud Powell and Lester Young.

Sarah Vaughan: The Divine One. Profile of the gifted jazz singer with the operatic range.

Space is the Place. A 1972 movie featuring Sun Ra and his Arkestra, it's an odd blaxploitation/science fiction film made at a time when Superfly and Shaft were all the rage.

Sweet Love Bitter. Comedian/social commentator Dick Gregory stars in this fictionalized account of saxophonist Charlie "Yardbird" Parker's final tragic years. In the movie, Bird become Richie "Eagle" Coles — although the name is different, some music aficionados prefer this flick to many others that attempt to translate jazz to the big screen.

Tenor Titans. Hosted by Branford Marsalis, this one takes a look — and listen — to several great saxmen including Coleman Hawkins, Lester Young, and John Coltrane.

The Ladies Sing the Blues. Several greats, together on one video: Billie, Bessie, Dinah, Lena, Ethel, Sarah, and others.

The Trumpet Kings. Hosted by trumpeter Wynton Marsalis, a look at great jazz trumpeters, from Louis Armstrong to Dizzy Gillespie.

Thelonious Monk: American Composer. Portrait of the quirky jazz pianist, including lots of rare footage of the master in action.

Thelonious Monk: Straight No Chaser. A profile of the pianist, executive produced by jazz lover Clint Eastwood.

Vintage Collection. (Volume 1: 1958-59, Volume 2: 1960-61). Dozens of jazz giants are captured in action in this video. This two-tape set offers a rare look at legends such as Coleman Hawkins, Count Basie, Thelonious Monk, Ben Webster, Roy Eldridge, Jo Jones, Milt Hinton, Jimmy Giuffre, Jim Hall, and many others. . . .

Web Sites

AACM.
www.centerstage.net/chicago/chicago/music/whoswho/AACM.html
This is the site for the Association for the Advancement of Creative Musicians, a support society for far-out music and its makers. Muhal Richard Abrams, Lester Bowie, and Anthony Braxton are among *avant garde* jazz players associated with AACM.

Blue Note Records.
www.bluenote.com
One of the biggies among jazz labels, Blue Note's Web site is a great place to keep up with leading jazz artists and their newest releases or re-releases on CD.

Double-Time Jazz.
www.doubletimejazz.com
Excellent online source of information about jazz, past and present — and a great place to buy CDs. Most titles on their all-time top 100 can be had for the bargain price of $9.95. This site also has regular updates on new releases.

Harmolodic.
www.harmolodic.com
Home page for Ornette Coleman, the *avant garde* saxophonist. This one features far-out animated graphics and info on a variety of topics related to Coleman and his music.

Jazz Central Station.
www4.jazzcentralstation.com
A wealth of information on jazz: news, history, links to Web sites dedicated to jazz heroes, plus plenty of music samples. Among related sites is one for *Jazz Times* magazine, with online versions of the monthly jazz magazine's contents.

Jazz Now Interactive.
www.jazznow.com
Web site for *Jazz Now* magazine, this place offers lots of good info on jazz.

Jazz Online.
www.jazzonln.com
Referencing Verve's extensive catalog of jazz recordings, this site's "Jazz 101" is a useful (although Verve-biased) primer to jazz.

Knitting Factory.
www.knittingfactory.com
Besides AACM, this is the other main organization supporting *avant garde* jazz. The Knitting Factory is a club in New York with nightly acts, as well as a music label which counts guitarist James Blood Ulmer, and Sam Rivers and Hamiett Bluiett among its artists.

The Jazz Store.
www2.thejazzstore.com
One of the best all-around jazz sites on the Web, this one includes dozens of links to other great sites on performers, books, videos, and so on.

WNUR Homepage.
www.nwu.edu/WNUR/jazz/
Extensive site maintained by WNUR, the jazz radio station at Northwestern University. Through links to other sites, this place delivers just about anything you could want to know about jazz: styles, history, labels, and dozens of musicians.

Appendix A

Starting a Collection

• •

In This Chapter

▶ Choosing CD, vinyl, or cassette

▶ Selecting a sound system

▶ Beginning your collection

▶ Discovering 100 recommended titles

• •

*Y*ou need to know only one rule about building a great music collection: There are no rules. Collecting music is a form of self-expression and your collection will ultimately reflect your personality and taste. The albums and artists you choose, the way you store and/or display them, the type of stereo equipment you buy, the way you incorporate music into your life, and whether or not you consider it a travesty to let Kenny G share shelf space with Coltrane — these are all decisions you must make yourself, and they will all help your collection make a colorful personal statement.

One Man's Story

My music collection is like a diary of my life. For me, certain music conjures certain memories. I almost never get rid of an album, unless it's any of the dozens of horrible supermarket-jazz CDs that anyone willing to label himself a music writer seems to receive by the truckload. (Luckily, these can be traded for credit toward more listenable music at many stores.)

I started collecting music in the 1960s — the pre-CD era. In orange crates are my early vinyl, an insecure adolescent mix that ranges from Miles Davis, Ahmad Jamal, and Herbie Hancock, to Led Zeppelin, the Rolling Stones, Jimi Hendrix, Edith Piaf, and some authentic African Pygmy music.

CD, Vinyl, or Cassette?

Although most of the best jazz is now available on CD, some has never been released in the new digital format — one good reason to keep an open mind to vinyl. Another reason is that clean vinyl albums sound *really good*. Some purists believe that pristine vinyl on a good turntable gives a more real representation of music than CDs that rely on many digital samples to construct a spectrum of sound. Most vinyl in reasonably good shape sounds fine to me. On the other hand, some mass-produced CDs sound horrible.

The rule seems to be that the more successful the artist, the lousier his or her CD sounds. Recording companies apparently lose quality control when they have to press 200,000 or 500,000 copies. Luckily, even successful jazz albums don't generally sell more than 100,000.

When shopping for CDs, watch for the word "remastered" on the cover. It means the sound has been cleaned up and optimized for CD. If a title you think you want isn't on a major label, you may want to read a review of it in a jazz magazine before you go out and buy it.

Good news for jazz fans: As part of the corporate rearranging of the music industry, major jazz labels have changed hands and many have set out to re-issue all their music on CD. Labels embarked upon such awe-inspiring ventures include EMD/Blue Note and GRP/Impulse!

Consider two more good reasons to build a portion of your music collection in vinyl recordings:

- **They're cheap.** Sometimes you only pay $2 or $3 for a vintage jazz album.
- **They're good lookin'.** At that price, many of these albums are worth buying just for the cover art. In fact, I like to display my vintage vinyl albums from the 1930s, 1940s, and 1950s, with their black and white photos and cool type styles, where people can see them. I don't believe that music collections should be hidden away. Visitors to your home should be able to examine your collection at their leisure.

What about cassettes?

So, CDs or vinyl are both okay. But cassettes are a last-ditch measure. I almost never buy them. Used ones are of questionable quality, because recording tape is prone to breaking, jamming, and damage from sun and moisture. Buying new cassettes is a bad investment. CDs cost about 50 percent more, but they are more durable, sound better, and last longer. Of course, every sound system should include a cassette deck. On many occasions, recording a copy of something borrowed from a friend or a library is the only way you'll be able to add that music to your collection.

Even for recording purposes, however, cassette decks are almost obsolete. For about $300, you can buy a digital mini-disc recorder that will make CD-quality recordings. Also, computer companies are marketing inexpensive "read/write" CD-ROM drives that can be used to record music on full-size CDs that will work in a CD player. As long as you copy music for personal use, and not for profit, you won't violate any laws.

The final question

A final consideration regarding formats: Where do you listen to music, and how often? In your car? At the gym? Rollerblading? Aboard your Harley? Depending on where you want to hear jazz, CDs or cassettes may be the best format. With costs dropping, though, CDs are superior to cassettes for almost every application. I'd guess that more than 80 percent (and rising) of the music you'll want in your jazz collection is available on CD, and car and portable CD players are now extremely affordable.

However, if you are a potential jazz fan on a modest budget, you can pick up a used turntable for less than $100 at a garage sale and assemble a decent collection of around 100 used vinyl LPs for under $300. That's about 100 hours of music, and if you played each album an average of six times over the next three or four years, that's 600 hours of entertainment for $300 — a steal at 50 cents an hour. These days, you can't even chew bubble gum at that price.

My Riff on Sound Systems

I'm not *Consumer Reports* so I won't review the pros and cons of all the various sound systems you can buy. If you're an aficionado, you won't take my advice anyway. You'll spend $5,000 or $10,000 or $15,000 to get exactly the sound you want. However, for less confident sound system purchasers, I can tell you my preferences.

CD changers and all-in-one systems

I think that the newest multi-CD changers are God's gift to music lovers. For $300, I bought a compact Pioneer stereo with a 25-CD changer, double cassette deck, and AM-FM. Now, what I do is, I load the changer up with whatever I feel like — all jazz vocals, all blues, all jazz saxophone, or, more likely, an eclectic mix that might include Charlie Parker, Jon Hendricks, and Jo Jones, but might also have Ravi Shankar, George Jones, and John Lee Hooker.

Then comes the best part. I press the *Random Play* button, and I have my own radio station. *Radio DIRK* coming at you with 50 watts of raw, Japanese-solid-state stereo power — no deejays, and plenty of surprises. Sitar raga followed by a bebop solo followed by deep blues. When I take my "station" to the next stage, I want to get one of those 200-CD changers. These days, they cost less than $300. What a concept for entertaining!

Turntables

But none of the new systems come with a turntable. In my opinion, as stated before, you *must* own one. You can pick up a used turntable from the 1970s at a garage sale or swap meet for around $25. Many used record stores also sell turntables, and you might also find one in newspaper classified ads, or in a store specializing in used equipment. Throw on a new cartridge for $75 or so (you absolutely should replace the cartridge on a used turntable before you play any records), and you're set. If you want a really good turntable, expect to pay $400 or more for one of several models available.

Other considerations

One other consideration is *Surround sound,* the successor to stereo. This system is especially good for music on television. You can buy good Japanese Surround-sound receivers for less than $500, or an audiophile Surround receiver by the Canadian company, Amfi, for about $500.

At the other extreme, you can get by quite nicely with a minimal system, like the one I use at my desk for reviewing CDs. Pick up a portable CD player for about $80, plug it into a pair of powered speakers for about $60, and you have pretty decent basic sound.

Starting Your Collection

At the end of this chapter, I include a list of jazz albums that would make an excellent start for anyone wanting to explore the history of jazz. Now, the first thing you should do is disregard some of my suggestions. The way you really discover jazz and build a great personal collection is not to listen to some so-called *expert* but to put it together piece by piece and learn as you go. By reading magazines and books, reading liner notes, talking to friends, listening to the radio, watching jazz programs on television, and wandering through music stores, garage sales, and swap meets, you are going to assemble a music library that only you could assemble.

Avoiding Greatest Hits packages

Here's a little advice about selecting albums. So many jazz titles are available today, even in a small music store, that deciding which ones to buy can be overwhelming. One type of CD I am cautious of is the *Greatest Hits* package. Dozens of these are out there, representing the careers of all the major jazz legends. Although some of them offer excellent selections of music that represent a musician's best moments, others do not. Major jazz music labels such as Blue Note, Columbia, Verve, and Impulse! built reputations for recording premium jazz, and they own the rights to that music. You'll get to know jazz's major, reputable labels, and some of their *Hits* packages are great. In other cases, small companies have acquired rights to inferior versions of songs and packaged them so that they look like something hot. Many's the time I've wasted money on CDs whose covers proclaim them to be the *Greatest* or *Best of.*

The other reason not to buy *Hits* packages is that they don't give the complete flavor of each period in a musician's growth.

So, even with Duke Ellington or Miles Davis or Charlie Parker, who all recorded dozens of albums, I recommend starting with one or two of their best, instead of an anthology.

Not included in my bias against compilation albums, though, are some of the beautiful boxed sets covering the careers of most of the major artists. Many of these are fanatically complete, including every take of a song recorded during a particular session. Most have excellent sound quality, and come with glossy booklets that include photos, detailed credits including lists of musicians for each song, and texts that help explain an artist's life and music. If you are really into one artist, and if you can afford these sets (many multi-CD sets go for more than $100), they offer classy crash courses.

Deciding which CDs or albums to buy

How do you know which albums to buy? I've recommended several later in this chapter. In addition, jazz magazines — Chapter 22 lists a few — regularly review dozens of new releases, and their reviews are generally more reliable than what you can find in your local paper (unless you live in a major city with a big, reputable paper such as Los Angeles or New York). Several books are also available that give reviews of thousands of jazz CDs. A good review will give you a sense of the music's sound, as well as a list of players. It sounds snotty, but I've found that a lot of the best jazz is also the jazz that gets the least attention. So you probably won't find some of the best music in magazines or newspaper.

To build a really cool collection, you have to go underground:

> ✔ **Listen to a college jazz station (like my beloved KSDS-FM in San Diego).**
>
> ✔ **Cultivate friends who like jazz.**
>
> ✔ **Talk to musicians between sets in clubs.**
>
> ✔ **Ask people who work in music stores.** I've found that your typical young clerk in a music store doesn't know much about jazz, so a better bet is to find a used record store, or a store that specializes in jazz.

Over time, you'll find out how to predict with surprising accuracy which recordings you will like. One additional trick is to pay close attention to credits and *liner notes* — the essays that comes with most CDs. This is an easy way to pick up important tips about jazz's history, and also to build your knowledge about which artists played together. If you buy a CD and find that you like it, chances are you may also enjoy CDs by some of the musicians who back the featured player.

Expanding your collection

If you're on the Net, you have access to a mind-blowing volume of information. While writing this book, I found Web sites (see Chapter 22) dedicated to jazz trombone, Benny Goodman, obscure guitarist Lenny Breau, as well as excellent retail sites that sell CDs by mail order and include complete lists of titles by artist.

Assembling a good collection is expensive — and risky. Expensive, because you will probably buy primarily CDs. Risky, because, especially in the early phase of your collecting, you probably won't like 10 to 15 percent of what you buy, and if you take a CD back on trade-in, you'll only get a fraction of the new price in credit. Many music stores, though, allow you to return any CDs you don't like, no questions asked — seek out those stores and support them.

Collecting music is, to me, one of life's great pleasures — the anticipation of finding a certain recording, the actual finding of it, possibly purchasing it at a bargain price, and the payoff: playing it for the first time. I can't describe what a rush I felt when, after a half-day search, I stumbled across a vinyl version of the Duke Ellington Orchestra's famous live *Fargo, N.D. 1940* album.

100 Recommended Jazz Titles

Keeping in mind that your collection should reflect your tastes and your own path into the music, I end this chapter with 100 titles that make the beginning of a great jazz collection. I have counted multi-CD sets of up to three CDs as a single title and have not included larger box-set compilations. If you can afford them, boxed sets are often a good place to start, although you need to do some research to make sure that the set represents an artist's best period or playing.

A few of my personal biases that you should keep in mind as you read this list (and before you call me up and tell me I'm out of my head):

- ✔ I love guitar music — I mean to the point of obsession.

- ✔ I generally favor jazz from the 1920s through 1950s.

- ✔ I believe that less is more, and I generally prefer to hear jazz's great soloists with as small a group as possible — or unaccompanied. Of course, there are several exceptions in the realm of great composing and arranging.

- ✔ I like abstract and *avant garde* jazz a lot, and don't consider it mere noise, as do some jazz purists.

I've tried to include several less-common choices here that demonstrate jazz's richness, such as bassist Jimmy Blanton's duets with Duke Ellington, French guitarist Philip Catherine's *Live,* and an inordinate amount of music made on the clarinet, which to me was jazz's original leading instrument.

So, here goes.

Early jazz/New Orleans

Louis Armstrong, *The Hot Fives* (Columbia)
Sidney Bechet, *Centenary Celebration — 1997: Great Original Performances 1924 To 1943* (Louisiana Red Hot Records)
Bix Beiderbecke, *Bix Beiderbecke, Vol. 1: Singin' the Blues* (Columbia)
Johnnie Dodds, *His Best Recordings 1923–1940* (Best of Jazz)
Earl Hines, *An Introduction to Earl Hines/His Best Recordings 1927–1942* (Best of Jazz)
James P. Johnson, *Running Wild (1921–1926)* (Tradition)
Scott Joplin, *The Elite Syncopations* (Biograph)
Eddie Lang, *Jazz Guitar* (Yazoo)
Jelly Roll Morton, *Birth of the Hot* (RCA/Bluebird)
Jimmie Noone, *His Best Recordings 1923–1940* (Best of Jazz)
King Oliver, *The Quintessence/1923–1928* (Fremeaux & Associates)
Original Dixieland Jass Band, *First Jazz Recordings, Vol. 1* (Jazz Archives)
Fats Waller, *The Fats Waller Piano Solos/Turn On The Heat* (BMG)

Swing/big band

Count Basie Orchestra, *The Essential Count Basie* (Sony)
Jimmy Blanton, on Duke Ellington's *Solos, Duets and Trios* (Bluebird)
Cab Calloway, *Cab Calloway (1939–1940)* (Classics)
Charlie Christian, *Solo Flight* (Jazz Classics)
Roy Eldridge, *Little Jazz* (Sony)
Duke Ellington Orchestra, *Okeh Ellington* (Sony)
Slim Gaillard, *Slim's Jam* (Drive Archive)
Benny Goodman, *Carnegie Hall Jazz Concert* (Sony)
Coleman Hawkins, *Body and Soul* (RCA/Bluebird)
Fletcher Henderson, *The Fletcher Henderson Story* (Sony)
Woody Herman, *Thundering Herds* (Sony)
Johnny Hodges, *Passion Flower* (Bluebird)
Lonnie Johnson, *Steppin' On The Blues* (Sony)
Jo Jones, *Essential Jo Jones* (Vanguard)
Jimmie Lunceford, *The Quintessence* (Fremeaux & Associates)
Django Reinhardt and Stephane Grappelli, *Django Reinhardt and Stephane Grappelli* (GNP Crescendo)
Artie Shaw, *Greatest Hits* (RCA)
Chick Webb and his orchestra, *Standing Tall* (Drive Archive)
Ben Webster, *Meet You At The Fair* (GRP/Impulse!)
Lester Young, *Master Takes* (Savoy)

Bebop, hard bop, and related

Cannonball Adderley, *Things Are Getting Better* (Original Jazz Classics)
Art Blakey, *Orgy In Rhythm* (EMD/Blue Note)
Clifford Brown, *The Beginning and the End* (Sony)
Duke Ellington, Charles Mingus, and Max Roach, *Money Jungle* (EMD/Blue Note)
Art Farmer and Benny Golson *Meet the Jazztet* (MCA/Chess)
Erroll Garner, *Body and Soul* (Sony)
Dizzy Gillespie, *The Chronological Dizzy Gillespie 1945–1946* (Classics)
Dexter Gordon, *Bouncin' with Dex* (SteepleChase)
Jimmy Hamilton, *Sweet But Hot* (Drive Entertainment)
Bobby Hutcherson, *Dialogue* (EMD/Blue Note)
J.J. Johnson, *The Eminent Jay Jay Johnson, Vols. 1 and 2* (EMD/Blue Note)
Barney Kessel, *The Poll Winners Straight Ahead* (Original Jazz Classics)
Yusef Lateef, *The Yusef Lateef Anthology* (Rhino)
Jackie McLean, *Jacknife* (EMD/Blue Note)
Joe Marsala, *Joe Marsala 1936–1942* (Classics)
Pat Martino, *All Sides Now* (EMD/Blue Note)
Charles Mingus, *Mingus Ah Um* (Sony)
Thelonious Monk, *Best of the Blue Note Years* (EMD/Blue Note)
Oliver Nelson, *Blues and the Abstract Truth* (GRP/Impulse!)
Charlie Parker, *The Complete Dial Sessions* (Jazz Classics)
Joe Pass, *Virtuoso* (Pablo)

Oscar Pettiford, *Deep Passion* (Impulse!)
Bud Powell, *The Amazing Bud Powell, Vol. 1* (EMD/Blue Note)
Max Roach, *To the Max!* (Blue Moon)
Sonny Rollins, *Saxophone Colossus* (Prestige)
Sonny Stitt, *Kaleidoscope* (Prestige)

Singers

Ella Fitzgerald, *The Best of the Songbooks* (Verve)
Billie Holiday, *The Quintessential Billie Holiday, Vol. 5 (1937–1938)* (Columbia)
Sheila Jordan, *One for Junior* (Muse)
Lambert, Hendricks & Ross, *Everybody's Boppin'* (Columbia)
Carmen McRae and Betty Carter, *Carmen McRae-Betty Carter Duets* (Great American Music Hall)
Anita O'Day, *Anita* (Verve)
King Pleasure, *Moody's Mood for Love* (Blue Note)
Frank Sinatra, *Come Fly with Me* (Capitol)
Bessie Smith, *The Complete Recordings, Vol. 1* (Columbia/Legacy)
Mel Tormé, *Fujitsu-Concord Jazz Festival (1990)* (Concord Jazz)
Sarah Vaughan, *At Mister Kelly's* (EmArcy)

Cool/post bop

Chet Baker, *Chet in Paris, Vol. 2: Everything Happens to Me* (EmArcy)
Miles Davis, *Birth of the Cool* (Capitol)
Miles Davis, *Miles and Coltrane* (Sony)
Lou Donaldson, *Lush Life* (Blue Note)
Bill Evans, *Sunday at the Village Vanguard* (Original Jazz Classics)
Jimmy Giuffre, *The Complete 1947–1953 Small Group Sessions, Vol. 1* (Blue Moon)
Chico Hamilton, *Man From Two Worlds* (GRP/Impulse!)
Herbie Hancock, *Maiden Voyage* (Blue Note)
Gerry Mulligan, *California Concerts, Vol. 2* (Pacific Jazz)
Wes Montgomery, *The Incredible Jazz Guitar of Wes Montgomery* (Original Jazz Classics)

Abstract/avant garde

Art Ensemble of Chicago, *Nice Guys* (ECM)
Alvin Batiste, *Late* (Columbia)
Anthony Braxton, *Dortmund (Quartet–1976)* (Hat Art)
Ornette Coleman, *The Shape of Jazz to Come* (Atlantic)
John Coltrane, *Live at the Village Vanguard* (Impulse!)
Duke Ellington and John Coltrane, *Duke Ellington and John Coltrane* (MCA)
Pierre Favre, *Window Steps* (ECM)

Charlie Haden, *Liberation Music Orchestra* (Impulse!)
Marc Johnson, *Right Brain Patrol* (JMT)
Albert Mangelsdorff, *Three Originals* (MPS)
Anthony Ortega, *New Dance* (Hat Hut)
Sam Rivers, *Involution* (EMD/Blue Note)
Sun Ra, *Holiday for Soul Dance* (Evidence)
Henry Threadgill and Very Very Circus, *Spirit of Nuff . . . Nuff* (Black Saint)
World Saxophone Quartet, *Plays Duke Ellington* (Elektra)

Electric

Philip Catherine, *Live* (Dreyfus Jazz)
Chick Corea and Return to Forever, *Light As a Feather* (Polydor)
Miles Davis, *Bitches Brew* (Sony)
Herbie Hancock, *Thrust* (Sony)
Mahavishnu Orchestra, *Birds of Fire* (Sony)
Grover Washington, Jr., *Mister Magic* (Motown)
Tony Williams and Lifetime, *Emergency* (Polydor)

Latin

Airto Moreira, *Virgin Land* (CTI)
Astrud Gilberto, *Look at the Rainbow* (PGD/Verve)
Joao Gilberto, *Amoroso/Brasil* (Warner Brothers)
Tito Puente, *El Rey* (Concord Picante)
Poncho Sanchez, *Para Todos* (Concord Picante)

Jazz from the '80s and '90s

Ray Anderson Alligatory Band, *Heads and Tales* (Enja)
Louie Bellson, *Their Time Was The Greatest* (Concord)
Benny Carter and Phil Woods, *My Man Benny, My Man Phil*
    (Music Masters)
James Carter, *Conversin' With The Elders* (Atlantic)
Clayton-Hamilton Jazz Orchestra, *Groove Shop* (Capri)
Eddie Daniels, *Beautiful Love* (Shanachie)
Kenny Garrett, *Songbook* (Warner Bros.)
Charlie Haden and Hank Jones, *Steal Away* (PGD/Verve)
Milt Hinton, *Old Man Time* (Chiaroscuro)
Branford Marsalis, *Trio Jeepy* (Sony)
Wynton Marsalis, *Blood on the Fields* (Sony)
James Moody, *Young At Heart* (Warner Brothers)
Marcus Roberts, *Blues For The New Millenium* (Sony)
Steve Turre, *Steve Turre* (PGD/Verve)
The Yellowjackets, *Four Corners* (MCA)

What's on the CD?

Jelly Roll Morton, "Thirty-Fifth St. Blues." As both band leader and pianist, Morton was one of jazz's early giants. Building on earlier ragtime, Morton composed, played, and led some of his era's top bands — most notably the Red Hot Peppers. This cut was recorded during the mid-'20s and catches Morton on the cusp of early New Orleans jazz and the swing era soon to follow. Several key elements of jazz are easy to detect, particularly the steady, swinging rhythms that sometimes overlap as his hands work in tandem, and catchy improvisations inspired by the song's melody. From the album *Jelly Roll Morton* (Milestone).

Louis Armstrong, "Riff Blues." Armstrong is considered jazz's first major soloist, and you can hear why on this song. In the mid-'20s, when jazz was still largely ensemble music, Armstrong emerged as a masterful improviser, spontaneously inventing long, new lines of melody over a tune's underlying chords, always with a swinging sense of rhythm. From the album *Mack the Knife* (Pablo).

Ella Fitzgerald, "St. Louis Blues." Since W.C. Handy published the tune in 1914, this song has been a staple of jazz, recorded by dozens of musicians. Here, it's given a fresh rendering by the legendary songstress, who does great things with the familiar melody and adds improvisations that prove she is one of the best vocalists, using her voice as an instrument. From the album *Bluella: Ella Fitzgerald Sings the Blues* (Pablo).

Miles Davis, "Oleo." Catching the chameleonic trumpeter in the prime of his mid-'50s hard bop period, this song is the epitome of Davis's cool, lyrical ways with a melody and solo. It also showcases one of Davis's all-time top bands: his quintet with saxophonist John Coltrane, drummer Philly Joe Jones, pianist Red Garland, and bassist Paul Chambers. From the album *Relaxin'* (Original Jazz Classics).

Clark Terry and Thelonious Monk, "In Orbit." One of jazz's underappreciated trumpeters teams with its all-time idiosyncratic pianist on this one. Terry's trumpet combines the swing era's loose, steady momentum and sense of melody with bop's more advanced chords, harmonies, and fleet improvisations. And of course Monk: His teetering piano, combining quirky chords and odd, choppy snatches of improvisation is one of jazz's all-time great instrumental voices. From Terry's album *In Orbit* (Original Jazz Classics).

John Coltrane and Red Garland, "Theme for Ernie." *Soultrane* (Prestige) is considered one of the great saxophonist's all-time top albums, and this cut from it also showcases pianist Red Garland, his constant collaborator at the time (1958). On tenor sax, Coltrane still shows hard bop leanings carried over from his mid-'50s stint in trumpeter Miles Davis's quintet, but his urgent improvisations foreshadow his soon-to-come explorations well beyond jazz's existing boundaries. The band is rounded out by bassist Paul Chambers and drummer Art Taylor.

Sonny Rollins, "Way out West." The title cut from Rollins's 1958 album catches him in peak form on his own original composition. Since his earliest recordings during the 1940s, Rollins has proven himself one of jazz's most inventive and durable players — and he's still going strong today. Although Rollins was a New Yorker, this session catches him with Californians Ray Brown on bass and Shelly Manne on drums. Rollins is a master of intricate, inventive, bebop-inspired saxophone who put a lot more urban verve into his 1950s music than some of the cooler California players. From the album *Way out West* (Original Jazz Classics).

Stan Getz, "Prezervation." By the title, you know this one's a tribute to earlier tenor sax legend Lester "Prez" Young — like Getz, Young was a master of warm, lyrical improvisations delivered in a gentle, honeyed tone. Recorded in 1949, this is one of Getz's earliest efforts, but it shows why he became one of jazz's most important tenor saxmen of the 1950s and 1960s. From the album *Prezervation* (Original Jazz Classics).

Wes Montgomery, "Tune Up." Jazz's all-time coolest guitarist, Montgomery said more with less than practically any other jazz fretman. Recorded in 1960, this song catches Montgomery early in his prime, with flutist James Clay, pianist Victor Feldman, bassist Sam Jones, and drummer Louis Hayes — plus a string section that points the way toward orchestrated mid-'60s soul jazz. From *Movin' Along* (Original Jazz Classics).

Art Tatum, "Danny Boy." Tatum is a rare blend of awesome technique and emotional nuance, all the more apparent when he goes it solo, as on this song. A swing stylist who started his career during the 1930s, Tatum also had blinding speed and an advanced knowledge of chords and harmonies that rank him among such leading bebop pianists as Thelonious Monk and Bud Powell. Here, he takes the old folk song and twists it into jazz form, proving that you don't even have to start with a new tune or a jazz standard to make a statement. Notice how his left and right hands work independently, so it sounds at times as if there couldn't be just one pianist. From *The Art Tatum Solo Masterpieces, Vol. 6* (Pablo).

Index

• A •

AACM (Association for the Advancement of Creative Musicians), 69, 328
Abrams, Muhal Richard, 187
abstract jazz, 14, 187–191, 339–340. *See also avant garde* jazz; free jazz
acid jazz, 14, 90–91
acoustic bass, 238. *See also* basses
Adams, Pepper, 56, 109
Adderley, Cannonball, 113, 338
Affif, Ron, 270
African American origins, 8–9, 20
African origins, 14, 20
Afro-Cuban All-Stars, 88
Afro-Cuban Jazz, 78. *See also* Latin jazz
Afro-Cubans, The, 79–80
Alden, Howard, 93, 258
Aleman, Oscar, 257
Alexander, Ray, 234
Allen, Geri, 193
Allen, Henry "Red," 134
Allison, Mose, 15, 165
Allyson, Karrin, 166
Almond, Peck, 92
altered ears, 7. *See also* listening to jazz
alto clarinets, 274. *See also* clarinets
alto saxophones, 98. *See also* saxophones
Altschul, Barry, 222
Ammons, Albert, 176
Ammons, Gene, 61, 113–114
Anderson, Ivie, 154
Anderson, Ray, 302, 340
Antoine, Mark, 93
Apfelbaum, Peter, 92
arco, defined, 238
Arkestra, 74
Armstrong, Louis
  CD-ROM contents, 341
  Chicago jazz, 28

Harden, Lil, 23
  music recommendations, 32, 337
  photograph, 134
  trombones, 294
  trumpets, 130–135
  vocalists, 148
Art Ensemble of Chicago, 74, 339
Austin High Gang, 30–31
Australian jazz clubs, 313
Author's Choice icons, 4
author's collection, 331
avant garde jazz. *See also* free jazz
  about, 67–68
  basses, 246–248
  Bley, Paul, 71
  Braxton, Anthony, 70
  Cherry, Don, 71
  clarinets, 281–282
  defined, 14
  Dolphy, Eric, 70
  drums, 219–220
  versus free jazz, 68–69
  Lydian Chromatic Concept of Tonal Organization, 68
  music recommendations, 339–340
  Russell, George, 68
  saxophones, 120–122
  Shepp, Archie, 70
  third stream, 68
  World Saxophone Quartet, 71
Ayers, Roy, 232
Azpiazu, Don, 78
Azymuth, 88

• B •

Bacon, Gilles, 198
Bailey, Derek, 267
Bailey, Mildred, 154–155
Baker, Chet, 58, 129, 142, 161, 339
Baker, Dorothy, 30
banjos, 253–254

Baquet, George, 22
Barbarin, Paul, 210
Barbieri, Gato, 84
baritone saxophones, 98. *See also* saxophones
Barnet, Charlie, 47
barrelhouse music, 23
Barretto, Ray, 84
Barron, Kenny, 192
bars, defined, 10
Basie, Count, 45–46, 175, 197, 338
  photograph, 45
bass clarinets, 274
bass drums, 208. *See also* drums
basses
  about, 237–238
  avant garde, 246–248
  big bands, 241–242
  Blanton, Jimmy, 237, 240–241
  Braud, Wellman, 239
  Brown, Ray, 237, 244–245
  Carter, Ron, 248–249, 252
  Clarke, Stanley, 249–250
  Duvivier, Charles, 251
  early jazz, 239–240
  electric jazz, 248–250
  Fambrough, Charles, 252
  Foster, Pops, 239
  Haden, Charlie, 237, 246–247
  Heath, Percy, 251
  Hinton, Milt, 241
  Hurst, Robert, 252
  improvisation, 240–241
  Jackson, Chubby, 242
  Kirby, John, 240
  LeFaro, Scott, 237
  McBee, Cecil, 245
  McBride, Christian, 252
  Mingus, Charles, 237, 243–244
  Mitchell, Red, 246
  Moffett, Charnett, 252
  Page, Walter, 240
  Pastorius, Jaco, 250
  Peacock, Gary, 247–248
  Pedersen, Niels-Henning Orsted, 247

Pettiford, Oscar, 242–243
Reid, Rufus, 251
Stewart, Slam, 242
swing, 241–242
Vitous, Miroslav, 251
Weber, Eberhard, 248
Williams, Buster, 251
Workman, Reggie, 251
Batiste, Alvin, 282, 339
Bauza, Mario, 79–80
beat, feeling, 16–17
bebop
  about, 49–51
  big bands and, 54–56
  clarinets, 279–280
  Clarke, Kenny, 53
  Dameron, Tadd, 53
  drums, 215–219
  Edison, Harry "Sweets," 53
  Garland, Red, 66
  Gillespie, Dizzy, 51, 54
  guitars, 263–265
  Hawkins, Coleman, 53
  Herman, Woody, 55
  Jamal, Ahmad, 66
  Kenton, Stan, 55
  Kessel, Barney, 53
  Killian, Al, 53
  Manne, Shelly, 53
  McGhee, Howard, 53
  Monk, Thelonious, 53
  music recommendations,
    53–54, 338–339
  Navarro, Fats, 53
  Parker, Charlie "Bird,"
    50–51, 54
  Pettiford, Oscar, 53
  piano trios, 65–66
  pianos, 177–179
  Powell, Bud, 53, 66
  Rich, Buddy, 53
  saxophones, 106–113
  Stitt, Sonny, 53
  Thornhill, Claude, 56
  traits of, 52
  trombones, 299–302
  trumpets, 136–140
  vocalists, 156–160
  Williams, Cootie, 53
  word origins, 52
Bechet, Sidney, 22, 99–100,
  275–276, 337
Beiderbecke, Bix, 29–30,
  130, 337

Bellson, Louie, 214–215, 340
bending notes, defined, 13
bending strings, 254
Benoit, David, 93
Benson, George, 270
Berigan, Bunny, 134
Berry, Chu, 103
Best Of packages, 335
big bands. *See also* swing;
    territory bands
  about, 34–35
  Barnet, Charlie, 47
  Basie, Count, 45–46
  basses, 241–242
  bebop and, 54–56
  Calloway, Cab, 38
  Carter, Benny, 38
  Casa Loma Orchestra, 38
  clarinets, 277–279
  Crosby, Bob, 47
  Dorsey, Jimmy, 47
  Dorsey, Tommy, 47
  drums, 211–215
  Ellington, Duke, 41–44
  Goldkette, Jean, 37
  Goodman, Benny, 46–47
  Hampton, Lionel, 38
  Henderson, Fletcher, 36–37
  Hines, Earl, 38–39
  James, Harry, 47
  Kirk, Andy, 39
  Krupa, Gene, 47
  Lunceford, Jimmie, 39
  McKinney's Cotton Pick-
    ers, 39
  Moten, Bennie, 40
  music recommendations,
    338
  Pollack, Ben, 37
  race relations, 43–44
  Redman, Don, 36
  Shaw, Artie, 48
  territory bands, 39–41
  trombones, 296–299
  vocalists, 153–156
  Webb, Chick, 39
  Whiteman, Paul, 38
  World War II and, 48
Bigard, Barney, 32
Bill Holman Big Band, 94
Black Saint record label,
  307–308
Blake, Eubie, 25, 172

Blakey, Art, 61, 82,
  216–217, 338
Blanchard, Terence, 145
Blanton, Jimmy, 237,
  240–241, 338
Bley, Paul, 71, 188
Blue Devils, 41
Blue Note Records, 308, 328
blue notes, defined, 13
Bluebird record label, 307
Blues For Dummies, 12
blues influence, 11–12,
  147–151
Blues Serenaders, 41
Bluiett, Hamiett, 274
Blythe, Arthur, 74
BMG Classics record label, 307
Bobo, Willie, 84
Boehm, Theobald, 284
Bolden, Buddy, 21–22,
  127–128, 253, 273, 294
Bongo Logic, 88
boogie-woogie piano, 176–177
books about jazz, 323–325
Bosco, Joao, 164
bossa nova, 78. *See also* Latin
    jazz
Bostic, Earl, 109
Boston jazz clubs, 314
Boswell, Connie, 151–152
Botti, Chris, 93
Bowden, Chris, 91
Bowie, Lester, 74, 143
boxed sets, 335
Brackeen, Joanne, 192
Brand, Dollar, 188
Brand New Heavies, 91
brass marching bands,
    influence of, 20
Braud, Wellman, 239
Braun, Rick, 93
Braxton, Anthony, 70, 120,
  281, 339
Brazilian music, 78, 163–164.
    See also Latin jazz
Breakstone, Joshua, 270
Breau, Lenny, 270
Brecker, Michael, 93, 124
Brecker, Randy, 93
Bridgewater, Dee Dee, 93
Brookmeyer, Bob, 294
Brooks, Lonnie, 12
Brooks, Roy, 222

Brown, Clifford, 61–62,
139–140, 338
Brown, Lawrence, 298
Brown, Ray, 237, 244–245
Brown, Tom, 26
Brubeck, Dave, 58, 180
Brunies Band, 26
Brunis, George, 26, 296
Bruno, Jimmy, 93, 270
Buckner, Milt, 197
Bunn, Teddy, 256
Burrell, Kenny, 263
Burton, Gary, 93, 230
Byard, Jaki, 193
Byas, Don, 104
Byrd, Donald, 76, 144

• C •

cadenza, defined, 12
Caldwell, Bobby, 93
Californian jazz clubs, 313,
317–318, 320–321
call and response, 12, 20
Callendar, Red, 56
Calloway, Cab, 38, 338
calypso. See Latin jazz
Canadian jazz clubs, 313, 322
Canned heat, 177
Carney, Harry, 274
Carter, Benny, 38, 100, 340
Carter, Betty, 149, 164, 339
Carter, James, 92, 124, 340
Carter, Ron, 94, 248–249, 252
Carver, Wayman, 285
Casa Loma Orchestra, 38
Casey, Al, 256
cassettes, choosing, 332–333
Catherine, Philip, 257–258, 340
Caymmi, Dori, 164
CD changers, 333–334
CD-ROM contents, 341–342
CDs, choosing, 332–333
cha-cha-cha. See Latin jazz
changes, defined, 10
Charles, Teddy, 229
"Charleston" composer, 172
Cheatham, Doc, 92
Cherry, Don, 71
Chestnut, Cyrus, 92, 192
Chicago jazz
Armstrong, Louis, 28
Austin High Gang, 30–31

Beiderbecke, Bix, 29–30
Bigard, Barney, 32
clubs, 315
free jazz, 69
Hines, Earl "Fatha," 31–32
history, 27
Morton, Jelly Roll, 29
Noone, Jimmie, 31–32
Oliver, Joe "King," 27–28
Russell, Luis, 32
Williams, Clarence, 32
Childs, Billy, 193
choke cymbals, 208. See also
drums
Christian, Charlie,
259–261, 338
Christopher, Evan, 282
Christy, June, 161
church music, influence of, 20
church pipe organs. See
organs
Cinelu, Mino, 94
circuit riders, 64
clarinets
about, 273–274
avant garde jazz, 281–282
Batiste, Alvin, 282
bebop, 279–280
Bechet, Sidney, 275–276
big bands, 277–279
Bluiett, Hamiett, 274
Bolden, Buddy, 273
Braxton, Anthony, 281
Carney, Harry, 274
Christopher, Evan, 282
Daniels, Eddie, 281
Davern, Kenny, 279
DeFranco, Buddy, 274, 280
Dodds, Johnny, 277
early jazz, 274–277
electric jazz, 281–282
Goodman, Benny, 274,
277–278
Hamilton, Jimmy, 280
Hampel, Gunter, 274
Herman, Woody, 279
Hucko, Peanuts, 279
Marsala, Joe, 279
Maupin, Bennie, 274, 282
Mintzer, Bob, 282
Mitchell, Roscoe, 274, 281
Murray, David, 274
New Orleans jazz, 274–277
Noone, Jimmie, 277

Peplowski, Ken, 279
Russell, Pee Wee, 278–279
Shaw, Artie, 278
Simeon, Omer, 274
swing, 277–279
Wilber, Bob, 279
Clarke, Kenny, 53, 215–216
Clarke, Stanley, 76, 249–250
classical music, 12, 20, 68
Clayton, Buck, 135
Clayton-Hamilton Jazz
Orchestra, 340
Cleveland jazz clubs, 316
Cline, Nels, 270
clubs
Boston, 314
calling ahead, 311, 313
Chicago, 315
Cleveland, 316
Denver, 316–317
finding, 312–313
Los Angeles, 317–318
Montreal, 318
New Orleans, 318–319
New York City, 319
Oakland, California, 320
Philadelphia, 320–321
preparing to go, 311–312
San Francisco, 321
Toronto, 322
Web sites, 313
C-melody saxophones, 98. See
also saxophones
Cobb, Arnett, 104
Cobb, Jimmy, 222
Cobham, Billy, 76, 220–221
Coda, Cub, 12
Cohen, Avishai, 92
Cole, Cozy, 210
Cole, Nat King, 161, 175
Cole, Richie, 126
Coleman, Ornette, 72–73,
117–118, 329, 339
photograph, 117
collecting jazz. See also music
recommendations
abstract selections, 339–340
artists, choosing, 335–336
author's collection, 331
avant garde selections,
339–340
bebop selections, 338–339
Best Of packages, 335
(continued)

collecting jazz *(continued)*
 big band selections, 338
 boxed sets, 335
 cassettes, choosing, 332–333
 CD changers, 333–334
 CDs, choosing, 332–333
 compilation albums, 335
 cool jazz selections, 339
 cost, 336
 early jazz selections, 337
 electric selections, 340
 format, choosing, 332–333
 greatest hits packages, 335
 hard bop selections, 338–339
 Latin selections, 340
 liner notes, 336
 media, choosing, 332–333
 New Orleans jazz selection,
  337
 1980s selections, 340
 1990s selections, 340
 remastered titles, 332
 risk, 336
 singers, 339
 sound system, choosing,
  333–334
 Surround sound, 334
 swing selections, 338
 turntables, 334
 vinyl, choosing, 332–333
 vocalists, 339
Collette, Buddy, 56, 114,
  283, 286
Coltrane, John, 73–74,
  118–120, 339, 342
 photograph, 119
Coltrane, Miki, 92
Coltrane, Ravi, 92
Columbia record label, 310
compilation albums, 335
Concord Jazz, 191, 308
Condon, Eddie, 31, 261
Conrad Herwig, 88
contemporary jazz, 92–93, 290
Cook, Will Marion, 34
cool jazz
 about, 56–57
 Baker, Chet, 58
 Brubeck, Dave, 58
 Davis, Miles, 58
 Desmond, Paul, 58
 Evans, Gil, 59
 Giuffre, Jimmy, 59
 guitars, 265–267

Latin jazz influences, 82–83
Lighthouse All-Stars, 60
Los Angeles, 57–60
Manne, Shelly, 59
Manne Hole club, 59
Modern Jazz Quartet
  (MJQ), 59
Mulligan, Gerry, 59–60
music recommendations,
  339
pianos, 179–183
Rogers, Shorty, 60
Rumsey, Howard, 60
saxophones, 113–116
Tristano, Lennie, 60
West Coast, 57–60
Cooper, Buster, 298
Corea, Chick, 75, 86, 192, 340
cornets, 129. *See also* trum-
  pets
Coryell, Larry, 76, 267
Costa, Eddie, 233
Costa, Gal, 164
Count Basic, 91
Cox, Anthony, 92
Cox, Ida, 149
creole, defined, 20
Crispell, Marilyn, 74, 188
Criss, Sonny, 110
Crosby, Bing, 152
Crosby, Bob, 47
Crusaders, 75, 192
Cuban music, 78. *See also*
  Latin jazz
cuboppers, 79–81. *See also*
  Latin jazz
Cugat, Xavier, 78
Cunliffe, Bill, 193
cymbals, 208. *See also* drums

• D •

Dameron, Tadd, 53
Daniels, Eddie, 281, 340
Dara, Olu, 94
Davern, Kenny, 279
Davis, Eddie "Lockjaw," 104
Davis, Jesse, 110, 126
Davis, Miles
 CD-ROM contents, 341
 cool jazz, 58
 electric jazz, 75
 hard bop, 62

music recommendations,
  339, 340
 photograph, 141
 trumpets, 140–142
Davis, Wild Bill, 197–198
Day, Doris, 155
DeArango, Bill, 263
DeDroit, Johnny, 26
DeFrancesco, Joey, 203–204
DeFranco, Buddy, 274, 280
DeJohnette, Jack, 94, 222
Dennerlein, Barbara, 204
Denver jazz clubs, 316–317
depression-era vocalists,
  151–152
Desmond, Paul, 58, 114
Dickenson, Vic, 298
Digable Plants, 91
DiMeola, Al, 76, 268
diversity, 90
Dixieland, 21, 25–26, 294–295
Dodds, Baby, 22, 209
Dodds, Johnny, 22, 277, 337
Doggett, Bill, 200
Dolphy, Eric, 70, 121
Donaldson, Lou, 339
Donegan, Dorothy, 175–176
Dorham, Kenny, 144
Dorian mode, defined, 13
Dorsey, Jimmy, 47
Dorsey, Tommy, 47, 299
Double-Time Jazz Web site, 328
doubling, defined, 253
Dowd, Charles, 234
Drew, Kenny, 180
drum kit, defined, 208
drums
 Altschul, Barry, 222
 avant garde, 219–220
 Barbarin, Paul, 210
 bebop, 215–219
 Bellson, Louie, 214–215
 big bands, 211–215
 Blakey, Art, 216–217
 Brooks, Roy, 222
 Clarke, Kenny, 215–216
 Cobb, Jimmy, 222
 Cobham, Billy, 220–221
 Cole, Cozy, 210
 DeJohnette, Jack, 222
 Dodds, Baby, 209
 drum kit, defined, 208
 early jazz, 207–211

electric jazz, 220–222
Foster, Al, 222
Hamilton, Chico, 218
Hanna, Jack, 222
Hart, Billy, 222
Hayes, Louis, 222
Haynes, Roy, 222
Higgins, Billy, 222
Jackson, Ronald Shannon, 220
Jones, Elvin, 219–220
Jones, Jo, 212–213
Jones, Philly Joe, 219
Krupa, Gene, 211–212
Lewis, Victor, 222
Manne, Shelly, 222
Mouzon, Alphonse, 221
Penland, Ralph, 222
Rich, Buddy, 213–214
Richmond, Danny, 222
Roach, Max, 217–218
Roker, Mickey, 222
Singleton, Zutty, 209–210
swing, 211–215
Tate, Grady, 222
Tough, Dave, 210
Watts, Jeff "Tain," 222
Webb, Chick, 211
Williams, Tony, 221
Wilson, Shadow, 222
Dudziak, Urszula, 149, 164
Dulfer, Candy, 93
Durham, Eddie, 259
Dutch jazz clubs, 313
Dutrey, Honore, 296
Duvivier, Charles, 251

• E •

Earland, Charles, 200–201
Earshot Jazz Web site, 313
Eckstine, Billy, 155
Edison, Harry "Sweets," 53, 135
Eldridge, Roy, 135–136, 338
electric jazz
  basses, 248–250
  Byrd, Donald, 76
  clarinets, 281–282
  Clarke, Stanley, 76
  Cobham, Billy, 76
  Corea, Chick, 75
  Coryell, Larry, 76

Crusaders, 75
Davis, Miles, 75
DiMeola, Al, 76
drums, 220–222
flutes, 290
guitars, 259–261, 267–269
Hancock, Herbie, 76
Henderson, Eddie, 76
Holdsworth, Allan, 76
Hubbard, Freddie, 76
Johnson, Alphonso, 76
McLaughlin, John, 76
Mouzon, Alphonse, 76
music recommendations, 340
pianos, 192
saxophones, 123
Smith, Johnny Hammond, 76
Tower of Power, 76
Washington, Grover, Jr., 76
Weather Report, 76
Elias, Eliane, 94, 184
Elling, Kurt, 92, 166
Ellington, Edward Kennedy "Duke"
  big bands, 41–44
  early years, 41–42
  legacy, 43
  music recommendations, 42–43, 338, 339
  photograph, 44
  pianos, 176
  signature sound, 42–43
  trombones, 297–298
Elliott, Richard, 93
Ellis, Dave, 92
Ellis, Herb, 263
EMD record label, 308
EM&I, 91
Essential Music icons, 4
Eubanks, Kevin, 94
Europe, James Reese, 34
European music, influence of, 12–13, 20
Evans, Bill, 180, 339
Evans, Gil, 59
Excelsior band, 22

• F •

Faddis, Jon, 135
Fambrough, Charles, 252
Fantasy record label, 309

Farlow, Tal, 266
Farmer, Art, 129, 144, 338
Farrell, Joe, 292
Favre, Pierre, 339
Feldman, Victor, 233
Ferrante, Russell, 192
f-holes, defined, 238
Fitzgerald, Ella, 39, 149, 157–158, 339, 341
  photograph, 157
Flanagan, Tommy, 180
flat seventh interval, defined, 13
Fleck, Bela, 93
floor toms, 208. *See also* drums
Floyd, Troy, 41
flugelhorns, 129. *See also* trumpets
flutes
  about, 283–284
  Boehm, Theobald, 284
  Carver, Wayman, 285
  Collette, Buddy, 283, 286
  contemporary jazz, 290
  design of, 284
  early jazz, 284–285
  electric jazz, 290
  Farrell, Joe, 292
  Fortune, Sonny, 292
  Hofmann, Holly, 283, 292
  Kirk, Rahsaan Roland, 283, 288–289
  Kujala, Steve, 292
  Lancaster, Byard, 292
  Lasha, Prince, 283, 290
  Lateef, Yusef, 289–290
  Laws, Hubert, 283, 290
  Lloyd, Charles, 283
  Mann, Herbie, 283, 286–287
  McNeil, Lloyd, 283
  Most, Sam, 283
  Newton, James, 283, 291
  overblowing, 283
  Rivers, Sam, 292
  Shank, Bud, 292
  Socarras, Albert, 284–285
  Steig, Jeremy, 283
  Tabackin, Lew, 291–292
  Valentin, Dave, 292
  Wess, Frank, 283, 285, 287–288
Forman, Bruce, 270
Forrest, Helen, 154

Fortune, Sonny, 292
Foster, Al, 222
Foster, Pops, 22, 239
Fourplay, 93
free jazz. *See also avant garde*
    jazz
    about, 14, 71–72
    Arkestra, 74
    Art Ensemble of Chicago, 74
    versus avant garde jazz,
        68–69
    Blythe, Arthur, 74
    Bowie, Lester, 74
    Chicago, 69
    Coleman, Ornette, 72–73
    Coltrane, John, 73–74
    Crispell, Marilyn, 74
    Hill, Andrew, 74
    Indian influences, 74
    Jenkins, Leroy, 74
    Lewis, George, 74
    modal jazz, 74
    Murray, David, 74
    Murray, Sunny, 74
    New York City, 69
    Pullen, Don, 74
    Ra, Sun, 74
    Sanders, Pharoah, 74
    saxophones, 120–122
    Shanker, Ravi, 74
    Sharrock, Sonny, 74
    Taylor, Cecil, 74
    Threadgill, Henry, 74
    Ulmer, James "Blood," 74
    Zorn, John, 74
Freelon, Nnenna, 166
Freeman, Bud, 31
French jazz clubs, 313
fretless, defined, 238
frets, defined, 258
front-line, defined, 31
Fuller, Curtis, 65, 303
funeral music, influence of, 20
fusion, 75–76. *See also* electric
    jazz

● *G* ●

Gaillard, Slim, 155, 338
Galliano, 91
Gang Starr, 91
Garland, Judy, 155
Garland, Red, 66, 342

Garner, Erroll, 185–186, 338
Garrett, Kenny, 92, 124, 340
Garson, Mike, 193
Getz, Stan, 85, 114, 342
Gibbs, Terry, 227–228
Gibson guitars, 259
Gil, Gilberto, 164
Gilberto, Astrud, 85, 163, 340
Gilberto, Joao, 85, 163, 340
Gillespie, John Birks "Dizzy"
    bebop, 51, 54
    Latin jazz, 80–81
    music recommendations,
        338
    and Parker, Charlie
        "Bird," 51
    photograph, 138
    trumpets, 136–139
    vocalists, 162
Giuffre, Jimmy, 59, 339
Glenn, Tyree, 298
glissandi, 238, 293
glockenspiels, 225. *See also*
    vibraphones
Goldings, Larry, 204
Goldkette, Jean, 37
Golson, Benny, 338
Gonzalez, Jerry, 87
Goodman, Benny, 31, 46–47,
        274, 277–278, 338
Gordon, Dexter, 62,
        110–111, 338
Grappelli, Stephane, 238, 338
Gray, Wardell, 111
greatest hits packages, 335
Green, Benny, 193
Green, Charlie, 296
Green, Freddie, 261–262
Green, Grant, 266
grenadilla, 274
Greyboy, 90–91
Griffin, Johnny, 111–112
Grillo, Frank, 79–80
Grimes, Tiny, 262
groove, 91, 198–203
GRP record label, 309
Gryce, Gigi, 112
guitars
    about, 253–254
    Affif, Ron, 270
    Alden, Howard, 258
    Aleman, Oscar, 257
    Bailey, Derek, 267
    bebop, 263–265

Benson, George, 270
Bolden, Buddy, 253
Breakstone, Joshua, 270
Breau, Lenny, 270
Bruno, Jimmy, 270
Bunn, Teddy, 256
Burrell, Kenny, 263
Casey, Al, 256
Catherine, Philip, 257–258
Christian, Charlie, 259–261
Cline, Nels, 270
Condon, Eddie, 261
cool jazz, 265–267
Coryell, Larry, 267
DeArango, Bill, 263
DiMeola, Al, 268
Durham, Eddie, 259
early jazz, 254–256
electric jazz, 259–261,
        267–269
Ellis, Herb, 263
Farlow, Tal, 266
Forman, Bruce, 270
Gibson, 259
Green, Freddie, 261–262
Green, Grant, 266
Grimes, Tiny, 262
hard bop, 265–267
Hunter, Charlie, 258
Johnson, Lonnie, 254–255
Kessel, Barney, 264–265
Lagrene, Bireli, 258
Lang, Eddie, 255
Leitch, Peter, 270
Loar, Lloyd, 259
Martino, Pat, 270
McDonough, Dick, 256
McLaughlin, John, 268
Metheny, Pat, 268
Montgomery, Wes, 265
Moore, Oscar, 256
Mumford, Jefferson, 253
Pass, Joe, 266–267
Paul, Les, 259, 262
Pizzarelli, Bucky, 258
Pizzarelli, John, 258
Reinhardt, Django, 256–257
Remler, Emily, 270
Rickenbacker, 259
Ritenour, Lee, 268
Rypdal, Terje, 269
Scofield, John, 269
seventh string, 258
Smith, Floyd, 259

Szabo, Gabor, 267
Thomas, Rene, 258
Van Eps, George, 258, 262
Walker, Aaron "T-Bone," 266
Wayne, Chuck, 262
Whitfield, Mark, 270
Gypsy Kings, 93

● *H* ●

habanera, 78
Haden, Charlie, 94, 237,
    246–247, 340
Hagans, Tim, 92
Hamilton, Chico, 56, 218, 339
Hamilton, Jimmy, 280, 338
Hammond B-3, 196. *See also*
    organs
Hampel, Gunter, 274
Hampton, Lionel "Hamp," 38,
    224–225
    photograph, 226
Hampton, Slide, 304
Hancock, Herbie, 76, 94,
    188–189, 192, 339, 340
    photograph, 190
Handy, Craig, 126
Handy, W.C., 78
Hanna, Jack, 222
Hanshaw, Annette, 152
Haque, Fareed, 92
hard bop
    about, 56–57, 60–61
    Ammons, Gene, 61
    Blakey, Art, 61
    Brown, Clifford, 61–62
    Davis, Miles, 62
    Fuller, Curtis, 65
    Gordon, Dexter, 62
    guitars, 265–267
    Henderson, Joe, 65
    Jazz Messengers, 61
    Johnson, J.J., 62
    Jordan, Clifford, 62
    Lateef, Yusef, 65
    Latin jazz influences, 82–83
    McLean, Jackie, 62
    Mingus, Charles, 63
    Mobley, Hank, 63
    Monk, Thelonious, 63
    Morgan, Lee, 63
    music recommendations,
        338–339

New York City, 60–65
    pianos, 179–183
    Roach, Max, 61–62
    Rollins, Sonny, 63–64
    saxophones, 113–116
    Shorter, Wayne, 65
    Silver, Horace, 64
    Stitt, Sonny, 64
    Waldron, Mal, 65
    Winding, Kai, 64
Hard Bop Cafe Web site, 313
Harden, Lil, 23
Hargrove, Roy, 145
Harmolodic Web site, 329
harmolodics, defined, 72
harmony, defined, 16
Harrell, Tom, 129, 143
Harris, Barry, 177
Harris, Eddie, 123
Harris, Gene, 191
Harrison, Jimmy, 296
Hart, Antonio, 92
Hart, Billy, 222
Hartman, Ed, 234
Hartman, Glenn, 198
Hatza, Greg, 204
Hawes, Hampton, 56, 177
Hawkins, Coleman "Hawk," 53,
    100–101, 338
Hayes, Louis, 222
Hayes, Tubby, 229
Haynes, Roy, 222
head arrangement, defined, 64
Headhunters, 192
Heath, Percy, 251
heaviosity, defined, 1
Hemphill, Julius, 121
Henderson, Eddie, 76
Henderson, Fletcher, 36–37,
    254, 338
Henderson, Joe, 65, 94,
    124–125
Henderson, Wayne, 304
Hendricks, Jon, 149, 160–161
Herman, Woody, 55, 82, 279,
    338
Hicks, John, 191–193
Higginbotham, J.C., 296
Higgins, Billy, 222
high-hats, 208. *See also* drums
Hill, Andrew, 74, 189–190
Hines, Earl "Fatha," 31–32,
    38–39, 173–174, 337
Hinton, Milt, 241, 340

Hodges, Johnny, 102, 338
Hofmann, Holly, 283, 292
Hoggard, Jay, 233
Holdsworth, Allan, 76
Holiday, Billie, 153–154, 339
Holland, Dave, 94
Holman, Bill, 94
Holmes, Richard
    "Groove," 201
honky tonk music, 23
Hooker, John Lee, 177
Horn, Shirley, 165
Howard, George, 93
Hubbard, Freddie, 76, 129, 143
Hucko, Peanuts, 279
Hunter, Alberta, 149
Hunter, Charlie, 92, 258
Hurst, Robert, 252
Hutcherson, Bobby,
    230–231, 338
Hyams, Marjorie, 229
Hyman, Dick, 188

● *I* ●

Ibrihim, Abdullah, 188
improvisation
    basses, 240–241
    classical music, 12
    jazz, 10–11, 16
Impulse! record label, 309
Incognito, 91
Indian influences, 13, 74
instrumental pop, defined, 14
Internet. *See* Web sites
Irvis, Charlie, 296
Italian jazz clubs, 313

● *J* ●

Jackson, Chubby, 15, 242
Jackson, Javon, 126
Jackson, Milt "Bags," 228–229
Jackson, Papa Charlie, 254
Jackson, Quentin, 298
Jackson, Ronald Shannon, 220
Jackson, Tony, 172
Jacquet, Illinois, 104
Jamal, Ahmad, 66, 181
James, Bob, 93
James, Boney, 93
James, Harry, 47
James Taylor Quartet, 91

Jamiroquai, 91
Jarret, Keith, 190
jazz
  elements of, 9–11
  first famous soloist, 27
  first jazz band, 21
  first recording, 25–26
  first soloist on vinyl, 22
  inventor of, 26
  race relations, 26
  roots of, 11–14
  spelling variations, 8
  Web sites, 328–329
  word origin, 8–9
Jazz Central Station
    Web site, 329
Jazz Clubs Web site, 313
Jazz in France Web site, 313
Jazz Italia Web site, 313
jazz labels. See labels
Jazz Messengers, 61, 94
Jazz Now Interactive
    Web site, 329
Jazz Online Web site, 329
Jazz Store Web site, 329
JazzNet Web site, 313
JazzWeb Web site, 313
Jefferson, Eddie, 149, 158
Jenkins, Leroy, 74, 238
Jiosa, Denny, 93
Jobim, Antonio Carlos, 163
Johnson, Alphonso, 76
Johnson, Bill, 254
Johnson, Budd, 104
Johnson, Bunk, 22, 172
Johnson, James P., 24, 34,
    172, 337
Johnson, J.J., 62, 300–302, 338
  photograph, 301
Johnson, Lonnie, 254–255, 338
Johnson, Marc, 340
Johnson, Pete, 176
Jones, Elvin, 219–220
Jones, Hank, 94, 191, 340
Jones, Jo, 212–213, 338
Jones, Leroy, 145
Jones, Philly Joe, 219
Joplin, Scott, 25, 78,
    170–171, 337
Jordan, Clifford, 62
Jordan, Sheila, 339

• K •

Kellaway, Roger, 193
Kelly, Wynton, 181
Kenny G, 92
Kenton, Stan, 55, 82
Keppard, Freddie, 22–23,
    128–129, 172
Kessel, Barney, 53,
    264–265, 338
keyboards. See also organs;
    pianos
  synthesizers, 192
Killian, Al, 53
Kirby, John, 240
Kirk, Andy, 39
Kirk, Rahsaan Roland, 121,
    283, 288–289
Kirkland, Kenny, 193
Knitting Factory, 69, 329
Konitz, Lee, 56, 115
Koz, Dave, 93
Krall, Diana, 166
Krupa, Gene, 31, 47, 211–212
Kuhn, Steve, 193
Kujala, Steve, 292

• L •

labels, 307-310
Ladnier, Tommy, 136
Lagrene, Bireli, 258
Lake, Oliver, 121
Lamb, Joseph, 24
Lambert, Hendricks
    & Ross, 149
Lancaster, Byard, 292
Land, Harold, 15, 115
Lang, Eddie, 255, 337
Larkins, Ellis, 191
LaRocca, Nick, 26
Lasha, Prince, 283, 290
Lateef, Yusef, 65, 289–290, 338
Latin jazz
  about, 77–78
  Afro-Cuban All-Stars, 88
  Afro-Cubans, The, 79–80
  Azpiazu, Don, 78
  Azymuth, 88
  Barbieri, Gato, 84
  Barretto, Ray, 84

  Bauza, Mario, 79–80
  Blakey, Art, 82
  Bobo, Willie, 84
  Bongo Logic, 88
  Conrad Herwig, 88
  cool jazz, 82–83
  Corea, Chick, 86
  cuboppers, 79–81
  Cugat, Xavier, 78
  early influences, 78–79
  Getz, Stan, 85
  Gilberto, Astrud, 85
  Gilberto, Joao, 85
  Gillespie, Dizzy, 80–81
  Gonzalez, Jerry, 87
  Grillo, Frank, 79–80
  Handy, W.C., 78
  hard bop, 82–83
  Herman, Woody, 82
  Joplin, Scott, 78
  Kenton, Stan, 82
  Libre, 88
  Machete Ensemble, 88
  Machito, 79–80
  Mann, Herbie, 85
  Matos, Bobby, 78, 88
  Mendes, Sergio, 87
  Morton, Jelly Roll, 78
  music recommendations,
    340
  O'Farrill, Chico, 81
  Oquendo, Manny, 88
  Perez, Danilo, 87
  pianos, 184–185
  Pozo, Chano, 80–81
  Prado, Perez, 82
  Puente, Tito, 83
  Rivera, Mario, 88
  Rubalcaba, Gonzalo, 88
  Ruiz, Hilton, 88
  Sanchez, Poncho, 86
  Sandoval, Arturo, 86–87
  Santamaria, Mongo, 85
  Santos, John, 88
  Sepulveda, Charlie, 88
  Shearing, George, 83
  Socarras, Alberto
    (Albert), 79
  Tjader, Cal, 83
  Valdes, Carlos "Patato," 88
  Valdes, Chucho, 88
  Valentin, Dave, 86
  vocalists, 163–164

Laws, Hubert, 283, 290
Lee, Peggy, 162
LeFaro, Scott, 237
Leitch, Peter, 94, 270
Lewis, George, 22, 74, 303
Lewis, John, 178
Lewis, Meade "Lux," 176
Lewis, Victor, 222
Libre, 88
licorice stick. *See* clarinets
Liebert, Ottmar, 93
Lifetime, 340
Lighthouse All-Stars, 60
Lincoln, Abbey, 164
Lincoln Center musicians, 92
liner notes, 336
listening to jazz, 16–17
    See also CD-ROM contents
    See also clubs
    See also collecting jazz
    See also music
        recommendations
lite jazz, 93
live jazz. *See* clubs
Lloyd, Charles, 283
Loar, Lloyd, 259
Loeb, Chuck, 93
Los Angeles jazz, 57–60,
    317–318
Louisiana Five, 26
Lovano, Joe, 110, 125
Lunceford, Jimmie, 39, 338
Lupri, Matthias, 234
Lydian Chromatic Concept of
    Tonal Organization, 68
Lyle, Bobby, 93
lynchings, song about, 153

• *M* •

Machete Ensemble, 88
Machito, 79–80
magazines about jazz, 325
Mahavishnu Orchestra, 340
Mahogany, Kevin, 92, 166
Mainieri, Mike, 232
mambo, 78
Mangelsdorff, Albert, 303, 340
Mann, Herbie, 85, 283, 286–287
    photograph, 287
Manne, Shelly, 53, 59, 222
Manne Hole club, 59
"Maple Leaf Rag," 170–171

Marable, Fate, 22
marches, influence of, 20
Mares, Paul, 26
Margolis, Kitty, 166
marimbas, 225. *See also*
    vibraphones
Marmarosa, Dodo, 182
Marsala, Joe, 279, 338
Marsalis, Branford, 125, 340
Marsalis, Delfeayo, 304
Marsalis, Wynton, 91, 145
Martin, Claire, 92
Martino, Pat, 270, 338
Matos, Bobby, 78, 88
Matsui, Keiko, 93
Maupin, Bennie, 274, 282
Maybeck, Bernard, 191
Maybeck Recital Hall record-
    ings, 191
Mazurek, Robert, 92
McBee, Cecil, 245
McBride, Christian, 92, 252
McCann, Les, 181, 192
McDonough, Dick, 256
McDuff, "Brother" Jack, 201
McFarland, Gary, 233
McFerrin, Bobby, 149
McGhee, Howard, 53
McGriff, Jimmy, 202
McKinney's Cotton Pickers, 39
McLaughlin, John, 76, 268
    photograph, 269
McLean, Jackie, 62, 115, 338
McNeil, Lloyd, 283
McPartland, Marian, 181–182
McPherson, Charles (quota-
    tions)
    on jazz, 15
    on Parker, Charlie, 110
    on saxophones, 97
McRae, Carmen, 162, 339
McShann, Jay, 176
measures, defined, 10
Medeski, John, 204
Medeski, Martin and Wood, 91
Mehldau, Brad, 92
melody, defined, 16
Mendes, Sergio, 87
Merrill, Helen, 162
metal-lophones, 224
Metheny, Pat, 94, 268
midwest territory bands. *See*
    territory bands
Miller, Mulgrew, 193

Mingus, Charles, 63, 237,
    243–244, 338
    photograph, 244
Mingus Big Band, 94
Mintzer, Bob, 282
Mississippi riverboat
    cruises, 22
Mitchell, Blue, 144
Mitchell, Red, 246
Mitchell, Roscoe, 122, 274, 281
Mobley, Hank, 63, 115
modal jazz, 13, 74
Modern Jazz Quartet
    (MJQ), 59
Moffett, Charnett, 252
Mole, Miff, 296
Moncur, Grachan, III, 303
Money Mark, 91
Monk, Thelonious
    bebop, 53
    CD-ROM contents, 341
    hard bop, 63
    music recommendations,
        63, 338
    photograph, 178
    pianos, 178–179
Monk, T.S., 92
Montgomery, Buddy, 191, 234
Montgomery, Wes,
    265, 339, 342
Montreal jazz clubs, 318
Moody, James, 110, 116, 340
Moore, Oscar, 256
Moreira, Airto, 340
Morgan, Lee, 63, 143
Morton, Benny, 299
Morton, Jelly Roll
    CD-ROM contents, 341
    Chicago jazz, 29
    invention of jazz, 26
    Latin jazz, 78
    music recommendations,
        29, 337
    New Orleans jazz, 23
    pianos, 172, 174
    trombones, 294
Most, Sam, 283
Moten, Bennie, 40
Mother Earth, 91
Mouzon, Alphonse, 76, 221
mulatto, defined, 20
Mulligan, Gerry, 59–60,
    116, 339
Mumford, Jefferson, 253

Murray, David, 74, 274
Murray, Sunny, 74
music recommendations. *See also* collecting jazz
  abstract jazz, 339–340
  Adderley, Cannonball, 338
  Anderson, Ray, 340
  Armstrong, Louis, 32, 337
  Art Ensemble of Chicago, 339
  avant garde jazz, 339–340
  Baker, Chet, 339
  Basie, Count, 46, 338
  Batiste, Alvin, 339
  bebop, 53–54, 338–339
  Bechet, Sidney, 337
  Beiderbecke, Bix, 337
  Bellson, Louie, 340
  big bands, 338
  Blakey, Art, 338
  Blanton, Jimmy, 338
  Braxton, Anthony, 339
  Brown, Clifford, 338
  Calloway, Cab, 338
  Carter, Benny, 340
  Carter, Betty, 339
  Carter, James, 340
  Catherine, Philip, 340
  Christian, Charlie, 338
  Clayton-Hamilton Jazz Orchestra, 340
  Coleman, Ornette, 339
  Coltrane, John, 339
  cool jazz, 339
  Corea, Chick, 340
  Daniels, Eddie, 340
  Davis, Miles, 339, 340
  Dodds, Johnnie, 337
  Donaldson, Lou, 339
  early jazz, 337
  Eldridge, Roy, 338
  electric jazz, 340
  Ellington, Duke, 42–43, 338, 339
  Evans, Bill, 339
  Farmer, Art, 338
  Favre, Pierre, 339
  Fitzgerald, Ella, 339
  Gaillard, Slim, 338
  Garner, Erroll, 338
  Garrett, Kenny, 340
  Gilberto, Astrud, 340
  Gilberto, Joao, 340
  Gillespie, Dizzy, 338
  Giuffre, Jimmy, 339

  Golson, Benny, 338
  Goodman, Benny, 338
  Gordon, Dexter, 338
  Grappelli, Stephanie, 338
  Haden, Charlie, 340
  Hamilton, Chico, 339
  Hamilton, Jimmy, 338
  Hancock, Herbie, 339, 340
  hard bop, 338–339
  Hawkins, Coleman, 338
  Henderson, Fletcher, 338
  Herman, Woody, 338
  Hines, Earl "Fatha," 337
  Hinton, Milt, 340
  Hodges, Johnny, 338
  Holiday, Billies, 339
  Hutcherson, Bobby, 338
  Johnson, James P., 337
  Johnson, J.J., 338
  Johnson, Lonnie, 338
  Johnson, Marc, 340
  Jones, Hank, 340
  Jones, Jo, 338
  Joplin, Scott, 337
  Jordan, Sheila, 339
  Kessel, Barney, 53, 338
  Lang, Eddie, 337
  Lateef, Yusef, 338
  Latin jazz, 340
  Lifetime, 340
  Lunceford, Jimmie, 338
  Mahavishnu Orchestra, 340
  Mangelsdorff, Albert, 340
  Marsala, Joe, 338
  Marsalis, Branford, 340
  Martino, Pat, 338
  McLean, Jackie, 338
  McRae, Carmen, 339
  Mingus, Charles, 338
  Monk, Thelonious, 63, 338
  Montgomery, Wes, 339
  Moody, James, 340
  Moreira, Airto, 340
  Morton, Jelly Roll, 29, 337
  Mulligan, Gerry, 339
  Nelson, Oliver, 338
  New Orleans jazz, 337
  Noone, Jimmie, 337
  O'Day, Anita, 339
  Oliver, Joe "King," 337
  Original Dixieland Jass Band, 337
  Ortega, Anthony, 340

  Parker, Charlie, 338
  Pass, Joe, 338
  Pettiford, Oscar, 339
  Pleasure, King, 339
  Powell, Bud, 339
  Puente, Tito, 340
  Ra, Sun, 340
  Reinhardt, Django, 338
  Rivers, Sam, 340
  Roach, Max, 338, 339
  Roberts, Marcus, 340
  Rollins, Sonny, 339
  1980s selections, 340
  1990s selections, 340
  Sanchez, Poncho, 340
  Shaw, Artie, 338
  Sinatra, Frank, 339
  Smith, Bessie, 339
  Stitt, Sonny, 339
  swing, 338
  territory bands, 41
  Threadgill, Henry, 340
  Torme, Mel, 339
  Turre, Steve, 340
  Vaughan, Sarah, 339
  Very Very Circus, 340
  vocalists, 339
  Waller, Fats, 337
  Washington, Grover, Jr., 340
  Webb, Chick, 338
  Webster, Ben, 338
  Williams, Tony, 340
  Woods, Phil, 340
  World Saxophone Quartet, 340
  Yellowjackets, 340
  Young, Lester, 338
musicals, influence of, 20
Musicians Speak icons, 4
musicologist, defined, 12
mutes, use of, 27

Nanton, Tricky Sam, 298
Nascimento, Milton, 163
National Public Radio (NPR) jazz show, 182
Navarro, Fats, 53, 139–140
Nelson, Oliver, 338
Nelson, Steve, 234
neo-traditionalists, 91–92
Netherlands, jazz clubs, 313

New Orleans jazz
  Baquet, George, 22
  Bechet, Sidney, 22
  Bolden, Buddy, 21–22
  clarinets, 274–277
  clubs, 318–319
  Dodds, Baby, 22
  Dodds, Johnny, 22
  Excelsior band, 22
  Foster, "Pops," 22
  Harden, Lil, 23
  history of, 20–21
  Johnson, Bunk, 22
  Keppard, Freddie, 22–23
  Lewis, George, 22
  Marable, Fate, 22
  Morton, Jelly Roll, 23
  music recommendations,
    337
  Nicholas, Albert, 23
  Oliver, Joe "King," 23
  Onward Brass Band, 22
  Original Creole Band, 22
  Ory, Kid, 23
  race relations, 26
  Ragtime, 23–25
  Robicheaux, John, 22
  Storyville, 21, 33
  Tio, Lorenzo, 22
  Tio, Louis, 22
New Orleans Rhythm Kings
    (NORK), 26
New York City
  Cook, Will Marion, 34
  Europe, James Reese, 34
  free jazz, 69
  hard bop, 60–65
  jazz clubs, 319
  Johnson, James P., 34
Newton, James, 283, 291
Nicholas, Albert, 23
Nichols, Red, 136
Night Trains, 91
1980s selections, 340
1990s selections, 340
Noone, Jimmie, 31–32, 277, 337
Norvo, Red, 225–227
Novus record label, 307
NPR (National Public Radio)
    jazz show, 182

• O •

Oakland, California jazz
    clubs, 320
octaroon, defined, 20
O'Day, Anita, 162, 339
O'Farrill, Chico, 81
Oliver, Joe "King," 23, 27–28,
    129–130, 294, 337
On The CD icons, 4
Onward Brass Band, 22
opera, influence of, 20
Oquendo, Manny, 88
organs
  about, 195–196
  Basie, Count, 197
  Buckner, Milt, 197
  Davis, Wild Bill, 197–198
  DeFrancesco, Joey, 203–204
  Dennerlein, Barbara, 204
  Doggett, Bill, 200
  Earland, Charles, 200–201
  early jazz, 196–198
  Goldings, Larry, 204
  groove (1960s), 198–203
  Hartman, Glenn, 198
  Hatza, Greg, 204
  Holmes, Richard
    "Groove," 201
  McDuff, "Brother" Jack, 201
  McGriff, Jimmy, 202
  Medeski, John, 204
  Patterson, Don, 202
  Patton, Big John, 202
  versus pianos, 196
  Ra, Sun, 202
  Scott, Shirley, 202–203
  Smith, Jimmy, 199–200
  Smith, Johnny
    "Hammond," 200
  Smith, Lonnie, 203
  Waller, Fats, 197
  Web site, 198
  Young, Larry, 203
Original Creole Band, 22
Original Dixieland Jass Band
    (ODJB), 25–26, 337
Ortega, Anthony, 340
Ory, Kid, 23, 295–296
overblowing, 71, 283
overdubbing, 184
Oz-Jazz Worldwide
    Web site, 313

• P •

Page, Hot Lips, 136
Page, Walter, 41, 240
Palmer, Roy, 296
Palmieri, Eddie, 184
parade music, influence of, 20
Parker, Charlie "Bird," 50–51,
    54, 106–109, 338
  photograph, 107
party bands, influence of, 20
Pass, Joe, 266–267, 338
Pastorius, Jaco, 250
Patterson, Don, 202
Patton, Big John, 202
Paul, Les, 259, 262
Payton, Nicholas, 92, 145
Peacock, Gary, 247–248
Pedersen, Niels-Henning
    Orsted, 247
Penland, Ralph, 222
Peplowski, Ken, 279
Pepper, Art, 116
Perelman, Ivo, 92
Perera, Roberta, 93
Perez, Danilo, 87, 92
Peterson, Oscar, 186
Pettiford, Oscar, 53,
    242–243, 339
Pettis, Jack, 98
PGD record label, 310
Philadelphia jazz clubs,
    320–321
Phillips, Flip, 104–105
Piano Jazz radio show, 182
piano trios, 65–66
pianos
  about, 169–170
  Abrams, Muhal Richard, 187
  abstract jazz, 187–191
  Allen, Geri, 193
  Ammons, Albert, 176
  Barron, Kenny, 192
  Basie, Count, 175
  bebop, 177–179
  Blake, Eubie, 172
  Bley, Paul, 188
  boogie-woogie, 176–177
  Brackeen, Joanne, 192
  Brand, Dollar, 188
  Brubeck, Dave, 180
  Byard, Jaki, 193
  Canned heat, 177

(continued)

pianos *(continued)*
Chestnut, Cyrus, 192
Childs, Billy, 193
Cole, Nat King, 175
Concord Jazz recordings, 191
cool jazz, 179–183
Corea, Chick, 192
Crispell, Marilyn, 188
Crusaders, 192
Cunliffe, Bill, 193
Donegan, Dorothy, 175–176
Drew, Kenny, 180
early jazz, 170–172
electric, 192
Elias, Eliane, 184
Ellington, Duke, 176
Evans, Bill, 180
Ferrante, Russell, 192
Flanagan, Tommy, 180
Garner, Erroll, 185–186
Garson, Mike, 193
Green, Benny, 193
Hancock, Herbie, 188–189, 192
hard bop, 179–183
Harris, Barry, 177
Harris, Gene, 191
Hawes, Hampton, 177
Headhunters, 192
Hicks, John, 191–193
Hill, Andrew, 189–190
Hines, Earl "Fatha," 173–174
Hooker, John Lee, 177
Hyman, Dick (quotation), 188
Ibrihim, Abdullah, 188
Jackson, Tony, 172
Jamal, Ahmad, 181
Jarret, Keith, 190
Johnson, James P., 172
Johnson, Pete, 176
Jones, Hank, 191
Joplin, Scott, 170–171
Kellaway, Roger, 193
Kelly, Wynton, 181
Kirkland, Kenny, 193
Kuhn, Steve, 193
Larkins, Ellis, 191
Latin jazz, 184–185
Lewis, John, 178
Lewis, Meade "Lux," 176
Marmarosa, Dodo, 182

Maybeck Recital Hall recordings, 191
McCann, Les, 181, 192
McPartland, Marian, 181–182
McShann, Jay, 176
Miller, Mulgrew, 193
Monk, Thelonious, 178–179
Montgomery, Buddy, 191
Morton, Jelly Roll, 172, 174
versus organs, 196
Palmieri, Eddie, 184
Peterson, Oscar, 186
Powell, Bud, 179
Pullen, Don, 191
Ragtime, 170–172
Return to Forever, 192
Roberts, Marcus, 193
Rosnes, Renee, 193
Rubalcaba, Gonzalo, 193
Ruiz, Hilton, 185
Sample, Joe, 192
Shearing, George, 182
Silver, Horace, 182
solos, 191
swing, 173–176
Tapscott, Horace, 191
Tatum, Art, 186
Taylor, Billy, 182–183
Taylor, Cecil, 191
Terrasson, Jacky, 193
Timmons, Bobby, 183
Tristano, Lennie, 183
Tyner, McCoy, 187
Valdes, Bebo, 185
Valdes, Chucho, 185
Waller, Fats, 174–175
Walton, Cedar, 193
Weather Report, 192
Weston, Randy, 183
Williams, Jessica, 191
Williams, Mary Lou, 176
Wofford, Mike, 191
Yancey, Jimmy, 176
Yellowjackets, 192
Zawinul, Joe, 192
Pine, Courtney, 125
pipe organs. *See* organs
Pizzarelli, Bucky, 258
Pizzarelli, John, 258
pizzicato, defined, 238
player piano rolls, 24
Pleasure, King, 149, 158, 339
plungers, use of, 27
Pollack, Ben, 37

Polygram record label, 310
polyrhythms, defined, 14
Potter, Chris, 92, 126
Powell, Bud, 53, 66, 179, 339
Pozo, Chano, 80–81
Prado, Perez, 82
Previn, Andre, 59
Prima, Louis, 156
Printup, Marcus, 92
Procope, Russell, 105
Puente, Tito, 83, 340
Pullen, Don, 74, 191
Purim, Flora, 164

• Q •

quadroon, defined, 20
quarter tones, defined, 12
Quebec, Ike, 105
quiet storm, 93
Quinichette, Paul, 105
Quintero, Juan Carlos, 93

• R •

Ra, Sun, 74, 202, 340
race relations, 26, 43–44
Ragtime
Blake, Eubie, 25
controversy, 23–24
Jackson, Tony, 172
Johnson, James P., 24
Joplin, Scott, 25
Lamb, Joseph, 24
New Orleans jazz, 23–25
pianos, 170–172
Scott, James, 24
Rainey, Ma, 150
Rappolo, Leon, 26
RCA record label, 307
recommendations. *See* collecting jazz; music recommendations
record labels. *See* labels
recording ban, 50
Red Hot Peppers, 29, 174
Redman, Don, 36, 149
Redman, Joshua, 126
Reeves, Dianne, 166
Regina, Elis, 164
Reid, Rufus, 251
Reinhardt, Django, 256–257, 338

remastered titles, 332
Remember icons, 4
Remler, Emily, 270
Reser, Harry, 254
Return to Forever, 192
Rhino Records label, 309–310
rhumba, 78
rhythm, listening to, 16–17
rhythm section, identifying, 17
Rich, Buddy, 53, 213–214
Richmond, Danny, 222
Rickenbacker guitars, 259
Rippingtons, 93
Ritenour, Lee, 268
Rivera, Mario, 88
Rivers, Sam, 292, 340
Roach, Max, 61–62, 217–218, 338, 339
Roberts, Marcus, 193, 340
Robicheaux, John, 22
Rogers, Shorty, 60, 144
Roker, Mickey, 222
Rollini, Adrian, 227
Rollins, Sonny, 63–64, 112, 339, 342
Roney, Wallace, 145
Rosnes, Renee, 193
Rowland, Dennis, 166
Rubalcaba, Gonzalo, 88, 193
Rudd, Roswell, 303
Ruiz, Hilton, 88, 185
Rumsey, Howard, 60
Rushing, Jimmy, 150
Russell, George, 68
Russell, Luis, 32
Russell, Pee Wee, 31, 278–279
Rypdal, Terje, 269

• S •

Saindon, Ed, 234
salsa, 78. *See also* Latin jazz
Salvatore, Sergio, 93
samba, 78
sample, defined, 90
Sample, Joe, 93, 192
Samuels, Dave, 231–232
San Francisco jazz clubs, 321
Sanchez, David, 92
Sanchez, Poncho, 86, 340
Sanders, Pharoah, 74, 122
Sandoval, Arturo, 86–87
Santamaria, Mongo, 85

Santos, John, 88
Sax, Adolphe, 12, 98
saxophones
  about, 97–99
  Adams, Pepper, 109
  Adderley, Cannonball, 113
  Ammons, Gene, 113–114
  avant garde jazz, 120–122
  bebop, 106–113
  Bechet, Sidney, 99–100
  Berry, Chu, 103
  Bostic, Earl, 109
  Braxton, Anthony, 120
  Brecker, Michael, 124
  Byas, Don, 104
  Carter, Benny, 100
  Carter, James, 124
  Cobb, Arnett, 104
  Cole, Richie, 126
  Coleman, Ornette, 117–118
  Colette, Buddy, 114
  Coltrane, John, 118–120
  cool jazz, 113–116
  Criss, Sonny, 110
  Davis, Eddie "Lockjaw," 104
  Davis, Jesse, 126
  Desmond, Paul, 114
  Dolphy, Eric, 121
  electric jazz, 123
  free jazz, 120–122
  Garrett, Kenny, 124
  Getz, Stan, 114
  Gordon, Dexter, 110–111
  Gray, Wardell, 111
  Griffin, Johnny, 111–112
  Gryce, Gigi, 112
  Handy, Craig, 126
  hard bop, 113–116
  Harris, Eddie, 123
  Hawkins, Coleman "Hawk," 100–101
  Hemphill, Julius, 121
  Henderson, Joe, 124–125
  Hodges, Johnny, 102
  inventor, 12, 98
  Jackson, Javon, 126
  Jacquet, Illinois, 104
  Johnson, Budd, 104
  Kirk, Rahsaan Roland, 121
  Konitz, Lee, 115
  Lake, Oliver, 121
  Land, Harold, 115
  Lovano, Joe, 125
  Marsalis, Branford, 125

McLean, Jackie, 115
McPherson, Charles (quotation), 97
Mitchell, Roscoe, 122
Mobley, Hank, 115
Moody, James, 116
Mulligan, Gerry, 116
Parker, Charlie "Bird," 106–109
Pepper, Art, 116
Pettis, Jack, 98
Phillips, Flip, 104–105
Pine, Courtney, 125
Potter, Chris, 126
Procope, Russell, 105
Quebec, Ike, 105
Quinichette, Paul, 105
Redman, Joshua, 126
Rollins, Sonny, 112
Sanders, Pharoah, 122
Sax, Adolphe, 98
Shepp, Archie, 122
Shorter, Wayne, 123
Sims, Zoot, 116
Smith, Willie, 105
Stitt, Sonny, 112
swing, 99–106
Tate, Buddy, 105
Threadgill, Henry, 122
Trumbauer, Frankie, 98
types of, 98
Washington, Grover, Jr., 123
Watson, Bobby, 126
Webster, Ben, 102
Wilber, Bob, 106
Woods, Phil, 125–126
Young, Lester "Prez," 103
scales, defined, 13
scat, 149. *See also* vocalists
Scofield, John, 94, 269
Scott, James, 24
Scott, Marilyn, 93
Scott, Shirley, 202–203
Seattle jazz clubs, 313
Sepulveda, Charlie, 88
seventh notes, defined, 13
seventh string, guitars, 258
Shank, Bud, 292
Shanker, Ravi, 74
Sharrock, Sonny, 74
Shaw, Artie, 48, 278, 338
Shaw, Woody, 143
Shearing, George, 83, 182
Shepp, Archie, 70, 122

Shim, Mark, 92
Shorter, Wayne, 65, 94, 123
Signature Sound icons, 3
Silver, Horace, 64, 182
Simeon, Omer, 274
Sims, Zoot, 116
Sinatra, Frank, 47, 163, 339
singers. *See* vocalists
Singleton, Zutty, 209–210
Slide Five, 91
slide trombone, 294. *See also*
    trombones
Smith, Bessie, 150, 339
Smith, Cecilia, 234
Smith, Floyd, 259
Smith, Jimmy, 199–200
  photograph, 199
Smith, Johnny "Hammond,"
    76, 200
Smith, Lonnie, 203
Smith, Mamie, 151
Smith, Willie, 105
smooth jazz, 93
snare drums, 208. *See also*
    drums
Snowboy, 91
Socarras, Alberto (Albert), 79,
    284–285
solos, 64, 191
songs. *See individual artists;*
    music recommendations
Sony record label, 310
soprano saxophones, 98. *See
    also* saxophones
Soul Bossa Trio, 91
Soul Note record label,
    307–308
sound system, choosing,
    333–334
South American influences, 78.
    See also Latin jazz
Spiritual Vibes, 91
spirituals, influence of, 20
Spyro Gyra, 93, 231–232
St. Cyr, Johnny, 253–254
standards, defined, 10
standup bass, 238, 249. *See
    also* basses
Steig, Jeremy, 283
Steps Ahead, 232
Stewart, Slam, 242
Stitt, Sonny, 53, 64, 112, 339
Stone, Jesse, 41

Storyville, 21, 33
Strayhorn, Billy, 43
string instruments. *See also*
    basses; guitars
  banjos, 253–254
  cellos, 242–243
  mandolins, 253
  violins, 238
string-bend, 254
Strozier, Frank, 56
Sullivan, Maxine, 156
Surround sound, 334
swing. *See also* big bands
  about, 32
  basses, 241–242
  clarinets, 277–279
  defined, 9–10
  drums, 211–215
  music recommendations,
    338
  pianos, 173–176
  saxophones, 99–106
  trombones, 296–299
  vocalists, 153–156
syncopation, defined, 10
synthesizers, 192
Szabo, Gabor, 267

● *T* ●

Tabackin, Lew, 291–292
tailgaters, 293
Tapscott, Horace, 191
Tardy, Greg, 92
Tate, Buddy, 105
Tate, Grady, 222
Tatum, Art, 186, 188, 342
Taylor, Billy, 182–183
Taylor, Cecil, 74, 191
Teagarden, Jack, 31, 297
television programs about
    jazz, 325–328
tenor saxophones, 98. *See also*
    saxophones
Terrasson, Jacky, 193
territory bands, 39-40. *See
    also* big bands
Terry, Clark, 129, 144, 341
third stream, 68
Thomas, Rene, 258
Thornhill, Claude, 56
Threadgill, Henry, 74, 122, 340
Timmons, Bobby, 183

"Tin Pan Alley" songs,
    influence of, 20
Tio, Lorenzo, 22
Tio, Louis, 22
Tip icons, 4
titles. *See individual artists;*
    music recommendations
Tizol, Juan, 294, 298
Tjader, Cal, 83, 234
Tolliver, Charles, 144
tom-toms, 208. *See also* drums
Tormé, Mel, 165, 339
  photograph, 166
Toronto jazz clubs, 322
Tough, Dave, 31, 210
Tower of Power, 76
Trent, Alphonse, 41
Tribe, 91
Tribe Called Quest, 91
Tristano, Lennie, 60, 183, 188
trombones
  about, 293–294
  Anderson, Ray, 302
  Armstrong, Louis, 294
  bebop, 299–302
  big bands, 296–299
  Bolden, Buddy, 294
  Brookmeyer, Bob, 294
  Brown, Lawrence, 298
  Brunies, George, 296
  Cooper, Buster, 298
  Dickenson, Vic, 298
  Dixieland, 294–295
  Dorsey, Tommy, 299
  Dutrey, Honore, 296
  early jazz, 294–296
  Ellington, Duke, 297–298
  Fuller, Curtis, 303
  Glenn, Tyree, 298
  Green, Charlie, 296
  Hampton, Slide, 304
  Harrison, Jimmy, 296
  Henderson, Wayne, 304
  Higginbotham, J.C., 296
  Irvis, Charlie, 296
  Jackson, Quentin, 298
  Johnson, J.J., 300–302
  Lewis, George, 303
  Mangelsdorff, Albert, 303
  Marsalis, Delfeayo, 304
  Mole, Miff, 296
  Moncur, Grachan, III, 303
  Morton, Benny, 299
  Morton, Jelly Roll, 294

Nanton, Tricky Sam, 298
Oliver, King, 294
Ory, Kid, 295–296
Palmer, Roy, 296
Rudd, Roswell, 303
swing, 296–299
tailgaters, 293
Teagarden, Jack, 297
Tizol, Juan, 294, 298
Turre, Steve, 304
Watrous, Bill, 304
Wells, Dickie, 299
Winding, Kai, 302
Woodman, Britt, 298
Young, Trummy, 299
Trumbauer, Frankie, 98
trumpets
about, 129
Allen, Henry "Red," 134
Armstrong, Louis, 130–134
Baker, Chet, 129, 142
bebop, 136–140
Beiderbecke, Bix, 130
Berigan, Bunny, 134
Blanchard, Terence, 145
Bolden, Buddy, 127–128
Bowie, Lester, 143
Brown, Clifford, 139–140
Byrd, Donald, 144
Clayton, Buck, 135
Davis, Miles, 140–142
Dorham, Kenny, 144
early jazz, 128–130
Edison, Henry "Sweets," 135
Eldridge, Roy, 135–136
Farmer, Art, 129, 144
Gillespie, John Birks "Dizzy,"
  136–139
Hargrove, Roy, 145
Harrell, Tom, 129, 143
Hubbard, Freddie, 129, 143
Jones, Leroy, 145
Keppard, Freddie, 128–129
Ladnier, Tommy, 136
Marsalis, Wynton, 145
Mitchell, Blue, 144
Morgan, Lee, 143
mutes, use of, 27
Navarro, Fats, 139–140
Nichols, Red, 136
Oliver, King, 129–130
Page, Hot Lips, 136
Payton, Nicholas, 145
plungers, use of, 27

Rogers, Shorty, 144
Roney, Wallace, 145
Shaw, Woody, 143
Terry, Clark, 129, 144
Tolliver, Charles, 144
Williams, Cootie, 136
trumpet-style voicings, 31
tubas, 237
tune, defined, 16
Turner, Mark, 92
turntables, 334
Turre, Steve, 304, 340
12-bar blues structure, 10–11
Twin Cities Jazz Web site, 313
Tyner, McCoy, 187

● U ●

Ubiquity record label, 310
Ulmer, James "Blood," 74
Uni record label, 309
upright bass, 238. See also
  basses

● V ●

Valdes, Bebo, 185
Valdes, Carlos "Patato," 88
Valdes, Chucho, 88, 185
Valentin, Dave, 86, 292
valve trombones, 294. See also
  trombones
Van Eps, George, 258, 262
Vaughan, Sarah, 159–160, 339
Venuti, Joe, 238
Verve record label, 310
Very Very Circus, 340
vibes. See vibraphones
vibraphones
  Alexander, Ray, 234
  Ayers, Roy, 232
  Burton, Gary, 230
  Charles, Teddy, 229
  Costa, Eddie, 233
  Dowd, Charles, 234
  early jazz, 223–227
  Feldman, Victor, 233
  Gibbs, Terry, 227–228
  Hampton, Lionel "Hamp,"
    224–225
  Hartman, Ed, 234
  Hayes, Tubby, 229
  Hoggard, Jay, 233

Hutcherson, Bobby, 230–231
Hyams, Marjorie, 229
Jackson, Milt "Bags,"
  228–229
Lupri, Matthias, 234
Mainieri, Mike, 232
McFarland, Gary, 233
Montgomery, Buddy, 234
Nelson, Steve, 234
Norvo, Red, 225–227
Rollini, Adrian, 227
Saindon, Ed, 234
Samuels, Dave, 231–232
Smith, Cecilia, 234
Spyro Gyra, 231–232
Steps Ahead, 232
Tjader, Cal, 234
Web site, 234
Winchester, Lem, 230
vibrato, 293
videos about jazz, 325–328
vinyl, choosing, 332–333
violins, 238
Vitous, Miroslav, 251
vocalists
  Allison, Mose, 165
  Allyson, Karrin, 166
  Anderson, Ivie, 154
  Armstrong, Louis, 148
  Bailey, Mildred, 154–155
  Baker, Chet, 161
  bebop, 156–160
  big band, 153–156
  blues influence, 147–151
  Bosco, Joao, 164
  Boswell, Connie, 151–152
  Brazilian singers, 163–164
  Carter, Betty, 149, 164
  Caymmi, Dori, 164
  Christy, June, 161
  Cole, Nat King, 161
  collecting jazz, 339
  Costa, Gal, 164
  Cox, Ida, 149
  Crosby, Bing, 152
  Day, Doris, 155
  depression-era, 151–152
  Dudziak, Urszula, 149, 164
  early jazz, 147–148
  Eckstine, Billy, 155
  Elling, Kurt, 166
  first jazz singer, 148
  (continued)

vocalists *(continued)*
  Fitzgerald, Ella, 39, 149, 157–158
  Forrest, Helen, 154
  Freelon, Nnenna, 166
  Gaillard, Slim, 155
  Garland, Judy, 155
  Gil, Gilberto, 164
  Gilberto, Astrud, 163
  Gilberto, Joao, 163
  Gillespie, Dizzy, 162
  Hanshaw, Annette, 152
  Hendricks, Jon, 149, 160–161
  Holiday, Billie, 153–154
  Horn, Shirley, 165
  Hunter, Alberta, 149
  Jefferson, Eddie, 149, 158
  Jobim, Antonio Carlos, 163
  Krall, Diana, 166
  Lambert, Hendricks & Ross, 149
  Latin jazz, 163–164
  Lee, Peggy, 162
  Lincoln, Abbey, 164
  Mahogany, Kevin, 166
  Margolis, Kitty, 166
  McFerrin, Bobby, 149
  McRae, Carmen, 162
  Merrill, Helen, 162
  music recommendations, 339
  Nascimento, Milton, 163
  O'Day, Anita, 162
  Pleasure, King, 149, 158
  Prima, Louis, 156
  Purim, Flora, 164
  Rainey, Ma, 150
  Redman, Don, 149
  Reeves, Dianne, 166
  Regina, Elis, 164
  Rowland, Dennis, 166
  Rushing, Jimmy, 150
  scat, 149
  Sinatra, Frank, 47, 163
  Smith, Bessie, 150
  Smith, Mamie, 151
  Sullivan, Maxine, 156
  swing, 153–156
  Torme, Mel, 165
  traits of, 148–149
  Vaughan, Sarah, 159–160
  Wallace, Sippie, 151
  Washington, Dinah, 162
  Waters, Ethel, 152
  Wilson, Cassandra, 166
  Wilson, Nancy, 165
voices, 11, 17

• W •

Waldron, Mal, 65
Walker, Aaron "T-Bone," 266
Wallace, Sippie, 151
Waller, Fats, 174–175, 197, 337
Walton, Cedar, 193
Washington, Dinah, 162
Washington, Grover, Jr., 76, 93, 123, 340
Washington, Kenny, 92
Waters, Ethel, 152
Waters, Kim, 93
Watrous, Bill, 304
Watson, Bobby, 126
Watts, Jeff "Tain," 222
wax recording cylinders, 21
Wayne, Chuck, 262
Weather Report, 76, 192
Web sites
  clubs, 313
  jazz, 328–329
  Knitting Factory, 329
  organs, 198
  vibraphones, 234
  WNUR Homepage, 329
Webb, Chick, 39, 211, 338
Weber, Eberhard, 248
Webster, Ben, 102, 338
Weckl, Dave, 93
Wells, Dickie, 299
Wess, Frank, 283, 285, 287–288
West Coast cool jazz, 57–60
Western chromatic scale, 12–13
Weston, Randy, 183
White, Peter, 93
white bands, 26
Whiteman, Paul, 38

Whitfield, Mark, 270
Wilber, Bob, 106, 279
Williams, Buster, 251
Williams, Clarence, 32
Williams, Cootie, 53, 136
Williams, Jessica, 191
Williams, Mary Lou, 176
Williams, Tony, 221, 340
Wilson, Cassandra, 166
Wilson, Nancy, 165
Wilson, Shadow, 222
Winchester, Lem, 230
Winding, Kai, 64, 302
WNUR Homepage, 329
Wofford, Mike, 191
Wollenson, Kenny, 92
Wolverines, 29
Woodman, Britt, 298
Woods, Phil, 56, 125–126, 340
word origins
  bebop, 52
  jazz, 8–9
Workman, Reggie, 251
World Saxophone Quartet, 71, 340
World War II, 48
World Wide Jazz Web site, 313

• X •

xylophones, 225

• Y •

Yancey, Jimmy, 176
Yellowjackets, 93, 192, 340
Young, Larry, 203
Young, Lester "Prez," 103, 338
Young, Trummy, 299
Young Lions, 91
Young Man with a Horn, 30

• Z •

Zawinul, Joe, 192
Zorn, John, 74

IDG BOOKS WORLDWIDE
BOOK REGISTRATION

Register This Book and Win!

We want to hear from you!

Visit **http://my2cents.dummies.com** to register this book and tell us how you liked it!

✔ Get entered in our monthly prize giveaway.

✔ Give us feedback about this book — tell us what you like best, what you like least, or maybe what you'd like to ask the author and us to change!

✔ Let us know any other *...For Dummies*® topics that interest you.

Your feedback helps us determine what books to publish, tells us what coverage to add as we revise our books, and lets us know whether we're meeting your needs as a *...For Dummies* reader. You're our most valuable resource, and what you have to say is important to us!

Not on the Web yet? It's easy to get started with *Dummies 101*®: *The Internet For Windows*® *95* or *The Internet For Dummies*®, 5th Edition, at local retailers everywhere.

Or let us know what you think by sending us a letter at the following address:

...For Dummies Book Registration
Dummies Press
7260 Shadeland Station, Suite 100
Indianapolis, IN 46256-3945
Fax 317-596-5498

BUSINESS AND GENERAL REFERENCE BOOK SERIES FROM IDG

COMPUTER BOOK SERIES FROM IDG